VOLUME 440

NOVEMBER 1978

# THE ANNALS

*of* The American Academy *of* Political
*and* Social Science

RICHARD D. LAMBERT, *Editor*

RALPH B. GINSBERG, *Acting Editor*

ALAN W. HESTON, *Assistant Editor*

# THE EUROPEAN COMMUNITY AFTER TWENTY YEARS

*Special Editor of This Volume*

PIERRE-HENRI LAURENT
*Professor of History*
*Tufts University*

*Adjunct Professor Diplomatic History*
*Fletcher School of Law*
*and Diplomacy*

PHILADELPHIA

*Copy Editor*

KIM HOLMES, PH.D.

International Standard Book Numbers (ISBN)

ISBN 0-87761-233-1, vol. 440, 1978; paper—$4.50
ISBN 0-87761-232-3, vol. 440, 1978; cloth—$5.50

*Issued bimonthly by The American Academy of Political and Social Science at 3937 Chestnut St., Philadelphia, Pennsylvania 19104. Cost per year: $18.00 paperbound; $23.00 clothbound. Add $2.00 to above rates for membership outside U.S.A. Second-class postage paid at Philadephia and at additional mailing offices.*

*Claims for undelivered copies must be made within the month following the regular month of publication. The publisher will supply missing copies when losses have been sustained in transit and when the reserve stock will permit.*

*Editorial and Business Offices, 3937 Chestnut Street, Philadelphia, Pennsylvania 19104.*

2031208

# CONTENTS

PREFACE ........................................... *Pierre-Henri Laurent*    vii

ORIGINS AND EVOLUTION OF THE EUROPEAN
    COMMUNITIES ......................................... *F. Roy Willis*    1

DECADE OF DIVERGENCE AND DEVELOPMENT ....... *Pierre-Henri Laurent*    13

FRANCE IN THE COMMUNITIES: PRESIDENTIAL AND
    PARTY ATTITUDES ....................................... *Joyce Quin*    21

THE PARLIAMENT AND THE COMMISSION ............. *Jean-Joseph Schwed*    33

THE COURT OF JUSTICE: THE INVISIBLE ARM ................ *Werner Feld*    42

DECISIONAL SYSTEMS, ADAPTIVENESS, AND EUROPEAN
    DECISIONMAKING .............. *Glenda Rosenthal* and *Donald Puchala*    54

ECONOMIC UNCERTAINTY AND EUROPEAN SOLIDARITY: PUBLIC
    OPINION TRENDS ........... *Ronald Inglehart* and *Jacques-René Rabier*    66

MONETARY POLICY: PROCESSES AND POLICIES ........... *Michael Brenner*    98

ENERGY POLICY IN THE COMMUNITIES .................... *Wilfrid L. Kohl*   111

EUROPEAN INDUSTRIAL POLICIES: BALANCING INTERDEPENDENCE
    AND INTEREST ....................................... *Doreen Ellis*   122

THE EXTERNAL RELATIONS OF THE EUROPEAN
    COMMUNITY ............... *Michael B. Dolan* and *James A. Caporaso*   135

THE COMMUNITY IN PERSPECTIVE ................... *Stuart A. Scheingold*   156

BOOK DEPARTMENT ...................................................   169

INDEX ............................................................   227

iii

## BOOK DEPARTMENT

### INTERNATIONAL RELATIONS AND POLITICS

BOYCE, PETER. *Foreign Affairs for New States.* Hans H. Indorf ..................... 169

FREEDMAN, LAWRENCE. *U.S. Intelligence and the Soviet Strategic Threat.* Russell F. Weigley ................................................................. 170

LA FEBER, WALTER. *The Panama Canal: The Crisis in Historical Perspective.* Lynn H. Miller ................................................................ 171

MADDOX, ROBERT J. *The Unknown War with Russia: Wilson's Siberian Intervention.* Dale La Belle ............................................................. 172

STOKMAN, FRANS N. *Roll Calls and Sponsorship: A Methodological Analysis of Third World Group Formation in the United Nations.* O. Zeller Robertson, Jr. ......... 173

YANARELLA, ERNEST J. *The Missile Defense Controversy: Strategy, Technology, and Politics.* Russell F. Weigley ................................................ 170

### AFRICA, ASIA, AND LATIN AMERICA

BARNETT, TONY. *The Gezira Scheme: An Illusion of Development.* Philip Carl Salzman ................................................................... 174

BISSELL, RICHARD E. *Apartheid and International Organizations.* Richard Dale ..... 177

BUTLER, JEFFREY, ROBERT J. ROTBERG, and JOHN ADAMS. *The Black Homelands of South Africa: The Political and Economic Development of Bophuthatswana and Kwazulu.* John M. MacKenzie ................................................ 175

CHANOCK, MARTIN. *Britain, Rhodesia and South Africa, 1900–1945: The Unconsummated Union.* John M. MacKenzie ......................................... 176

FELDMAN, HERBERT. *The End and the Beginning: Pakistan 1969–1971.* Norman D. Palmer .................................................................... 179

HAVENS, THOMAS R. H. *Valley and Darkness: The Japanese People and World War Two.* Hilary Conroy ............................................................. 180

PRYBYLA, JAN S. *The Chinese Economy Problems and Policies.* Albert E. Kane ....... 181

AL SAYYID MARSOT, AFAF LUTFI. *Egypt's Liberal Experiment, 1922–1936.* Robert L. Tignor ................................................................... 182

SILVERSTEIN, JOSEF. *Burma: Military Rule and the Politics of Stagnation.* Frank N. Trager .................................................................... 183

SUTTER, ROBERT G. *China-Watch: Toward Sino-American Reconciliation.* Joseph Earle Spencer .............................................................. 184

CHIN O. CHUNG. *P'yongyang Between Peking and Moscow: North Korea's Involvement in the Sino-Soviet Dispute 1958–1975.* Joseph Earle Spencer .................. 184

TSURUTANI, TAKETSUGU. *Political Change in Japan: Response to Post industrial Challenge.* Yi C. Wang ......................................................... 185

WHITE, LYNN T. III. *Careers in Shanghai: The Social Guidance of Personal Energies in a Developing Chinese City, 1949–1966.* Alan P. L. Liu .......................... 186

WIRSING, ROBERT G. *Socialist Society and Free Enterprise Politics: A Study of Voluntary Associations in Urban India.* Norman D. Palmer ............................. 179

WIRTH, JOHN D. *Minas Gerais in the Brazilian Federation, 1889–1937.* S. Ramirez-Horton ................................................................... 188

# CONTENTS

PAGE

## EUROPE

ADAMTHWAITE, ANTHONY. *France and the Coming of the Second World War, 1936–1939.* Joel Colton ......................................................... 189

PARKER, GEOFFREY. *The Dutch Revolt.* William A. Weary ......................... 190

MARCEAU, JANE. *Class and Status in France: Economic Change and Social Immobility 1945–1975.* Jacques Fomerand ................................................ 191

SAFRAN, WILLIAM. *The French Polity.* Jacques Fomerand .......................... 191

## UNITED STATES

DAVIS, S. RUFUS. *The Federal Principle: A Journey Through Time in Quest of Meaning.* W. T. Generous, Jr. ....................................................... 192

DEVINE, DONALD J. *Does Freedom Work? Liberty and Justice in America.* David Spitz ..................................................................... 193

DINKIN, ROBERT J. *Voting in Provincial America: A Study of Elections in the Thirteen Colonies, 1689–1776.* Richard S. Sliwoski ..................................... 194

DOMHOFF, WILLIAM G. *Who Really Rules? New Haven and Community Power Reexamined.* Leonard Blumberg ................................................ 195

KALODNER, HOWARD I. and JAMES J. FISHMAN, eds. *The Courts' Role in School Desegregation.* Robert Neil Johnson ........................................... 195

POLE, J. R. *The Pursuit of Equality in American History.* William M. Simons ........ 196

RABINOWITZ, HOWARD N. *Race Relations in the Urban South, 1865–1890.* Donald H. Stewart ................................................................... 198

REED, JAMES. *From Private Vice to Public Virtue: The Birth Control Movement and American Society Since 1830.* Joseph J. Spengler .............................. 197

ROSE, LISLE A. *The Long Shadow: Reflections on the Second World War Era.* Jacques Szaluta ................................................................. 199

## SOCIOLOGY

AARON, HENRY J. *Politics and the Professors: The Great Society in Perspective.* Richard N. Swift .............................................................. 200

CONNOLLY, HAROLD X. *A Ghetto Grows in Brooklyn.* Nelson Wikstrom ............. 201

INSEL, PAUL M. and HENRY C. LINDGREN. *Too Close for Comfort: The Psychology of Crowding.* Joseph W. Weiss ..................................................... 201

JONES, ROCHELLE. *The Other Generation: The New Power of Older People.* Kenneth G. Summersett .................................................................. 202

KAISER, HARVEY H. *The Building of Cities: Development and Conflict.* Alvin Boskoff ..................................................................... 203

LEE, ALFRED MCCLUNG. *Sociology For Whom?* Jerry L. L. Miller .................. 204

NAPIER, AUGUSTUS Y. and CARL A. WHITAKER. *The Family Crucible.* Theodore Abel and Veğa Lalire ................................................................ 205

PORTERFIELD, ERNEST. *Black and White Mixed Marriages: An Ethnographic Study of Black and White.* Jetse Sprey .................................................... 206

PAGE

BAKER, BOBBY, and LARRY L. KING. *Wheeling and Dealing: Confessions of a Capitol Hill Operator.* Francis M. Wilhoit ............................................... 207

BENSON, GEORGE C. S., STEVEN A. MAARANEN, and ALAN HESLOP. *Political Corruption in America.* Francis M. Wilhoit .................................... 207

RAVITCH, DIANE. *The Revisionists Revised: A Critique of the Radical Attack on the Schools.* Frederick Shaw ....................................... 208

REISER, STANLEY JOEL. *Medicine and the Reign of Technology.* Vaughn D. Bornet ... 209

SALVADORI, MASSIMO. *The Liberal Heresy: Origins and Historical Development.* Thomas J. Knight ............................................. 210

SCHUMAN, DAVID. *The Ideology of Form: The Influence of Organizations in America.* Thomas J. Knight ............................................. 210

## ECONOMICS

EWEN, LYNDA ANN. *Corporate Power and Urban Crisis in Detroit.* Harry W. Reynolds, Jr. ............................................... 212

GARMS, WALTER I., JAMES W. GUTHRIE, and LAWRENCE C. PIERCE. *School Finance: The Economics and Politics of Public Education.* Charles H. Boehm ............. 213

KENESSEY, ZOLTAN. *The Process of Economic Planning.* Nicolas Spulber ............ 214

MCFARLAND, M. CARTER. *Federal Government and Urban Problems HUD: Successes, Failures, and the Fate of Our Cities.* Wallace F. Smith ......................... 215

PUSHKAREV, BORIS S. and JEFFREY ZUPAN. *Public Transportation and Land Use Policy.* W. Bruce Allen ......................................... 216

RANGARAJAN, L. N. *Commodity Conflict: The Political Economy of International Commodity Negotiations.* Stanislaw Wasowski ................................. 217

SEIDEL, STEPHEN R. *Housing Costs And Government Regulations: Confronting the Regulatory Maze.* Joseph F. Zimmerman ........................................ 219

TUFTE, EDWARD R. *Political Control of the Economy.* Michael D. Reagan .......... 220

WEBER, ARNOLD R. and DANIEL J. B. MITCHELL. *The Pay Board's Progress: Wage Controls in Phase II.* Charles E. Jacob ........................................ 220

# PREFACE

The need for periodic reassessment of major institutions in an era of swift change explains this collection on the Western European Community after twenty years of operation. It has developed less vibrantly than its framers had hoped, but it has survived several momentous crises, and even grown in scope, size, and influence. The experiment of economic cooperation and integration has resulted in a vast common market of workers, capital and goods—a flourishing concern. Admittedly, issues and sources of conflict from the first decade continue, and new problems arise, obstructing the road toward that 'ever closer union' that the Treaties of Rome forecasted.

The attempts to illuminate the past, clarify the present, and project into the future contained in this issue are the products of specialists from numerous disciplines and backgrounds. They disagree openly and frequently, but are in accord that the results of research into the nature and mechanisms of this regional integration venture require greater exposure and discussion in the United States. Hopefully, this series of papers will broaden knowledge and understanding about the Community which is, with all its imperfections, a great and growing weight and authority in global politics and the new world economy.

This issue focuses on institution building and policymaking, reviewing many of the causes for the Community's uneven record and emphasizing the new issues of the seventies. Various obstacles have impeded progress toward harmonization, coordination, and integration in the fields of energy, transfer of technology, monetary, and foreign policies. Accomplishments have been limited and real Community linkage has been based on sound structural foundations and economic stability-growth. For certain specific goals, the member-states are cooperative and have demonstrated a capacity to expand. But ambitions are in fact more modest and priorities more carefully and realistically set. Often, the Nine find that they must fight the tendency merely to retain past gains and achievements.

Those obstacles that will inevitably deter advances are the economic ills—inflation, unemployment, the balance of payments deficits, shortage of energy, the appeal of protectionism, and the widening gap of economic divergencies among the partners. But the prevailing crises are not all economic in character. Structural failings in the Community remain. Institutional evolution must be geared and adapted to the newer problems, such as creating greater connections to the grass roots. The authors point out the achieved strategy areas of joint policy and the arena where there are encouraging signs of progress, but they also delineate the failures of the uneven, spotty, almost woeful institutional apparatus.

With all its imperfections, the Community is alive, basically well, outward-looking in most cases, certainly open minded and liberal, and a greater weight in the globe today. Yet it remains too bureaucratic, is too frequently a reflection of strong nationalistic instincts, and lacks direct democratic accountability. It is a growing concern that at times flourishes, but usually labors hard to make nine independent states into a community of regional cooperation, an essentially unique political enterprise.

It should be noted that all the articles were finished in May and June, 1978, with the exception of the Scheingold, Kohl, and Laurent contributions, completed in late July.

PIERRE-HENRI LAURENT

ANNALS, AAPSS, 440, Nov. 1978

# Origins and Evolution of the European Communities

By F. ROY WILLIS

ABSTRACT: Although its historical antecedents have been traced back as far as the Roman Empire, the movement to integrate Europe politically and economically took contemporary form during the second World War when resistance groups proposed plans to avoid future wars by federating Europe. Early postwar efforts at consultative federation, like the Council of Europe, failed to create a supranational authority. In 1950, Jean Monnet and Robert Schuman proposed the formation of the European Coal and Steel Community, which was the predecessor of the European Economic Community, or Common Market, and Euratom. By 1968 the Common Market had achieved its goal of creating a customs union of its six members, protected by a common external tariff, and common policies for such sectors as agriculture were introduced. Many Communitywide organizations helped create widespread commitment to cooperative action in the economic sphere. Great increases in production and trade were recorded by all six members during the 1960s and early 1970s. Moves toward closer political integration were not successful, however, largely due to the pressure of French President Charles de Gaulle who, in 1965–66, blocked plans for increasing the powers of the E.E.C. Commission and the European Parliament. As a result, European public opinion, while respecting the economic benefits gained from E.E.C., became increasingly disinterested in the possibility that the Community might eventually become a United States of Europe.

---

F. Roy Willis is Professor of Modern European History at the University of California, Davis. He graduated from King's College, Cambridge, and took his Ph.D. in 1959 at Stanford University. He was a Rockefeller Foundation Fellow in Paris in 1962–63 and a Guggenheim Fellow in Rome in 1966–67. His books on contemporary Western Europe include The French in Germany, 1945–1949, France, Germany, and the New Europe, 1945–1967, and Italy Chooses Europe. He recently edited European Integration, and is now writing a study of regional underdevelopment in France since 1750.

JEAN MONNET, president of the High Authority of the European Coal and Steel Community, told the Council of Europe, on March 28, 1953: "Our Community is not an association of producers of coal and steel; it is the beginning of Europe." Later, when he published his collected speeches, he gave them the title, *The United States of Europe Has Begun*. And in 1955, seeking to found a pressure group that would hasten the coming of genuine political integration in Europe, he called it the Action Committee for the United States of Europe.[1] Monnet's determination to emphasize the political character of the movement for European integration raises the central question of interpretation of the history of the European Communities—whether the process of integration in Western Europe since the second World War has been a political movement that became unwittingly involved in economics, or an economic movement with a little political window dressing, or perhaps an uneasy compromise—even a mariage de convenance between mismatched mates. At all stages of the process of integration, the political and economic facets have been closely interrelated.

## THE FEDERALIST MOVEMENTS

The idea of Europe was in vogue during the 1940s and early 1950s.[2] As Walter Lipgens has shown, during the second World War the non-

communist liberation movements in occupied Europe were imbued with the idea that the Nazis were both a product of the anarchistic nature of the European state system and a betrayal of the deepest ideals of European civilization.[3] A struggle against Nazism and Fascism became for them a struggle for a European federation in which the traditional European values could be safeguarded. The newspapers of the liberation movements, like *L'Unità Europea* in Italy, *Franc-Tireur* in France, and *Het Parool* in the Netherlands, were filled with plans for European directorates, European economic councils, and even a European police power.

These plans were largely ignored when the Allied armies, both in eastern and western Europe, handed over power piecemeal to individual national governments in 1944–45; but disappointment at the loss of this opportunity of remolding the European state system made many more than ever determined to seek the creation of a European federation. In the immediate postwar years, federalists presented persuasive historical precedents for union. Some saw precursors of their goal in the Catholic Church, the Roman Empire, or Charlemagne's Holy Roman Empire. Scholars described the plans of statesmen who had proposed union, such as the Duc de Sully, the Abbé de Saint-Pierre, Giuseppe Mazzini, and, in the interwar years, Aristide Briand. Influential federalists of the interwar years reappeared. Count Coudenhove-Kalerghi revived his European Par-

---

1. Jean Monnet, *Les Etats-Unis d'Europe ont commencé: Discours et allocutions, 1952–1954* (Paris: Laffont, 1955), p. 65; Action Committee for the United States of Europe, *Joint Declaration* (Paris, 1955).

2. Henri Brugmans, "L'Idée européenne, 1920–1970," *Cahiers de Bruges*, No. 26 (Bruges, 1970).

3. Walter Lipgens, "European Federation in the Political Thought of Resistance Movements During World War II," *Central European History*, Vol. I (1), (March 1968) pp. 5–19.

liamentary Union. Luigi Einaudi, who had written the most persuasive economic defense of European union in the 1930s, was even elected president of Italy.

Great propaganda efforts on behalf of European integration were made by the European Movement, a union of federalist groups founded at The Hague in May 1948; and in the summer of 1949, as a result of this pressure, ten West European governments agreed to form a Council of Europe.[4] The Council was to be a consultative federation which would satisfy the federalist demands, give Western Europe an identity separate from the Soviet bloc and from the United States, but, it soon appeared, not require the cession of sovereignty by any individual government.[5]

## THE CREATION OF THE EUROPEAN COAL AND STEEL COMMUNITY

Disillusionment with the Council of Europe drove Jean Monnet to conceive the plan for a European Coal and Steel Community, which he presented to the French Foreign Minister Robert Schuman in May 1950. As head of the National Planning Commissariat, Monnet was aware of difficulties suffered by the reviving French economy as a result of Western Europe's autarkic economic planning since 1945. As former deputy secretary-general of the League of Nations, he was deeply committed to international cooperation. In him, the political and economic motives for unifica-tion were inseparable. In Robert Schuman, who saw in his native Lorraine the sufferings provoked by "the ancient antagonism of France and Germany," Monnet found a statesman of moral stature and insight, willing to sponsor his plan for an integration of the coal and steel industries of France and Germany in a community open to the participation of all western European countries.[6] As Schuman declared on May 9, 1950, for him the moral element of the plan was supreme. The goal was to make war between France and Germany not merely "unthinkable, but impossible." The new community would "mean the immediate establishment of common bases of industrial production, which is the first step toward European federation and will change the destiny of regions that have long been devoted to production of war armaments of which they themselves have been the constant victims."[7]

The Schuman Plan was immediately welcomed by German Chancellor Konrad Adenauer and by Italian Premier Alcide De Gasperi, and by the governments of Belgium, the Netherlands, and Luxembourg, but was quickly rejected as too great an infringement on national sovereignty by the Labour government of Great Britain. The treaty creating the European Coal and Steel Community (E.C.S.C.) was signed in 1951, and the Community of the Six began functioning in July 1952.

4. European Movement, *The European Movement and the Council of Europe* (London, 1950).

5. Charles Melchior de Molènes, *L'Europe de Strasbourg: Une première expérience de parlementarisme international* (Paris: Editions Roudil, 1971), pp. 14–29.

6. Richard Mayne, "The Role of Jean Monnet," *Government and Opposition*, vol. 2, no. 3 (April–July 1967), pp. 349–71; Robert Rochefort, *Robert Schuman* (Paris: Editions du Cerf, 1968), pp. 267–86.

7. *L'Année politique, 1950* (Paris: Editions du Grand Siècle, 1951), pp. 306–307.

## THE THEORY OF ECONOMIC INTEGRATION

The E.C.S.C. was in a real sense the precursor of the Common Market because almost all the principles of its operation were taken up in the Market's constitutional documents, the Treaties of Rome. The crucial economic agreements allowed free movement within the community of goods (coal, iron ore, iron, and steel), workers, and capital. Tariffs and import quotas were to be abolished, as were the many ingenious methods of discriminating against imports from other members—by transport rates, differential pricing, or monopolistic sales cartels. It was also recognized that workers, unemployed as a result of the collapse of weaker industrial groups under the harsh blast of the new competitive conditions, should be financially aided for retraining and relocation. Thus, E.C.S.C., in spite of its restriction to two segments of the economy, set out to achieve those gains that economic theorists like Jakob Viner, James E. Meade, and Bela Balassa were promising from the integration of essentially similar national economies.[8]

In brief, Viner and Meade held that it was not the linking of complementary economies that enabled a customs union or common market to be successful, but rather the linking of competitive economies. Trade creation occurs as the result of the refinement of specialization, due to the shift of production from a high-cost to a low-cost producer within the union. This shift is beneficial to all members only when there is a high degree of "substitutability of factors and of products" within each member country. These static economic effects are also accompanied by dynamic effects. Increased competition reduces oligopolistic or monopolistic distortions. Technological innovation is encouraged. Labor productivity has to be raised. A larger market makes possible economies of scale. The inflow of foreign capital is encouraged, especially when the union is protected from outside competition by the establishment of a common external tariff, a uniform tariff on imports into all member countries. Finally, internal factor flows make possible a more effective use of the union's resources.

Warnings of the economic dangers of such a union were not lacking, however. Viner himself pointed out that increased competition might inflict damage on weaker members of the union, if labor or capital could not be transferred easily into a viable sector of the economy. Infant industries, especially in the less developed regions of Europe, might be wiped out. The common external tariff might encourage trade diversion rather than trade creation, or the shift of purchases from low-cost producers outside the union to high-cost producers within the union. Perhaps worst of all, as Gunnar Myrdal warned, in a process of "cumulative causation," the union might encourage polarization of development within the already advanced members of the union, or even within the advanced regions of one member.[9]

8. Jacob Viner, *The Customs Union Issue* (New York: Carnegie Endowment for International Peace, 1950); James E. Meade, *Problems of Economic Union* (London: Allen and Unwin, 1953); Bela Balassa, *The Theory of Economic Integration* (Homewood, IL: Richard D. Irwin, 1961).

9. Gunnar Myrdal, *Economic Theory and Underdeveloped Regions* (New York: Harper and Row, 1971), pp. 23–38.

## STRUCTURE AND FUNCTIONING OF E.C.S.C.

The political structure of E.C.S.C. was also taken up in the Treaties of Rome. A nine-member executive body, known as the High Authority, was to administer E.C.S.C., its revenue provided by a tax of up to one percent of the coal and steel production of the union. The member governments were represented on a Council of Ministers. The national parliaments sent representatives to a 78-member Common Assembly. Individuals and governments could appeal to a Court of Justice.[10] The choice of Jean Monnet as first president of the High Authority underlined the determination of the Community's founders that their creation should seek more than the material benefits of freer trade.

The European Coal and Steel Community was an immediate success. Installed in Luxembourg, the multinational bureaucracy quickly established responsive methods of work. Barriers to trade were dismantled. Difficult problems like the restriction of the powers of the German coal sales agency (GEORG) and the French coal-import monopoly (A.T.I.C.) were handled effectively, and the Community came through the recession of 1953 without great difficulty. Yet, in 1954, Monnet suddenly resigned in despair and opponents of the Community mounted a powerful campaign for its demolition. The reason for this renewed attack on Europeanism was the ill-handled and overly hasty attempt to bypass economic integration in 1950–54 by a sudden rush into military and political integration, for which Western Europe— and especially France and Germany —were not yet prepared.

## THE EUROPEAN DEFENSE COMMUNITY AND THE EUROPEAN POLITICAL COMMUNITY

In 1950, the United States government, deeply involved militarily in Korea, had warned that West Germany would have to take its part in the military defense of Europe. To avoid the rearmament of her traditional enemy, France's Premier, René Pleven, proposed the creation of a European Defense Community (E.D.C.), modeled upon E.C.S.C., which would administer a European Army to which the Germans would be permitted to supply contingents. Two years later, Schuman and De Gasperi proposed that an enlarged Common Assembly draw up a treaty for the creation of a European Political Community (E.P.C.). This body would be able to command the European Army and would be nothing less than the nucleus of a European government. After vicious, procrastinating debate in all the parliaments of the Six, the French Assembly, primarily to avoid German rearmament, dealt E.D.C. its deathblow on August 30, 1954; and the Political Community was shelved as a result.[11]

Western European Union, the military alliance proposed by the British as a substitute for E.D.C., involved no cession of sovereignty to a supranational body and permitted German rearmament on a national basis; it was approved in 1955. In June of that year, the foreign

10. Louis Lister, *Europe's Coal and Steel Community: An Experiment in Economic Union* (New York: Twentieth Century Fund, 1960), pp. 9–15.

11. Raymond Aron and Daniel Lerner, eds., *France Defeats EDC* (New York: Praeger, 1957).

ministers of Belgium, the Netherlands, and Luxembourg brought a memorandum to the Council of Ministers meeting in Messina which contained the proposal for a European Common Market. It was, in part, their attempt to save faltering European supranationalism by utilizing and expanding the economic goals set forth in the Schuman Plan.

## NEGOTIATING THE TREATIES OF ROME, 1955–57

The Benelux memorandum proposed the extension of integration to all sectors of the European economy in gradual stages, during which barriers could be eliminated, national policies harmonized, and new institutions, such as a European investment fund, created. At the same time it called for urgent action on nuclear and conventional energy and monetary policy. The ministers recognized that "the constitution of a European common market, excluding any right to customs and any quantitative restrictions, is the objective of their action in the economic field." They appointed the energetic, farsighted Belgian foreign minister, Paul-Henri Spaak, to head an Intergovernmental Committee charged with drawing up plans for a common market and for energy and transport policies. The Committee reported back to the ministers at Venice in 1956, and was commissioned to draw up treaties for establishment of a European Economic Community (E.E.C.), or Common Market, and for a European Atomic Energy Community (Euratom).

The negotiations were long and difficult.[12] It was agreed that customs barriers should be gradually eliminated in three stages of four years each, with provisions for acceleration or slowing of the process if necessary. A common external tariff was to be erected, with protective rates for products like those of Italy's underdeveloped southern regions. A European investment bank and a social fund were to be created, to help provide large-scale investment for backward regions and aid worker readaptation. After great battles, in which France's partners attempted to disassociate themselves from the French war in Algeria, it was agreed that preferential treatment should be given to the French and Belgian overseas territories and that a Development Fund should be created to help them.

The greatest battles occurred over agriculture, and these were to continue through the whole existence of the Common Market. European agriculture was to a large extent subsidized, through price controls and other means, by the industrial sector, and was politically influential because of the family character of production in many regions. France, with half of the arable land in the Community, was especially interested in winning secure outlets behind the common external tariff for its cereals, beef, dairy products, and wine. The negotiators, after many arguments, included agriculture within the treaty but left to later negotiation the exact provisions for its administration.

Euratom was to include only peaceful uses of fissionable materials, was to establish common research and laboratories, and promote exchange of knowledge and health regulations.[13]

12. F. Roy Willis, *France, Germany, and the New Europe, 1945–1967*, rev. ed. (Stanford: Stanford University Press, 1968), pp. 242–51.

13. On the weaknesses of Euratom, see Altiero Spinelli, *The Eurocrats: Conflict and Crisis in the European Community*, trans. C. Grove Haines (Baltimore: Johns Hopkins Press, 1966), pp. 33–45.

The institutions of the two Communities were similar. E.E.C. was to be administered by a nine-member Commission, Euratom by a five-member Commission. Member states were to be represented by a Council of Ministers, which soon became the most powerful of the Communities' institutions; the Council's work was to be prepared by a Committee of Permanent Representatives. The Common Assembly established as a 78-member body by E.C.S.C. negotiation, was to be expanded and later renamed European Parliament. The Court of Justice was to serve E.E.C. and Euratom as well as E.C.S.C.

The Treaties of Rome, establishing the European Economic Community and Euratom, were signed on the Capitol Hill on March 25, 1957. In the colorful ceremonies, Italian President Antonio Segni pointed out that the new Communities had moral and political as well as economic facets: "It was not without deep significance that the treaties . . . should be signed in Rome, in this city that, even through the mouths of illustrious foreigners, has been recognized as the cradle, the seat of that great European civilization that these treaties themselves aim to advance in its economic development in order to make it take again its political importance in the world."[14]

## EARLY ACHIEVEMENTS OF THE COMMON MARKET

The abolition of customs barriers among the Six, and the erection of a common external tariff, was achieved on July 1, 1968, two years ahead of schedule. The acceleration was made possible by a vast business boom, stimulated in large part by industrial groups' expectations of the benefits they would reap from freedom of trade within a community of 180 million people. All statistics showed that the first decade of operation of the Common Market was one of the most prosperous in all European history. Growth rate of product per worker for the Community as a whole, in 1958–68, had been 4.9 percent annually, and gross national product had risen 5.2 percent annually. The Common Market outstripped the United States, which had an annual increase of only 2.7 percent per worker and 4.7 percent of G.N.P. Trade within the Community increased more than 400 percent.[15] Italy in particular realized a dramatic economic boom, seeing its annual per capita income in constant (1968) dollars rise from $805 to $1358, and its G.N.P. from $41.9 to $71.6 billion.[16]

During this first decade, industrial integration advanced rapidly. According to Leon N. Lindberg, "business circles, after initial reactions ranging from cautious support to outright hostility, had accepted the Common Market as a *fait accompli* and jumped in with almost breathtaking speed to form a network of agreements within the Six."[17] Mergers, cooperation agreements, and, less frequently, investment in member countries had begun to effectuate a genuine European business community. The pro-

14. Italy, Presidenza del Consiglio dei Ministri, Servizio delle Informazioni, *Comunità Economica Europea* (Rome, 1958), p. 99.

15. European Economic Community, Commission, *Rapport général sur l'activité des Communautés, 1969* (Brussels, 1970), pp. 24, 31.

16. United States Department of State, *Research Memorandum, REU-27 REU-41*, 1969.

17. Leon N. Lindberg, *The Political Dynamics of European Economic Integration* (Stanford: Stanford University Press, 1963), p. 170.

liferation of organizations, such as the Council of Federations of Commerce, the Union of Industries of the European Community, the Union of the Handicrafts of E.E.C., and the League for European Economic Cooperation, which brought together business groups from all members of the Community, played its part in creating a European frame of mind. Carl J. Friedrich concluded in 1969 that "it is the businessman-entrepreneur who has had the largest share in building the new European community, after the framework of institutions had been erected by the politicians."[18]

Business prosperity encouraged labor migration until the recession of 1973–75. Large numbers of unemployed Italians moved northward, in the 1950s to the Belgian coalmines, and in the 1960s to the factories of Germany. By 1961, over one million Italians had moved to the other countries of the Community. Since vast numbers of workers were also being welcomed from Spain, Portugal, Turkey, Greece, and other countries of the Mediterranean Basin, the Italian government was granted preferential treatment for its migrants within the Community. Community regulations issued in 1961 and 1964 permitted Italians to bring their families and secure education for their children, and even to be elected to workers' boards in their host countries. The migrant worker, however, usually remained alien to the way of life and social relations of his host country and was ready to return home if suitable employment be-

came available. In 1966, for example, the excess of migrants from Italy over returnees was only 3,000.[19]

## THE PROBLEM OF EUROPEAN AGRICULTURE

Agriculture provided the greatest problem for the new Community. Germany, with a heavily protected agricultural sector, preferred to buy its necessary imports, which reached $2.5 billion annually, from clients for its industrial exports. Rather than shift its purchases from South America and Scandinavia to the higher-priced producers in France, the Germans fought to avoid the rapid opening of an agricultural common market of the Six. The French, however, seeking secure markets within the Community, were determined to block progress on the timetable for tariff reduction on industrial goods unless satisfied in agriculture. French President Charles de Gaulle, by his open threats to use his veto power, compelled the Community negotiators to engage in marathon negotiating sessions in 1962 and 1963, from which a workable but expensive agricultural policy finally emerged.

The keystone of the agricultural policy was a system of levies on imports from outside the Community. For each class of agricultural production, a different form of levy was adopted. By an extremely complicated system, involving "target prices," "intervention prices," and "sluicegate prices," a common price level for each product was achieved in the Community by 1967. Since the prices were eventually established at very high levels, in the

18. Carl H. Friedrich, *Europe: An Emergent Nation?* (New York: Harper and Row, 1969), p. 47. *See also* Dusan Sidjanski, "Pressure Groups and the European Economic Community," *Government and Opposition*, vol. 2, no. 3 (April–July 1967), pp. 397–416.

19. The problems of migration are reviewed annually in European Communities, Commission, *Exposé sur l'évolution de la situation sociale dans la Communauté* (Brussels: 1959—).

1970s the Community found itself compelled to buy up surplus production and to accumulate huge stocks of cereals and other products. The common agricultural policy, which was costing the Community over $2 billion annually by the 1970s, satisfied nobody fully. Consumers were disappointed that the Common Market had not led to a lowering of prices, even if it had made available a greater variety of foodstuffs at all seasons of the year. Farmers were angered in times of surplus production when prices fell, and on several occasions engaged in violent demonstrations in Brussels and in their own regions.[20]

## THE EUROPEAN POLICY OF CHARLES DE GAULLE

In 1965–66, the Community was shaken, and probably permanently damaged, by the conjunction of an agricultural and a constitutional crisis, provoked primarily by President de Gaulle. Freed of the entanglements of the Algerian war after 1962, de Gaulle moved forcefully to impose his conception of Europe on the Community. He entirely accepted the economic goals of the Treaties of Rome and his principles were coherent. The civil servants he dispatched to Brussels, many of them brilliant young graduates of the National School of Administration, were the most highly qualified of any national group. At every crisis period in the formulation of detailed policies for the Community his pressure compelled his partners to an agreement.[21]

However, de Gaulle disapproved totally of the supranational goals that were so important to the framers of the Treaties of Rome. The Europe he proposed to build was a Europe of States. "To imagine that something can be built that would be effective in action, and that would be approved by the peoples outside and above the states—this is a dream," he declared. "I do not believe that Europe can have any living reality if it does not include France and its Frenchmen, Germany and its Germans, Italy and its Italians, and so forth. Dante, Goethe, and Châteaubriand belong to all Europe to the very extent that they were respectively and eminently Italian, German, and French. They would not have served Europe very well if they had been stateless or if they had thought and written in some kind of integrated Esperanto or Volapück." He therefore proposed to foil any of the forces, within or without the Community, that might try to turn it into some kind of supranational entity.

Further he held that the Community must be a "European Europe." The greatest danger in the postwar period had been of becoming an appendage of the "Atlantic colossus," the United States. An excessively enlarged Community, spreading to include Scandinavia, Britain, and other countries would "in the last resort emerge as a colossal Atlantic community dependent upon and controlled by the United States, which would soon have absorbed the community of Europe."[22]

20. Documentation Française, "L'Europe agricole et l'élargissement du Marché Commun," Notes et Etudes Documentaires, Nos. 4061–4063 (12 Feb. 1974), pp. 8–49.

21. Alfred Grosser, "General de Gaulle and the Foreign Policy of the Fifth Re-

public," International Affairs (April 1963), pp. 298–313.

22. Press conferences of 5 September 1960, 15 May 1962, and 14 January 1963, cited in French Embassy Press and Information Service, Major Addresses, Statements, and Press Conferences of General Charles de Gaulle, May 19, 1958—January 31, 1964 (New York, 1964), pp. 92–93, 173–77, 211–216.

### The veto on British membership, 1963

His objections to British entry into the Community, formulated in the veto of January 1963, were primarily political. In his view, Britain was the subservient ally of the United States, the Trojan Horse that would introduce American dominance onto the continent of Europe, and would thereby pervert the European vocation of the new Community, which was to stand between and, if possible, aid the dissolution of the two competing blocs of the Cold War. As an economic issue, the difficulties of Britain's entry had been, to a large extent, settled by the long negotiations of Edward Heath's delegation with the representative of the Six in 1961–62. The veto of Britain's membership was the first great intrusion of political calculations into the economic working of the Community.

The reaction to the veto among all five of France's partners was equally political. The Belgians and the Dutch had seen Britain as a necessary counterweight to the heavy-handed diplomacy of France. The Italians had seen de Gaulle as a spoiler—attempting to enlist the Germans by the Franco-German Treaty of Friendship of 1963— in his attempt to exercise political hegemony in Europe. The Germans saw his veto as a crude effort to sever them from their American ties. In the months following the veto the Community lay in the doldrums until German Foreign Minister Gerhard Schröder proposed a "synchronization" program, which was a realistic recognition that in the future all economic progress would be made by a balancing of concessions among national delegations.

### The Empty Chair Crisis, 1965–66

In 1965, the Common Market moved to settle the problem of long-term financing of the agricultural fund (F.E.O.G.A.) whose dual purpose was to guarantee the producers the receipt of the Community price for their products and to aid the structural adaptation of agriculture. On March 23, 1965, the Commission infuriated the French government by proposing that F.E.O.G.A. should be financed not only from the receipts on levies on agricultural imports but from tariffs on industrial goods as well. Both levies and customs duties were to be considered Community revenue, administered by the Commission. Since the Commission would then be administering a revenue of over $2 billion, the European Parliament should be given control over the Community budget.

The effect of these proposals would have been to convert the Commission into an independent, supranational government with a large autonomous financial base, and the European Parliament into a powerful legislature. When the French attempted to separate the agreement on agricultural financing from the other proposals, they were opposed by their five partners. The meeting broke up in anger, and the next day de Gaulle withdrew the French representatives from Brussels. French ministers stopped taking part in the Council of Ministers, and French experts were forbidden to make important decisions in any Community negotiations. Apart from day-to-day business, the Community was effectively paralyzed.

De Gaulle then dropped any pretense that it was agricultural financing that concerned him. In his September press conference he denounced the supranational goals of the Commission, and made clear his opposition to the provisions of the Treaty of Rome that introduced majority voting during the third stage of the Treaty. When compromise was finally reached in January 1966, the French made only minor concessions on financing, and were granted almost all their political demands. The language of the agreement did not conceal the fact that the French had destroyed any possibility in the foreseeable future that the Commission could be converted into a supranational government. The following May Hallstein resigned, after the French refused to support the renewal of his presidency of the Commission.[23]

## THE EXPANSION OF THE COMMUNITY

This method of resolving the most fundamental constitutional crisis the Community had faced restricted it to economic activity, and thus made easier the expansion of the Community to include Britain, Ireland, and Denmark. With the separation and, in reality, the elimination of the supranational political goals of the Community, by de Gaulle and his successor

Georges Pompidou, the British could consider membership for its economic significance alone, without fear of entering a political Community which historical memories would lead them to distrust. The exacerbated debate in Britain was precipitated almost exclusively by uncertainty as to the economic consequences of membership. For the Danes and Irish the decision was easier, since their economies were so tightly tied to that of Britain that they could not afford to be left outside the common external tariff once Britain joined.

What is significant about the debate over expansion of the Community in 1971–72 is the lack of political context. When Britain first sought membership in the Common Market in 1961–63, the Conservative government was able to present its decision as a political as well as an economic one. It had the duty and the right, it claimed, to share in the political remodeling of Western Europe. None of this could-be alleged with much conviction in 1972. Europeans in general, and would-be members in particular, had become cynical about the political evolution of the Community.[24]

In the summit meeting of heads of government in 1972, on the eve of the Community's expansion, the political paralysis was dramatized by the rejection of a Dutch proposal for increasing the powers of a directly elected European Parliament and of a French proposal for a political secretariat separate from the Commission and located in

23. John Newhouse, *Collision in Brussels: The Common Market Crisis of 30 June 1965* (New York: W. W. Norton, 1967); John Lambert, "The Constitutional Crisis, 1965–66," *Journal of Common Market Studies* (May 1966), pp. 195–228.

24. Roger D. Hansen, "European Integration: Forward March, Parade Rest, or Dismissed?" *International Organization* (Spring 1973), pp. 225–54.

Paris. The energy crisis of the 1970s was to emphasize even more blatantly the lack of a political will that was the consequence of the crises of the 1960s. A political blockage existed which prevented the nine from taking the crucial decisions on monetary and other policies necessary to transform the Community into an economic union. Removal of the blockage would require extraordinary surgery by nine doctors in honest disagreement as to their diagnosis.

# The Decade of Divergence and Development

By PIERRE-HENRI LAURENT

ABSTRACT: Economic events, particularly the energy crisis, inflation, and recession, have had an impact on both the successes and failures of the European Community in the seventies. Accomplishments, such as the 1973 enlargement and the evolution of a global development cooperation policy, cannot be cited without the mention of EC setbacks in forming joint economic, monetary, and energy policies. The record of contemporary Community policy, with its disagreements and inaction, reflects both worldwide economic disorder and growing divergent views within the Nine. Europe has moved from a relatively insignificant status in international affairs to that of a global power, utilizing the partnership concept embodied in the pioneering Lomé agreement, the world's largest regional economic organization. The European Community has furthermore devised extensive new lines of cooperation with two other zones of major interest through the creation of the Euro-Arab dialogue and the EC-Mediterranean grand design. These new "foreign policies" are the outgrowth of new German influence, Commission initiative, and Third World global significance. Put in perspective, these achievements are limited by the recurrent inability to construct common Community policies and/or bring about structural reform. In order to liberate the Nine from a state of disunity, there has emerged a drive to make the European Parliament more powerful and directly elected. A democratic European legislature, with more competences, may break the deadlock but will not achieve the mandatory coherence between internal and external policies and procedures of the Community.

*Pierre-Henri Laurent is Professor of History at Tufts University, and Adjunct Professor of Diplomatic History at Fletcher School of Law and Diplomacy. His articles, mostly on the Common Market, have appeared in* Current History, Journal of Contemporary History, Political Science Quarterly, World Affairs, Review of Politics *and other publications. He has both studied and observed the EC, has been the recipient of a grant from the National Endowment for the Humanities, and fellowships from NATO and Fondation Paul-Henri Spaak.*

CONTEMPORARY historians of the European Community must review the second decade of its existence in the context of changes that emerged from 1969 to 1975. They must also note the persistence of problems that have plagued any serious movement toward internal common policies. Community progress and failure in the post-1973 years became heavily influenced by the various repercussions of the OPEC price decisions. Thus, a mixture of external variables and internal reorientations combined to alter the EC in terms of some basic methods of procedure and general goals. The end result was the creation of the Community of Nine, a recast and expanded relationship with the Third World, and a commitment in the direction of democratic legitimacy by means of increased authority for and direct elections of the European Parliament.

There is however another side to Community evolution. Even the strong outlines of an EC foreign policy cannot divert attention from the decade-long quarrels over policy formation on matters of energy, money, industrial technology, and social policies. Whereas a habit of consultation and a proclivity to joint positions often grew into common external fronts in some questions, constructive advancement has been negligible on paramount political and economic issues. The major shortcoming is the absence of a permanent system of effective communication and interaction between the Community and the general European public.

Beset by the world economic slump, which diverted the march toward integration called for in 1969–72, the EC has slowly come to recognize that significant internal preconditions must exist in order to fulfill a genuinely common and comprehensive external policy. As Corrado Pirzio-Biroli said in 1977, what became apparent in the struggles of the EC was the need for greater coherence between the emergent active foreign policies and certain economic issues, and the political process of decision formation.[1] To some observers, the central drive of the EC, so often failing to turn aspiration into practice, has become the imperative task of extending its competences and bypassing the obstacles that barricade most of the Brussels ventures. Enhancing the power and altering the composition of the community's Parliament has surfaced as one means to that end. Since the record of the seventies is one of wide disparities among member states' interest, and a lack of national sacrifice in forging collective answers, some observers say the integration dreams will remain just that. Others see an alternative route to free the EC of unproductive haggling and bickering. They advocate a "revolution" that would make the Parliament truly representative of the people.

## ENLARGEMENT

Once the three communities of the Treaties of Paris and Rome were merged into the European Community in 1969, which marked the achievement of most of the original 1957 goals, the new organization experienced several important changes. The first was the waning of French influence and power, and the rapid ascendency of German leadership. These were not mere per-

1. Corrado Pirzio-Biroli, "Foreign Policy Formation within the European Economic Community" (Unpublished, 1977). The author wishes to thank Signor Pirzio-Biroli for his extensive assistance.

sonnel shifts, although Pompidou and later Giscard D'Estaing and Claude Cheysson differed from De Gaulle as did Willy Brandt and Helmut Schmidt from Ludwig Erhard. What appeared was a novel sense of Community mission and rededication to the unfinished tasks.

German assertiveness was expressed in a broad range of issues as early as the enterprising milestone summit at The Hague, December 1969. Bonn determined to apply its dynamic pressure by proposing three priority points to her partners at that meeting, and later at the Paris summits in 1972 and 1974. The first and most critical issue was enlargement, which was finally possible to negotiate without French opposition.[2] In 1972, the Federal Republic, with the Dutch, pressed for redefinition of EC ties with the developing nations in a manner that averted the French inspired concepts of the Yaoundé agreements in 1963 and 1969.* Two years later, in December 1974, again at Paris, in a bid to jolt a beleagured Community into a positive renewal step, Bonn, with strong support from the Benelux Countries, sought to reform the institutional arrangement of the Nine with additional competences to the European Parliament.

None of these measures was exclu-

sively German, but Bonn did mobilize the member states and frequently assumed the initiative against the reluctant French. Nor were these the only notable goals in the seventies. Before enlargement the EC worked periodically to form joint programs, especially in monetary and financial union; however, interests collided in what were really half-hearted efforts made while awaiting the conclusion of enlargement negotiations.

The parallel-in-time debate over transforming EC development principles of aid, investment, and trade began with the enlargement of the Community from Six to Nine. The British sine qua non for entry, and German-Dutch sentiment, both worked toward a global approach, aiding a sympathetic Commission. More committed, bold, and creative Commissioners (first Dahrendorf and Deniau and later Cheysson, Soames, and Haferkamp) supported by talented, highly efficient and industrious Directorate-Generals (I-External Relations and VIII-Development) began to prod the member states to action. They urged the use of the Commission's right of initiative to promote a novel EC program of worldwide development cooperation negotiations. Transforming rather than amending the French-oriented Yaoundé model, the EC experts proposed a partnership arrangement with the poverty-ridden, nonaligned, often socialist states. The package they conceived contained not only a system of generalized preferences in trade, but also a unique system of guarantees for the developing countries and their export earnings, in addition to other innovative programs.[3]

2. Uwe Kitzinger, *Diplomacy and Persuasion: How Britain Joined the Common Market* (New York: Transatlantic Arts, 1973), 35–146; Katherine Savage, *The History of the Common Market* (London: Krestrel, 1976), 114–126.

* The first Yaounde Convention invited the AASM (associated African states and Madagascar) with the EC. These were essentially the former French colonies (Burundi, Cameroun, Central African Republic, Chad, Congo, Benin, Dahomey, Gabon, Ivory Coast, Madagascar, Mali, Mauritania, Niger, Rwanda, Senegal, Somalia, Togo, Upper Volta, and Zaire).

3. Julian West, ed., *Alternatives in Development: Is Europe Responding to Third*

Even before expansion in 1973, or the energy crises, certain forces in Brussels and other national capitals argued the necessity to renew and revitalize ties with more of the Third World than just the former European colonies. The question of the Commonwealth countries became central, because the British pushed the Commission to initiate principles for the replacement of Yaoundé II with the Afro-Caribbean-Pacific (ACP) bloc *and* the former British territories. Central was the notion of no discrimination against the anglophones with respect to early associates. Bonn and The Hague put their weight behind rejecting the older associational model with its neocolonial overtones.[4]

## DEVELOPMENT

Once the U.K., Ireland, and Denmark made the EC a Community of Nine, in January 1973, serious EC-ACP talks could commence. British participation in planning was crucial, but the February 1973 Accra talks established the prerequisites for complete negotiations. At these Ghana conferences, skeptical African anglophone ministers were convinced of EC good faith and the ACP bloc merged into one negotiating team with Nigeria leading the way. For the first time, the forty-six states saw the full STABEX idea. This mechanism guarantees Third World exports against fluctuations in world commodity prices, should they fall below an agreed reference

level and was, in effect, a stabilization scheme with its focal point in an EC financed compensation system. This idea was to become the major innovation of all North-South relations in the seventies, because it provided greater security for the poor economies against harsh climate conditions and global price changes, and afforded them a greater opportunity to engage in long range planning.

Based on the Accra breakthrough, Commission contributions, and the Bonn-London concert, EC-ACP negotiations started in the summer of 1973.[5] When the fall brought the Arab petroleum price hikes, the EC displayed two faces to the outside world. The disarray of the Nine was illustrated in the various national responses. Less obvious were the Community decisions not only to accelerate and deepen its ACP exchanges, but also to embark on redesigning external relations with two other major zones of interest—the Arab states and the Mediterranean basic countries.

On the heels of the crude oil price rise came a succession of Commission-led maneuvers aimed at more extensive cooperation packages.[6] Although not completed and signed until February 1975, the Lomé agreement was a stunning array of contractual interconnections between nearly fifty developing states and the EC.[*] The rapidly

5. The *Times* (London), February 16, 19, 1973; Pirzio-Biroli, "Foreign Policy Formation," pp. 30–32.

6. Horst Mendershausen, *Coping with the Oil Crisis: The French and German Experiment* (Baltimore: Johns Hopkins University Press, 1976).

*World Needs?* (Oxford: Pergamon Press, 1974) contains essays reflecting EC ideas of 1970–73. See also I. William Zartman, *The Politics of Trade Negotiations between Africa and the European Economic Community* (Princeton: Princeton University Press, 1971) on the Lomé concepts.

4. Pirzio-Biroli, "Foreign Policy Formation," pp. 22–30.

* The Lomé Convention was composed of: the 19 AASM states; the Arusha Agreement Commonwealth states, Kenya, Tanzania, and Uganda; 21 additional Commonwealth states, including Botswana, Gambia, Ghana, Lesotho, Malawi, Nigeria, Sierra Leone, Swaziland,

changing global politics of 1973–74 had their impact on the final terms of Lomé, which proclaimed in precise clauses the importance of *developed* nations in the future life of *developing* countries. The new power of the poorer states was visible in numerous terms, but none so evident as the stabilization fund, and free access to European markets for ACP exports, guaranteed with *no* reciprocity for European commodities. Lomé was an immediate landmark, for the Nine had stepped into a front rank position in the world vis à vis the Third World. In essence, the capital, technology, skills, and markets of the Nine—those elements so scarce in the South—were opened up to the ACP. The Community employed a wide range of cooperation mechanisms comprised of food and financial aid, technical assistance, promotion of exports, price stabilization, and aid to industry in exchange for access to the rich resources, foodstuffs and raw materials of the ACP. For the administration of the agreement and to maintain a continuous dialogue, joint institutions were formed which were to be models for later EC–Arab and EC–Mediterranean pacts.[7]

The fragmented response of the EC to the Arab oil actions permeated the snowbound Copenhagen summit in December 1973. This Council gathering, as summits are officially called, had a somber tone which illustrated the outward shock and disunity of the Nine. Yet, it was the locale for deciding to build a permanent structure to cope with Euro–Arab problems. Suffering with the rest of the oil consuming world, and unable to escape the immediate impact of the oil embargo and increasing food prices, the Community nevertheless assumed a positive outlook and began creating machinery for a dialogue. The structure was completed in mid 1974 but the first meeting of the Euro-Arab General Committee did not meet, because of aggravated political issues, until May 1976. The way was open to tackle complex issues: protecting investments, locating and funding a Euro–Arab center of technology transfer, industrial model contracts, and agricultural and infrastructure projects.

The range of disagreements was enormous, and the future uncertain; two world forces, who aspired to avoid the super-power orbit by achieving mutually beneficial economic advantages, produced no overriding panaceas but did achieve some tangible results. Despite some objections from friends (mainly the United States), the Nine put forth its ideological flexibility, technology, vast market, and most significantly, its willingness to enter into long range commitments with the Arab states. Rather than papering over their problems, or exacerbating them by direct confrontation, the Nine selected a wise path of slow, arduous diplomacy, seeking to locate affinities and overcome differences.

By early 1974, the Community produced its new overall policy

---

and Zambia; in the Caribbean, Barbados, Guyana, Jamaica, the Bahamas, Grenada, Trinidad, and Tobago; in the Pacific, Fiji, Western Samoa, Tonga; plus six other African states, Ethiopia, Guinea, Guinea-Bissau, Equatorial Guinea, Liberia and the Sudan, for a total of 46 African, Caribbean, and Pacific states.

7. "The European Community and the developing countries," *European Documentation*, no. 1 (1977). Also see the interesting essays of Carol Cosgrove-Twitchett in Kenneth Twitchett, ed., *Europe and the World: The External Relations of the Common Market* (New York: St. Martins Press, 1976), and those in Frans A. M. Alting von Geusau, ed., *The Lomé Convention and the New International Economic Order* (Leyden: A. W. Sijthoff, 1977).

program aimed at the countries on the rim of the Mediterranean that had historical, economic, and cultural links to the Nine. In the sixties, a series of separate arrangements had evolved with diverse states such as Greece, Yugoslavia and Spain, but by the mid-seventies the geographical scope had been enlarged to include all the Mediterranean coastline states plus Jordan and Portugal. The cooperation agreements needed a coherent framework, which the Nine formulated in 1974, with a free trade area and the principle of reverse preferences. The nondiscriminatory economic conventions were noteworthy for they reflected a Community no longer gazing south to appease or accommodate the Franco-Italian combination. Now the Nine were genuinely convinced of the need to deploy more efforts and energies into that region.

The nearly concurrent emergence of democratic experiments in Greece, Portugal, and Spain have since resulted in their applications for full membership in the EC. This second enlargement, which will be a centerpiece of the third decade, is not simply an outgrowth of EC magnetism and its past successes, but a reflection of the grand design to intensify contacts of various kinds between the two neighboring regions.[8]

8. On the dialogue, see the excerpts of Henri Simonet in "The Third Meeting of the General Committee of the Euro–Arab Dialogue," European Information Memo, P-100 (October 1977); on the Mediterranean design, see Phillipe Petit-Laurent, Les fondements politiques des engagements de la communauté européenne en Mediterranée (Paris: Presses Universitaires de France, 1976). By 1978, the EC announced that economic and monetary union plans and their completion were preconditions to enlargement, adding that the resources and stability needed to carry out expansion would come only with such common policies and the streamlining of the EC institutional mechanisms. Le Monde, 4 June 1978.

The thrust of post-Lomé EC activity has accentuated the fact that by mid-decade the developing states provided one half of EC imports, and were the largest export market for the Nine. This new pattern of economic relations was partially the result of changed perceptions. First, the nonwesterners had come to see the Nine as more understanding and less rigid than the superpowers when it came to the requirements of the developing countries. European ideological sympathy and economic capability, mostly modern European principles of resource allocation and income distribution, are seen as blending easily and positively with the less-developed outlooks. To put it bluntly, the nonaligned wanted to remain that way and saw the Community as the best, biggest, and most generous alternative open to them. From the European viewpoint, the new ties were seen, pragmatically, as the best avenue for recovery from recession, with the same impact on European production but without the direct inflationary effect that added consumption would have on the Nine. In a broader sense, the Europeans aspired to regain some of their sovereignty, lost since 1945, and to participate with more of a leadership role in a new international economic order. Tactically, there are those in Brussels who felt these bonds would strengthen the instruments of common action by ultimately transferring national development aid appropriations to Brussels supranational control.

## CONVERGENCE AND THE PARLIAMENT

As expansion and development policy were worked out, the far-reaching and extremely expensive Community projects of the cheap energy and steady growth era of 1969–73 receded from view. With Europe in deep recession, it was much less feasible to labor on monetary union, common industrial enterprises, and the transfer of resources through regional and social policies. The world economic crises and the trauma of recession made these ideas nearly impossible, for the Nine became preoccupied with their own battles against inflation.

One of the consequences of inflation-riddled Europe, and the slow recovery from stagflation which followed, has been internal squabbles so strong that they deadlock the Nine. Divergences have forced the postponement of serious talks, and the search for convergence has only just begun. Further integration has not prevailed because outright resistance, myopia, foot-dragging, and *attentisme* all reflect the formidable, even immense, problems of floating currencies and soaring inflation.[9] These contemporary events have strained the bonds that held the Community together. Nevertheless, the similarities and common purpose have held fast, as witness the too-easily-forgotten June 1975 British referendum on staying in the Nine.

In the midst of all the setbacks, only one *major* attempt to prevent the EC from coming unstruck has been initiated.[10] This priority project, to give the Parliament real teeth and a democratic base, has become the

single venture aimed at structural reform. The other institutional novelty of the seventies—the Council with its summits—has turned out to be almost as ineffectual as the maze of ministerial groups, or the Brussels technocrats, primarily because these heads of state have not even attempted to overhaul Community operations.

The supranationality that follows in the wake of a democratic European legislature is seen by many as the best means to a more viable Community. When earlier efforts to empower the Parliament gained only limited success, the Commission acted as the friend and ally of that body and advocated increased budgetary powers. In 1974 at Paris, the member states agreed to direct elections. With little enthusiasm by the British and French, the Community decided to get the people of the Nine more involved. A partial motivation was the belief that a grassroots connection in the Community would foster a genuine three way power and responsibility distribution. Although incremental increase in Parliament authority, like interpellation rights and the Court of Auditors, gave the parliamentarians some greater part in the legislative and foreign policymaking processes, they represented limited gains. Co-control over the budget and finances would improve the Community's structure and operations but would hardly be the full answer. Giving the EC a more lustrous focus of democratic legitimation might help bring out the long thwarted rationalization of Community decisionmaking and sponsor more solidarity of action.

The impasse of the EC and the benefits of the triumph of democracy have been interwoven by those who see the directly elected Parliament as a counterweight means to release the EC from the divergence dilemma.

9. See *The New York Times*, 18 July 1978, for the Copenhagen II summit and Bonn meeting declarations of intent, as examples of the possible cooperation in the summer of 1978.

10. Marion Bywater and Paul Kemizis, "The Parliament Today," *European Community*, no. 196 (Aug.–Sept. 1976), pp. 14–17; Pierre-Henri Laurent, "The European Elections and the Making of Europe," *World Affairs*, vol. 140, no. 4 (Spring 1978), pp. 273–83.

The idea is that if this institution is composed of the peoples' representatives, they can and will flex their new political muscles and assert a "codetermination" role.

## THE PRICE OF SUCCESS

Certain developments in the seventies have forced the EC into a "coherence exercise" which would work toward some of the same ends, theoretically, as would a democratic parliament. Since the domestic economic policies of these nine industrial states are considerably closer now to many non-European states, and since the EC external trade is greatly liberalized, the Nine must pursue structural adjustments of their own production, distribution, and exchange system. The almost natural tendency, in times of economic ills, has been the national route of protectionism. The member states have been ambivalent in that they have used this approach, but it has become clear that this is indulging in an illusion. The benefits of coordinating the separate systems by collective policies, especially in manpower, regional development, and technology transfer became evident, but the actual means difficult to select. The burdensome, expensive, illogical, and protectionistic common agricultural policy remains the most clear cut example of needed reform to adjust to new realities.

The Community political structure has hammered out some harmonized and coordinated positions, but not faced the divergences in inflation, trade, and growth that are still enormous and, in fact, increasing in the present economic circumstances. The essence of stagnation for the EC is the way in which that condition magnifies and adds to the inability to formulate a coherence between internal and external EC policies.

The world's largest trading bloc has become, in this decade, a greater force of worldwide significance, engaged in a closer partnership with more of the developing world and its neighbors. It has enlarged once, and faces again the process of long accommodative diplomacy in order to expand. Furthermore, it has taken the first concrete move toward creating a democratic organ which *might* be at the center of Community action. At the same time, the EC has failed to bridge national and Community systems. Even though the gloomy paralysis may end with international economic revival, there will still be an urgent need for more will and impetus to collaborate and compromise. And the Europeans will have to face, straight on, the political necessity of finding new ways out of the divergences that have checked their progress in the seventies.

ANNALS, AAPSS, 440, Nov. 1978

# France in the Communities: Presidential and Party Attitudes

By JOYCE QUIN

ABSTRACT: The founding of the European Community was followed, shortly afterwards, by the death of the Fourth Republic in France and the establishment of the Fifth Republic under de Gaulle. Since then the attitude of France to the EC has been well known for its idiosyncratic qualities. Formerly one of the main inspirators for unity, France became, under the Fifth Republic, the enfant terrible of the European family. However, when in 1974 the first non-Gaullist President of the Republic, Valery Giscard d'Estaing was elected—reputedly more "European-minded" than his predecessors—a different approach was expected. This article describes the way French presidential and party attitudes have evolved in recent years. While French political differences over European integration have been deep, it will be shown that, due partly to experience gained through the workings of the EC, divisions have become less marked, and occasionally pronouncements by major political spokesmen on European matters have an uncanny similarity. Where differences still exist—as they undoubtedly do—they cause as much disunion within each of the major political groupings of Right and Left as between them.

---

*Joyce Quin is a member of the academic staff of the University of Durham (UK) where she lectures in both the French and Politics Departments. A graduate of the University of Newcastle-upon-Tyne she subsequently obtained her Master's degree at the London School of Economics. From 1972–1977 she was Lecturer in French at the University of Bath. Her main interest is French politics, in which field she has written articles and book reviews, and is currently preparing her doctoral thesis.*

SINCE 1973 France seems to have been dominated by elections and by the frantic political atmosphere which they engender. The seemingly inexorable rise of the parties of the Left (from their good showing in the Legislative elections of 1973, their near win in the Presidential confrontation of 1974, to their victories in the cantonal and municipal elections of 1976 and 1977) served to heighten political tension and create a competitive climate in which all issues, including European ones, tended to be exploited for domestic political advantage, frequently proving an excuse for one or other of the parties within each alliance to play politics, to maneuver, to apply pressure, or to appear conciliating towards partners and rivals.

President Giscard d'Estaing's own position, since his election, has not been a particularly easy one. While stating firmly, shortly after his arrival in office, that France wished to be governed from the Centre, he has had to rely on a Parliamentary majority in which the Gaullist Party (RPR) has been the largest component.[1] He has thus had a far from free hand in the conduct of the nation's affairs.

Now that the legislative elections are over and the union of the left is in some disarray, there has been speculation about the possibility of some new kind of Parliamentary majority emerging, including perhaps the President's own Republican party, its Centrist allies within the UDF and some, if not all, of the Socialists.[2] Even if such a re-

alignment took place, however, President Giscard would still need to rely upon the parties concerned; for this reason, in order to understand France's approach to EC questions, a knowledge of party as well as presidential attitudes is crucial.

## PRESIDENTIAL ATTITUDES

The accepted view of the differences between the three Presidents of the Fifth Republic is: of the three, de Gaulle was the most hostile to European integration; Giscard d'Estaing is the most European; with Pompidou occupying an intermediate position. The reality, however, is more complex. The terms "pro-" and "anti-European," while useful terms of political shorthand, are notoriously imprecise and are subject to widely differing interpretations. They are closely bound up, too, with attitudes on other questions, such as Europe's relationship with the United States, and its role within the Western alliance and the Western economic system. While many consider that de Gaulle, with his stress on French national independence, was an anti-European, the opposite has been claimed; far from hindering the EC's development it was he who helped to build it up in a realistic manner, determined to create a Europe which would be truly independent of both superpowers.[3]

Did de Gaulle and his successor Pompidou differ substantially in

---

1. The Gaullist Party, formerly called the Union of Democrats for the Republic (UDR), became the Rally for the Republic (RPR) in December 1976.

2. The Union for French Democracy (UDF) was formed in February 1978 by the

Republicans and the Centre parties primarily in order to prevent competition between themselves in the electoral constituencies. Its creation meant that, in the 1978 elections, the main parties were grouped in four political families: Gaullists; UDF; Socialists (and Left Radicals); and Communists.

3. Notably in Gilles Gozard, *De Gaulle, face á l'Europe* (Paris: PLON, 1976).

their attitude towards the EC? It would appear so, since Pompidou allowed the entry of Great Britain into the Community, supported the plan for Economic and Monetary Union, and made public utterances in favour of a rather ill-defined European Union to be achieved by 1980. It can be argued, however, that his approach did not represent a marked departure from what had preceded. Regarding the entry of Britain, for example, rather than this being the result of selfless Europeanism on Pompidou's part, it seems likely that he agreed to it because he felt that the time had come when it would serve France's interests. Firstly, the Common Agricultural Policy, de Gaulle's special concern, was by then firmly established and stood in contrast to the lack of common policies in other spheres. This meant that the other member countries would be unwilling to see it disintegrate, and although Britain disliked it she would accept it as an inevitable part of entry and as something not to be immediately challenged. Secondly, French political dominance in the Community vis-a-vis Germany no longer seemed secure. The economic giant was looking less and less the political dwarf and the addition of Great Britain might, therefore, be a welcome counterweight.

The transition from Pompidou to Giscard d'Estaing may be similarly viewed from the angle of continuity. Indeed Giscard himself has frequently stressed the continuity, claiming to be "Pompidolian" to the extent that he and his predecessor both saw the European option as the best way of strengthening French influence. For both, the independence of France could best be protected within an independent united Europe. Has there been nothing more, therefore, than the celebrated change of style in the attitude of Giscard d'Estaing to the EC? A brief review of the policies pursued since 1974 may be helpful.

## The energy crisis

There appears to have been little difference in the attitudes of Pompidou and Giscard d'Estaing to the world energy crisis of 1973–74. Both determinedly kept France aloof from Washington's initiatives in organizing the industrialized countries in response to the problem; and under Giscard, France refused to become a member of the IEA, regarding it as an "energy NATO."[4] Both urged a common EC approach to the problem and advocated the pursuance of closer relations with Arab countries.

## Attitude to the European institutions

Giscard, like his predecessors, seems to favour summitry within the EC, preferring the meetings of heads of state, as a way of deciding new policies, to the innovative and policy-formulating role of the Commission. Indeed, on his initiative, the Paris Summit of December 1974 institutionalized summits in creating the European Council—a development which was certainly in line with proposals for altering the EC's institutional structure made earlier by de Gaulle and Pompidou. At the same time, however, the heads of government, including Giscard, did decide that there should be less insistence on obtaining unanimity for all Community decisions, although in practice the effects of this have not turned out to be farreaching.

4. *Keesings Contemporary Archives* 1974, p. 26848.

Giscard's attitude to the Commission seems to have been one of indifference, even dislike. In the spring of 1977 he expressed strong opposition to the proposal that Roy Jenkins, the Commission President, should represent the EC at the London economic summit. This stance may be partly explained by a desire to placate Gaullist opinion at the time of the French municipal elections, and it is true that when the elections were over he agreed, reluctantly, to Jenkins being present for some of the agenda of the conference.

### Direct elections

The commitment to direct elections to the European Parliament, taken at the December 1974 European summit, aroused much controversy in France, and the President experienced considerable difficulty in seeking to obtain Gaullist support for the measure. For lack of space the events surrounding the issue cannot be analyzed in full here. Suffice it to say that eventually, in view of the opposition within France, Giscard submitted the matter to the Constitutional Council which ruled that although direct elections did not infringe on the French Constitution, any further increase in the European Parliament's powers would necessitate a Constitutional amendment. Because of this, and in order to lessen Gaullist hostility, a clause was included in the legislation giving French consent to the elections but stipulating that, save in the case of a revision of the Constitution, France would accept no further increase in the European Parliament's powers. This legislation was passed by virtue of Article 49 of the French Constitution: this allows a bill, which has been made an issue of confidence, to pass without a vote if no censure motion has been tabled. It should be noted, therefore, that no *positive* vote in favor of direct elections was accorded by French parliamentarians.

The issue of direct elections provides an example of the President espousing a "European" cause. However, there seems to be little evidence of enthusiasm on his part for any significant transfer of powers to the European Parliament from the national legislatures.

### Economic and monetary union

Giscard d'Estaing, as Finance Minister under Pompidou, was associated with the first European attempts to establish an Economic and Monetary Union, as was Raymond Barre, the present Prime Minister and former Vice-President of the European Commission. The President is still in favor of European initiatives in this sphere, although in light of the previous failure, he is aware of the difficulties involved. Whether his advocacy of such a union is motivated primarily by a desire to create a supranational Europe is uncertain. It can more readily be explained by the wish, fully shared by his predecessors, to lessen the dominance of the United States in international monetary affairs.

### Enlargement

The President seems sympathetic toward the applications of Greece, Spain, and Portugal for EC membership, because of the need to strengthen democracy in those countries. However, because of the affects of their economies on French agriculture, he has urged caution, indicating that a lengthy transition period will be involved. The French defense of the Common Agricultural Policy remains as firm as ever under Giscard d'Estaing.

## Summary

In the above brief account of the Presidents' policies it can be seen that on most aspects there has been little substantive change from preceding approaches. For Giscard political impetus within the EC must come primarily from the national governments and initiatives can only be approved if these conform to a rigorous definition of French interests.

## ATTITUDES OF THE PARTIES OF THE RIGHT AND CENTER—THE PRESIDENTIAL MAJORITY

### The Republicans

The Republican Party has been, from the time of its creation in 1966, very much the instrument and means of support for the political ambitions of Giscard d'Estaing.[5] It has consistently defined itself as being in favour of a distinct form of "Europeanism" which it describes as neither "*l'Europe des Etats*," the confederal Europe of the Gaullists, nor the "*Etats-unis d'Europe*" of the federalists, but "l'Europe existentielle"—an existential Europe built slowly but surely on the mutual compatibilities and lasting common interests of the members.

### The Center parties

The two main center parties of President Giscard's coalition, the Centre of Social Democrats[6] (CDS) and the Radical Party have always been the most obviously European parties. The CDS is particularly proud of its European heritage, revering the memory of Robert Schuman, one of the EC's founding fathers, who had belonged to the CDS' predecessor the Popular Republican Movement (MRP). Both CDS and the Radicals are enthusiastic about the ideal of integration, seeing it as a way of breaking down harmful nationalistic barriers between peoples.

### Gaullists

The Gaullists supported de Gaulle's policies throughout the sixties, praising his championing of French interests and his attitude to the "nonsense" of supranationalism. Underlying this staunch defense of France, however, was the realization that intergovernmental cooperation at least was important within Europe in order to provide a counterweight to the superpowers and, so long as French interests could never be overridden, the EC should therefore be supported. This explains the ease of adaptation to Pompidou's less abrasive approach and the acceptance of enlargement to include Britain, although it is true that some Gaullist diehards, represented most vigorously by the former Prime Minister Michel Debré and Alexandre Sanguinetti, were dubious about Pompidou's policies. With the advent of Giscard d'Estaing to the Presidency, this suspicion has increased and the Gaullists have set themselves up as the watchdogs of what they see as

5. Created formally in June 1966, as the National Federation of Independent Republicans (FNRI), it became the Republican Party in May 1977.

6. Formed in May 1976 because of a merger between the Democratic Centre (CD) and the Centre for Democracy and Progress (CDP).

French vital interests, prepared to cry out loudly if French sovereignty seems to be imperiled.

While the differences between the parties, as described, seem clear-cut, in recent years they have become less marked because of the way the integration process has slowed down. The Gaullists, having seen their leader successfully safeguard French interests within the Community in the sixties, have come to view the EC as a positive good. The Centrists, disappointed at the slowness of integration, have come to accept the fact that the goal of unity will not be achieved overnight and cannot be forced on unwilling governments jealous of their sovereignty. The Republicans consider that the slowness of the process has justified their initial analysis. There still remains, however, the important difference in how unity is viewed. For the Centrists it remains a desirable end in itself, while Gaullists, and to a lesser extent Republicans, see it as desirable insofar as it promotes French political and economic well-being.

## ATTITUDES TO CURRENT ISSUES

### Attitudes to the European institutions and the issue of direct elections

For the Gaullists the only really valid European institution is the Council of Ministers whose work is supplemented and enhanced by that of the European Council. Their suspicion of the political ambitions of the Commission is deep-rooted and not surprising. Although they participate actively in the work of the European Parliament, as do Republicans and Centrists, the idea of that Parliament as an embryonic European legislature is unaccept-

able to them.[7] The Republicans are less hostile to the supranational institutions but feel that for the foreseeable future initiative must lie with national governments. The Centre parties, however, consider that a strengthening of the supranational institutions is what European unity is all about. For them such a strengthening is necessary in order to counteract the essentially "egotistical" Council of Ministers.[8]

Differences between the parties of the Right and Centre on European issues have recently been seen most clearly in the question of direct elections. Internally the Gaullists were the most divided. A majority of them was prepared to accept the elections but was suspicious of where they might lead. A small minority (Michel Debre and his supporters) expressed total hostility, feeling that it would be highly regrettable to endow the Parliament with a spurious legitimacy; another minority (represented by Jacques Chaban-Delmas and Olivier Guichard) was in favor. The position of the leader Jacques Chirac was somewhat ambiguous. He denied that he had ever given his approval to the idea when he had been Prime Minister, and declared that the elections created a "dangerous illusion" but that he was not opposed to them in principle.[9] He was, however, opposed to the granting of

7. The Gaullists, together with the Irish Fianna Fail Party and the Danish Progress Party, have formed a rather curious political group in the European Parliament entitled the Group of European Progressive Democrats. The Republicans and Radicals are part of the *Liberal and Democratic Group* and the CDS is in the *Christian Democratic Group* whose members, in July 1976, joined to found the *European People's Party* (EPP).
8. From notes for Speakers, issued by the Radical Party to its 1978 election candidates.
9. Speech by Jacques Chirac in the National Assembly, 15 June 1977.

further powers to the Parliament and welcomed the ruling of the Constitutional Council which removed enough Gaullist doubts about the project for them to refrain from voting against the Government in a censure motion. The Centrists were certainly disappointed at this outcome since, in their opinion, the legitimacy conferred by direct elections would automatically entitle the Parliament to be given greater powers.

## Economic and Monetary Union

On this question all the parties are in favor. For the Gaullists, and to a lesser extent the Republicans, it is seen as a way of promoting a long wished for change in what is seen as the American-dominated international monetary situation, whereas for the Centrists it is an essential stage in the building of a united Europe.

## Enlargement

All parties of the Right and Centre have expressed varying degrees of caution. The Gaullists, while so far not formally opposing enlargement, feel that, particularly as concerns Spain and Greece, it is likely to have serious consequences on the workings of the Common Agricultural Policy; and have expressed determination to safeguard French farming interests. The Republicans, for similar reasons, are also wary, although their 1978 Election manifesto does state that in order to strengthen democracy in these countries it would be "unthinkable" to bar the door to their applications. The CDS and the Radical Party also express support for French farmers but add another dimension to the problem by saying firmly that there should be no enlargement until further steps towards integration have been made by the exist-

ing members. They are voicing the concern, felt by many Europeans, that enlargement without some concomitant strengthening of the EC would only exacerbate existing tensions and possibly bring about the collapse of the Community completely.

## Summary

To sum up the attitudes of the parties of the Right and Centre, it can be seen that European issues are not such a bone of contention in the seventies as they have been in the past; and that despite some common aspects, important and substantial differences do persist.

## THE QUESTION OF THE LEFT

Until the results of the 1978 Legislative elections were known, there was considerable speculation about what policies in European affairs a government of the Left would pursue, the EC being an area which had traditionally divided Communists and Socialists, and in which important differences still remained.

## General party attitudes—the Communists

Early Communist Party suspicion of the EC as a capitalist plot, which was reflected in an initial party policy of noninvolvement in the Community, gave way during the course of the sixties to a more positive approach. Seeing the Community as a reality, albeit a rather unpleasant one, they sought to make the Communist presence felt at the Community level. Hence the eventual Communist participation in Community institutions. The search within France for a common front with the Socialists, seen as the only way to come to power, also led to a change in Communist attitudes.

French membership in the EC became accepted therefore but, in Communist eyes, the EC should not become so powerful that it could threaten the policies of a Communist-Socialist coalition in France. This attitude explains why, in the Left's Common Programme of Government, signed in 1972, the commitment to participating in and constructing further the European Community was counteracted with the conflicting statement that the Community should not be allowed in any way to impede the left-wing government in the implementation of its policies. It should be noted that in Communist Party publications the concept of the nation-state, far from being outdated, is considered to be more valid than ever, and national independence is stressed as ardently as by the Gaullists.

## The Socialists

Firm supporters of integration in the fifties and sixties (although divided about the proposed creation of the European Defense Community in 1954), the Socialists, while still being pro-European, have in recent years increasingly criticized the present nature of the EC as being insufficiently socialist.[10] The Party's views on European policies were discussed in detail at a special party conference held at Bagnolet in December 1973 where different opinions on the subject could be seen. As on most issues, however, the clearest division was between the majority (Mitterrand) faction and the left-wing minority CERES (Centre d'Etudes, de Recherches et d'Education Socialistes)

10. For a more detailed treatment of Socialist attitudes see Joyce G. Quin, "The French Socialist Party and the EEC: Attitudes and Policies 1971–1974," *Journal of European Studies*, vol 6, part 3, no. 23, pp. 209–227.

which accounts for approximately 25 percent of Party membership. CERES is much more critical of the way the EC has evolved up to the present and, while it sees the Community as a potentially suitable framework for European socialist cooperation, it considers that immediate prospects of the Community moving in the desired direction are poor. Like the Communists, therefore, it feels that a left-wing government in France must preserve its independence in order to carry out its socialist program at home. Having been staunch advocates of the Socialist-Communist alliance, CERES seems to be somewhat demoralized because of the strains undergone by the Union of the Left in the past year, and—because of the election defeat—the amount of pressure it will be able to exert on future party developments is therefore uncertain.

## The Left Radicals (MRG)

A small group of Left Radicals broke away from the main Radical Party in 1972 and signed the Common Program of the Left shortly afterwards. True to their Radical tradition, they are proud of the role Radicals played in the EC's early years. There has been no conflict between the MRG and the Socialists over European issues although the MRG is somewhat less critical of the way the EC has developed to date. Between the Left Radicals on the one hand, and CERES and the Communists on the other, however, differences are noticeable.

## Attitudes to the European institutions and the question of direct elections

Communists and Socialists have very different attitudes toward the supranational community institutions. Socialists and Left Radicals wish to democratize and strengthen them whereas Communists are opposed to any increase in their powers. For this reason the two main parties of the Left fell out over the question of increasing the budgetary powers of the Parliament in December 1976.[11] In the Left's Common Program the only strengthening of the European institutions which could be agreed on, despite the objective stated therein of building up the EC, was a modest democratization of the (consultative) Economic and Social Committee and of FEOGA, the Agricultural Guidance and Guarantee Fund.

The French Socialists have always cooperated actively with their fraternal parties within the Socialist group of the European Parliament (the only group to have member parties in all nine EC countries), and in the course of 1977 helped draft a European Socialist manifesto, an action which was criticized by the French Communists who claimed that its content conflicted with the provisions of the Common Programme of Government.[12]

During the early part of 1977 the issue of direct elections seemed as if it would severely damage the unity of the French Left. Socialists and Left Radicals were in favor, whereas Communists had long since been opposed to the idea. Indeed the Communist leader Georges Marchais had claimed that they constituted a "crime against France." In April 1977, however, the Communist Party announced a sudden and major change of policy by stating that, since the French Government (after the Constitutional Council's ruling) was committed to refusing any further powers to the European Parliament, the way of electing that Parliament was no longer important and they would no longer oppose direct elections as such.

*Enlargement*

The possible enlargement of the Community to include Portugal, Spain, and Greece is another contentious issue between the forces of the Left. In that part of the Common Program which was *actualisé* (brought up to date) for the 1978 elections, a compromise formula was worked out which states that "Any new application for membership in the Community from democratic countries shall be examined, taking into account, as a priority, French agricultural and industrial interests."[13] The Socialist official position had been that, in principle, they were in favor of enlargement so long as a transition period would allow necessary adjustments to be made in the economies of the applicants. The Communists had voiced formal opposition to enlargement, giving as their reason the intolerable competition for French Mediterranean agriculture. It seems likely also that, privately, the Communists felt that their own influence would be even further diluted within an enlarged Community at the expense of Socialist and Social-Democratic tendencies.

*Summary*

It can be seen that on certain issues compromises between the parties of the Left have been made and, in some respects, they are

---

11. *Le Monde*, 9 December 1976.
12. Communist Party pamphlet, "*Les Communistes Francais et l'Europe.*"

13. *Le Programme commun de gouvernement de la gauche: propos socialistes pour l'actualisation* (Paris: Flammarion 1978) p. 118.

closer on EC matters than they were a decade ago. Again, however, much of this has been due to the slowing down of the European integration process which has meant that the contradiction of aims expressed in the Common Program has not been fully exposed. Tactical reasons have also played their part in making compromises possible. Furthermore, many of the issues which could cause very thorny problems, such as the question of defense within the EC, have been largely ignored in the quest for unity.

PUBLIC OPINION

Public opinion in France has remained constantly, although somewhat placidly, in favor of Europe since the integration process began, and there seems to have been little change in this overall attitude in the seventies. In an opinion poll taken in September 1977, by the Louis Harris (France) Institute, the following results were obtained.[14]

While it is not surprising that Communist supporters appear less enthusiastic than any of the other groups, even in their ranks more favor than oppose integration, indicating a considerable degree of national consensus on the subject. The distinction between supporters of the parties of the Right and Centre are seen here to be minimal. Indeed, by a slight margin, it is the reputedly anti-European RPR which has the greatest percentage in favor! This may be explained in various ways, none of which are wholly conclusive. First, it may indeed indicate a genuine evolution on the part of RPR supporters, since the days of de Gaulle, towards a pro-European stance. Second, it may illustrate nothing more than the elasticity of the term pro-European; or third, it may mean that although European integration commands general support among the French public, it is not an issue which is important in determining party loyalty.

*Poll on European Integration*

| | Very Much in Favour or Moderately in Favour Percent | Very Much Opposed or Moderately Opposed Percent | Don't Knows Percent |
|---|---|---|---|
| TOTAL of Those Questioned | 59 | 17 | 24 |
| *Party affiliation* | | | |
| Communists | 45 | 32 | 23 |
| Socialists | 65 | 16 | 19 |
| Left Radicals | 63 | 22 | 15 |
| Centrists | 67 | 16 | 17 |
| Republicans | 67 | 13 | 20 |
| Gaullists | 71 | 14 | 15 |

14. Published by the newspaper *Le Matin* in its *Dossier des Legislatives 1978*, p. 37.

## CONCLUSIONS

In the past few years it has been possible to detect certain common threads in the pronouncements of the major parties of Right and Left about European affairs. All parties see French involvement in the EC as necessary and desirable but all (even the Centrists, although less insistently) stress at the same time the value of national independence. Communists, Socialists, Gaullists and Republicans, from their different perspectives and to different degrees, stress the need for French sovereignty to remain intact. While lip service is paid to the ideal of European unity, it is seen very much as a long-term prospect.

All (with the possible exception of the Centrists) feel that any form of united Europe should assert its independence, politically and economically, from the United States. Gaullists and Communists are particularly vocal on this point, as is the left-wing minority CERES in the Socialist party. It is certainly true that French parties, even though most acknowledge America as an ally, are much more wary of American economic and political involvement in Europe than are the major parties in the other EC countries. To this extent all the French parties have been influenced by, and live in the shadow of, de Gaulle.

Not surprisingly, the need to safeguard French economic interests is widely emphasized, and among these interests agriculture is paramount. All parties firmly support the Common Agricultural Policy, although Communists and Socialists would like to see it provide more adequately for the needs of the less well-off farming sector. All express considerable reservations (or, in the case of the Communists, formal opposition) concerning the accession of Greece, Portugal and Spain to the Common Market, although the Portuguese economy is considered as less of a threat.

None of the major parties (Centrists apart) express much enthusiasm for the existing supranational institutions of the Community. The Commission is seen as too bureaucratic or too meddlesome, the Parliament as inadequate or, in the Gaullist and Communist view, as potentially, dangerously powerful!

Yet, in analyzing the similarities between the major parties, differences become quickly apparent and European matters continue to divide internally each bloc of Right and Left. The similarities noted do not derive, for the most part, from any fundamental consensus. Neither have these similarities prevented considerable discord within each bloc, particularly on the issue of direct elections; although a compromise was eventually arrived at on this question it looks to be a fragile creation.

On European issues the paradoxes in French political life are still striking. The coincidence of views between Communists and Gaullists still occurs. Yet the impression overall is that the Gaullist hardliners are dwindling and, with the slowing down of the integration process, Europe is seen as less of a supranational threat. This has had the effect of blurring the distinctions between Gaullists and Republicans.

However, the way that European issues still prove contentious within blocs—and in some cases within parties—serves to explain why, notwithstanding the generally favourable attitude of public opinion, European integration was largely ignored during the recent legislative election campaign.

Finally, despite the calmer political climate prevailing after the elections, divisions over Europe, within the Parliamentary majority upon which President Giscard at present relies, mean that (with the possible exception of economic and monetary matters where differences seem to be least acute) the Government is unlikely to be in a position to pursue a dynamic European policy in the near future.[15]

15. While the emergence of some new and possibly more pro-European majority (such as Republicans, Centrists and some, if not all of the Socialists) around the President, mentioned at the beginning of this article, cannot entirely be ruled out, at the time of writing it appears remote. In any case, of course, even with such a majority in France, external circumstances and the attitudes of France's EC partners could still preclude any swift progress towards unity.

# The Parliament and the Commission

By JEAN-JOSEPH SCHWED

ABSTRACT: In the European Community, relations between the Institutions — Parliament, Council, Commission, Court of Justice, Court of Auditors — are determined by the treaties which established the European Communities. Relations between the Commission and the European Parliament have developed considerably over the last 20 years and are coming increasingly to resemble those between a national government and its Parliament. The election of the European Parliament by direct universal suffrage in June 1979 will give a new dimension to these essentially political relations. The Institutions will continue to evolve during the coming decade and relations between the Commission and the Parliament will undoubtedly be strengthened. Similarly, the Council will probably change shape in ways that cannot yet be foreseen.

*Jean-Joseph Schwed is Head of the Division for Liaison with the European Parliament at the Commission of the European Communities. He has held this post for over 15 years and is thus a close observer of institutional relations in the Community. Mr. Schwed holds French Law and Arts degrees and is a Master of Arts of the University of Chicago. He is the author of a number of publications on institutional matters and, more especially, on the European Parliament.*

THE THEME of this issue of *The Annals*—the European Community after 20 years—provides an excellent opportunity for speaking of the European Parliament. It has taken 20 years of change for the Community to implement the intentions of its founding fathers, as laid down in the Treaties of Paris and Rome.

When the European Parliament met in March 1958, it replaced the European Coal and Steel Community's Assembly, and had the same form it still has today. But, 20 years later, on 7 April 1978, in Copenhagen, the heads of state of the different governments fixed the date on which the Parliament was to be elected by direct universal suffrage, thus giving concrete effect to Article 21 of the Treaty establishing the European Coal and Steel Community, ECSC, Article 138 of the Treaty establishing the European Economic Community, EEC, and Article 108 of the Treaty establishing the European Atomic Energy Commission, EAEC. It has taken 18 years to reach agreement; 21 will have elapsed by the time the elections are held. Voting is now to take place in the nine Member States of the Community between 7 and 10 June 1979.

This does not mean, however, that it has needed the election of the European Parliament for democratic community control suddenly to be brought into existence. The Community conceived by Jean Monnet, Robert Schuman, Konrad Adenauer, and Alcide de Gaspari was already a democratic community. For the founding fathers of Europe it was unthinkable that a state structure be established among the six original member countries without a representation of their peoples, which, albeit at one remove, would play the same role as parliaments do in democratic systems of government.

Pending the direct elections, Parliament is composed of delegates from the national parliaments, whose task thus becomes European in scale, and who approach it in the same spirit and with the same demands as in their home Parliaments. Their role, like that of Parliament itself, is important—today it is instrumental in preserving the balance of power within the Community, tomorrow it will be essential.

With the Commission representing the Community interest and the Council the national interests, it is just as well that the Parliament exists as a balancing element. In the near future direct elections will give this institution a new face.[1] In the Community's constitutional system, the Parliament will be the only institution whose political nature is fundamentally different. While the Council, the Commission, the Court of Justice, and the Court of Auditors have ties with the member states—some because they represent them, others because their members are drawn from them— the elected Parliament will receive its mandate directly from the peoples of the Community. It will be independent and autonomous with respect both to governments and states, deriving its legitimacy from the popular vote.

This situation will cause a shift in the relationships between the Community's institutions. In relation to the Council, which is a Community

1. For a general background on the development of the direct elections idea, see Pierre-Henri Laurent, "The European Elections and The Making of Europe," *World Affairs*, no. 4 (Spring 1978), 273–284.

institution but represents the governments and is composed of their members, the elected Parliament will undoubtedly wield greater authority. Confrontation between those elected by the people and those representing governments is bound to become more acute. The terrain and the weapons adopted will give a new dimension to relations between the Council and Parliament.

There will be no fundamental transformation of the relationship between Parliament and the Commission, but the change brought about by the direct elections will put it in a new light and should remove a certain number of ambiguities. The representative function of the Member of Parliament will then be perfectly clear, which often has not been the case in the past. The Commission will continue to be fully independent in the exercise of its functions, actuated by a concern to defend and promote the Community interest. The Parliament, which has been directly elected by the peoples of Europe, will have the same interest at heart, but considered equally from both the specifically national and the general Community aspects. Both institutions will have to arbitrate between the interests, however legitimate, of the member states and the higher interest of the Community; and the two will not necessarily coincide. After direct elections, the two institutions may more frequently disagree on interpretations of what is the higher interest of the Community.

The close relationship between the Commission and the Parliament enhances the power of each body. The Commission gains necessary political dimension and impetus for its programs from the Parliament,

to which it is responsible. Although there have been two attempts, the Commission has never been dismissed, the ultimate sanction on which parliamentary control is based. The control Parliament exercises over the Commission has been its chief means of influencing community affairs. Thus the two are integrally related, deriving mutual benefit and exerting a kind of conjugal control. After the popular elections, the function of the Parliament will expand beyond legislation and control to include providing stimulus for programs and utilizing the political power possessed by an institution emanating directly from the people.

## PARLIAMENTARY PARTICIPATION IN COMMUNITY DECISIONMAKING

The Commission, which alone has the right to initiate legislation, has a delicate role to play. It has to allow for the Council's reluctance to act, the member states varying in the extent to which they are willing to accept its ideas, and it must, at the same time, effect the policies it has outlined in the Annual Programme presented to and discussed by the Parliament. Faced with the hesitations of the institution which is to make the decisions, and the intentions expressed by the institution to which it is responsible, the Commission must choose the appropriate terms and tactics. Once it has defined its position, it must defend it, cognizant of the fact that once the Council's procedures have been completed its proposal can be amended only by unanimous decision of the member states.

At this stage in the procedure it is, therefore, just as important for mutual confidence to reign between the Commission and the Parliament as it is vital for the Commission to be fully aware of the situation in the Member States. This mutual confidence is established in the course of a number of informal procedures agreed upon between the Parliament and the Commission, though these do not appear in the Treaties.

Consultation of the elected Parliament is provided for in 22 Articles of the EEC Treaty and 11 Articles of the EAEC Treaty. Any Community act based on one of these Articles, which had not had parliamentary consultation would, under EEC Article 173, be invalid. Any member state, or even any private person, could rely on this irregularity before the Court of Justice. Since 1963, the Commission and the Council have, of their own initiative, widened the scope of consultation, being convinced that Parliament's opinion needed to be obtained on any proposal which had political, economic or social implications. Thus, the European Parliament is consulted by the Council, on a proposal from the Commission, on all Community regulations which are to have force of law in the member states. Just as governments lay down rules, the Commission acts independently in adopting regulations and taking decisions of more limited scope.

When a Commission proposal is put before the Parliament, the Commission, like any Government dealing with its Parliament, tries to defend its text as a whole. Close collaboration is established, both in the parliamentary committees and at the plenary session, to convince Parliament of the merits of the Commission's proposals. The debates at the plenary session provide a unique opportunity for the commission to see its texts debated in public, thus receiving coverage by the press and the various media, and obtaining wider audience. One example is the annual proposal on farm prices, which is an occasion for public debate where all opinions can be voiced.

Public discussion also serves the purpose of clarifying the positions of both the Commission and the Parliament. The fact that they take the same attitude, or that their opinions diverge, is not without interest to the public, or even for the Council, which may have to face a united front if it wants to change a Commission proposal.

The Commission's independence, deliberately established by the authors of the Treaties, even includes having complete freedom to appraise parliamentary amendments. It was important for this institution, whose sole concern is the Community interest, to have the fullest autonomy. Neither the Council, which must be unanimous if it is to oppose the Commission's point of view, nor the Parliament, whose opinions are not binding on it, can interfere with its freedom of judgment, unless, in the Parliament's case, it institutes the censure procedure. However, some members consider that censure can only be used, as specified in Article 144, to attack "the activities of the Commission." But it is obvious that at this stage in a conflict the two institutions will reason more in political than in legal terms, and that each will draw its own conclusions from the situation.

If the Commission accepts the Parliament's opinion and amends its original proposal under the second paragraph of EEC Article 149, its new proposal can be amended only by unanimous decision of the Council. Thus, where Parliament and the Commission are in agreement, the Parliament's point of view benefits from the guarantees which the rules concerning dialogue between the Council and the Commission give the latter, and the Commission's point of view is reinforced by having the support of the Parliament.

If, having gone over them, the Commission is unable to accept the Parliament's amendments, the latter's position is weaker. The Council might accept them, but the chances of persuading it are reduced. This situation, which was doubtless detrimental to the Parliament, was altered with the revision of the Treaties in 1975, when the Parliament received budgetary powers. Concertation is arranged between the Council and the Parliament, where the former wants to depart from the opinion delivered by the latter, on "general Community acts having notable financial implications, whose adoption is not required in pursuance of acts already in existence." Such concertation (where the Commission acts as a mediator) is likely to expand following the direct election of the Parliament. It may develop slowly into a system of codecision, giving the Parliament and the Council the right to decide on certain matters, if possible by joint agreement, with the Council's viewpoint prevailing in the event of conflict. These two institutions could then become the Community's two legislative bodies.

## Budgetary powers

In one field, however, the Commission has thought it right to depart from the principle of its independence. It considers that the Parliament should have real powers of decision with regard to expenditure and revenue. Thus, in one matter where the Commission acts alone—the fixing of the rate of levy on coal and steel production—it has subordinated the exercise of its right to parliamentary approval.

"No taxation without representation" is a principle which finds expression in the Community also. When the use of its own resources to provide budget revenue was accepted by the Council in 1970, the Parliament was given budgetary powers. These were made more explicit and increased when the Treaties were further revised in 1975. Budgetary power is now the keystone of Parliament's powers and authority. The Institution's evolution over almost 10 years, and the role it will play following direct elections, stem directly from this.

The Commission, which proposes the budget in the form of a preliminary draft, and implements it, is drawing all the political conclusions from this new situation. It notes that in this field the workings of the institutions confront it with two authorities which take their decisions in conjunction. Parliament even has the right to reject the budget. Both at the political level of budgetary options and the more technical level of decisions on financing, the Commission's position must be clear and consistent; it will have to be defended before both the Parliament and the Council.

The budgetary procedure demonstrates with particular clarity the different spheres of competence occupied by the Parliament, the Council, and the Commission, each having its own responsibilities. The differences will become even more marked with the popularly elected Parliament, where member and tax-payer will be in direct confrontation. It was in fact precisely in order to deal with the difficulties to which such confrontation could give rise that the Parliament was also given powers of control over the budget. It is for the Parliament, whose task was lightened by the establishment in 1977 of the Court of Auditors, to give a discharge to the Commission in respect to its implementation of the budget.

With the exercise of budgetary powers, the notion of parliamentary confidence, which is necessary to the Commission in the legislative process, takes on new meaning. Since Parliament, like the Council, holds the pursestrings—the means required by the Commission to carry out Community policies—the Commission's relations with both must be exemplary. Even if Parliament did not have the means of persuasion that its powers to grant financial resources furnish, it would still have powers of control which have developed considerably over the past 20 years.

*Censure*

Like many parliaments throughout the world, the European Communities' Parliament has not escaped the general tendency to expand powers of control, even to the detriment of legislative powers. In point of fact, it is precisely because the authors of the Treaties, for reasons of political expediency, were unwilling to grant the Parliament normal legislative power, that it was compensated by extremely developed powers of control. The Treaties of Rome even increased the right to censure the Commis-

sion, which is now general, while the Treaty of Paris only gave the Parliament this right once a year, when the High Authority's General Report came up for consideration.

Parliament's powers of control, strengthened by its right to censure the Commission, have been expanded considerably over the past 20 years. Aware of the importance of democratic control in the Community, the Commission has deliberately accepted this control and its expansion. Moreover, it regards possible dismissal by the Parliament —parliamentary control of its activities—as the corollary of its freedom, and its necessary independence.

The motion of censure itself has not developed notably, for a long time the Commission did not fall from grace in the eyes of the Parliament, its actions did not prompt any motions of no confidence. It was in 1972 that the first motion of censure (later withdrawn) was tabled against the Commission, which was accused of not having presented in due time its proposal for increasing the Parliament's powers. Since that time three motions have been tabled, only two were put to the vote: in June 1976, a motion by the Conservative Group against the Commission's milk policy; and in 1977, a motion by the EPD Group concerning the sale of butter for which refunds had been paid to the Soviet Union.

If Parliament has been little inclined to dismiss the Commission, there are pragmatic reasons for this. What affect can a gesture have, in fact, if it cannot influence the composition of the Commission succeeding the one dismissed? Parliament does not, at present, have any means of swaying the governments' choice of members of the Commission. It is perhaps also the case that the special majority required to pass a motion of censure is so rigid a condition that use of this weapon has not been highly developed.

It may be, however, that greater political involvement in the directly elected Parliament, and the fact that a given political family, either alone or through alliances, can hold the majority, will give substance to Parliament's repeated request to participate in the choice of members of the Commission.

The motion of censure may also come to be used for purposes other than the dismissal of the Commission. The tabling of a motion and the vote (the result becomes less important here) can be considered the most severe form of criticism and the most public form of disapproval. It was probably this view of the motion of censure that the Conservative and the EPD Groups had in 1976 and 1977. Lastly, the threat of a motion of censure can also be an effective means of obtaining something from the Commission.

## PARLIAMENTARY SCRUTINY OF COMMISSION POLICY

The European Parliament has at least three opportunities each year to subject Commission policy to scrutiny, apart from the debate on the budget, which probably gives the Parliament the most effective means for penalizing Commission action. Every year, in February, the Commission presents to Parliament its actions program for the coming year. This "governmental program" is very thoroughly discussed, giving Parliament an opportunity to appraise the Commission's options, and hence, to influence Community action. The General Report that the Commission presents every year also furnishes the Parliament with a unique instrument for controlling Commission action. The Report, which is published in February, covers the past year. A few years ago it used to be carefully examined by Parliament, but this came to be considered pointless in view of the time elapsing between the event and Parliament's reaction. Finally, the discharge which, in association with the Council, the Parliament gives in respect to the Community budget, provides another opportunity for control. In considering how the budget has been implemented, Parliament is also able to consider how the common policies are being administered, and Commission management in general.

## Written and oral questions

Apart from these isolated occasions, Parliament keeps a check on the Commission and the Council through the written and oral questions which its members put to them. The use of written questions has increased somewhat over the years. They give Parliament a unique instrument for checking up on Commission action, on all the operations for which it is exclusively responsible and, more especially, on its administration of the common policies. The written questions relate to a wide variety of subjects, ranging from the protection of songbirds to the impact of American investments in the Community. The pertinence of many of the questions, and the persistence of some members, have given great weight to this procedure. Thus, in its everyday activities, in all the decisions which it takes on its own initiative, the Commission must bear in mind that it may have to justify itself to Parliament and, hence, to public opinion. Questions and replies are published in full in the Official Journal of the Communities.

The object of written questions may go beyond just keeping check. The author of a question may be trying to apply political pressure to force the Commission to act, either by using its own powers or by putting proposals to the Council. A parallel may thus be drawn between what is done here and what the Council does when it asks the Commission to act in a given field.

Oral questions, with or without debate, and the questions put during Question Time have the same object but use different means. The Commission may have every reason to welcome or regret debate, particularly public debate, which can have very real advantages—or disadvantages—compared with polished written replies. Thus, over the years, the debates on questions and the Question Time sessions have become a major element animating parliamentary proceedings, and the way they have developed shows how important Parliament considers this form of dialogue with the Commission and the Council.

## Committees in camera

Parliamentary checks on the Commission can also take more discreet forms. Not all subjects are suitable for discussion in the House. Either because of the confidential nature of the subject, or because Members are not in a position to discuss it, or for some other reason, it is often thought preferable for the Commission to talk things over with members in the parliamentary committees, which usually meet in camera. This, in fact, is where most

exchanges of views take place. All matters for which the Communities have a responsibility, including those connected with political cooperation, are discussed very freely by both sides. The Commission informs members of its immediate intentions; it may be said to sound them out. In this way the Parliament can exercise some control before the event, and the Commission, for its part, is more aware of what the Parliament's reactions to its proposals are likely to be. This procedure has the advantage of enabling each of the institutions to preserve its own freedom: freedom of action for the Commission, freedom of judgment for the Parliament.

In the field of external relations, to which the European Parliament has traditionally attached great political importance, it is information given at parliamentary committee meetings, in a confidential context, that allows Parliament to follow day by day the evolution of the relations which the Community has established throughout the world.

## POLITICAL NATURE OF THE PARLIAMENT

Lastly, there is one role which the present Parliament plays discreetly, but will develop considerably with the new popularly elected Parliament: that of providing political stimulus. The fact that the political power of the Parliament stems neither from states nor governments will give its views an originality which can only be beneficial to the Community.

Here, too, Parliament and the Commission are going to be in competition as to which one is going to provide what Leibnitz called the flick of the finger. At the same time they are interdependent: to see its ideas converted into legislative measures, the Parliament must go through the Commission; to find the support which it needs to create new common policies, the Commission must turn to the Parliament.

## CONCLUSIONS

The Commission cannot be what it is, or what it wants to be, without the Parliament. The greatest danger for it would be to see its role reduced to that of a European technocracy, powerful but out of touch with its roots. But the very fact that the Commission is responsible to a political authority— whose legitimacy will soon be based on universal suffrage—means that it, too, shares in this aura: it will receive the charisma enjoyed by political institutions. For the Commission, democratic control is thus an absolute necessity, and strengthening it a duty.

The Parliament, which tomorrow will be a Parliament elected by direct universal suffrage, will not create an image for itself unless, facing it, it has a strong and dynamic Commission and a forceful Council. Powers are only created by opposition. A diabolical pair for some, for others, an ideal couple, Parliament and the Commission go forward hand in hand.

The past twenty years show clearly how an institution such as the European Parliament can develop. The Commission, and the Council, with reluctance, have assisted in its growth. Tomorrow universal suffrage will do the rest. Between 7 and 10 June 1979, the nine Member States will finally see the realization of Victor Hugo's sagacious prophecy:

"The day will come when cannon balls and bombs will be replaced by votes, by popular universal suffrage, by the real arbitration of a sovereign Parliament which will be for Europe what the Commons are for England, what the Diet is for Germany, what the Legislative Assembly is for France."[2]

2. Victor Hugo—Opening address to the Peace Congress (1849), in "Actes et Paroles" —Paris: Michel Levy, 1875.

# The Court of Justice—The Invisible Arm

By WERNER J. FELD

ABSTRACT: The Court of Justice of the European Communities is an essential part in the equilibrium of powers among the major Community institutions. Over the years the Court has contributed significantly to the progress of economic, social, and perhaps political integration through its vigorous development of Community law. Its decisions have a truly supranational nature: they are directly binding on individuals, business enterprises, and governments in the Community member states, without the necessity of additional independent affirmative action by the national authorities. One of the most significant jurisdictional assignments made to the Community Court is the responsibility for treaty interpretations. The extensive jurisprudence of the Court in this area has led to the gradual acceptance of the supremacy of Community Law over conflicting national law. Controversies between Community institutions and member governments about treaty violations have also led to repeated court intervention. In all cases the decisions of the Court have eventually been obeyed. Disputes between member states have up to now not resulted in any Court decisions. A large number of suits filed with the European Court involve matters of administrative law. As a consequence, the administrative law functions of the Court have assumed considerable importance, especially since complaints can be brought by individuals and enterprises regarding actions or inactions of the Commission. Although the power of the Court is considerable, the justices have always denied that the European Community has been subjected to a government by the judges.

Werner J. Feld is a Professor of Political Science at the University of New Orleans. He received a degree in law after attending the University of Berlin and has a Ph.D. in Political Science from Tulane University. He has published extensively on political and legal problems of the European Community. His books include: The Court of the European Communities: New Dimensions in International Adjudication (1964); Transnational Business Collaboration Among Common Market Countries (1970); The European Community in World Affairs (1976); and Domestic Political Realities and European Unification, with John K. Wildgen (1977).

THE COURT of Justice of the European Communities is an essential part in the equilibrium of powers among the major Community institutions and fulfills crucial functions in the reciprocal distribution of institutional authority and responsibilities. Over the years the Court has contributed significantly to the progress of economic, social, and perhaps political integration through its vigorous development of Community law. Its decisions have a truly supranational nature: they are directly binding on individuals, business enterprises, and governments in the Community member states without the necessity of additional independent affirmative action by the national authorities. In fact, these authorities must make available national resources if enforcement of Court decisions against private parties should become necessary.

## THE GENEALOGY OF THE COURT

The present Court is the direct successor to the Court of Justice of the European Coal and Steel Community (ECSC) which had been in operation since December 1952. When the European Economic and Atomic Energy Communities (EEC and Euratom) were established in 1958, the Coal and Steel Community Court was transformed into the judicial organ for all three Communities. This transformation did not entail any major organizational changes. The new court took from its predecessor the majority of the judges, most of its personnel, its physical plant, and its docket of nearly 40 cases.[1] Located in Luxembourg,

the Court initially occupied an unprepossessing, modern office building, devoid of any of the ornate architecture which normally characterizes the home of a high tribunal. However, in the early 1970's it was moved to the outskirts of Luxembourg into an imposing new edifice commensurate with its authority and prestige as the chief tribunal of a potentially powerful regional political system.

## ORGANIZATION

### The judges

Initially, the Court was composed of seven judges, but after the accession of Great Britain, Ireland, and Denmark, their number was increased to nine. The constituent treaties do not specify the nationality of the judges. However, the personnel statutes of the Communities require all civil servants—and the judges are civil servants in a broad sense—to be nationals of the member states, although exceptions to this rule can be made. So far, only nationals of the member states have occupied seats on the bench.

The judges are appointed for a term of six years. They must be chosen from among persons of "indisputable independence" who are qualified to hold the highest judicial office in their respective countries, or who are jurists of high standing.[2] Their removal from office is possible only if, in the unanimous opinion of the other members of the Court, they no longer fulfill the required conditions or meet the obligations of their office.[3]

1. *Journal Officiél des Communautés Europeènnes*, 19 October 1958, pp. 453/58 and 11 November 1958, pp. 467/58 and 468/58.

2. ECSC Treaty arts. 32, 32b; EEC Treaty arts. 165, 167; Euratom Treaty arts. 137, 139.
3. ECSC Treaty art. 32b; EEC Treaty art. 168; Euratom Treaty art. 139; Protocol on the Statute of the Court of Justice (EEC Treaty) arts. 5, 6. The Protocols of the other treaties on the statute have similar provisions.

The president of the Court, elected for a term of three years, possesses important powers. Among them are the suspension of a decision of the Communities' executive organs imposing pecuniary obligations on private persons, and staying the execution of an action against which an appeal has been lodged with the Court. However, the rulings of the president are provisional and in no way prejudge the decisions of the Court on the substance of the matter before it.[4]

The judges are appointed with the common consent of the member governments. This method and the provisions concerning their terms of office have been subjected to criticism. It has been claimed that a term of office lasting six years was too short and that, as a minimum, the Statute of the International Court of Justice should have been emulated, which stipulates a term of nine years for the judges of that Court.[5] Further, it has been asserted that a six-year term, coupled with the possibility of reappointment, might tend to operate against the independence of the judge since for a reappointment the judge must look to his government.[6] Although the appointment of a judge requires the common consent of all nine governments, which implies the possibility of a veto, in practice the consent is a formality.

4. Statute of the EEC Treaty art. 36; EEC Treaty arts. 185, 186, 187, 192. Similar provisions are found in the other Treaties. See also Rules of Procedure art. 6.
5. Statute of the International Court of Justice art. 13.
6. Henry L. Mason, *The European Coal and Steel Community: Experiment in Supranationalism* (The Hague: Nijhoff, 1955), p. 25, relates the thoughts of the French Economic Council in 1951; and Hans-Ulrich Bächle, *Die Rechtsstellung der Richter am Gerichtshof der Europäischen Gemeinschaften* (Berlin: 1961), pp. 126–30, who also cites other critics.

## The advocates-general

The judges of the Court are assisted by four advocates-general who must meet the same professional qualifications as the judges and who are also appointed for six years by the governments of the member states. Their functions are "to present publicly, with complete impartiality and independence, reasoned conclusions on cases submitted to the Court of Justice with a view of assisting the latter in the performance of its duties . . ."[7] Although the institution of the advocate-general is unknown in common law systems, it is extensively used in French administrative law procedure.[8]

The advocates-general represent in no way either the Communities or the public; they function only in the interest of justice. Their sole, but vital, task is to prepare for the Court an opinion on the legal aspects of any question submitted to it. Although not necessarily accepted, these opinions strongly influence the Court, and their conclusions are always published next to the judgment in the collection of jurisprudence of the Court. Indeed, in the more than twelve hundred judgments rendered by the Court by the end of 1977, the opinions of the advocates-general have been accepted by the justices in the majority of cases. If they are not accepted, they take on the character of dissenting opinions and, as such, frequently offer alternative solutions which may influence the development of future case law. The advo-

7. ECSC Treaty arts. 32a, 32b; EEC Treaty arts. 166, 167; Euratom Treaty arts. 138, 139.
8. Bernard Schwartz, *French Administrative Law and the Common Law World* (New York: New York University Press, 1954), pp. 23–31 and 138–9.

cates-general may be removed from office under the same conditions as the judges. The power of removal is now vested in the Court itself.

## The registrar of the Court

The registrar of the Court is elected for a term of six years by the judges of the Court from among the candidates nominated by one or more of the justices. He is not only the chief administrator of the Court, but also assists in the conduct of the Court's judicial business. During the public sessions he wears a robe as do the judges and advocates-general. Requests to bring actions before the Court must be addressed to the registrar. He prepares the official record of each session of the Court which must be signed by him and the president.[9]

## The chambers of the Court

In principle, the Court sits in plenary session. However, it is authorized to set up chambers composed of three or five judges and, soon after its establishment, the Court created two chambers of three judges each.[10] The functions of these chambers are to undertake preliminary examinations of evidence or to decide certain categories of cases. The division of tasks between the two chambers is made by the President of the Court.

## Pattern of appointments

Early in the history of the Court a pattern was developed according to which the positions of judges and other court personnel were assigned to different countries and which

appeared to allocate special weight to the Court presidency. Before enlargement, France, Italy, and Germany were assigned two positions each, either two judgeships or one position of one judge and one advocate-general. The other countries were given one judgeship each, and initially the Netherlands held the presidency for a number of years, while the registrar was Belgian and, in fact, still is. Following the accession of the three new member states, the British obtained two Court positions and Ireland and Denmark each one. At the end of 1977 the Germans held the presidency of the Court and had one judgeship, the British, Italians, and French each furnished one judge and one advocate-general, and each of the remaining five countries were allotted one judgeship.

A number of judges and advocates-general appointed to the Court had political backgrounds. Some held ministerial positions in their countries, a few were active in party politics, while others were law professors, but political backgrounds have been more common.[11]

## JURISDICTIONAL POWERS

If the constituent treaties of the ECSC, EEC, and Euratom are considered the "Constitution" of the three Communities, and if the Community system as a whole is viewed as an incipient federation, one might well label some of the jurisdictional powers of the Court as having a constitutional nature. Clearly, the three treaties accomplish what is normally accomplished by the constitution of a federal state: they delineate the basic goals of the Communities;

9. Statute of the EEC Treaty arts. 19, 30, 34; Rules of Procedure arts. 47(6), 53.
10. ECSC Treaty art. 32; EEC Treaty art. 165; Euratom Treaty art. 137.

11. For some details see Werner Feld, *The Court of Justice of the European Communities* (The Hague: Nijhoff, 1964), pp. 18–33.

they regulate the relationship of the Community institutions to the governments of the member states; they stipulate the powers and obligations which these institutions have in relationship to the governments; and they specify the competences and duties which the member governments have regarding the organs of the Communities. For disputes between Community institutions and the member states, the Court is the supreme arbiter, the guardian of common interests, as well as the guarantor of national prerogatives.[12] In addition, the Court decides disputes between member states for which it has exclusive jurisdiction and which, therefore, cannot be submitted to the International Court in The Hague.[13]

Another type of jurisdiction given to the Court is essentially of an administrative nature and concerns such questions as whether the Community institutions have made valid decisions in suits for damages against the Communities and their officials.[14] Pursuant to this jurisdictional assignment the Court also decides disputes between the Community organs, for example, suits filed by the Commission against the Council. This type of dispute has been rare, but one has produced a landmark decision.[15] Finally, the

Court may act as an internal administrative tribunal in cases concerning civil servants of the Communities.[16]

Perhaps one of the most significant provisions of both the EEC and the Euratom Treaties grants to the Community Court the responsibility for treaty interpretations.[17] In order to prevent nine different interpretations and applications of the Community treaties, as well as the quasi-legislative and other acts of the Communities, the Court has powers to insure uniformity of law.[18] Similar provisions are also contained in the ECSC Treaty, but their application is more limited. It should be noted that the pronouncements of the Court on uniform treaty participation are not "advisory opinions," but in special instances, under the EEC and Euratom Treaties, the Court can render such opinions regarding the compatibility of prospective international agreements with the Treaty provisions.[19]

The judgments of the Community

12. See ECSC Treaty art. 88; EEC Treaty arts. 169–71; Euratom Treaty arts. 141, 143.

13. ECSC Treaty art. 87; Euratom Treaty art. 193; EEC Treaty art. 219.

14. ECSC Treaty arts. 33–40; EEC Treaty arts. 173–73; Euratom Treaty arts. 146, 148, 156. In some member states, particularly Great Britain and Ireland, suits against the government for damages are tried by the civil courts even though administrative courts may be available for other sorts of cases. In other member states all such suits against the governments are tried by the administrative courts.

15. *EC Commission* v. *EC Council*, Case #22/70, Commercial Clearing House (CCH) Common Market Reports para. 8134 (1971).

16. See EEC Treaty art. 169, and the Staff Regulations for the European Communities art. 91, paragraphs 1 and 2.

17. EEC Treaty art. 177; Euratom Treaty art. 150.

18. Under the EEC and Euratom Treaties, "acts" may be "regulations," "decisions," or "directives." "Regulations" resemble American statutes inasmuch as they are binding on and directly applicable to private parties in the member states. A "decision" binds only the addressee named therein. "Directives" are addressed to and binding on member states only. See Euratom Treaty art. 161; EEC Treaty art. 189. The ECSC Treaty distinguishes between "general" and "individual" decisions, which are somewhat similar to the "regulations" and "decisions" of the EEC and Euratom Treaties. In addition, an "act" may also be a "recommendation" which resembles the "directive" of the EEC and Euratom Treaties, except that it may also be addressed to private parties who then will have the choice of means for attaining the desired objectives. ECSC Treaty arts. 14, 33.

19. See EEC Treaty art. 228; Euratom Treaty arts. 104, 105.

Court are enforceable in the member states against private parties in the same manner as judgments of national courts. Judgments against governments of member states, however, can only be enforced pursuant to the ECSC Treaty under certain conditions.[20] The later EEC and Euratom Treaties do not contain such provisions, but up to now all of the Court's decisions eventually have been obeyed.

## MAJOR ISSUES

### Supremacy of community law

An overview of the Court's jurisdictional activities can be gained from Table 1 which provides a subject matter analysis of the 1266 cases decided by the Court up to the end of 1977. Among the cases arising from the EEC Treaty (the most important of the three), more actions were brought for uniform interpretation of the Treaty (463 out of a total of 1608 actions) than under any other jurisdictional assignment, and 407 opinions were rendered.[21] This is an interesting and very important development, since through this kind of jurisprudence, the Community Court basically performs the role of federal supreme court.

Under both the EEC and Euratom Treaties, national courts of last resort *must* refer all cases which require interpretation of the treaties, or acts of Community agencies, to the Court.[22] Lower courts may also request such determinations which then bind the national courts. Under the ECSC Treaty, national courts must refer to the Court those cases in which the validity of an act by the High Authority or Council is

contested,[23] but otherwise the national courts' interpretations are not restricted.

Perhaps the most significant opinion delivered by the Court was in the case of *Costa* v. *E.N.E.L.*[24] It involved a serious conflict of legal views between the Community Court and the Italian Constitutional Court. A resident of Milan had refused to pay an electric bill of slightly more than three dollars, claiming the nationalization of the electric utilities contravened certain articles of the EEC Treaty.[25] The matter was referred by the trial court to both the Community Court and the Italian Constitutional Court. The latter court upheld the validity of the nationalization, examining only the constitutional question of whether a law ratifying an international treaty, which imposed certain restrictions on Italy's sovereignty, could be altered by a subsequent Italian law changing such restrictions. Acknowledging that the Italian constitution specifically permitted such a limitation of sovereignty,[26] the Italian Court nevertheless gave precedence to the subsequent nationalization over the law instituting the EEC Treaty.[27]

20. ECSC Treaty arts. 44, 88, 92.

21. See EC Commission, *11th General Report*, p. 331.

22. See Euratom Treaty art. 150; EEC Treaty art. 177, 298.

23. See ECSC Treaty art. 41. This article speaks of "resolutions" of these organs, but this term has been accepted as meaning the same as "acts."

24. Case #9, 25/64 10 Recueil de la Jurisprudence de la Cour p. 1141. (1964).

25. EEC Treaty arts. 37, 53, 93, 102, allegedly were violated. These articles deal with member state obligations in connection with enactments of laws likely to distort the Common Market, state aids, restrictions on the right of establishment, and state monopolies.

26. See *Constitution of Italian Republic* art. 11.

27. For a partial text of the judgment, see 2 *Common Market Law Review* (1964), pp. 224–5. For an analysis of this decision by Nicola Catalano, former Justice of the Court of the European Communities, see ibid., pp. 225–35.

TABLE 1

CASES ANALYZED BY SUBJECT MATTER[1] SITUATION AT 31 DECEMBER 1977

| TYPE OF CASE | ECSC | | | | EEC | | | | | | | | OTHER[2] | EURATOM | PRIVILEGES AND IMMUNITIES | PROCEEDINGS BY STAFF OF INSTITUTIONS | TOTAL |
|---|---|---|---|---|---|---|---|---|---|---|---|---|---|---|---|---|---|
| | SCRAP COMPENSATION | TRANSPORT | COMPETITION | OTHER[2] | FREE MOVEMENT OF GOODS AND CUSTOMS UNION | RIGHT OF ESTABLISHMENT FREEDOM TO SUPPLY SERVICES | TAX CASES | COMPETITION INCL. AIDS | SOCIAL SECURITY AND FREE MOVEMENT OF WORKERS | AGRICULTURAL POLICY | TRANSPORT | CONVENTION ARTICLE 220 | | | | | |
| All actions brought | 169 | 36 | 62 | 20 | 127 (25) | 14 (2) | 36 (2) | 103 (10) | 123 (19) | 361 (61) | 7 (2) | 12 (5) | 22 (11) | 4 | 8 | 802 (25) | 1,607[4] (162) |
| Cases not resulting in a judgment | 22 | 6 | 21 (2) | 9 11 | 16 (2) | 1 | 6 | 6 (1) | 4 (1) | 13 (2) | | | 1 (1) | 1 | 1 | 94 (3) | 208[4] (12) |
| Cases decided | 147 | 30 | 41 | (1) | 96 (20) | 13 (3) | 28 (2) | 89 (7) | 110 (20) | 277 (38) | 6 (2) | 11 (4) | 12 (4) | 3 | 7 | 385 (17) | 1,266 (118) |
| Cases pending | | | | | 15 | | 2 | 8 | 9 | 65 | 1 | 1 | 9 | | | 23 | 135 |

N.B. The figures in brackets represent the cases dealt with by the Court in 1977.

[1] Cases concerning several subjects are classified under the most important heading.

[2] Levies, investment declarations, tax charges, miners' bonuses.

[3] Staff Regulations, Community terminology, Lome Convention, short-term economic policy, commercial policy, and relationship between Community law and national law.

[4] In one of which no service was effected and the case was removed forthwith from the register.

SOURCE: *11th General Report of the EC Commission*, p. 330.

In its decision, the Community Court strongly disagreed with the views expressed in the Italian judgment:

Contrary to other international treaties, the Treaty instituting the EEC has created its own legal order which was integrated with the national order of the member states the moment the Treaty came into force and which the domestic courts have to take into account; as such it is binding upon them. In fact . . . the member states, albeit within limited spheres, have restricted their sovereign rights and created a body of law applicable both to their nationals and to themselves. The integration, with the laws of each member state, of provisions having a Community source . . . have as their corrolary the impossibility for the member states to give precedence to a unilateral and subsequent measure which is inconsistent with . . . a legal order accepted by them. . . . [T]he rights created by the Treaty by virtue of their specific original nature, cannot be judicially contradicted by an internal law, . . . without undermining the legal basis of the community. . . .[28]

Despite the explicit and comprehensive nature of the *E.N.E.L.* decision, the Italian courts were at first reluctant to abide by its command, but the concepts of the Community Court gradually have been accepted.

Germany also has encountered difficulties with the application of the Community law supremacy doctrine. The German courts, perhaps more than any others, have referred a number of cases to the Community Court but have had problems in reconciling the supremacy doctrine of Community law with certain basic constitutional principles and fundamental rights of German individuals.[29] The vital question has been whether the delegation of powers stipulated in article 24(1) of the German Basic Law might allow delegation to the Community of fundamental constitutional principles and rights—and if so, to what extent? The Court held that

[t]he validity of a Community instrument or its effect within a member state cannot be affected by allegations that it strikes at either the fundamental rights formulated in that State's constitution or the principles of a national constitutional structure.[30]

At the same time, the Court stated that while Community legislation infringing upon the human (fundamental) rights provisions of a member state's constitution is not necessarily valid, respect for such rights is an integral precept of the common law of the Community and, indeed, is derived from the constitutional principles common to the member states.[31] This issue is not settled. In the meantime, in April 1977, the Presidents of the Council of Ministers, the Commission, and the European Parliament signed a Joint Declaration stressing the prime importance of these fundamental rights and agreeing to respect them. While this Declaration is not a substitute for codification, it is viewed as having legal effects by reenforcing the Court's rulings on fundamental rights in individual cases, thereby

29. See for example the decision of the Administrative Court in *Frankfurt am Main, Internationale Handelsgesellschaft GmbH* v. *Einfuhr-und Vorratsstelle für Getreide und Futtermittel,* Case #11/70, *CCH Comm. Mkt. Rep.* para. 8126 (1972).

30. Ibid., p. 7424.

31. Ibid., p. 7425. See also Gerhard Bebr, "How Supreme is Community Law in the National Courts?" *Common Market Law Review* vol. 11, no. 3, 1974, pp. 24–34.

28. See Supra n. 24, pp. 1158–60 of decision cited.

enhancing the status of judge-made law.[32]

Whatever the outcome of the human rights issue, national courts in all member states have submitted a rising number of interpretation questions to the Community Court. An interesting result of the procedure for preliminary decisions is the fact that it opens the way for citizens in the Community countries to activate the judiciary machinery of the Community. Although a citizen first must convince the national judge of the seriousness and pertinency of his contentions, the procedure has served to awaken Community citizens to the spreading web and interdependence of Community and national law.

## CONTROVERSIES BETWEEN COMMUNITY ORGANS AND MEMBER GOVERNMENTS

Before controversies between the institutions of the Community and member state governments come to the official attention of the Court under the EEC and Euratom Treaties, usually a request must be made by the Commission that a member meet its treaty obligations. Failure to comply within a certain period authorizes the Commission to refer the matter to the Court. If the Court finds a treaty violation, the state government is obliged, as a signatory to either treaty, to implement the Court's decision.[33] Under the ECSC Treaty, the Commission has similar

32. EC Commission, *11th General Report*, p. 280.

33. See EEC Treaty arts. 169, 171; Euratom Treaty arts. 141, 143. See also EEC Treaty art. 225, which permits the Commission to appeal immediately to the Court without first consulting the State concerned if the alleged treaty violation has the effect of distorting conditions of competition in the Common Market.

powers but can impose certain economic sanctions against the offending state without a Court decision if the state involved does not appeal to the Community Court, or if such an appeal fails.[34]

Among the cases charging member governments with treaty violation a considerable number have involved the free movement of goods within the common market (see Table 1). Many others related to the delayed or incomplete transposition of Community directives into national law. Indeed, in 1977, sixty-eight new infringement proceedings were initiated by the Commission and eight new cases were brought before the Court of Justice.

In the majority of cases submitted to the Court, its decisions have confirmed the infringement of Community law. In no case has a member state government failed to comply with these judgments, although at times compliance took an unreasonably long period of time.[35] One might ask why member states permit obvious violations of the EEC Treaty to reach the Court. Strong national interest groups may have pressured a member government into instituting measures protecting an industry or commodity, or there may have been strong dissension within the government in regard to a proposed protective measure. The potentially violative measure was then instituted with the full knowledge that the Court would act as the final arbiter. Whatever the reasons, this conceivably intentional shifting of final decisionmaking from the state to the Community tends to enhance the authority of the Court and thereby

34. See ECSC Treaty art. 88.

35. Henry G. Schermers, "The European Court of Justice: Promotion of European Integration," *American Journal of Comparative Law* vol. 22 (1974), pp. 444–68.

may contribute, in a small way, to the process of integration.

The Court seems to have understood these motivations for treaty violations and has been very patient in dealing with them. For example, in late 1968 the Court issued a judgment holding that Italy had failed to fulfill its treaty obligations by continuing to impose a tax on the exportation of art treasures to other member states. It took four years for the Italian government to remedy the situation.[36]

Disputes over the relationship of the Communities to the member states, resulting from decisions of the former High Authority or the EEC Commission, can also be brought before the Court by the member governments.[37] For example, Germany complained about insufficient import quotas for oranges[38] and raw materials for the manufacture of brandy from countries outside the Common Market.[39] Although the Court sustained the German claim in the brandy case, primarily on procedural grounds, the Commission's actions were supported in the other case. Admittedly, such decisions may not have great economic and political significance. However, they do reveal acceptance of the Court as a fair and equitable arbiter of conflicts involving national economic interests.

*Controversies between member states*

Any dispute between member states which cannot be settled by any other method provided by the ECSC Treaty may be submitted to the Court by one of the parties.[40] Such a general clause was omitted in the EEC and Euratom Treaties, both of which allow member states to bring interstate disputes before the Court only after the alleged treaty violation has been referred to the Commission. The Commission must then ask the states concerned for comments and thereupon issue an official opinion.[41] However, the Court has never rendered any decision in such matters because the Commission has been able to settle the disputes.[42]

ADMINISTRATIVE LAW MATTERS

A large number of suits filed with the European Court involve matters of administrative law. As a consequence, the administrative law functions of the Court have assumed considerable significance, especially since complaints can be brought by individuals and enterprises regarding actions or inactions of the Commission.

The major grounds for lodging an administrative law complaint against the Community organs are lack of legal competence or action ultra vires. The second ground consists of a major violation of established procedure such as a failure to adopt an administrative action by the requisite number of votes, or the failure to articulate sufficient reasons for an act. This ground for appeal may be available not only in the case of a violation of a procedural requirement set forth in the Treaties, but also in the case of a violation of the inherent procedural requirement of fair play, which may be viewed as

36. See *EC Commission v. Italy*, case #7/68, *CCH Comm. Mkt. Rep.* para. 8056 (1968); Schermers, "The European Court of Justice," pp. 542–53.

37. See ECSC Treaty arts. 33, 35; Euratom Treaty art. 148; EEC Treaty arts. 173, 175.

38. *Germany v. EEC Commission*, case #34/62, *CCH Comm. Mkt. Rep.* para. 8016 (1963).

39. Ibid., para. 8012.

40. ECSC Treaty art. 89.

41. EEC Treaty art. 170; Euratom Treaty art. 142.

42. See EC Commission, 9th *General Report*, p. 284.

somewhat similar to the American concept of procedural due process. A third ground, an infringement of the Treaty or of any legal provision relating to its application, such as an implementing regulation, is used to contest an administrative act because of an improper interpretation of the treaties or regulations, or because of a complete absence of facts to support the challenged act. This ground has been invoked in many cases before the Court and has resulted in extensive jurisprudence in the area.

An administrative act may also be attacked on appeal for what the English text of the treaties calls "abuse of power."[43] It applies to situations in which an organ has exercised its power to achieve an end not envisioned in the grant of power. Finally, complaints filed in civil service matters, which have been frequent (see Table 1), also fall under the category of administrative law.

In most cases, the Commission's decisions have been attacked, but in civil service suits other institutions were also the target. In an unusual, albeit significant, case the Council was the defendant and the Commission the complainant.[44] The Council had taken the position that the international treatymaking power of the Community existed only where it was expressly provided for in the constituent treaties, while the Commission had argued that the EC had

broader international competences. The Court held that when there is a correspondence between internal and external Community action, the member states could no longer enter into international agreements on their own, but had to act through Community channels. In a later opinion, the Court confirmed its concept of parallelism between the Community's internal and external powers. Where the Community has internal powers of action, its institutions may opt between exercising these powers by autonomous internal actions, possibly followed by external actions, or directly by broader-based external actions with non-member countries.[45]

## CONCLUSIONS

We shall conclude this article with some observations of how the Community Court justices view their roles and strategic options in regard to constitutional issues. In conformance with continental practice, the Court has adopted the principle of formal unanimity and does not permit the publication of any dissenting opinions to the decisions. While this has been deplored by some observers,[46] it has been argued that the absence of dissenting opinions helps to strengthen the position of the Court within the complex operations of the Communities, and at the same time promotes consensus building within the Court.

In its relationship to the national judiciaries, the Court has always

43. The Court defines "abuse of power" as those actions through which an organ "by its grave lack of foresight or of circumspection, amounting to a disregard of legal objectives, pursued other aims than those for which the powers were provided. *Fédération Charbonnière de Belgique* v. *High Authority*, Case #8/55, 2 Recueil de la Jurisprudence de la Cour (1956), pp. 199, 310.

44. *EC Commission* v. *EC Council*, Case #22/70, *CCH Comm. Rep.* para. 8134 (1971).

45. Case #1/76, reported in *Common Market Law Review* vol. 14, no. 4, 1977, pp. 639–649.

46. See Feld, supra, n. 11, pp. 99–100. See also Valerio Germentieri and Cornelius Joseph Golden, Jr., "The United Kingdom and the European Court of Justice: An Encounter Between Common and Civil Law Traditions," *American Journal of Comparative Law* vol. 22, (1973), pp. 664ff.

avoided explicitly presenting itself as a superior tribunal.[47] It has stressed repeatedly that it is a special court with a specific task that operates on an equal footing with the national courts, which in turn have their own specific missions. When a request for preliminary rulings is received, the Court has always sought to reply as quickly as possible and to avoid usurping the prerogatives of the national courts. In no case has a request for preliminary ruling been declared inadmissible. This concern for good relations with the national courts also has been reflected in periodic conferences between groups of national judges and justices of the European Court. Several times each year national judges are invited to visit the European Court in Luxembourg for mutual discussions and for receiving information on the Community legal system.

The justices of the Court have been very sensitive to the accusation that they are developing the European Community into a government by judges.[48] According to the continental legal theory of Western Europe, the task of the courts is to *apply* the law to specific cases, not to *make* laws. In practice, however, every such application necessarily includes interpretation. Consequently, even in Western Europe, supreme courts and constitutional courts cannot avoid a limited law making function; their decisions obviously will have some impact upon public policy formulation and implementation.

47. See Schermers, "The European Court of Justice," p. 448.

48. See the comments of former President of the Court, A. M. Donner, who is still a judge, in "The Constitutional Powers of the Court of Justice of the European Communities," *Common Market Law Review* vol. 11, no. 2, (1974), pp. 131–134.

ANNALS, AAPSS, **440**, Nov. 1978

# Decisional Systems, Adaptiveness, and European Decisionmaking

By GLENDA G. ROSENTHAL AND DONALD J. PUCHALA

ABSTRACT: Decision formation in the Community has reflected an adaptability responding to different times and circumstances. The process of decisionmaking has grown in capacity, complexity and sophistication. It evolves slowly, however, to allow the diversity of its component parts to adjust and adapt. The actual EC decisional performance record indicates both the expansion of cooperative initiatives and the long range increase in joint action. The overall consensus formation capacity appears not to lead to political federation but has produced numerous noteworthy and viable means to collective programs. Some limited definitions of "European interests" have emerged in the summitry, ministerial and Commission decisions of the seventies, which illustrate the evolution of a flexible and viable decisionmaking structure as the Community faces a more demanding set of problems.

---

*Glenda Goldstone Rosenthal received her academic training at Oxford University, the College of Europe and Columbia University, where she received a Ph.D. in Political Science in 1973. She has worked as an information officer at the French Embassy Press and Information Service, at the European Community Information Service in New York, and was Executive Secretary of the Council for European Studies. She has taught International Politics and European Politics at Rutgers University, Vassar College, New York University, and Columbia University, where she is currently Assistant Professor of Political Science and a member of the faculty of the Institute on Western Europe.*

*Donald James Puchala is Professor of Government at Columbia University and Director of Columbia's Institute on Western Europe. He is the author of numerous articles on Western European Integration and Integration Theory, a co-author of* American Arms and a Changing Europe, *and an editor of* Western European Perspectives on International Affairs. *He received his doctorate from Yale University in 1966 and has since held Social Science Research Council, Carnegie Endowment and Ford Foundation fellowships for the study of European Integration.*

A NALYSTS who studied the European Communities (EC) from an "integration" perspective viewed changes in the Brussels policy process as signals of advancing or retreating supranationality.[1] Whether or not such tests of integration are valid, and indeed whether or not integration in Europe is occurring, are not the concern of this paper. We begin with the observation that decisionmaking in the European Communities, whatever its changing nature, has been highly adaptive over time, and has yielded a continuing flow of commitments, agreements and collaborative ventures under a variety of internal and external political-economic conditions.

## DECISIONAL SYSTEMS IN THE EUROPEAN COMMUNITIES

Consensus-building is both the goal and the essence of policymaking in the European Communities. Since no participant or coalition has the capacity to effectively coerce others, and since EC authorities have limited means of enforcing compliance from national governments, whatever collaborative outcomes emerge from Community policymaking, and whatever collective behavior follows, are largely the results of consensus.

Structurally speaking, the European Communities embody at least four consensus-building systems. These are conceptually distinct, though they may operate simultaneously and complimentarily in a single issue area, in sequence in a single area, simultaneously in two or more areas, in sequence in several areas, or intermittently. We call these four systems: (1) the Rome System, (2) the Concert System, (3) Summitry, and (4) Political Cooperation. As we shall show, each has evolved over time, and each has been more or less functional under varying conditions.

### The Rome System

The first EC decisional system resulted directly from the institutional designs and assignments of the Rome Treaty, though, as might be expected, what actually emerged after 1959 was considerably different from textbook notions of a "proposing Commission" and a "disposing Council."[2] Nonetheless, the Rome system is in many ways a Commission-dominant system in which the Eurocracy and its leaders function in supranational fashion as promoters of the aims of the Treaty and custodians of the "European" interest. The Commission acts in this system to initiate policy and to defend and shepherd its proposals. Concurrently it acts to mediate among national interests and conciliate amidst national clashes and confrontations.

Consensus-building in the Rome System is accomplished in consociational fashion, that is, by allowing for prolonged and inclusive consultation among all parties, and accumulating agreement by moving from less to more controversial issues and from lower to higher political-bureaucratic levels. Structurally, the system involves myriads of intra- and inter-bureaucratic committees and co-

1. Ernst B. Haas, "International Integration: The European and the Universal Process," *International Organization* 15 (1961), pp. 93–129; Leon N. Lindberg, "Political Integration as a Multidimensional Phenomenon Requiring Multivariate Measurement," *International Organization* 24 (1970), pp. 649–731.

2. W. Hartley Clark, *The Politics of the Common Market* (Englewood Cliffs, NJ: Prentice-Hall, 1967), pp. 15–54. Compare, Leon N. Lindberg, *The Political Dynamics of European Economic Integration* (Stanford: Stanford University Press, 1963), pp. 49–106.

ordinating groups that progressively integrate first national positions and then transnational ones.[3] Study, consultation and negotiation in the networks of groups and committees are generally prolonged—sometimes upwards of five years—and considered by participants a "ripening stage," when "we all learn each others' problems and discover that the only way out is along lines indicated by the Commission."[4] Consensus-building usually culminates in the Committee of Permanent Representatives (COREPER) where final national positions are presented and integrated, and where differences between the Commission's preferences and those of the member states are negotiated. "Difficult" or politically charged issues, left outstanding after COREPER deliberations, may be passed on to the Council of Ministers, but in the Rome System the Council functions more frequently to legitimize COREPER recommendations and to authorize EC action.[5]

## The Concert System

So named because it may easily be likened to the Nineteenth Century Concert of Europe, the second EC decisional system is a continuing multilateral diplomatic conference.[6]

The participants are ministers who represent their national governments and their national interests, plus the EC Commission, which in this context participates as a tenth member state (though usually with second class status). The Concert System is Council-centered and consensus is built through intergovernmental bargaining and exchanged concessions frequently embodied in policy packages negotiated in marathon sessions. Aside from the less authoritative role of the Commission, and its lessened ability to buffer national confrontations, what is distinctive about the Concert System is that it is not consociational. The consensus it generates is among governments, but not necessarily between them and the Commission. Nor is it a consensus that includes all of the relevant subnational and transnational interests involved in particular issues. Indeed, issues often get into the Concert System because no Community solution can be conceived or engineered that will not alienate some important interests somewhere in the EC and thereby threaten some government's bases of political support. Under such conditions, only *political* officials able and empowered to make *political* calculations about domestic support and opposition can negotiate for their member states. As a Brussels respondent phrased it, "Only high-level national politicians are able to do the appropriate "arithmetic" on the spot that permits weighing anticipated political gains against anticipated costs, and therefore only such officials are able to modify national policies in order to facilitate international agreement."[7] Like the Rome System,

3. Lindberg, *Political Dynamics*, pp. 97–103; Helen Wallace, *National Governments and the European Communities* (London: Chatham House/PEP, 1973); Helen Wallace, "The Impact of the European Communities on National Policy-Making," *Government and Opposition* 6 (1971): 520–38.

4. Leon N. Lindberg, "Decision-Making and Integration in the European Community," *International Organization* 19 (1965): 64.

5. Lindberg, *Political Dynamics*, pp. 53–54.

6. Glenda G. Rosenthal, *The Men Behind the Decisions: Cases in European Policy-Making* (Lexington, MA: Lexington Books, 1975), pp. 1–14.

7. Interview with an official in the Secretariat of the Council of Ministers, Brussels, 20 January 1977.

the Concert System frequently pro-
longs the discussion of issues over
months and years, basically to allow
consensus to congeal, and to permit
unfavorable national political conditions to dissipate. In essence, the
Concert System functions to permit
the redefinition of national interests,
and this is sometimes imperative for
consensus-building.

## Summitry

The structure of the Summit
System of EC decisionmaking is
uncomplicated. Nine heads of government and the President of the
European Commission, with their
principal advisors, gather periodically
at an EC capital to discuss problems
of Community concern. What distinguishes Summitry from other EC
decisional systems is obviously the
status of the actors involved. But, in
addition, summit conferences within
the EC are also to be distinguished
by their agendas, since, as a rule,
European summits have a recurrent
central theme: "Efforts should be
undertaken to promote cooperation
and enhance unity!" Embellished as
they are with high political symbol-
ism, summit conferences can initiate
or check movement in given policy
areas, bestow or deny legitimacy,
foster enthusiasm or dampen it,
elicit commitment or block it. In
their positive impacts, they are
highly functional to the operations of
the EC in that they serve as antidotes
to the periodic *crise de conscience*
which Brussels suffers. They are also
occasions for exhibiting philosophic
consensus when practical problems
cannot be immediately solved, and
they are useful in showing activity
when such shows are necessary for
cooperative momentum.
Consensus-building via Summitry

has a mystery about it that is not
easily penetrated, partly, of course,
because most summit sessions are
held behind closed doors. Certainly,
we can suppose that bargaining and
political arithmetic are as prominent
and functional at the summit as at the
ministerial level. But in addition, the
summit provides an almost unique
setting for international political
communication, inasmuch as the
similar stations and responsibilities
of the participants open the way to
mutual understanding, though not
always to empathy and agreement.
All of those who gather at the summit
uniquely understand the political
stakes that underlie their agendas;
all are political pros in their respective systems; all feel the pressures
and responsibilities of ultimate office;
all personify their states.[8] Dynamics
at the summit are also affected by
imperatives to agree that are linked
to high public visibility of success or
failure. Because of the expectations
that summit conferences tend to
generate in public opinion, and
because cooperation strikes sympathetic chords among European
publics, failed consensus at the
summit is an outcome that participants
strive steadfastly to avoid.[9]

## Political Cooperation

What we have in mind, in identify-
ing Political Cooperation as a separate
decisional system within the EC, are
the initially ad hoc and increasingly
regularized structures erected to
permit Community governments to
discuss and act in concert in issue-
areas removed from the strict con-

8. The *Economist*, 15 April 1978, pp.
57–58.
9. Annette Morgan, *From Summit to
Council: Evolution in the EEC* (London:
Chatham House/PEP, 1976).

cerns of the Common Market. Political Cooperation as imagined at The Hague Summit Meeting in 1969, and then more specifically proposed in the Davignon Report of 1970, represents the most elaborate form of extra-treaty decisionmaking. While Political Cooperation is not formally EC decisionmaking, since neither its structure nor agenda are mandated by the Rome Treaty, it is certainly decisionmaking by the EC. Its Conference of Ministers is identical to the Council of Ministers, and its agenda concerns the collective action of the Nine in global affairs.

Structurally, the Political Cooperation System is strictly intergovernmental and rather amorphous. Its institutions are a Conference of Foreign Ministers, as noted, and a Political Committee composed of the Political Directors and other senior officials from national foreign ministries. In addition, various subcommittees, study groups, working groups, and other ad hoc bodies come into and pass from existence as consultative needs and priorities dictate. Channels of fairly regular liaison now link all of the foreign offices of the Nine, and counterpart channels tie in the Commission and the COREPER (though loosely in these last instances). While consultation is the avowed purpose of this extra-treaty system, consensus-building, as for example on EC positions at the European Security Conference (CSCE), and on European attitudes towards the United States, has been its outcome.

Like the Summit System, consensus-building via Political Cooperation follows in some measure from the small group dynamics generated during the interactions of similarly experienced and stationed officials who have learned to com-municate intimately under relaxed conditions. Unlike Summitry, Political Cooperation, at least at present, tends to involve very little intergovernmental bargaining, exchanged concessions, package deals or the like. There seems no strong imperative to agree, so that when agreement does emerge, it tends to represent minds meeting after long discussion, or convergence toward some logical European position.[10] Then, too, somewhat like Summitry, Political Cooperation fills up time functionally, in the sense that it lends the Communities a capacity for continuing activity, even when other decisional systems are blocked. It is difficult to estimate the exact importance of this capacity to generate cooperative activity for its own sake, though judging from EC experience we would reckon it significant. Finally, and obviously, Political Cooperation lends the Nine capacity to respond to challenges and opportunities posed by issues beyond the Rome Treaty, and this capacity has become increasingly important as the EC has become a recognized global actor.

## THE GROWTH OF EC DECISIONAL SYSTEMS

In light of what we see as the coexistence of several different EC decisional systems, we must take issue with those who have contended that Community policymaking has evolved from a supranational form to an intergovern-

10. William Wallace and David Allen, "Political Cooperation: Procedure as Substitute for Policy," in Helen Wallace, William Wallace, and Carole Webb, eds., Policy-Making in the European Communities (London: John Wiley, 1977), pp. 227–248.

mental one.[11] We would argue that, from the beginning, decisionmaking has displayed both supranational and intergovernmental forms, and that this continues to hold true. To the extent that there have been changes in EC decisionmaking structures, they have moved toward more complexity and subtlety in all four decisional systems, and increased institutionalization of Summitry and Political Cooperation. The Rome System has adjusted to the emergence of European interest groups and national interest groups that have focused their attentions on Brussels. Recognition and access have been accorded to these subnational and transnational groups, and their lobbying has been integrated into the consultative networking of the Rome System.[12] Similarly, the system has grown to accommodate more explicit and harder fought intrabureaucratic struggles within the Eurocracy and among Commissioners.

The Concert System, for its part, has grown to accommodate ever closer liaisons and interpersonal linkages among representatives in the national delegations and in the national capitals. Over the years, such interpersonal responsiveness has extended even to the ministers themselves. In addition, what was initially a somewhat ceremonial casting of the Council Presidency

has evolved, over time, into an important leadership role in the Concert System.[13] There has also been a maturing of the Council's secretariat, heightening in the quality of its personnel, and assumption of an increasingly effective role in the preparation of Council meetings in liaison with other Brussels organs. As noted, growth in both Summitry and Political Cooperation has taken the form of regularization and institutionalization. Summit conferences have been a part of EC decisionmaking since 1961, but they increased in frequency and importance from 1969 onward, and they have recently been institutionalized as the European Council, a body which now meets regularly three times each year. Political Cooperation, as already noted, has evolved from a series of ad hoc interministerial discussions to a program of regular conferences carefully prepared by a network of national political directors.

## ADAPTIVENESS IN EUROPEAN DECISIONMAKING

Not without fits and starts, crises and failures, the last 20 years of EC decisionmaking have been experiences in adaptation. Agreements or commitments to initiate, expand, or accelerate common programs or collective actions have been continually generated under varying constitutional, ideological, political and economic conditions within Europe and without. An important key to this adaptiveness in EC decisionmaking has been its abun-

11. This argument, for example, is one of the central thrusts of Frans A. M. Alting von Geusau's *Beyond European Community* (Leyden: A. W. Sijthoff, 1969), pp. 179–191.

12. James A. Caporaso, *The Structure and Function of European Integration* (Pacific Palisades, CA: Goodyear, 1974), pp. 23–86; Cf. Jean Meynaud and Dusan Sidjanski, *Les Groupes De Pression Dans La Communaté Européenne, 1958–1968* (Brussels: Editions de L'Institut de Sociologie de l'Université Libre de Bruxelles, 1971).

13. Helen Wallace, *National governments and the European Communities* and "The Impact of the European Communities on National Policy-Making."

dance of consensus-building capacity. Only rarely in EC experience have all four decisional systems been blocked simultaneously. Also important has been the unhurried pace of EC decisionmaking. It is true that none of the EC decisional systems operate very well under strong pressures for immediate action, and none function very effectively in the context of crisis. Still, the virtue of all of them is that they force extended consultation and negotiation, they are hospitable to delays, inasmuch as postponements are not taken as breakdowns, and they almost never force participants into domestically or internationally untenable political positions. While it is true that certain timing devices, like deadlines and marathon negotiations, are used to force closure in EC systems, these are employed tactically only at the very end of prolonged processes during which EC participants are allowed ample time to cooperate.[14] In this lies part of the durability of European cooperation, and such durability has been much in evidence over time.

### ACCOMPLISHMENT AND DECISIONMAKING, 1958–1965

Since few have questioned the accomplishments of the European Communities during these initial years, we shall not dwell upon the record but simply highlight it. The Rome Treaty committed signatories to the creation of a free trade area among themselves. The first steps were taken in January 1959 and repeated in 1960 and 1963, both times ahead of schedule. Concurrently, in 1960, agreement was reached on the initiation of a Common External Tariff, and alignments toward the CET were also twice accelerated. The first steps toward a Common Agricultural Policy were taken in 1960, and major agreements on the whole framework of the CAP were reached at the end of 1962. In external relations, association agreements were negotiated with Greece in 1961 and Turkey in 1963. Also in 1963, the Yaoundé Convention linked 18 newly independent African countries with the Common Market.

The steady record of accomplishment during the period 1958–1965 has led some analysts to look upon these early Community years as the golden age of emergent supranationalism.[15] There is no question that the profusion of agreements during this period enhanced functional integration among the Six. However, more relevant to our analysis is the steady increase in the authority of all Community institutions, most notably the Commission. As intended by the architects of the Rome Treaty, for most of the period 1958–1965, the Rome System of decisionmaking was the Community mode. The Commission served as innovator, initiator, package-builder, arbitrator, overseer, and enforcer of the Community interest. Even during this period, however, the Concert System was intermittently activated because political questions arose which could only be negotiated and resolved by politicians. Some of the agricultural issues, for example, were of this nature. Nor should we omit mention of the Paris and Bonn

14. Donald J. Puchala, "Domestic Politics and Regional Harmonization in the European Communities," World Politics 27 (1975): 496–520.

15. Leon N. Lindberg and Stuart A. Scheingold, Europe's Would-Be Polity: Patterns of Change in the European Community (Englewood Cliffs, NJ: Prentice-Hall, 1970), pp. 24–63, 279–310.

summits in 1961, where moral initiatives were taken which prompted action toward a political Europe to compliment the economic one being built in Brussels. However, 1958–1965 must be looked upon as the heyday of the Rome System of EC decisionmaking.

By almost every measure, conditions were appropriate for the quasi-supranationality emanating from Brussels during 1958–1965. Constitutionally, the Rome Treaty itself committed signatories to prescribed courses of actions and to relative acquiescence in Commission tutelage. Ideologically, the spirit of Europeanism captured elites (especially the Centrist and Center-Right factions who held power in every major EC member state) and masses alike, and created strong imperatives to subdue and settle national conflict. This could be readily accomplished by following the advice and accepting the packages wrapped by the Commission. Economically, during this early period, every indicator of national growth pointed upward in EC member states, so that governments could reasonably argue, and believe, that horsetrading in Brussels was doing no harm to their domestic welfare and the political stability which followed from it. Internationally, most of the world were friends of European integration, and those who opposed it—the Russians—abetted it by their very opposition. Since no member state was asked during this period to trade among Westpolitik, Ostpolitik, Europeanism, Atlanticism, and Globalism, endorsing European unity accomplished a number of foreign policy ends, and supporting the supranational undertakings of the Commission confirmed this endorsement.

French policies under DeGaulle began to create some disharmony by the end of the period, especially after 1963, but French challenges to the Rome System were yet to come.

## ACCOMPLISHMENT AND DECISIONAL ADAPTATION, 1966–1972

In Community history, the years 1966 to 1972 are commonly interpreted as a period of crisis and relaunching. They were also years of noteworthy accomplishments in European cooperation, though these were slower-paced and somewhat less heralded than those of the earlier period. In 1967 the executives of the three European Communities were merged into a single Commission. Final agreements on directives for the Community's Value-Added Tax were affirmed in that same year, and all restrictions on the freedom of workers in the Communities were abolished in July 1968. In December 1968, the Mansholt Memorandum for the structural reform of agriculture was announced. Between 1969 and 1972 initiatives were taken to move toward establishing an economic and monetary union, a common industrial policy, and Community-wide environmental, scientific, and technological policies. By 1972 most of the commitments concerning enlargement were finally in place.

In external relations, agreement on the outstanding issues of the Kennedy Round was reached in 1967. In July 1968, the Community signed the Arusha Agreements with new East African associates, and in 1969, association agreements were reached with Morocco and Tunisia. Between 1969 and 1972 the global

Mediterranean Policy was mapped, aid to developing countries was systematized and increased, and the common commercial policy toward the Soviet Bloc countries was established. Not least important, Political Cooperation was endorsed and launched during this period, thus giving Europe a foreign policy voice on issues beyond the confines of the Rome Treaty.

The significance of citing EC accomplishments between 1966 and 1972 rests not only in the fact that the flow of initiatives, commitments, and agreements continued despite institutional turmoil in the Common Market. What is perhaps more important in the context of our analysis is that these accomplishments continued because EC consensus-building was able to shift to the Concert and Summit systems when the Rome System became blocked in high politics areas. Decisionmaking via the Rome System was stymied after 1965 due to changes in the political and economic environment. However, the result of blockage in the Rome System was neither stagnation nor degeneration, but renewed consensus-building, via hard bargaining, on the basis of newly and rather narrowly defined national interests. Likewise, as the Commission's stature waned, after the French assault on Walter Hallstein, its functions as innovator, initiator and mobilizer of movement toward unity were taken over in the Summit System. Top-level meetings, at The Hague in 1969 and Paris in 1972, set the tone and built the framework for the relaunching of "Europe" in the early seventies under the banner "completion, consolidation and enlargement."

The shift from consensus-building via the Rome System to consensus-building via Concert and Summit can be looked upon as an adaptive response to changing economic and political conditions surrounding the EC in the mid and late 1960s. Constitutionally, most of the time-tables embodied in the Rome Treaty had run their course by the late 1960s, and the one concerning voting in the Council had run afoul, so that the Treaty became both less of a constraint on member-state conflict and a source of conflict in and of itself.[16] Ideologically, "Europeans" in the member states and in Brussels grew older and less influential. Pragmatists entered to replace them in Brussels. Nationalists replaced them in member-state elites. Commitment to unity in mass opinion ebbed. Economically, recession threatened and then occurred in the mid-1960s, everywhere dampening the euphoria in growth and affluence that characterized earlier years. Externally, Community member states were being pressed by third countries to choose between Community partners and new ones. French foreign policy under DeGaulle could not be accepted as "European" policy, but there could be no "European" policy without France. Neither could there be one without West Germany whose governments became preoccupied with Ostpolitik, partly out of frustration with Westpolitik.

In overview, these conditions in the mid and late 1960s rendered almost all Community questions high politics issues. In economic matters, domestic stress raised political risks for governments in any community concessions, and national political interests thereby clashed

16. John Newhouse, *Collision in Brussels: The Common Market Crisis of 30 June 1965* (New York: W. W. Norton, 1967), pp. 151–60, passim.

with Community economic interests. In external relations, divergent positions and political investments in them made concession impossible at any but ministerial and summit levels. Equally significant, there was little role in this period for an articulator and overseer of the European common interest because there was no self-evident transcendent common interest (except, perhaps everyone's interest in continued cooperation). Under such circumstances, the common interest became defined as "those terms and ends in community diplomacy which best secured the political tenure of member governments." Such a common interest could only be the product of difficult and domestically sensitive bargaining among top-level political figures. This was abundantly provided for in both the Concert and the Summit Systems, which functioned modally during these middle years.

## CONTINUING ACCOMPLISHMENT AND FURTHER DECISIONAL ADAPTATION, 1973–1978

The years 1973 and 1974 were admittedly years of crisis, not only in western Europe, but throughout the western world. European cooperation suffered extensively under the pressures of energy shortage, related stagflation, and global monetary disarray. All of the EC decisional systems exhibited their common weakness, the incapacity for consensus-building amid crisis, and for immediate response to rapidly changing conditions. The destructiveness of 1973–1974 is well known. But, what is noteworthy is that EC decisionmaking, and the cooperative outcomes from it, recovered rather markedly from 1975 onward.

In 1975 the Communities signed the Lomé Agreement with 46 African, Caribbean and Pacific states. Between 1975 and 1977, all the countries of the Mediterranean, save Libya, entered into arrangements with the EC, thereby all but completing the global Mediterranean policy mapped in 1972. With regard to the Soviet Bloc, the EC finally implemented its common commercial policy with state traders; in the Middle East the Euro-Arab dialogue was introduced and actively pursued; in the Far East a trade agreement with the People's Republic of China was framed. Internally, commitments were affirmed with regard to the direct election of a European Parliament, and the Copenhagen Summit of April 1978 finally fixed a June 1979 date for these elections. That same meeting registered new and concrete commitments to a European Monetary Union. It also affirmed that a "declaration on democracy" be inserted in future treaties of accession. This latter move emerged in the context of a serious Community commitment to pursue further enlargement by negotiating with Greece, Spain and Portugal.

Except to say that it has proven adaptive, as evidenced by continuing cooperation, it is difficult to clearly characterize EC decisionmaking in the post–1972 period. There is no question but that the Summit System has become increasingly central, and that it is now the primary source of European initiative. Neither can one fail to note the newly important functioning of the Political Cooperation mechanism, especially as the EC's well-being becomes entwined in manipulations of interdependence at the various nodes of the global political and economic systems. Still, the Concert System continues in full gear. Much of the consensus-building surrounding direct elections, and most of the internal negotiation about enlargement, have been centered in the Council and handled via the Concert System. What is interesting, too, is that the Rome System has also reemerged with some effect in recent years. Not only has the Commission under Roy Jenkins demonstrated renewed capacities for initiative, but, in addition, a good deal of the consensus-building on external economic questions—North-South ones in particular—is coming via Commission guidance. Recent years, then, have seen the simultaneous functioning of all of the EC decisional systems.

In many ways, the amorphous decisionmaking structure of the Communities in the early 1970s also reflects adaptation to conditions surrounding the EC. The Treaty of Rome is no longer a source of initiative, and Summitry has replaced it because continued European cooperation requires both leadership and legitimating authority. Political ideology in Western Europe, including ideology of the Left, remains essentially nationalistic, despite European slogans and symbols. This, combined with the obvious fact that unfavorable national economic conditions are threatening the tenure of incumbent governments in almost all EC countries, makes it unlikely that Common Market issues will be resolved at levels below the ministerial, and by means other than bargaining among national interests. Most issues remain high politics and these keep the Concert System continually operative. On the other hand, global conditions, such as divergences between the United States and Western Europe on postures toward the Third World, approaches to OPEC, and international market sharing—as well as apparent movements toward economic protectionism almost everywhere—suggest that a recognizable, transcedent "European" interest may have reemerged in the mid-1970s. To the extent that this common interest requires an articulator and a promoter, opportunity is newly opened to a dynamic Commission with a President of stature. Under such conditions, it is less than surprising to see Roy Jenkins and the Eurocracy acting independently and energetically on questions like Monetary Union.

### CONCLUSIONS

We are the first to recognize that the thrust of our analysis has been contrary to much conventional wisdom which contends that "the EC decisionmaking machinery is creaking badly," or that "the trouble with decisions in Brussels is that they are made at snail's pace."[17] By contrast, we are led to the conclusion first, that EC decisionmaking machinery is growing in capacity, complexity and sophistication. Second, the durability of the whole edifice of Western European cooperation is closely related to the fact that EC decisionmaking is able to move at snail's pace, for it is at this cautious tempo that international consensus-building becomes possible. Third, we would suggest that our conclusions follow much less from counter-intuition than from accurately observing and reflecting upon the 20–year record of EC decisional outcomes. In light of the

17. The *Economist*, 3 September 1977, p. 49.

data, the best assessment of EC decisional performance must be that: (1) cooperative initiatives are regularly taken and these are expanding in substantive scope, and (2) in longer-run perspective most cooperative initiatives *eventually* yield commitment or agreement to collective or collaborative action.

Finally, returning to our opening point, it is quite true that decisional processes in the European Communities have not driven the Nine (or the Six for that matter) toward political federation, as some expected they would. But it is probably misleading to make progress toward federation the primary criterion for evaluating Western European unity. An alternative, and perhaps more revealing, test of European unity is in the state system's capacity to produce consensus on programs of common action. By this test, the consensus-building capacity of EC processes and institutions, regardless of their intergovernmental or supranational character, suggests notable accomplishment in European unity.

ANNALS, AAPSS, **440**, Nov. 1978

# Economic Uncertainty and European Solidarity: Public Opinion Trends

By RONALD INGLEHART AND JACQUES-RENÉ RABIER

ABSTRACT: Impressive growth in public support for the European Community took place during the decade following its founding; there is reason to believe that this development was partly due to the exceptional prosperity then prevailing in the Community's member nations. Conversely, there is evidence that the troubled economic conditions present since expansion of the Community in 1973 have had the opposite effect—subject to some important limiting factors. Analysis of public opinion survey data reveals a positive correlation between support for Community membership and a given nation's level of industrial production at a given time point; and a negative correlation with rates of inflation. Nevertheless, long-term influences seem to dominate the effects of the immediate economic context. Among these long-term factors, length of membership in the Community seems particularly important. But the presence of "Post-Materialist" value priorities, and of relatively high levels of "Cognitive Mobilization" also show significant linkages with public support for European integration.

*Ronald Inglehart is Professor of Political Science at The University of Michigan and currently Visiting Professor of Political Science at the University of Mannheim, Germany. Author of* The Silent Revolution: Changing Values and Political Styles among Western Publics, *he has collaborated with Rabier since 1969 in the design and analysis of European public opinion surveys.*

*Jacques-René Rabier is a special advisor to the Commission of the European Communities. Since 1974, he has been responsible for the Community's program of public opinion research, conducting surveys in each of the nine nations twice each year. The author of numerous articles on mass attitudes and European integration, he has served in a variety of posts, most recently as Director-General for Information of the Commission of the European Communities.*

IN THE Spring of 1979, the electorates of nine nations will vote for their representatives in the first directly-elected European Parliament in history. This event constitutes a major advance for public involvement in shaping the European Community, for European integration was initially a process that was almost exclusively restricted to collaboration between a relative handful of highly-placed elites. With the national referenda of 1972 and 1975, when membership or non-membership in the European Community for Ireland, Norway, Denmark and Great Britain was decided by the electorates of the four respective countries, it marked the first public ratification of a European integration effort. The European Parliament will place the affairs of the Community under the permanent scrutiny of representatives elected by the voters of all nine member countries. It is a good time to take stock of the evolution of mass attitudes toward Europe's supranational institutions.

To date, these institutions have been all too remote from the general public, being guided exclusively by appointed officials. As a result, they have lacked the political base and the democratic legitimacy that might justify their playing a more important role in dealing with some of the major problems that currently beset the European Community as a whole. By themselves, direct elections will not clear the way for a greater degree of European decision-making, but they could facilitate this development. Whether they do so or not depends on how much backing the publics of the nine nations accord the European institutions, and whether they are ready to support decisionmakers who act at the European level, with an eye to the interests of the European Community as a whole rather than an exclusive focus on the interests of a particular nation. This article will analyze relevant trends in mass attitudes toward European integration, in an effort to interpret these trends and some of the factors underlying them.

## PUBLIC EVALUATIONS OF MEMBERSHIP IN THE EXPANDED EUROPEAN COMMUNITY

The decade following the founding of the European Economic Community in 1958 was a period of unprecedented prosperity and high expectations. During these years, support for European unification among the publics of the original six member nations showed a clear tendency toward upward convergence. At first, sharply divided along Left-Right lines, the French and Italian publics gradually moved toward a pro-European consensus that extended across the political spectrum, bringing them up to the initially higher levels of support that prevailed among the publics of Germany, The Netherlands, Belgium and Luxembourg. This evolution seems to have been favored by the prosperity then prevailing, which tended (rightly or wrongly) to be attributed in part to membership in the European Community.

The British public remained outside the Community during this period, at first by the choice of their own government, and subsequently as a result of two successive Gaullist vetoes of British entry. The general contours of the flow of public opinion from 1952 to 1975 are indicated by Figure 1; the process

FIGURE 1

THE EVOLUTION OF SUPPORT FOR EUROPEAN UNIFICATION, 1952–1975.
Based on percent "for" "efforts to unify Europe." Missing data are included in percentage base; thus, in 1952, 70 percent of the German public was "for," 10 percent "against" and 20 percent "undecided" or "no opinion."

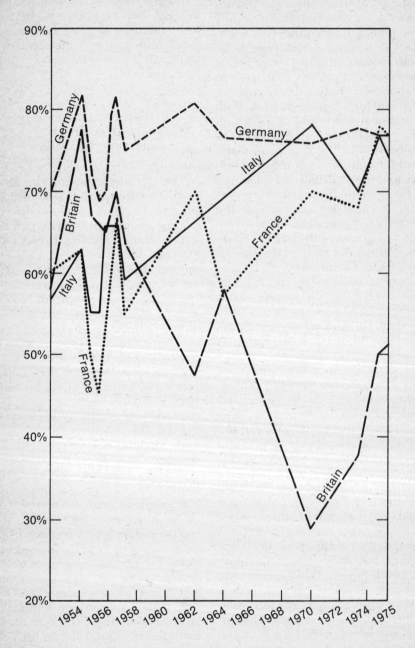

has been examined elsewhere in greater detail.[1]

The expanded nine-nation European Community came into being in 1973, on the eve of the most serious economic recession since the 1930s. In sharp contrast to the prosperity of the Community's early years, the publics of the expanded Community have experienced varying degrees of economic stagnation, accompanied by extraordinarily high inflation, and the highest levels of unemployment since the immediate postwar era.

Though they differ in detail, almost all of the major theorists who have worked in this area concur that favorable economic payoffs are conducive to—and perhaps even essential to—the processes of national and supranational integration.[2] Similarly, David Easton views mass support for a political system as the result of positive governmental outputs. In time, a series of outputs that are perceived as beneficial may build up a reservoir of "diffuse support" that is not contingent on immediate payoffs, but the generation of diffuse support can be traced back to favorable outputs at an earlier time, with economic outputs being the most obvious type and perhaps the most widely appreciated one.[3] Has mass support for the European Community institutions continued to develop in the uncertain economic climate that has prevailed since 1973, or has there been a growing sense of disenchantment?

It seems that both things have occurred in connection with different aspects of mass attitudes. In order to grasp what has been happening, it is important to distinguish between diffuse or "affective" support and "utilitarian" support—a calculated appraisal of the immediate costs and benefits of membership in the Community.[4] The latter seems to have moved downhill to some extent from 1973 to 1977, though with important cross-national differences in how far it went. But along with this development, a sense of solidarity among the nine nations of the European Community has emerged among all nine publics— a solidarity that includes a sur-

1. See Ronald Inglehart, *The Silent Revolution: Changing Values and Political Styles Among Western Publics* (Princeton: Princeton University Press, 1977), Chap. 12.

2. See Ernst B. Haas, *The Uniting of Europe* (Stanford, CA: Stanford University Press, 1958); Ernst B. Haas and Phillipe C. Schmitter, "Economics and Differential Patterns of Political Integration: Projections About Unity in Latin America," *International Organization*, vol. 18 (Autumn 1964), pp. 705–37; Karl W. Deutsch, *et al.*, *Political Community and The North Atlantic Area* (Princeton: Princeton University Press, 1957); Leon N. Lindberg and Stuart A. Scheingold, *Europe's Would-Be Polity* (Englewood Cliffs, NJ: Prentice-Hall, 1970); Joseph S. Nye, Jr., "Comparative Regional Integration: Concept and Measurement," *International Organization*, vol. 22 (Autumn 1968), pp. 855–80; Lindberg and Scheingold, eds., *Regional Integration: Theory and Research* (Cambridge, MA: Harvard University Press, 1971); Amitai Etzioni, *Political Unification* (New York: Holt, Rinehart and Winston, 1965); Philip E. Jacob and James V. Toscano, eds., *The Integration of Political Communities* (Philadelphia: Lippincott, 1964); and Charles Pentland, *International Theory and European Integration* (New York: The Free Press, 1973).

3. See David Easton, *A Framework for Political Analysis* (Englewood Cliffs, NJ: Prentice-Hall, 1965), pp. 124–26. Cf. Seymour M. Lipset, "Some Social Requisites of Democracy: Economic Development and Political Legitimacy," *American Political Science Review* 53, 1 (March, 1959).

4. For a discussion of utilitarian support versus affective support, see David Handley, "Public Support for European Integration" (Ph.D. diss., University of Geneva, 1975); cf. Werner Feld and John Wildgen, *Domestic Political Realities and European Integration* (Boulder, CO: Westview Press, 1976).

prisingly widespread willingness to share economic burdens in time of difficulties, and a certain readiness to place the interests of the Community as a whole above those of one's own nation. It may be that the sheer passage of time under common supranational institutions —provided they are entered into voluntarily—gradually instils the habit of viewing things from a perspective broader than that of the nation-state, even in the absence of material rewards.

As Deutsch has suggested, symbolic rewards can sometimes substitute for economic ones, and the experience of struggle against common difficulties can encourage a sense of solidarity even in times of adversity.[5] In short: unfavorable economic conditions seem to have engendered a decline in the prevalence of positive assessments of membership, but they have not prevented the growth of a sense of European Community solidarity. Let us examine the evidence on both points.

In late October and early November of 1977, representative national samples of the publics of the nine European Community countries were interviewed as part of a regular program of surveys carried out twice each year under the sponsorship of the Commission of the European Community.[6] The respondents were

asked: "Generally speaking, do you think that (your country's) membership in the Common Market is a good thing, a bad thing, or neither good nor bad?" This question is phrased in a way that makes it easy for those who have no clear opinion to select the neutral option. Dimensional analysis of data from earlier surveys indicated that this item was a good indicator of responses to a broad cluster of attitudes concerning support for, or opposition to, European integration. Consequently, this item was included as a standard question in all subsequent European Community surveys. The distribution of responses in Fall, 1977 appears in Table 1.

In the Community as a whole, a clear majority felt that their country's membership was a good thing,

---

5. See Karl W. Deutsch, *Political Community*, Chap. 3.

6. Field work for the Euro-Barometer series has been carried out by the European Omnibus Survey—a consortium consisting of the European affiliates of the Gallup survey group—except in Belgium and Luxembourg where the surveys were conducted by INRA. In these surveys, samples of approximately 1,000 respondents are interviewed in each country except Luxembourg, where the N is approximately 300; and in the United Kingdom, where 1,000 respondents are interviewed in Great Britain and 300 respondents are interviewed in Northern

Ireland. The organizations responsible for fieldwork in each country are: DIMARSO/INRA (Luxembourg and Belgium); Gallup Markedanalyse (Denmark); EMNID-Institut (Germany); Institut Francais d'Opinion Publique (France); Irish Marketing Surveys (Ireland); Instituto per le Richerche Statistische e l'Analyisi dell'Opinione Publica (DOXA-Italy); Nederlands Institut voor de Publieke Opinie (NIPO-Netherlands); and Social Surveys Ltd. (Gallup Poll-Great Britain). Fieldwork in Northern Ireland is conducted jointly by Irish Marketing Surveys and Social Surveys (Gallup Poll). In Germany, fieldwork for the 1973 survey was carried out by Gesellschaft für Marktforschung and for the 1970 survey by Institut für Demoskopie. In Britain, the 1970 survey was conducted by Louis Harris Research, Ltd. In the Netherlands, the 1973 survey was carried out by Nederlandse Stichting voor Statistiek. International coordination of the Euro-Barometer surveys is directed by Helène Riffault of IFOP and Norman Webb of Social Surveys (Gallup Poll). Fieldwork for the Fall, 1977 survey took place from October 24 to November 8, 1977. For a more detailed report of findings from this survey, see Commission of the European Communities, *Euro-Barometer Number 8: Public Opinion in the European Community* (Brussels: European Community [mimeo], 1978).

TABLE 1

PUBLIC APPRAISAL OF THEIR NATION'S MEMBERSHIP IN THE EUROPEAN
COMMUNITY: FALL, 1977

| FEEL THAT THEIR NATION'S MEMBERSHIP IS: | FRANCE | BELG. | NETH. | GER- MANY | ITALY | LUX. | DEN- MARK | IRE- LAND | UK | EURO- PEAN COM- MUNITY* |
|---|---|---|---|---|---|---|---|---|---|---|
| Total Respondents | (1004) | (1006) | (943) | (999) | (1155) | (344) | (992) | (997) | (1351) | (8791) |
| A Good Thing | 57% | 60 | 74 | 59 | 70 | 73 | 37 | 59 | 35 | 56 |
| A Bad Thing | 9 | 5 | 5 | 7 | 5 | 3 | 33 | 19 | 37 | 14 |
| Neither Good Nor Bad | 28 | 19 | 16 | 24 | 18 | 17 | 24 | 19 | 23 | 23 |
| Don't Know | 6 | 16 | 5 | 10 | 7 | 7 | 6 | 3 | 5 | 7 |

* Each national sample weighted in proportion to that nation's population.

with positive assessments outweighing negative ones by a four-to-one ratio even in this relatively uncertain economic context. But a marked contrast is apparent when we compare the appraisal given by the publics of the six original member countries with those of the three new members. In both Denmark and the United Kingdom, positive and negative evaluations are almost evenly balanced, with negative ratings actually outweighing positive ones in the latter country. The third new member public, the Irish, manifest a much more favorable attitude but even there negative appraisals are more than twice as numerous as in any of the original six nations. The fact that Ireland is relatively favorable is not particularly surprising: adherence to the Common Market has secured entry on favorable terms to a large market for Irish agricultural products— something particularly important for a country that is still heavily agrarian. Moreover, Irish membership seems to have encouraged a boom in industrial development, linked with the fact that Ireland has one of the lowest costs for industrial production of any region within the European Community.

Nevertheless, the overall pattern cannot be attributed solely to differences in currently prevailing economic conditions. All nine countries have suffered seriously from the effects of the recent recession. The striking difference in the balance of positive and negative appraisals between the original six and the three new member countries seems to reflect the presence or absence of a reservoir of diffuse support built up over a long period of time, raising evaluations among the six well above the level that would be expected on the basis of current economic factors alone.

How resistant is such support to decay in the face of adverse current conditions? Table 2 shows the percentage making a positive appraisal of their country's membership in the Common Market, in each nation, for each of the nine time points at which the current series of surveys has been conducted. As a detailed inspection of these results shows, positive evaluations remained at relatively high levels in each of the original six member nations throughout the period from 1973 through 1977. Positive appraisals have, on the whole, been much less widespread in the three new member countries; and their support levels have shown somewhat greater volatility over time, as if they were more responsive to current influences. Figure 2 provides a graphic presentation of the data in Table 2, combining the results from the six in an average weighted according to population. The graph reveals a pattern that may be more difficult to see in Table 2. Though the oscillations are greater among the publics of the three new members than among the six, there is a certain parallelism in the rise and fall of attitudes toward Common Market membership in both sets of countries: favorable assessments reach a peak in Fall 1975, plummet to a low point in 1976 and then show a tendency to recover in 1977. This pattern bears an interesting relationship to the rise and fall of the Index of Industrial Production for the respective nations, which is shown in Figure 3.

Let us assume that public assessments of the Common Market have been influenced, at least to some extent, by the economic fortunes of the respondent's country, of which the Index of Industrial Pro-

duction is one indicator. If this is the case, we must note that there is a lag of about a year between changes in our economic indicator and changes in mass attitudes. With the onset of the recent recession, the Index of Industrial Production declined, sometimes precipitously, in all nine countries, reaching a low point in 1975—the year in which positive evaluations of the Common Market were at a peak. Industrial production made a subsequent recovery, with most nations regaining or surpassing their 1973 levels by the Fall of 1976—when public assessments in most countries were at their low point. Needless to say, there were cross-national deviations from the general pattern; on the whole, they reflect changes in industrial production reasonably well. On one hand, the recovery of favorable attitudes has been relatively weak and occurred relatively late in Britain—which accords with the fact that British industrial production in 1977 was still below its 1973 level. Conversely, the recession had a comparatively mild impact on Ireland's economy. To be sure, her per capita

TABLE 2

PUBLIC APPRAISAL OF MEMBERSHIP IN THE EUROPEAN COMMUNITY, 1973–1977
(PERCENTAGE SAYING THAT THEIR COUNTRY'S MEMBERSHIP
IS "A GOOD THING")

|  | FALL 1973 | SPRING 1974 | FALL 1974 | SPRING 1975 | FALL 1975 | SPRING 1976 | FALL 1976 | SPRING 1977 | FALL 1977 |
|---|---|---|---|---|---|---|---|---|---|
| France | 61% | 68 | 63 | 64 | 67 | 57 | 52 | 64 | 57 |
| Belgium | 57 | 68 | 60 | 57 | 59 | 62 | 66 | 69 | 60 |
| Netherlands | 63 | 66 | 70 | 64 | 67 | 75 | 74 | 80 | 74 |
| Germany | 63 | 59 | 62 | 56 | 61 | 48 | 57 | 54 | 59 |
| Italy | 69 | 77 | 82 | 71 | 75 | 63 | 68 | 71 | 70 |
| Luxembourg | 67 | 79 | 73 | 65 | 78 | 66 | 77 | 84 | 73 |
| Denmark | 42 | 35 | 33 | 36 | 41 | 36 | 29 | 30 | 37 |
| Ireland | 56 | 48 | 50 | 50 | 67 | 50 | 50 | 57 | 59 |
| UK* | 31 | 33 | 36 | 47 | 50 | 39 | 39 | 35 | 35 |

* Surveys were carried out in Great Britain only, in 1973 and 1974; from 1975 on, the figures for the "United Kingdom" include Northern Ireland as well.

FIGURE 2

APPRAISAL OF MEMBERSHIP IN COMMON MARKET, 1973–1977.
PERCENTAGE SAYING THAT THEIR COUNTRY'S MEMBERSHIP
IS "A GOOD THING."

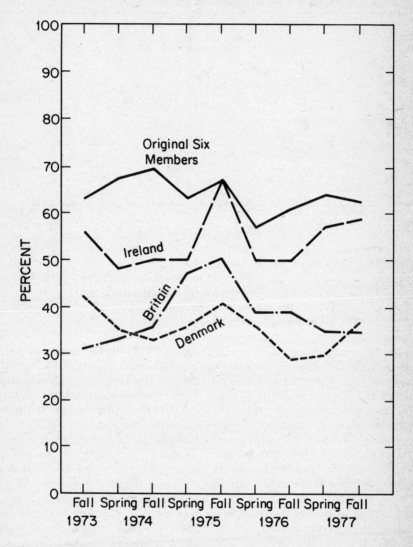

income was low by comparison with the rest of the European Community, and her unemployment level relatively high, but both of these things have been true of Ireland for decades. Presumably, it is *changes* from one's accustomed condition that influence public appraisals of the benefits of membership in the Community. In terms of recent change, Ireland fared relatively well. Her Index of Industrial Production showed only a modest decline by 1975, and made an exceptionally strong recovery thereafter, standing far above her 1973 level in 1977.

If there is, indeed, a lag of a year

FIGURE 3

INDUSTRIAL PRODUCTION RATES IN EUROPEAN COMMUNITY COUNTRIES,
1973–1977 (SEASONALLY ADJUSTED, 1970 = 100).

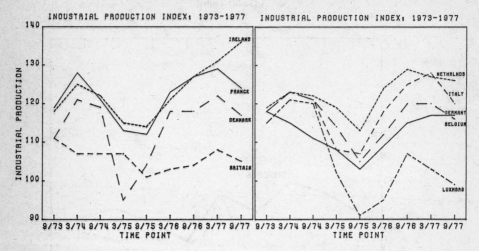

or so between changes in industrial production and changes in mass attitudes toward the Community, the next surveys should show a further rise in favorable appraisals of Common Market membership in Ireland and several other European Community countries. The existence of such a lag seems entirely plausible: one would expect to find some such delay, since the consequences of changing rates of production do not immediately impinge upon the general public, and there might well be some further delay before the public began to attribute these effects to any given cause.

The regression of our attitudinal variable on a given nation's index of industrial production one year before the given survey yields a correlation of .253.[7] This lag provides our best fit: the correlations

7. For these regression analyses, evaluations of membership were coded as follows: Bad = 1, Neither = 2. Good = 3. The mean score for a given nation at a given point in time was the input to our aggregate data set. Missing data were excluded from calculations of the mean scores.

with the index at earlier points in time yield lower values and the correlation with the index at the time of the survey is only .194. Though a correlation of .253 is scarcely overwhelming, it is significant at better than the .05 level when dealing with 81 data points, as we are here. Public evaluations of membership in the Community seem linked with economic growth or decline.

Can we explain more of the variance in attitudes by utilizing additional economic indicators? Yes. The best such measure, for present purposes, seems to be an indicator of inflation. Figure 4 shows the Consumer Price Indices for the nine European Community countries from 1973 to 1977. Since these indices show a steady upward trend while our attitudinal measure does not, it is evident that we need to use the *change* in this index, during some specified period preceding a given survey, rather than the index itself, as a predictor of attitudes. Empirically, our best fit proves to be the rise in a nation's Consumer Price Index during the two years

FIGURE 4

INFLATION RATES IN EUROPEAN COMMUNITY COUNTRIES, 1973–1977 (1970 = 100).

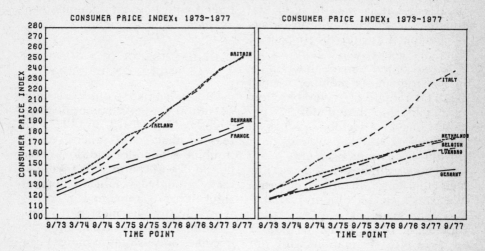

preceding the given survey. The lag involved here is longer, in a sense, than that connected with the Index of Industrial Production. This fact is somewhat surprising: the average consumer buys things almost every day. One might expect that he or she would become aware of inflation almost immediately. This may be true, but apparently it takes the public a certain period of time to connect inflation with EEC membership. Once this connection is made, however, its impact is slightly stronger than that associated with rising or falling rates of industrial production: our indicator of inflation shows a −.268 correlation with assessments of membership in the Common Market. The negative polarity, of course, indicates that relatively high rates of inflation are linked with negative assessments of membership.

Utilizing our indicators of both inflation and industrial production in the regression equation, we obtain a multiple correlation of .376. Additional economic indicators (including measures of the change in unemployment rates) increase the amount of variance explained only very slightly; but our results do seem to indicate that economic conditions have a significant impact on public appraisals of membership in the E.E.C. These results support the idea that favorable outputs tend to enhance support for membership in a political community, while unfavorable ones have the opposite effect—but only in a loose way. It is unclear whether these "outputs" really come from the political system in question: the recession and inflation of the 1970's and their subsequent abatement were worldwide phenomena that probably were affected only marginally by any actions taken by the European Community institutions. However, the publics concerned here *did* seem to attribute prevailing economic conditions to their membership in the European Community, to some extent, and if they did, it is a significant fact. Given the relatively low rates of economic growth and high rates of inflation that were present most of the time since 1973, the net result was a slight decline in favorable assessments. But it is important to distinguish between long-term effects of membership and the impact of immediate economic conditions.

As we noted above, the publics of the original six member nations retained a relatively favorable view of membership throughout this period. Long-term factors—perhaps a reservoir of diffuse support built up during the pre-1973 era—were eroded only slightly. Let us put this statement into quantitative terms. We constructed a dummy variable based on whether a given nation joined the Community in 1958 or in 1973. Its correlation with our dependent variable is .896: this variable alone explains considerably more of the variance in attitudes than any available economic indicator or any combination of them. It seems unlikely that anything would greatly affect a correlation of this size. And, when this variable is used together with the economic indicators described above, in a multiple regression, neither the partial correlation (.863) nor the multiple correlation (.892) differ much from the zero-order correlation. It is impossible to prove, with the present data base, that the publics of the six make relatively positive evaluations of membership *because* they have been members for a relatively long time: it is conceivable (though it seems unlikely) that we are dealing with some cultural predisposition that just happens to be much more prevalent in the six than in the three. But the results of these analyses do clearly demonstrate the preponderance of long-term effects over those of the current economic environment, at least as measured by these standard economic indicators.

The economic context is important. Nation-specific effects, apparently linked with long-term membership, are even more important.

## THE EMERGENCE OF A SENSE OF COMMUNITY SOLIDARITY

Public evaluations of EEC membership remained static or declined slightly from 1973 to 1977, for reasons that seem related to the troubled economic conditions of that period. Those publics that were already strongly favorable to membership in 1973 remained relatively favorable, for the most part, while those that had recently entered had become only slightly more favorable or even a little less so by 1977.

We have dealt with only one aspect of public attitudes toward the Community, however. Assuredly it is a crucial one, for if a people conclude that their membership in a given political community is no longer a good thing, the next step might well be to leave it. Still, the appraisal of membership as measured here does not tell the whole story. The question we have been dealing with is framed in a way that tends to evoke an assessment of the utilization aspects of membership: one would expect such assessments to reflect the current economic context to a significant degree. Let us examine a less utilitarian, more affective aspect of mass attitudes toward the Community.

At three points in time, representative samples of the nine European Community publics have been asked: "If one of the countries of the Common Market (European Community) finds itself in major economic difficulties, do you feel that the other countries, including (your country), should help it or not?" This question evokes responses concerning what *should* be done, not simply an appraisal of what has happened. The responses obtained from each public in 1973 appear in Table 3. By comparison with appraisals of the benefits of EEC membership, the levels of support for Community solidarity were strikingly high. There was a good deal more opposition in Denmark and the United Kingdom than in any of the original six member nations, but the principle of aiding other European Community countries in time of need was endorsed by strong majorities in all nine countries.

In a sense, these high levels of support for European Community solidarity are not surprising. The Danish and Irish publics had just voted to join the Community in 1972, in national referenda that evoked intense and widespread discussion of the choice being made. There would seem to be little sense in joining, unless one were committed to a certain degree of solidarity. The British electorate had not yet been consulted on the subject, but their representatives in Parliament had debated extensively and finally voted in favor of joining the European Community by a conclusive majority: cues from the political elites tended to encourage

a sense of solidarity—which was endorsed by a 2:1 majority among the British public. The ratio was almost 7:1 in the Community as a whole, however. These high levels of support for Community solidarity were expressed during the first year of membership for the three new countries. The very fact that the Community had just been expanded, after years of debate and difficult negotiations, may have given the Community a psychological boost that would not necessarily last; all of this took place before the Arab oil embargo of October, 1973 and the sharp economic decline of 1974 and 1975. Would this remarkably high level of public support for economic solidarity collapse in the fact of real, rather than hypothetical, economic difficulties? For the Community as a whole, the answer is a clear-cut "No."

Table 4 shows the levels of support for Community solidarity at each of the three points in time when this question was asked. The same data are summarized in graphic form in Figure 5, with results from the original six members combined in an average weighted according to national populations. The overall pattern is not one of collapse, but of upward convergence. Among the original six, sup-

TABLE 3

SENSE OF EUROPEAN COMMUNITY SOLIDARITY, FALL, 1973: IF A MEMBER COUNTRY IS IN MAJOR ECONOMIC DIFFICULTIES, SHOULD THE OTHER COUNTRIES—INCLUDING YOUR OWN—HELP IT? (RESPONSES FROM SURVEY IN LATE SEPTEMBER AND EARLY OCTOBER, 1973)

|  | FRANCE | BELG. | NETH. | GER-MANY | ITALY | LUX. | DEN. | IRE. | UK | EUROPEAN COMMUNITY* |
|---|---|---|---|---|---|---|---|---|---|---|
| Should Help It: | 78% | 78 | 79 | 77 | 88 | 87 | 62 | 80 | 59 | 76 |
| Should Not Help It: | 9 | 9 | 9 | 7 | 2 | 8 | 25 | 10 | 28 | 11 |
| Don't Know | 13 | 13 | 12 | 16 | 10 | 5 | 13 | 10 | 13 | 13 |

* Weighted in proportion to national populations; unweighted N = 13,484.

TABLE 4

SENSE OF EUROPEAN COMMUNITY SOLIDARITY,
1973–1975 (PERCENTAGE SAYING THEIR
COUNTRY SHOULD HELP ANOTHER
E.C. NATION IN DIFFICULTY)

| | FALL 1973 | FALL 1976 | FALL 1977 |
|---|---|---|---|
| France | 78 | 75 | 76 |
| Belgium | 78 | 82 | 74 |
| Netherlands | 79 | 84 | 85 |
| Germany | 77 | 74 | 72 |
| Italy | 88 | 95 | 92 |
| Luxembourg | 87 | 86 | 83 |
| Denmark | 62 | 68 | 75 |
| Ireland | 80 | 83 | 83 |
| UK | 59 | 77 | 75 |

port for economic solidarity remained at very high levels, with
little overall change. And among the
three new member publics, support
for Community solidarity showed a
substantial rise. Ireland, which already ranked high in 1973, rose to
a level slightly higher than the
average for the original six; while
the British and Danish publics
showed substantial gains that left
them only slightly below the six.

It seems significant that the German level of support showed a
moderate but appreciable decline,
while the Italian level showed a
comparable rise—during this period
Germany was called upon to provide
actual economic aid to Italy, and
did provide it. Nevertheless, even
in Germany the proponents of economic solidarity prevailed over its
opponents by more than 7:1 in
November 1977; and for the Community as a whole there was an
upward shift. Its magnitude, weighted
according to the size of national
populations, is a net gain of three
percentage points from 1973 to 1977.
This is a modest figure, to be sure,
but we tend to run into ceiling
effects. In the case of the original
six, the percentages favoring soli-

darity simply cannot rise very much
farther; outright opposition was
already very low in 1973 and a certain proportion of nonresponse seems
inevitable in any national public
opinion survey. The gain was concentrated almost entirely in the
three new member nations. The fact
that there has been a pattern of
upward convergence, with the new
members catching up with the original six, seems more significant than
the absolute size of the overall
upward movement.

Despite the uncertain economic
climate that has prevailed since expansion of the European Community in 1973, there have been
important gains in the prevalence of
a sense of Community solidarity.
As was suggested earlier, the sheer
passage of time under common
supranational institutions may tend
to instill the habit of viewing things
from a broader perspective than
that of the nation-state, even in the
absence of material rewards. The
Fall 1977 survey provides another
piece of evidence that helps explain the surprising fact that a
sense of Community solidarity became more widespread from 1973
to 1977, while public appraisals of
the benefits of membership were
stagnant or showed a tendency to
decline. In addition to asking each
respondent whether he or she felt
that membership was a good or bad
thing, they were asked, "And do you
think that (your country's) membership in the Common Market is a
good thing, a bad thing or neither
in the light of (your country's)
future in the next ten or fifteen
years?" Pluralities (and in most
cases, clear majorities) of the publics of all nine countries felt that
their country's membership would
prove to be a good thing in ten
or fifteen years time. For example,

while only 35 percent of the British public felt that British membership was a good thing in the Fall of 1977, 48 percent felt that it would be a good thing in the long run.

It is, of course, impossible to say what actually will have happened by 1988 or 1993. But the difference between the two responses suggests that, while the various publics were quite aware of the troubled circumstances of the recent past, they had not lost hope for the Community's future.

## DIRECT ELECTIONS TO EUROPEAN PARLIAMENT

There is additional evidence of a growing sense of European Community solidarity. It concerns the forthcoming direct elections to the European Parliament. Public support for holding such elections has, itself, shown impressive growth. Earlier a matter of controversy, particularly in the new member nations, by 1977 a consensus had emerged throughout the Community in favor of them. Over time, the idea of holding such elections has evolved from a hypothetical proposal to a coming reality, which has probably encouraged public acceptance. It has also required certain changes in the wording of the survey items designed to measure public support or opposition to the European elections.

In 1970, representative samples of the publics of the six countries that were then members were asked: "Are you for or against the election of a European parliament by popular vote of all the citizens of the member states of the European Community?" A similar question was asked in Great Britain, but since it was not then a member of the Community, it was placed in the context of hypothetical British entry. The question was repeated in 1973, except that this time four categories of response were offered: "completely in favor," "favor on the whole," "disagree in general," and "disagree completely." By Spring, 1975, a concrete proposal was being discussed to hold direct elections to the European Parliament in 1978, and the question was worded: "One of the main proposals is to elect a European Parliament in May 1978, by a popular vote of all the citizens in the member states of the European Community (Common Market). Are you, yourself, for or against this proposal? How strongly do you feel about it?" The same four response categories were offered as in 1973; and this question was repeated in each survey through May 1976. By Fall 1976, agreement had been reached on the goal of holding direct elections in May 1978 (although important details remained to be worked out that, in fact, delayed the elections until Spring 1979). Accordingly, in Fall 1976 the question was phrased: "The governments of the member countries of the Common Market have reached agreement to hold the first elections to the European Parliament by universal suffrage, that is, by direct vote of all citizens, in May 1978. Are you, yourself, for or against this particular election?"

The same four response categories were offered as stated above. In Spring and Fall 1977, the introductory wording was simplified to read: "In 1978, elections for the European Parliament are planned in every country of the Common Market including (your country). Everybody will be entitled to vote. Are you, yourself, for or against this particular election?" Again, four

FIGURE 5

SENSE OF EUROPEAN SOLIDARITY, 1973–1977. PERCENTAGE SAYING THAT THEIR COUNTRY
SHOULD HELP ANOTHER EUROPEAN COUNTRY IN DIFFICULTY.

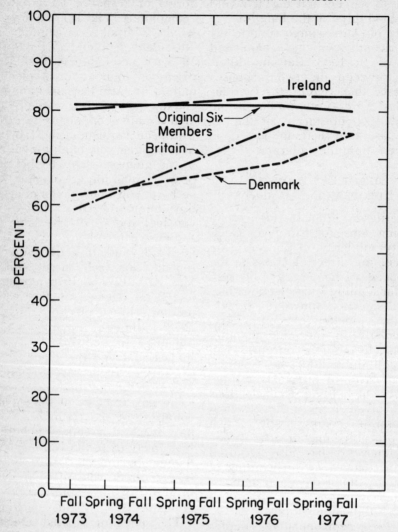

response categories were offered. Figure 6 shows the changes over time in the percentage completely favorable, or to some extent favorable, to a directly-elected European Parliament. Despite the various changes in wording of the question, and the shift from a distant possibility to a measure that had been approved by the respective governments, support for a directly-elected European Parliament changed only gradually in the original six member countries, rising from a weighted average of 60 percent favorable in 1970, to 74 percent favorable in Fall 1977. Changes among the publics of the three new member coun-

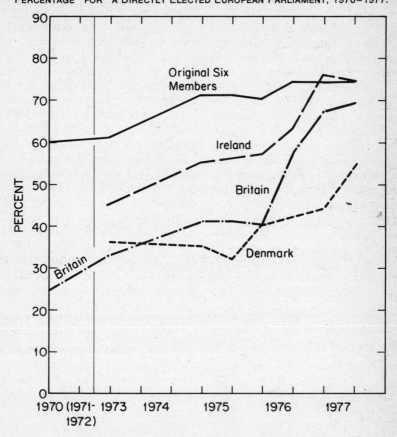

tries were dramatic by comparison. In 1970, only 25 percent of the British public were favorable, while a 55 percent majority were opposed to a directly elected European Parliament. By late 1977, support was voiced by 69 percent and opposition by only 18 percent. In our earliest Danish survey, nine months after Danish entry, only 36 percent were favorable while 43 percent were opposed. By 1977 these figures had shifted to 54 percent and 29 percent, respectively. In Ireland, a 45 percent plurality were already favorable to a directly elected European Parliament in 1973, but this figure rose to 74 percent in 1977.

Once again, we find the phenomenon of upward convergence, with the three new member publics catching up with the original six, but here the evidence is far stronger than anything we have seen above. It seems likely that much of the change since 1975 is due to a process in which the publics became aware of, and influenced by, decisions made by national elites. But if this were the case, it illustrates forcefully the extent to which these publics can be mobilized in support of European institutions when their generally favorable predispositions are reinforced by positive action on the part of political leaders.

The growth of public backing for direct elections to the European Parliament is impressive, but it is probably a relatively soft indicator of a sense of European solidarity. One might favor such elections in the belief that the European Parliament will remain unimportant; or because one sees it as a forum for the defense of national interests. The 1977 surveys included a question that enables us to examine the latter possibility. It is also a relatively "difficult" question that helps provide an indication of the distribution of hard-core Europeans, because it explicitly pits the national interest against that of the Community as a whole. The item is: "Which of the following attitudes would you expect a (British, French, etc.) member of the European Parliament to have?

—He should support things that are good for Europe as a whole, even if they are not always good for (my country) at the time.
—He should support the interests of (my country) all the time whether or not they are good for Europe as a whole.

The responses to this item in Fall 1977 appear in Table 5.

The proportion according priority to the interest of Europe as a whole above the national interest is far smaller than the proportion favoring a directly-elected European Parliament, as one would expect. In the three new member countries the national interest is clearly preponderant over that of the Community. In Belgium, the two are in nearly even balance. But in the remaining five of the original six member countries—and in the Community as a whole—the predominant attitude is to feel that one's representative in the European Parliament should support measures

that are good for Europe as a whole, even if they run counter to the immediate national interest.

This question has not been asked over a sufficient period of years to enable us to draw any conclusions about long-term trends. The fact that the publics of the older member countries are substantially more likely to give priority to European interests suggests that the formation of a European outlook is something that develops rather slowly. It does not, however, necessarily indicate the direction in which the three newer publics are moving.

In a sense, this item provides a test of whether an individual is prepared to become a citizen of Europe. And the results indicate that Europeans do exist. They are outnumbered by those who are citizens of a given country first and foremost, among the three newer members of the Community. But among those publics that had experienced almost twenty years of membership in the Community by Fall 1977, the Europeans seemed to comprise a majority.

## INDIVIDUAL-LEVEL DIFFERENCES IN ASSESSMENT OF MEMBERSHIP AND A SENSE OF COMMUNITY SOLIDARITY

Up to this point we have focused entirely on variations in public attitudes across nations and across time. Nations are not monolithic, however; within each country, one finds substantial differences in support for European integration between people of different sex, age, occupation, political loyalties and educational levels. In order to understand changes over time in the support levels of given nationalities, we must analyze these individual-level differences as well as the political and economic environment of given nations at given times. For example, the upward convergence of the French and Italian publics with the other publics of the original six-member European Community can be attributed, in large part, to the conversion of the communist electorates of these countries from hostile to favorable orientations toward integration.[8]

Among those individual-level characteristics that show substantial associations with support for European integration, education is probably the most pervasive: the highly-educated are consistently more favorable than the less-educated. This finding emerges from virtually every nationwide survey that has ever been conducted on the subject. The fact itself is clear and unmistakable. But it can be interpreted in a variety of ways.

On one hand, it could be attributed to the fact that the more educated tend to have higher incomes and more desirable jobs than the less educated. Accordingly, the argument might plausibly be developed that education is linked with support for integration because the more educated respondents tend to be of higher social class level; European integration benefits the upper and middle classes more than the working class; thus the fact that the more educated are relatively favorable to integration is simply an expression of social class interest.[9] Carried a bit farther, one could argue that support for European integration is inherently a Right-wing political position, while opposition to integration is the natural stance of the Left. In support of this argument one could marshal evidence that the electorates of the Left tend to be less favorable to integration than those of the Right. This is frequently, but by no means universally true—but one might save the hypothesis by arguing that in some countries, the electorates of the Left have fallen prey to delusions. The implication of this general interpretation is that the future growth or decline of mass support for European integration depends essentially on whether the Left or the Right ultimately triumphs.

The foregoing interpretation makes the assumption that the more educated are relatively pro-European because they tend to come from higher social class backgrounds. But education is a complex variable that taps many things. It is indeed an indicator of one's social class. It is also an indicator of the presence or absence of certain cognitive skills, for the more educated tend to know more, and are more accustomed to dealing with abstractions and remote objects than the less educated. Finally, education is an indicator of one's social milieu: the more educated tend to move in different circles, read or view different media, and become exposed to different influences from the less educated. It may be true that the

8. See Inglehart, *The Silent Revolution*, Chapter 12; and Robert D. Putnam, "Interdependence and the Italian Communists," *International Organization*, 32, 2 (Spring, 1978), forthcoming.

9. In practice, it is difficult to demonstrate that integration benefits the middle class more than the working class. The former unquestionably *do* have higher incomes and social status, but there is very little evidence that these differences would be smaller if

the Community did not exist. An alternative version of the argument might therefore be that, regardless of whether they actually *do* benefit more, middle class respondents are more likely to *think* that they do and this explains their higher levels of support for integration.

TABLE 5

EUROPEAN COMMUNITY SOLIDARITY: SHOULD PRIORITY BE GIVEN TO YOUR COUNTRY'S
NATIONAL INTERESTS OR TO THOSE OF EUROPE AS A WHOLE? (RESPONSES
TO FALL, 1977 SURVEY)

| A (BRITISH, FRENCH, ETC.) MEMBER OF THE EUROPEAN PARLIAMENT SHOULD: | FRANCE | BELG. | NETH. | GER. | ITALY | LUX. | DEN. | IRE. | UK | EURO-PEAN COM-MUNITY* |
|---|---|---|---|---|---|---|---|---|---|---|
| Support things that are good for Europe as a whole, even if they are not always good for (my country) at the time | 48% | 39 | 65 | 49 | 54 | 48 | 36 | 35 | 42 | 48 |
| Support the interests of (my country) whether or not they are good for Europe as a whole | 40 | 41 | 27 | 36 | 39 | 43 | 52 | 58 | 52 | 41 |
| Don't Know | 12 | 20 | 8 | 15 | 7 | 9 | 12 | 7 | 6 | 11 |

* Weighted in proportion to national populations.

more educated are relatively pro-European simply because this is the best way to pursue a distinctive class interest. But it could work the other way around: it might be that any observed social class differences in levels of support for European integration result from the fact that middle class respondents have, on the whole, received more education than working class respondents.

Let us compare the relative strengths of the relationships between support for European integration and the respondent's educational level on one hand, and the occupation of the head of the respondent's household, on the other. Table 6 shows the percentages making positive appraisals of European Community membership by education and occupation in the European Community as a whole, as of Fall 1977. Though there is some cross-national variation in the strength of these relationships, these figures are reasonably representative of the pattern that is found in each of the nine member nations (though not, of course, of the absolute levels). They are also fairly

typical of those found at other points in time, though it seems worth mentioning that both of these relationships were somewhat stronger in 1977 than they were in 1973.

The first thing that we might note is the fact that respondents in households headed by manual workers do, indeed, make less favorable appraisals of EEC membership than those in households headed by a person with a non-manual occupation. The impression that these data convey, however, is scarcely one of social class polarization: a majority of the respondents in both manual and non-manual households made favorable appraisals; there is simply a difference in degree and the difference is not overwhelming. Furthermore, when we compare the responses of all four broad occupational categories, there is no monotonic relationship between income and the proportion making favorable appraisals: those from farm households have the lowest mean family income but they prove to be fully as favorable as our highest income group, those from nonmanual house-

TABLE 6

APPRAISAL OF EUROPEAN COMMUNITY
MEMBERSHIP BY EDUCATION AND BY
OCCUPATION, HEAD OF HOUSE-
HOLD* (PERCENTAGE SAYING
THAT THEIR COUNTRY'S
MEMBERSHIP IS A
GOOD THING)

1. *By Education*

Respondent left school at:

| | | |
|---|---|---|
| Age 15 or younger | 54% | (4179) |
| Ages 16–18 years | 63 | (2308) |
| Age 19 or older | 73 | (1885) |
| Eta = .154 | | |

2. *By Occupation, Head of Household*

| | | |
|---|---|---|
| Farmer | 68% | (291) |
| Manual worker | 53 | (2421) |
| Nonmanual | 68 | (3454) |
| Inactive | 57 | (2204) |
| Eta = .136 | | |

* Fall, 1977 nine-nation survey, weighted according to population. Weighted N's are shown in this and subsequent tables.

holds. Finally, the apparent impact of education on one's attitude proves to be stronger than the apparent impact of one's occupation. A simple comparison of the size of the percentage differences between the various groups suggests that this is the case, and the relative size of the Eta coefficients confirms it. When we enter both variables into a Multiple Classification Analysis that adjusts for the effects of nationality, income, age, and political party preferences, as well as the effects of education and occupation on each other, we obtain Beta coefficients of .090 and .045 for education and occupation, respectively. Education proves to be a more powerful predictor of attitudes than does occupation. In other words, our data give more support to the hypothesis that middle class respondents are relatively favorable to European integration because

they tend to have relatively high levels of education than to the converse hypothesis.

But this still leaves unanswered the question of why the more educated tend to be relatively favorable. Could it be due to the influence of distinctive political party preferences? In general, the more educated are more likely to support relatively conservative political parties than the less educated; and, as we have noted, in most (though not all) of the European Community countries the parties of the Right give more support to European integration than those of the Left. Could this be a cause of spurious correlation? Again, the answer seems to be no. Table 7 shows the distribution of favorable appraisals of EEC membership among those who support political parties of the Left and Right respectively, at four points in time in the Community as a whole.

The electorates of the Left consistently make less favorable assessments of membership than do those of the Right, although the gap seems to have narrowed since 1973, but the percentage differences found here are even smaller than those associated with manual versus nonmanual occupations. There are major cross-national differences in the explanatory power of this variable, which we will touch on later. On the whole, the partisan differences are modest (the Eta coefficient for this variable in Fall 1977 was only .064). This fact suggests, and more detailed statistical analysis confirms, that the attitudinal differences by education and occupation could be attributed to differential political party preferences to only a limited extent. The fact remains that the more educated are consistently more favorable to Euro-

TABLE 7

APPRAISAL OF EUROPEAN COMMUNITY
MEMBERSHIP BY POLITICAL PARTY
PREFERENCE: 1973–1977 (PER-
CENTAGE SAYING THAT THEIR
COUNTRY'S MEMBERSHIP
IS A GOOD THING)

| RESPONDENT SUPPORTS A PARTY OF THE: | FALL 1973 | FALL 1975 | FALL 1976 | FALL 1977 |
|---|---|---|---|---|
| Left | 60% | 57 | 55 | 58 |
| Right | 73 | 69 | 65 | 65 |

pean integration than the rest of their compatriots, and this is one of the most important attitudinal cleavages within the respective countries. Why?

## TWO ANALYTICAL HYPOTHESES

Earlier analyses have suggested two distinct types of underlying causes. They might be described as the "Cognitive Mobilization" hypothesis and the "Materialist/Post-Materialist" hypothesis, respectively. Both hypotheses have been developed in considerable detail in previously published work. We will provide only a brief summary of them here.[10]

The Cognitive Mobilization hypothesis argues that the rising educational levels of recent decades, coupled with the growing availability of information about things happening in distant places, is conducive to an increasingly cosmopoli-

10. For a fuller discussion of "Cognitive Mobilization" see Inglehart, "Cognitive Mobilization and European Identity," *Comparative Politics* 3, 1 (October 1970) pp. 45–70; the Materialist/Post-Materialist hypothesis was first developed in Inglehart, "Changing Value Priorities and European Integration," *Journal of Common Market Studies* 10, 1 (September 1971) pp. 1–36. Both themes have been explored further in Inglehart, *The Silent Revolution*, Chaps. 2, 11, 12.

tan outlook on the part of Western publics. The ability to handle abstractions, to process information about remote and complex entities (such as the European Community) lies at the heart of the Cognitive Mobilization process, and formal education tends to increase these skills. The illiterate peasant tends to be a parochial whose horizons are limited to the village or rural area in which he lives.[11] His involvement in politics tends to be based on personal loyalties and word-of-mouth communications. The relatively well-educated publics of contemporary Western Europe are far better equipped to understand and take part in politics at the national level. To a greater degree than was true in the past, they are able to process information about what is happening in Europe as a whole, and the penetration of electronic communications media makes such information readily available. One consequence is that these publics are relatively likely to know about and discuss European politics and to view things from a European perspective. For

11. The classic empirically based study of parochial versus cosmopolitan worldviews among mass publics is that of Daniel Lerner, *The Passing of Traditional Society* (New York: Free Press, 1958). In their seminal study, *The Civic Culture* (Princeton: Princeton University Press, 1963), Gabriel Almond and Sidney Verba document the importance of formal education in promoting a sense of "subjective political competence" and a participant role in politics. We view Cognitive Mobilization as an extension of the social mobilization process that continues within the individual after the external landmarks of social mobilization (such as urbanization, universal suffrage, industrialization and compulsory education) have been completed. See Karl W. Deutsch, "Social Mobilization and Political Development," *American Political Science Review* 55, 2 (September, 1961) pp. 493–514.

many (especially among the publics of the original six member countries) the European Community has become a familiar object rather than something strange and threatening.

The Materialist/Post-Materialist hypothesis holds that people have a variety of needs, ranging from needs for subsistence and physical safety, to needs for belonging, solidarity, esteem and realization of one's intellectual and esthetic potential. Though all of these things are valued, people give priority in their values and behavior to those needs that are in relatively short supply.

Throughout most of recorded history, most people have been preoccupied by the struggle for material survival. But the unprecedented prosperity of western countries in recent decades has led to the emergence of substantial numbers of Post-Materialists—people who give top priority to the needs for belonging and self-realization. A Materialist value type (that gives top priority to the sustenance and safety needs) remains far more numerous, however.

One's basic value priorities tend to crystalize during pre-adult years and change relatively little thereafter. Accordingly, one's relative emphasis on survival or higher-order needs is a relatively fixed characteristic and not simply a response to the immediate environment. In a given setting, the Materialist value type tends to focus mainly on the pursuit of economic and physical security, while the Post-Materialist type places more emphasis on belonging and intellectual pursuits. One consequence is that, quite apart from their relative levels of Cognitive Mobilization, the Post-Materialists are more likely to take an interest in remote and abstract causes—European integration being one of many possibilities—and to place relatively heavy emphasis on a sense of European solidarity (as one of numerous possible ways to satisfy the need for belonging).

The two hypotheses that we have just sketched out imply that relatively well-educated and economically-secure groups will tend to be relatively favorable to European integration, other things being equal. This is not an iron law of universal determinism, merely a probable relationship. It is possible, for example, that a Post-Materialist might seek to attain a sense of belonging through involvement in some cause aimed at political disintegration rather than integration: Belgium's Flemish separatists seem to constitute a case in point. Nevertheless, those with Post-Materialist value priorities have a relatively high potential for mobilization in support of such causes as European integration; and the higher their level of Cognitive Mobilization, the greater their potential for involvement.

The implications for European integration of these two hypotheses were subjected to empirical tests based on survey data from 1970 and 1973, and the results generally support the interpretation just given.[12]

12. For a detailed account of the operationalization and testing of these hypotheses, see the sources cited in n. 11. Very briefly, we hypothesized that those who had spent their formative years in economic and physical security would be most likely to have Post-Materialist values. Accordingly, the indicator of value type used in this article is based on responses to the following questions:

If you had to choose among the following things, which are the *two* that seem most desirable to you?"
—Maintaining order in the nation
—Giving the people more say in important political decisions

—Fighting rising prices
—Protecting freedom of speech.

The first item, Order, was designed to tap concerns for physical safety; the third item, rising prices, was designed to tap a concern for economic stability. The two other items reflect nonmaterial, expressive concerns. On the basis of their two choices, our respondents thus fell into three categories: the Materialists (those who chose the first and third items together); the Post-Materialists (those who chose the second and fourth items together); and the Mixed types (those choosing any of the four remaining combinations). While this simple 4-item battery provides a parsimonious and fairly effective indicator of value priorities, a 12-item battery has been developed that is more accurate and reliable. It is more difficult to measure skills than attitudes in a public opinion survey. For practical reasons, our measures of cognitive level are indirect. The Cognitive Mobilization indicator used here is based on responses to two questions that have become standard items in the European Community surveys. They are:

When you get together with your friends, would you say that you discuss political matters frequently, occasionally, or never?

When you, yourself, hold a strong opinion, do you ever find yourself persuading your friends, relatives or fellow workers to share your views? (if yes): Does this happen often, from time to time or rarely?

Our reasoning in using these items as indicators of *skills* (which clearly, they do not measure directly) is that those who know and understand something about political life are most likely to discuss it; and that those most skilled in argumentation are most apt to attempt to persuade others to adopt their opinions. Needless to say, this is not always true. But overall, the "Mobilized" responses to these items show strong positive correlations with one's level of political information, sense of political competence and education, as is demonstrated in Inglehart, *The Silent Revolution*, Chapter 11. We dichotomized between relatively "High" and "Low" levels of Cognitive Mobilization by classing as "high" those who discuss politics "frequently" or "occasionally," *and* persuaded other people "often" or "from time to time." Those who discussed politics "frequently" were ranked "high" even if they *didn't* persuade others to accept their views. The remaining respondents were classed as "Low" on Cognitive Mobilization. Obviously, this is a generous definition of "High" levels of Cognitive Mobilization—

One wonders, however, how well the empirical relationships observed in the early 1970's would hold up in the changed socioeconomic environment of the late 1970's.

In order to examine the current relevance of mass publics' value priorities and cognitive skills to support for European integration, we set out to develop a typology that would enable us to measure the combined effects of the two variables. A typology seemed useful because, while the Post-Materialist type tends to rank high on Cognitive Mobilization, there is nothing that approaches a one-to-one relationship, empirically. Moreover, the effects of the two variables are not necessarily additive: they display some interesting interaction effects, as we will see below.

A series of typological analyses were carried out in order to examine the relative homogeneity of various groups in regard to values, levels of Cognitive Mobilization and certain related attitudes.[13] The results of these analyses support the construction of a typology based on two sets of three groups: the six types consist of, on one hand, the Materialist, Post-Materialist and Mixed (or intermediate) value types among those with relatively *low* levels of Cognitive Mobilization; and the Materialist, Post-Materialist and Mixed value types among those respondents having relatively high levels of Cognitive Mobilization.

But in addition to these six groups,

---

but even by this liberal standard, the majority of the public fell into the "Low" category.

13. Much of the groundwork for the Political Orientation Typology used here was laid by Bruno Roche of the Institut Francais d'Opinion Publique, who carried out an initial series of typological analyses. The authors are indebted to M. Roche for his contributions.

the typological analyses point to the existence of a seventh group, having such distinctive characteristics that it should be treated as a separate category in the typology. The respondents in this seventh group were identified by their responses to the question:

On this card are three basic kinds of attitudes toward the society in which we live. Please choose the one which best describes your own opinion:
1. The entire way our society is organized must be radically changed by revolutionary action.
2. Our society must be gradually changed by reforms.
3. Our present society must be valiantly defended against all subversive forces.

As shorthand terms one might refer to the three respective options as Revolution, Reform, and Reaction. In November 1977 the percentages choosing each option in the Community as a whole (weighted according to population) were 6 percent, 55 percent and 32 percent respectively—with 7 percent giving no answer.

While those who choose the first or Revolutionary option constituted only six percent of the European public, they are a particularly interesting and highly distinctive group. In regard to both value priorities and Cognitive Mobilization, there was considerably more difference between the Revolutionaries and the Reformists than between the Reformists and the Reactionaries or nonresponding groups. Specifically, the Revolutionaries have disproportionately high levels of political interest and activity in discussions; and a quite disproportionate tendency to be Post-Materialists. We hasten to emphasize that it would be a serious error to conclude that all Post-Materialists are potential Revolutionaries. There is a Reformist majority among all three value types. But when we focus our attention on the two extremes of the Revolutionary-Reactionary continuum, we find striking differences according to value type. Among the Materialists, Reactionaries outnumber Revolutionaries by an overwhelming 10:1 ratio. Among the mixed value types Reactionaries outnumber Revolutionaries by 4:1. But among the Post-Materialist group, the ratio is approximately 1:1—with Revolutionaries more numerous than Reactionaries. The Revolutionaries resemble the Post-Materialists in being considerably younger and better educated than the population at large. Furthermore, the two groups are similar in showing a decided preference for the political parties of the Left. But in other crucial respects they are dramatically different, as we will see shortly. Consequently, we constructed a Political Orientation Typology containing seven, rather than six groups, using the procedure shown in Figure 7.

Figure 7 shows the percentage of the European Community public (weighted according to population) falling into each of the seven types in Fall 1977. We replicated this procedure using data from the Fall 1976 surveys. The distribution of the respective types proved to be quite stable: in Fall 1977 six of the seven groups were within one percent of their Fall 1976 distributions. The seventh group—the Mobilized Materialists—increased from 12 percent of the total in 1976 to 14 percent in 1977. There was a shift toward Materialism from 1976 to 1977, and it was concentrated among those ranking high on Cognitive Mobilization. The Non-Mobilized Materialists showed no gain.

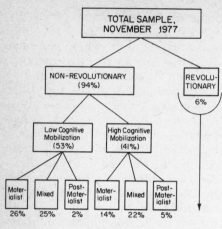

FIGURE 7

CONSTRUCTION OF POLITICAL ORIENTATION
TYPOLOGY. PERCENTAGES IN EACH CATEGORY
ARE BASED ON FALL, 1977 SURVEY.

Let us examine some of the politically relevant characteristics of the seven groups in our typology. A standard item in the European Community surveys is the question:

In political matters people often talk of 'the Left' and 'the Right.' How would you place your own views on this scale?" [The respondent is given a scale divided into ten boxes, running from Left to Right. At the left end of the card, the word "Left" appears and at the right end, the word "Right". The ten boxes are numbered from 1 to 10 and the respondent is asked to give the number of the position at which he would place himself. If he or she hesitates, he or she is asked to try again].

Table 8 shows the mean score on the Left-Right ideology scale for each of the seven groups in our typology. At a given level of Cognitive Mobilization, Materialists are substantially more likely to place themselves on the Right than are Post-Materialists—with the mixed types falling in between. But note that Cognitive Mobilization drives the Materialists and Post-Materialists in *opposite* directions: the mobilized

Materialists fall at the extreme Right of our seven groups, while the mobilized Post-Materialists place themselves to the Left of any group except the Revolutionaries. Not surprisingly, the Revolutionaries fall well to the Left of any other group. The fact that Cognitive Mobilization moves the Materialists and Post-Materialists in opposite directions seems logical: The Post-Materialists have, according to our hypotheses, emerged only recently and still constitute a minority group in societies that have, for some time, been largely oriented toward maximizing Materialist values. The Post-Materialists' basic priorities differ from those that predominate in their societies—and consequently, they are relatively likely to support social change, despite their relatively affluent backgrounds. The Materialists are in the opposite situation. Thus, Cognitive Mobilization drives the two groups in opposite directions because those with relatively high levels of cognitive skills presumably find it easier to select the ideological position that best expresses their underlying values.

This is only the first of several interaction effects associated with

TABLE 8

SELF-PLACEMENT ON LEFT-RIGHT SCALE BY
GROUPS IN POLITICAL ORIENTATION TY-
POLOGY* (MEAN SCORE SHOWN FOR
EACH GROUP: 1.00 = EXTREME
LEFT, 10.00 = EXTREME RIGHT)

| | | |
|---|---|---|
| Non-Mobilized | Materialists | 6.00 (1920) |
| | Mixed | 5.74 (2011) |
| | Post-Materialists | 5.13 (224) |
| Mobilized | Materialists | 6.13 (929) |
| | Mixed | 5.70 (1699) |
| | Post-Materialists | 4.78 (486) |
| | Revolutionaries | 3.89 (606) |

* Fall, 1976 nine-station survey.

our typology. We find a similar pattern in response to the question: "If there were a General Election tomorrow [to respondents under 18, add: "And you had a vote"], which party would you support?" For purposes of cross-national comparisons, the political parties of the nine countries are coded as belonging to the Left, the Right, or as unclassifiable on this basis. In most countries the task is reasonably simple. In Great Britain and Germany, for example, the Labour and Social Democratic parties respectively are viewed as the Left, while the Conservative and Christian Democratic Parties make up the Right. In France, the parties of the Giscardien —Gaullist governing coalition—are considered to constitute the Right, while all major opposition parties make up the Left. In Italy, the picture is more complex, but there is general agreement that the Communists, Socialists and Social Democrats (and, usually, the tiny Republican Party) make up the Left, while the Christian Democrats, Liberals and Neo-Fascists are coded as Right. In the remaining countries, apart from Ireland, informed observers are able to say, with high intercoder reliability, which parties comprise the Left or Right. For Ireland the Left-Right dimension is almost meaningless, but we coded the Fine Gael party as Left on the grounds that it was allied with the Irish Labour Party—which can be placed on the Left with some confidence. By the process of elimination, this implied that the Fianna Fail must constitute the Irish Right.

Table 9 shows the percentages voting for the Right in the European Community as a whole.[14] We

14. Table 9 combines results from the Fall 1976 and Fall 1977 surveys in order to

TABLE 9

POLITICAL PARTY PREFERENCE OF GROUPS IN POLITICAL ORIENTATION TYPOLOGY*
(PERCENTAGE SUPPORTING PARTIES OF THE RIGHT)

| | | | |
|---|---|---|---|
| Non-Mobilized | Materialists | 59% | (2882) |
| | Mixed | 53 | (2746) |
| | Post-Materialists | 43 | (289) |
| Mobilized | Materialists | 62 | (1643) |
| | Mixed | 54 | (2591) |
| | Post-Materialists | 33 | (669) |
| | Revolutionaries | 28 | (801) |

* Combined Fall, 1976 and Fall, 1977 survey results.

find exactly the same type of interaction effect here as in connection with the respondents' description of their political views. The mobilized Materialists are the most conservative of any group (62 percent of them reporting that they would vote for a party of the Right) while the mobilized Post-Materialists are the most Left-oriented of any group —except the Revolutionaries. Figure 8 gives a graphic presentation of the effects of values and Cognitive Mobilization on Left-Right ideological self-placement and on Left-Right voting interactions. The interaction effects visible here indicate that in a simple additive model, the political impact of both values and cognitive skills would tend to be underestimated.

In everything we have seen up to this point, the Revolutionaries resemble the Post-Materialists—especially the mobilized ones. Similar in social background characteristics, in ideological self-placement,

compensate for relatively large amounts of missing data due to nonresponse and because Centrist parties, such as the British Liberals, or nonclassifiable parties, such as the Belgian ethnic separatists, are excluded from these tables.

(a) Mean Self-Placement on Left-Right Ideology Scale:

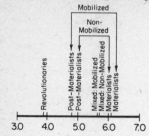

(b) Percentage Voting for Parties of the Right:

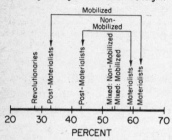

FIGURE 8

LOCATION ON LEFT-RIGHT DIMENSION OF
GROUPS IN POLITICAL ORIENTATION
TYPOLOGY.

and in their political party preferences, one might be tempted to conclude that the Revolutionaries are just like the Mobilized Post-Materialists, only more so. This conclusion would be mistaken. Though they overlap in many respects, the Revolutionaries are a highly distinctive type—and in some ways they lie at the *opposite* end of the continuum from the Mobilized Post-Materialists. This fact is particularly relevant to our central interest in this article—public attitudes toward European integration. For the European integration movement is a Reformist strategy par excellence. It is supported by those who wish to improve the existing social order, more than by those who seek to defend the status quo. But the Revolutionaries constitute a group that is dedicated to *abolishing* the existing system,

not repairing it. For the Revolutionary Left, reforming the system is merely a way to ward off total overhaul: viewed in this light, European integration may seem counterproductive.

Table 10 shows the percentages making positive assessment of Common Market membership among the seven groups in our typology. In contrast with the two preceding tables, in which Revolutionaries and Mobilized Post-Materialists occupy adjacent positions, here they fall at opposite ends of the spectrum. Another contrast with the preceding tables is the fact that here, Cognitive Mobilization and value priorities have additive effects, with favorable assessments rising in a smooth progression as we move from the nonmobilized Materialists, at the low extreme, to the Mobilized Post-Materialists, who make the most favorable assessments. But the Revolutionaries rank *lowest* of any group, with a percentage of favorable assessments that puts them substantially below the non-Mobilized Materialists—in other respects the group they resemble least.

Is this an isolated phenomenon?

TABLE 10

APPRAISAL OF EUROPEAN COMMUNITY MEM
BERSHIP BY GROUPS IN POLITICAL ACTION
TYPOLOGY* (PERCENTAGE SAYING
THAT THEIR COUNTRY'S MEM
BERSHIP IS A GOOD THING)

| | | | |
|---|---|---|---|
| Non-<br>Mobilized | Materialists | 55% | (2023) |
| | Mixed | 57 | (2105) |
| | Post-Materialists | 63 | (190) |
| Mobilized | Materialists | 64 | (1172) |
| | Mixed | 69 | (1962) |
| | Post-Materialists | 78 | (400) |
| | Revolutionaries | 43 | (518) |

* Fall, 1977 Survey, weighted according to
population.

Let us compare the proportions who feel that their representatives in the European Parliament should act for the good of the Community as a whole, even if it conflicts with the national interest. Table 11 provides the relevant data. And the basic pattern is similar to what we have just seen. Willingness to give priority to the interests of the Community is lowest among nonmobilized Materialists and reaches its peak among the mobilized Post-Materialists. But the impact of value type dominates that of Cognitive Mobilization: the mobilized Materialists are more European than nonmobilized ones, and the same thing is true of each of the other value types when we compare the mobilized with the nonmobilized group. But the effect of Cognitive Mobilization alone is not great enough to raise *all* of the mobilized types above the nonmobilized ones.

The results of these analyses help clarify the complex relationship between support for European integration and Left-Right dimension. For both Left and Right have several distinct constituencies, drawing varying amounts of support

TABLE 11

NATIONAL INTEREST VS. EUROPEAN COMMUNITY INTEREST BY GROUPS IN POLITICAL ORIENTATION TYPOLOGY* (PERCENTAGE GIVING PRIORITY TO EUROPE AS A WHOLE)

| | | | |
|---|---|---|---|
| Non-Mobilized | Materialists | 45% | (1963) |
| | Mixed | 51 | (2013) |
| | Post-Materialists | 66 | (185) |
| Mobilized | Materialists | 56 | (1164) |
| | Mixed | 63 | (1854) |
| | Post-Materialists | 78 | (389) |
| | Revolutionaries | 50 | (499) |

* Fall, 1977 survey, weighted according to population.

from each of our seven types. One major group is Materialist, concerned primarily with attaining—or defending—economic and physical security. For this group, it seems likely that support for European integration has had particularly strong linkages with the perception that it was associated with prosperity. In the uncertain setting of the late 1970's, this component of support was relatively weak. Both mobilized and nonmobilized Materialists made comparatively negative assessments of Community membership, and were relatively hesitant to let the interests of the Community as a whole take precedence over their own country's immediate interests. For the Post-Materialists, on the other hand, European integration's appeal may be rooted to a greater extent in concerns for human solidarity, even apart from its economic effects. This is not to say that concerns for solidarity were unimportant to those with Materialist or Mixed values; it is simply a question of the relative weights.

The Revolutionaries are a special case. Like the Post-Materialists, they tend to support social change; accordingly, both groups place themselves on the Left of the political spectrum. But the two groups' ideological perspectives differ. For the Reformist Left, the construction of a supranational European Community, aimed at superseding the nation-state, may seem a major advance having farreaching implications. For the Revolutionary Left, it may seem like a diversion or even a hindrance to more drastic forms of change. The two groups part company on this issue, with the Revolutionary Left taking a position adjacent to that of the nonmobilized Materialists. Ironically, a Reactionary impulse was particularly strong among the latter group. Although its members have lower levels of income and education than any other group, which previously might have tied them more strongly to the Left, in 1977 advocates of "a valiant defense of the present society against all subversive forces" vastly outweighed proponents of revolutionary change. The nonmobilized Materialists were concerned by the current crisis, but were more apt to see the solution in a restoration of the prosperous industrial society they had known in the recent past, than in revolutionary change. For opposite reasons, the Revolutionaries and nonmobilized Materialists were reluctant to support European integration.

The relationship between Left-Right political preferences and support for European integration is complex. While the Reformist Left is markedly favorable, the Revolutionary Left tends to be suspicious. But the complexity does not end there, because one finds striking cross-national differences in the degree to which the supporters of the Left and Right hold positive attitudes toward the Community. Table 12 gives some evidence on this score. In Italy, the country with the largest Communist Party in Western Europe, the Left is highly favorable to EEC membership; this holds true of both Communist and Socialist electorates, when we analyze them separately. Clearly, we cannot equate the Revolutionary Left with support for the Communist Party. Most Italian Communists are non-Revolutionary. In Germany, where the Social Democrats have been in power since 1969 (and have shared power since 1966), the electorate of the Left is somewhat *more* favorable to the Community and to European solidarity than the electorate of the Right. Overall, there is a clear correlation between support for the parties in office—whether of the Left or the Right—and support for the Community. When the Left has been in power for some period of time, there is a tendency for its supporters to identify with its policies, including support for European integration, if that is one of them. Accordingly, in the Netherlands, where a coalition headed by the Left was in office from 1972 to 1977, the differences between supporters of the Left and Right are negligible; in earlier surveys, the electorate of the Left was slightly more favorable to European integration than that of the Right.

Political party cleavages on this issue are greatest by far in Denmark,

TABLE 12

APPRAISAL OF EUROPEAN COMMUNITY MEMBERSHIP BY POLITICAL PARTY PREFERENCE BY NATION* (PERCENTAGE SAYING THEIR COUNTRY'S MEMBERSHIP IS A GOOD THING)

| RESPONDENT SUPPORTS A PARTY OF THE: | FRANCE | BELG. | NETH. | GER. | ITALY | DEN. | IRE. | UK |
|---|---|---|---|---|---|---|---|---|
| Left | 58% | 63 | 77 | 67 | 72 | 26 | 59 | 33 |
| Center | 61 | 77 | — | 74 | 58 | 38 | — | 33 |
| Right | 72 | 84 | 80 | 61 | 80 | 66 | 64 | 45 |
| Don't Know | 58 | 65 | 74 | 70 | 73 | 28 | 60 | 29 |

* Fall, 1977 survey, weighted according to population.

one of the new member countries. Here, the polarization between Left and Right is immense; a gulf of 40 percentage points separates the two electorates. This polarization dominates all other variables, including the Political Orientation typology. In the nine nations as a whole, this typology is the strongest individual-level predictor of one's assessment of membership and of support for European over national interests. In Denmark, both political party preference and occupation of head of household have stronger explanatory power than does the typology. In general, the effects attributable to the Political Orientation typology are weaker in the three new member countries than in the original six. As was noted above, the impact of the immediate environment tends to be greater in the new member countries than in the old; and both value type and level of Cognitive Mobilization are, theoretically, relatively stable characteristics of given individuals.

To a limited extent—though only a limited one—our indicators of values and cognitive levels help explain the long-term continuity in favorable assessments of EEC membership that was noted in the first part of this article. When we aggregate mean scores on our values index to the national level, the result shows a correlation of .457 with favorable assessments of membership across the nine nations across time. Similarly aggregated to the nation level, our index of Cognitive Mobilization has a .356 correlation.[15]

These correlations are somewhat stronger than those obtained with any of the economic indicators discussed in the earlier section.

Both Post-Materialist values and high levels of Cognitive Mobilization are somewhat more prevalent among the publics of the original Six than among the Three—probably a reflection of the fact that the three new members have somewhat lower economic levels: while Denmark is highly prosperous, both Ireland and Britain rank at or near the bottom of the Community rankings in gross domestic product per capita. Nevertheless, we should not make too much of these findings. When we add these two variables to a multiple regression that includes the economic indicators discussed previously, *and* the dummy variable based on early versus late membership, the latter variable remains—by far—the strongest predictor of favorable or unfavorable assessments of the Community.[16] The effects attributable to value type and to Cognitive Mobilization levels may contribute to the stability of attitudes observed at the aggregate level. They do not explain away the effects associated with sheer length of membership.

We have examined the degree to which various groups make favorable or unfavorable assessments of membership in the EEC, and the degree to which they feel that representatives to the European Parliament should work on behalf of Com-

---

15. It should be noted that these figures are somewhat less reliable than those in our earlier aggregate analyses, because neither the values indicator nor the Cognitive Mobilization indicator was included in all the surveys conducted since 1973. Our N's in the present correlations fall to 45 and 63,

respectively. Even with these reduced N's, the relationships are significant at better than the .01 level, however.

16. In principle, a multistage causal model would be desirable here, but in view of our reduced N's we will not press the data any farther. It seems advisable to wait until the results from additional surveys become available.

TABLE 13

EXPECTED RATE OF PARTICIPATION IN ELECTIONS
TO EUROPEAN PARLIAMENT, BY POLITICAL
ORIENTATION TYPOLOGY* (PERCENTAGE
SAYING THEY WILL CERTAINLY
OR PROBABLY VOTE)

| | | | |
|---|---|---|---|
| Non-Mobilized | Materialists | 70% | (2272) |
| | Mixed | 67 | (2359) |
| | Post-Materialists | 73 | (206) |
| Mobilized | Materialists | 84 | (1227) |
| | Mixed | 84 | (1997) |
| | Post-Materialists | 89 | (410) |
| | Revolutionaries | 65 | (556) |

* Fall, 1977 survey, weighted according to population.

munity interests, or those of one particular nation. In 1979 the publics of the nine countries will have a chance to elect representatives pledged to act on behalf of given viewpoints. Will they take this opportunity?

One might expect those who are least enthusiastic about Community membership to show the lowest rates of turnout in the elections to the European Parliament, and to some extent this is the case. Table 13 shows the percentage saying (in Fall 1977) that they would certainly or probably vote in these elections, among each of the seven groups in our typology. Here, the effects of Cognitive Mobilization dominate those of value type, but within each cognitive level the Post-Materialists are most likely to vote, and the Revolutionaries seem least likely to vote. Being a group that otherwise shows quite high levels of political interest and partisan attachment, this tendency on the part of the Revolutionaries may change as the election campaign gets under way.[17] A year and a

17. This statement needs to be qualified. In the Community as a whole, the Revolu-

half before the elections, the Revolutionary type showed a markedly low intention to vote.

This was *not* true of the Left in general, however. Though they were somewhat less favorable than the Right in their assessments of Community membership, the supporters of the Left showed a slightly higher rate of certain or probable voting expectations. The Left's relatively high expected turnout seems to reflect differential rates of party identification—for whether or not one will vote seems to depend, above all, on whether or not one feels a sense of attachment to some political party. Table 14 shows the expected rates of turnout, according to strength of party attachments. It appears that partisan cues will play a double role in shaping the

TABLE 14

EXPECTED RATE OF PARTICIPATION IN ELECTIONS
TO EUROPEAN PARLIAMENT, BY PARTY
IDENTIFICATION* (PERCENTAGE
SAYING THEY WILL CERTAINLY
OR PROBABLY VOTE)

Question: "Do you consider yourself a supporter of any particular political party? (If YES): Do you feel yourself to be very involved in this party, fairly involved or merely a sympathizer?"

| | | |
|---|---|---|
| Very involved | 85% | (867) |
| Fairly involved | 83 | (1647) |
| Merely a sympathizer | 80 | (3146) |
| No affinity with any Party | 63 | (2922) |

* Fall, 1977 survey, weighted according to population.

tionaries show substantially higher levels of Cognitive Mobilization and attachment to political parties than does the population at large. Neither of these characteristics applies to the Revolutionaries in our samples from the United Kingdom or the Republic of Ireland. The relative weakness of a Marxist tradition in the British Isles seems to give support for revolutionary change a different significance from what it has on the Continent.

character of the new European Parliament. To an extent that varies greatly from nation to nation, they seem relevant to whether one emphasizes a European or a national frame of reference. In all nine countries, they seem highly relevant to whether or not one will vote in the European elections.

## CONCLUSION

Public assessments of the benefits of membership in the Common Market wavered in the face of the economic crisis that took place shortly after expansion of the Community, and it seems possible to attribute some of the ups and downs to specific economic factors. But these assessments showed more stability than one might have expected, given the severe economic perturbations that took place. In part this stability seems linked with long-term developments in the values and cognitive skills of Western publics. To an even greater degree it seems to reflect whether a given public has experienced membership in the Community for a relatively long or a relatively short period of years. Even among the publics of the three new countries, there are indications of a growing sense of Community solidarity. A readiness to pursue the common good rather than simply the immediate interests of a particular nation is already fairly widespread among the publics of the European Community. Whether the political leaders of the nine nations will act to encourage or to diminish this sense of solidarity remains to be seen.

# Monetary Policy: Processes and Policies

By MICHAEL BRENNER

ABSTRACT: Monetary integration has had an ill-starred journey throughout the twenty year life of the European Community. The issue has been raised most recently by Commission President Roy Jenkins. Its repeated revival, along with the recurrent failures to achieve a sustained success, reveal both its central place in Community affairs and the peculiar difficulties of harnessing monetary policy to the Community team of coordinated policy instruments. Whether the European Economic Community achieves more substantial integration in the future depends on whether it meets three conditions indicated by our account of past experiences: a political decision by members to accelerate progress toward unification; stable, roughly parallel economic performance among member countries; and the abatement of present turbulence in the international monetary system which, in turn, requires a recommitment of the United States to major reform.

---

Michael Brenner is Associate Professor in the Graduate School of Public and International Affairs, The University of Pittsburgh. He is the author of The Politics of International Monetary Reform: The Exchange and Technocratic Politics, The Functionalist Theory of European Integration.

MONETARY integration is the phoenix of the European Economic Community. Periodically it rises from the ashes of previous incarnations to hover uncertainly over the Community landscape, only to falter and to consume itself, not in fire but in self-doubt. After an interment far shorter than the mythical 500 years, the idea re-emerges, impelled upward by the force of need and assisted by the faithful midwives to the Community ideal.

In a postmortem on the last abortive attempt at flight, the study group appointed to do the examination (the Marjolin Committee) issued the death certificate with the unequivocal pronouncement that "the efforts undertaken since 1969 add up to a failure."[1] Yet, within two years, the trumpets were once again to be heard heralding the rebirth of moves toward economic and monetary union (although in more muted tones than in the past). This time the spirit has been imparted by Commission President Roy Jenkins' fervent call for a fresh start at forging the institutional bonds of monetary integration to match the practical realities of interdependence.[2] The major steps taken in response to his plea signify little about the chances of ultimate progress. They do attest to the singular resilience of monetary integration as a goal. Its repeated revival, along with the recurrent failures to achieve a sustained success, reveal much about

the life of the European Community, its requirements for growth and development, the forces that constrain it, and the larger global environment in which it exists.

## THE NATURE OF THE BEAST:

For a topic that has received widespread attention for so long, the meaning of monetary integration is surprisingly difficult to pin down. It has been thought of as both process and outcome, in terms of institutions and of policies. This multiplicity of conceptions reflects the several ways in which money creation and money values bear on the economic life of the Community. The regulation of domestic credit, its volume and terms of availability, the functioning of capital markets, external balances and rates of currency exchange, are all integral parts of the monetary domain. They affect economic performance in member states and the transmission of those effects to other members. They also play a major role in shaping the relationship between the EEC as a whole and the rest of the world economy. Moreover, these facets of monetary activity cannot readily be separated one from the other. To touch one is to set in motion the entire chain. This intricacy of monetary conditions and monetary policy makes it peculiarly unamenable to a piecemeal, incremental mode of integration, and is one reason why efforts to date have been tentative, restrained, and abandoned under stress. On the other hand, their critical importance to economic management is a constant spur to renewed attempts at harnessing monetary policy to the Community team of coordinated policy instruments.

One analyst has found it useful to

1. Report of the Study Group, Marjolin Committee, "Economic and Monetary Union 1980" (Brussels: EEC, March 1975), p. 1.

2. Speech by The President of The Commission, The Rt. Hon. Roy Jenkins, at the European Institute in Florence, Italy, 27 October 1977.

distinguish three different meanings of monetary integration:[3] *currency integration, financial integration,* and *unification at the level of policy.* By currency integration is meant the fixing of exchange rates among the currencies of member states, while permitting them to move together against other currencies. This arrangement describes the currency "Snake," the ill-fated experiment of the Community to achieve internal stability by pegging their currencies to par values in a world of floating rates. Currency integration, such as is still maintained in a truncated Snake led by West Germany and including nonmembers, has properly been called an "exchange rate union."[4] Exchange rate unions can take two forms: the more ambitious type locks currencies into unchanging rates supported by "unlimited, automatic, and undisputed financing" of deficits and market interventions, and is strengthened by a central monetary policy; the looser formulation views the member currencies as being in association, but with limited reserve backing and a tolerance of rate changes.[5]

Financial integration is the consolidation of financial markets, removing controls on capital to allow free movement across national boundaries. Creation of a free capital market does not mean that regulatory authority would be completely uprooted, but rather that all rules that affect the market, such as divi-

dend taxes, would be made uniform. The remarkable level of financial integration reached, without governmental intent, by Euro-currency banking institutions, has already produced a substantial measure of consolidation. De facto Euro-market integration is partial, however, and leaves noticeable irregularities, not only as to accessibility and effects, but also with regard to the ability of different national authorities to manage the capital flows it facilitates. Principal incentives for monetary union, in all or any of its forms, are: to control the consequences of freely moving capital on the Euro-currency market, to iron out current inconsistencies in effectiveness of regulation, and to lay the basis for a common approach to alleviating adverse effects where they appear.

The most farreaching aspect of monetary integration is unification at the policy level. It implies not just exchange rate union and the opening of capital markets, but the more drastic step of harmonizing the instruments of monetary policy: credit formation and money management. Policy unification can take various forms according to the level and scope of integration sought and thought feasible. It might entail the coordination of nationally focussed policies in the interest of complementarity; the harmonization of policies to achieve parallel economic circumstances; or the transfer of policymaking authority to a single agency in a full economic union. At each level, there is the further option of extending the range of integration to cover those aspects of fiscal policy—budget and taxes—that affect money creation. Features of all three forms of monetary integration can be detected in the plans and rudimentary programs that have

3. Benjamin J. Cohen, in Lawrence B. Krause and Walter Salant, eds., *European Monetary Integration and It's Meaning for the United States* (Washington, DC: The Brookings Institution, 1973). p. 32.

4. W. Max Corden, "The Adjustment Problem" in *European Monetary Integration*, p. 159.

5. Ibid., p. 161.

been a staple of the Community for a generation.

## SCHEMES, PROPOSALS & PLANS: A CAPSULE HISTORY

From its inception, the EEC has set as its goal pure monetary union— the harmonization of domestic as well as external policies, leading to and facilitating the eventual creation of a single economic and political entity. As a practical matter, constructive integration (even that so modest as the coordination of nationally focussed actions) has taken a back seat to a negative interest in preventing monetary frictions from obstructing progress toward the unification of trade and commerce. Concern has centered on the disruptive potential of balance of payments problems. Acute deficits encountered by one member could create severe pressures to impose trade controls—quotas, levies, export subsidies—that could undermine the still insecure structure of a common market. Exchange rate adjustments, when made in response to chronic imbalances, were the more appropriate response. But frequent rate realignments were themselves a challenge to the fragile institutions of free trade since it was assumed that trade flows were highly sensitive to even relatively small price shifts. Moreover, authorities, with the interwar experience still fresh in their memory, were keenly aware of the latent danger of competitive devaluations. Better, therefore, to prevent balance of payments crises than to deal with the effects of revaluations. Hence the incentive to achieve a measure of monetary cooperation as a support and reinforcement to the establishment of a customs union.

If the avoidance of chronic balance of payment difficulties was the primary Community objective in the monetary sphere, then logically it would have to pay some attention to the causes of payments disequilibria. They inevitably were to be found in the internal conditions and domestic monetary management of the member countries— differential price trends, interest rates, money supply. Consequently there has been a constant pressure, of varying intensity, to pull monetary policy deeper into the orbit of EEC authority. It has been counteracted just as consistently by the centrifugal tendency of national governments to guard these prized instruments of economic policy. The history of European monetary integration records the tug of war between these opposed forces, with the strains growing as progressive commercial integration—and or unruly external environment—generates stronger incentives for a consolidation of monetary institutions and policies without commensurate slackening of nationalist resistance.

Under the circumstances, the stress quite naturally has been on consultation. Lacking a central rule-making authority, and for want of agreed rules for harmonizing monetary policies, the only way to minimize the risk of contradiction and conflict was to create a web of communication among national officials, under Community auspices. The resulting heightened consciousness of monetary interactions and reciprocal effects, it was hoped, would encourage coordination of otherwise independent policies. The Treaty of Rome indicated the direction in calling upon member governments to "consider their policy relating to economic trends . . . and to treat its policy with regard to exchange rates . . . as matter(s) of common interest" and "to consult with each other and the Commission on measures to be taken in response to current circumstances."[6] The proximate goal has been a progressive approximation of the member states' economic policies, and, through coordination, "to remedy disequilibria in the balance of payments." Coordination is not stated as end in itself, but something to be pursued . . . "to the extent necessary . . . for the functioning of the Common Market."[7] As for means, collaboration among central banks and finance ministries is prescribed. In support of its hortatory declaration, the Treaty urged members to create an EEC Monetary Committee, to be composed of finance ministers, which would concern itself with such balance of payments problems as might threaten Community stability. Duly constituted at the EEC's inauguration, it was soon complemented by the establishment of a Committee on Short-term Economic Policy intended as a consultative forum on business cycle trends.

In keeping with its principal monetary concern, that payments strains might erode the foundations of an integrated market, the Treaty was more explicit about collaboration to ward off crises. Here, too, it was advisory rather than compulsory and emphasized procedure over substantive commitment. The approach advocated is summarized in one chronology of Community monetary policy. When a payments crisis impends:

The Commission shall recommend measures to be taken. If these prove insufficient, it shall after consultation with the EEC Monetary Committee recommend to the Council of Ministers the granting of mutual assistance in the form, for example, of limited credits by and with the consent of other members. If such assistance is not granted, or if it and other actions are inadequate, the Commission shall then authorize the member in difficulties to take its own safeguard measures, but these in turn shall be subject to amendment or suspension by the Council.[8]

These vague recommendations were given more substance in 1962 with the issuance of a Commission memorandum making the case for rigorous adherence to fixed parities and spelling out the conditions for doing so. It urged the members to agree on specific support commitments, under mutual assistance arrangements, that would accompany the "very narrow limits on the (rate) variations" which were foreseen.[9] To implement the recommendations, and to serve as a mechanism for wider coordination of monetary policies, a Committee of Governors of member Central Banks was added to the galaxy of consultative institutions.

The loose mesh of mutual obligations and support arrangements that have grown up under Community auspices is, in major respects, a microcosm of the international monetary system founded at Bretton Woods. The similarity is revealing both of the Community's modest expectations, its preoccupation with exchange stability and orderly adjustments, and the qualitative jump

---

6. *Treaty Establishing the European Economic Community*, Articles 105, 103 (Brussels: EEC, 1962).

7. Ibid art 106.

8. Arthur I. Bloomfield, "The Historical Setting" in *European Monetary Integration*, p. 2.

9. EEC Commission, *Memorandum of the Commission on the Action Programme of the Community for the Second Stage* (Brussels: October 1962).

represented by a move from loosely structured intergovernmental co-operation to a more thoroughgoing harmonization of monetary policies and institutions. It also underscores the obvious point that the state of monetary affairs within the Community is inseparable from conditions in the international monetary system at large. The reluctance or inability of member countries to achieve a greater measure of integration makes the Community enterprise vulnerable to the monetary distress of any member, a condition that may well be aggravated by relationships and developments outside the E.E.C.

Few in the Community deluded themselves about the threat to economic integration represented by independent national monetary policies, and the inherent danger of payments difficulties that, at best, could be mitigated by the rudimentary support measures at the Community's collective disposal. A sense of urgency about integration was not visible in the first eight years of the EEC's existence thanks to the very favorable circumstances that prevailed. The Bretton Woods system, generally, functioned during a period of extraordinary stability because of the near parallel movement of the major national economies. The contrast with the more recent past is startling. Between 1960 and 1972, inflation rates among Community members varied by an average of barely 1 percent. Rates of growth in GNP showed an only slightly wider differentiation. Productivity increases were similarly comparable. It is not surprising that the period saw nary an exchange rate adjustment. An exchange rate union apparently had been achieved with little strain or commitment. How starkly the picture has changed.

The years of remarkable stability gave way to a period of equally remarkable disparities in prices and money values. From 1973 through 1976, price trends within the Community were sharply divergent. Rate differentials reached a high of 21 percent between Germany and the United Kingdom in 1975. In all cases, they were several times greater than during the earlier period.[10] Real growth in GNP varied by up to 4 percent, with the high and low growth positions shifting among member countries. It was to be expected that balance of payments crises were a constant of monetary life, rate adjustments recurrent, and stable money values only a remembrance of a rapidly fading past.

THE PERIOD OF CRISIS

The Community survived for nearly the first decade of its life without having to confront the issue of its monetary Achilles heel. The period of grace came abruptly to end with the deutsche mark crisis of 1968 and 1969, that signalled the onset of exchange rate turbulence for the EEC, and for the international monetary system at large. Eventual devaluation of the French franc by 11.1 percent in August, 1969, under pressures originating with the events of May-June 1968, and Germany's decision to float the deutsche mark the following month, marked the end of the era of complacency, and ushered in a period of great activity, if not lasting innovation on the monetary front. Only the barest outline of landmark initiatives is possible in the

10. These calculations are based upon figures presented in the *Annual Reports* of the International Monetary Fund, and *International Financial Statistics*.

compass of this essay. A detailed recounting must make room for an assessment of why things happened and their consequences for Community construction.

For the last decade, reform efforts have moved in tandem with the recurrent crises that have punctuated the history of monetary relations generally. The Community's dilemma is that the strained circumstances that spotlight the need for joint action are also the most inauspicious for dramatic ventures in institution building. It is then that governments are least inclined to take the long view, and most vulnerable to domestic pressures. A crisis atmosphere encourages proclamations of intent to get at underlying causes, institutions and policies, but it provides little of the flexibility needed to meld interests, institutions and policies. Hence, the now familiar cycle: considered analysis and sound recommendations embodied in an impressive official report; awareness of its importance sharpened by disturbing monetary developments; agreement to launch a new collaborative program; desultory or partial implementation gravely handicapped by divergent national interests and complicating external factors.

The first of those cycles is associated with the *Barre Report*, issued in February 1969 and named after its Chairman, the present French Premier, Raymond Barre.[11] That Report, spurred by the approaching of the Community's ten-year transition period, concentrated on the need for a closer coordination of

short-term policies within the framework of medium-term guidelines. It recognized that monetary coordination was an essential condition for avoiding payments crises, the threat of which was underlined by developments in France. It also offered specific proposals to put some flesh on the skeletal arrangements for mutual financial assistance, which were cited as a necessary adjunct to international support mechanisms. The Barre proposals were acted on by the conference of heads of state that met at year's end. With the welcome and unexpected backing of French President Pompidou, they committed themselves to moving by stages to full monetary union. A Committee chaired by Pierre Werner of Luxembourg was given the job of drafting a plan for its achievement.

For the interim, a "mini-swaps" scheme was installed among member control banks that provided credits totalling $2 billion for financing countries facing balance of payments strains. The measure was a stockpiling of ammunition for future battles with the speculative capital movements that had forced realignment of the franc and mark, and were ensconcing themselves as a prominent feature of the international monetary life. Revaluations were themselves unwelcome to the Community; to have them imposed by speculators was doubly dangerous. The disruptive effect of rate changes had been magnified with development of the common agricultural policy which calculated the costs and benefits to members by reference to prevailing rates of exchange. Any alteration in national money values upset the calculations and caused particular consternation to France who, as the principal beneficiary, stood to suffer most

11. EEC Commission, *Memorandum of the Commission to the Council on the Coordination of Economic Policies and Monetary Cooperation Within the Community*, (Brussels: EEC, February 1969).

from a devaluation of the franc. This last point goes far to explain why France has shown a stubborn inclination to link its chronically weak currency to the deutsche mark, and even to voice support—if not always extending it—for collaborative efforts with the taint of supranationalism about them.

A common plan of defense against unwanted and/or unwarranted rate changes, however necessary and useful, represented the lowest common denominator of monetary cooperation. It did not speak to the more fundamental issue of harmonizing domestic policies and achieving roughly parallel courses of economic expansion. The *Werner Report*, issued in October 1970, tackled the tough questions of integration. It drew boldly and explicitly the route to monetary union. By 1980 full integration was projected. That meant an inflexible fixing of member currencies that would be totally convertible, with the effect of: a) creating a Community monetary standard; b) establishing a central banking system responsible for both internal credit creation and external monetary management backed by a pooling of reserves; c) the freeing of all capital movements; and d) formation of an ambiguously labelled "center of decision for economic policy" that would be accountable to the soon to be popularly elected European Parliament.[12]

However persuasive the logic of monetary union was to the Werner Committee, it was less than compelling for the national political leaders who convened to act on the former's recommendations. While accepting in principle the objectives as outlined, firm commitments were made only to the immediate measures for narrowing the exchange rate bands and reinforcing collaboration among central bank authorities. From the perspective of governments struggling with an increasingly unruly monetary environment, in which position, vulnerability, and policy preference differed from that of partners, there was good reason for caution. France could not permit herself to relinquish the power of monetary decision to a supranational entity. This was not only politically abhorrent but also gave no assurance of satisfying French concerns about the commercial consequences of an overvalued franc or the loss of agricultural support funds resulting from an undervalued franc. Germany, for her part, had little enthusiasm for assuming an open-ended commitment to bankroll the defense of interlocked Community currencies unless there were firm assurances that her partners would observe uniformly disciplined fiscal and monetary policies. Ultimately, monetary union would produce the centralized policies that are the essence of integration. In the intermediate stages, though, before that end was reached, Bonn saw itself as being asked to take on obligations made excessively risky by the failure to reach prior agreement on coordinated policies. The problem lay not in disagreements over the time frame for achieving monetary union. Rather, it was the timing of stages and the question of interdependence between concerted national policies and commitments to maintenance of rate parity that were the source of conflict and the cause of irresolution.

12. *Report to the Council and the Commission on the Realization by Stages of Economic and Monetary Union in the Community* (Luxembourg: October 1970).

Both the urgency of the case for monetary integration, and the threat posed to its attainment by unsettled international conditions, were dramatized by the currency crises of 1971. They had the immediate effect of putting the Werner plan for monetary union on the shelf. The events associated with the dollar devaluation and the closing of the gold window, ending the convertibility of the dollar, did give rise to the famous monetary Snake—on which attention has since been concentrated as the only surviving element of the aborted integration project.

## The Snake

The Community's painfully slow progress toward monetary integration, characterized more by the deliberate assessment of means than decision and commitment to ends, had been overtaken by the global crisis. It forced a shift in attention from programs for advancing Community unity through monetary union to protecting the existing structures of economic integration from the storms on the world's exchange markets. With the dollar no longer acting as the stable anchor for a fixed rate system, and the forecast calling for a period of fluctuating rates, the priority consideration for the EEC was to tighten its own monetary bonds to avoid having money values among member currencies undergo continual changes. There was little faith that the realignment of rates embodied in the Smithsonian Agreement of December 1971 had restored exchange stability, whatever individual views on the appropriateness of the new rate structure.[13]

With attention now concentrated on a manifest external danger, member governments reached agreement on the terms of a more formal exchange rate union. In March 1972 the six stated their commitment to maintain their exchange rates within a band of 2¼ percent, which meant that swings between any two currencies were permitted within a range of 4½ percent. Common Market currencies, tied in this way, could move together against the dollar within the wider margin of 4½ that the Smithsonian Agreement had established as the outer limits for shifts from a given parity. Thus the image of an undulating Community Snake moving within the Smithsonian tunnel, which itself was not as rigid as the term connotes. Member central banks undertook to coordinate interventions in Community currencies to maintain the 2¼ percent band. Liabilities incurred as a result of intervention would be settled monthly, a provision that limited the credit obligations of members. The credit facilities set up earlier would be available to bolster the reserves of any country whose currency was under pressure. When the U.K., Ireland, and Denmark joined the Snake in May, an earnest was given in support of their application to membership that no restriction be placed on the right to alter parities, with the prior condition of consultation with partners.

The Snake now had its constituent elements in place, plans had been set for a concerted attempt at preserving rate stability, and, perhaps, the basis laid for fashioning a single Community position on the out-

13. Robert Solomon offers a knowledgeable and perceptive account of the diplo- macy during this period in *The International Monetary System 1945–1976* (New York: Harper & Row, 1977).

standing issues of international monetary reform, and for a closer coordination of domestic policies. Any optimism encouraged by the Snake's creation was short-lived. Its rough journey through the precarious terrain of world monetary instability began almost immediately. By June, Britain and Ireland had to abandon the Snake when sterling came under irresistible speculative pressure. Denmark followed shortly thereafter. Italy also sought to float free, but was kept tenuously aboard by liberalizing the regulations on debt settlement. Early in 1973, the lira became the target of a speculative wave that culminated in the second dollar crisis of March. The collapse of the Smithsonian pseudo-system was the prelude to the abandonment of fixed rates and the introduction of generalized floating. The Snake molted and reappeared in a new guise, shed of its Italy member and now composed of the mark, guilder, French and Belgian francs, and a restored Danish crown. Currencies of three non-Community members—Austria, Norway and Switzerland—were informally associated with the Snake.

The fate of this new monetary personality was no better than that of its predecessor. The March crisis inaugurated a new period of even greater instability on the exchange markets. Rapid growth in the volume of mobile capital, whose flows were unpredictable and often uncontrollable, stacked the deck against central bank authorities seeking to maintain stable parities. Accentuation of inflationary trends, resulting in wider rate differentials, encouraged rate fluctuations and compounded the difficulty of achieving parallel monetary policies. And the dramatic oil price rise of late 1973 dealt the crushing blow to the Snake

by accentuating all the unfavorable conditions: divergent trends in inflation and employment, expansion of liquid capital on the money markets, and fluctuating exchange rates.[14]

Understandably, Community efforts in the monetary field have taken on the character of a holding operation, at times desperate, often suffering losses, yet maintaining the threads of cooperation and making effective use of mutual support where possible. France, unable to maintain the franc at fixed parity with the mark, and unwilling to make the sacrifices domestically that might permit her to do so, dropped out of the Snake in January 1974, returned in July 1975, and then was constrained to leave again six months later. Some encouragement might be taken from her perseverence. The Paris government's repeated pledges in support of the Snake are not just a manifestation of pride. It shares with other Community members a concern over a threatened split between chronically surplus and deficit countries. In a world of floating exchange rates, there is a pronounced tendency for differential inflation rates to be quickly registered in depreciations and appreciations. In the former case, depreciation gives a new impetus to inflation by raising the costs of imported goods, while motivating wage claims and price rises to maintain real income levels. The reverse logic is seen in the economies of surplus countries. The current phenomena of the vicious and the virtuous circle create incentives for Community governments to hold their currencies to

14. I analyze the March crisis and the switchover to floating rates in Michael Brenner, *The Politics of International Monetary Reform: The Exchange Crisis* (Cambridge, MA: Ballinger, 1978).

fixed parities, and to achieve a synchronization of domestic money management to mitigate differences in economic performance and price trends. The responsibilities of a surplus country like Germany and a deficit country like France or Italy are symmetrical, or at least matching, even though their economic circumstances are asymmetrical. Consequently, the policies they should pursue differ in their expansionary or contractionist orientation.[15]

The situation with regard to monetary cooperation, then, is desperate but not hopeless; there are even a few bright rays. The truncated Snake struggles along, now reduced to a German-led deutsche mark zone whose number of extra-Community members—Norway, Austria, and Switzerland de facto—equals the combined Community membership of Germany and the Benelux countries. Alignments must constantly be altered to keep participating currencies within their bands. Of the several initiatives incorporated in the 1971 program for monetary union, only those directed at the maintenance of exchange rate stability show much life. The latter have, however, grown and developed, albeit as emergency steps to ward off monetary disintegration. An impressive level of cooperation has been reached in the concerted central bank interventions on the exchange markets and in the management of reserves. Germany, as the dominant monetary member, has swallowed some of its opposition to assuming commitments in defense of its partners' currencies,

15. These aspects of the current situation are discussed by Otmar Emminger of the Deutsche Bundesbank in Robert A. Mundell and Jacques J. Polak, eds., *The New International Monetary System* (New York: Columbia University Press, 1977) pp. 3–18.

extending two bilateral loans totalling $2.5 billion to Italy at the time of its dire payments deficit in 1974 and 1975. Bonn has joined in the Community initiative to provide EEC backing for private bank consortia created to raise loans on the money and bond markets in aid of deficit members. Ireland and Italy have successfully utilized the procedure. No less concerned than before about external commitments that could curb her own monetary autonomy, interventions that could produce an involuntary increase in domestic money supply, the German government nonetheless sees her own economic security as dependent on orderly monetary conditions within the EEC, which in turn require her to act on behalf of rate stability, as well as in encouragement of complementary domestic policies.

## THE JENKINS RELAUNCH

It is this recognition of an essential common interest in monetary order that gives Commission head Roy Jenkins hope that the campaign for integration can be successfully relaunched. He keys on the undeniable benefits: to cushion the impact of the recurrent exchange rate crises centered on the dollar by spreading the effects over a wider currency area; to create a larger financial market that, more ambitiously, could absorb and neutralize capital flows; to remove the balance of payments constraint on members in chronic deficit by avoiding automatic depreciations; and ultimately, to achieve simultaneously a "rationalization of industry and commerce" and "a smooth regional distribution of the gains from increased economic integration."[16]

16. Jenkins, speech to European Institute.

The benefits accrue, however, only if genuine monetary union is achieved, embracing a European currency, a unified central bank, and the central political authority to legitimize it. Promised gains alone will not assure that the necessary intermediate steps are taken, or that concern over the short and middle-term distributional effects of a move toward monetary union would be acceptable to member governments. The apparent discrepancy between high expectations from future attainments and the current strained circumstances explains reports that "The Jenkins monetary initiative . . . has been greeted with indifference bordering on hostility."[17] This assessment might well exaggerate negative reaction. On the other hand, it would be premature to celebrate the very modest agreements on monetary cooperation that arose from Council consideration of Jenkins' proposals. The establishment of a European unit of account for the Community budget, and commitment to a further strengthening of credit mechanisms hardly constitute a turning point in the march toward monetary union.[18]

The volte-face of German Chancellor Helmut Schmidt, who offered a plan for monetary union at the April 1978 meeting of heads of state in Copenhagen, keeps open the possibility of more substantial progress. His surprisingly farreaching scheme would include an enlargement of the currency Snake while allowing wider margins for the weaker currencies, a par-

tial pooling of reserves, and creation of a de facto Community reserve money. The "boa" proposal, as it has been dubbed, has yet to elicit any firm commitments on anyone's part. It does though testify to the underlying attraction of monetary union.

Whether the Community can use the present feelings about a convergence of monetary interest, and the existing network of consultative arrangements, as a springboard to substantial integration will depend on whether it meets a number of conditions highlighted by our account of past trials and tribulations. First and foremost, the logic of union can only be activated by a political decision by national leadership to accelerate progress toward unification. In 1969 at The Hague, and then in the creation of the Snake, it was appreciation of an urgent need that could only be met through unified action that gave a boost to collective ventures. Second, stable, roughly parallel economic conditions must be achieved domestically. Wide differences in price and employment trends not only create technical obstacles to the integration of policies, they also sensitize governments to the possible adverse effects on economic interests and electoral constituencies. Third, the present turbulence in the international monetary system would have to abate. Of course, European monetary union is often seen as a necessary protection against externally induced disturbances, and as strengthening Europe's power to foster necessary reforms globally. In truth, world trends, as a primary cause of domestic economic troubles and rate fluctuations, now do not permit the Community members to catch their breath long enough to put their

17. *The New York Times*, 2 November 1977.
18. *European Community*, European Community Information Service, no. 31/1977, 16 December 1977.

houses in order and construct a larger monetary entity. Some easing of external pressures is a requirement for the Community institution building. Finally, only a major commitment by the United States to rather drastic renovation, or replacement, of the present jumble of in-effective monetary institutions can alleviate current strains and instabilities. Without a turnabout in its inner-directed policies, reform is impossible; with it, a reform partnership with Europe would be compelling, and a critical spur given to European monetary integration.

ANNALS, AAPSS, 440, Nov. 1978

# Energy Policy in the Communities

By WILFRID L. KOHL

ABSTRACT: Energy policy in the European Community has been limited, thus far, to the collection of information, the setting of objectives, support for some research and demonstration projects, and the making of recommendations to member countries. This situation is likely to continue in the near future, because the institutions of the Community were not set up to cope with the complexities of a common energy policy. More importantly, there are major differences in resource endowments and energy policies of the member states, which inhibit cooperation, since energy is an extremely sensitive area of national sovereignty. Since the 1973–74 oil crisis, more energy policy has been made at the national level than at the European level. However, on the whole, west European countries have responded more rapidly with revisions and improvements in their energy policies than has the United States. They have acted to set objectives whereby Community dependence on imported energy would be reduced by 1985, and to encourage adjustment of the mix of energy sources. Even if these objectives are achieved, the EC will remain an area dependent on the outside world for approximately 50 percent of its energy needs in the mid–1980s.

---

Wilfrid L. Kohl is Director and Associate Professor of International Relations at the Johns Hopkins University Center in Bologna, Italy. Previously, he taught political science and was Associate Director of the Institute on Western Europe, Columbia University. He also served on the staffs of the National Security Council and the Ford Foundation, and he has been an International Affairs Fellow of the Council on Foreign Relations and the Woodrow Wilson International Center for Scholars. The author of French Nuclear Diplomacy, and the editor of Economic Foreign Policies of Industrial States, he has also written numerous articles on American foreign policy and U.S.–European relations.

Appreciation is expressed to Daniel S. Lipman for assistance in researching background materials used in the preparation of this article. The author is also grateful to a number of energy policy officials in the EC and member governments with whom he held interviews in 1978 to discuss these problems.

THE OIL crisis of 1973–74 revealed the vulnerability of the European Community, which had become highly dependent upon imported petroleum to meet its energy needs. The crisis also demonstrated the fragility of the Community structure, given the total lack of political will to agree on a common response to the oil embargo.[1] But what has happened since? In view of the rethinking of energy policies that has been going on in all western industrial countries, has the Community spirit revived in Western Europe? Have the Europeans made progress in formulating a common energy policy for the Nine?

### THE PRESENT STATE OF COMMUNITY ENERGY POLICY

With few exceptions, energy policy in the European Community has been limited to the collection of information, the setting of objectives, support of some research and demonstration projects, and the making of recommendations to member countries. There are many reasons for this. To begin with, it is well to recall that the institutions of the Community were not set up to cope with the complexities of a common energy policy. Also, we must remember that it is only recently—since the 1973–74 oil crisis—that there has been recognition of a need for a common energy policy.

In the 1950s coal was the predominant source of Europe's energy needs. The European Coal and Steel Community, established in 1951, did produce a reasonably successful policy in the coal sector, at least for a time. The other sector receiving early attention was nuclear energy, viewed then as a relatively undeveloped resource that might provide for Europe's expanding future energy needs; hence, the founding of the European Atomic Energy Community (Euratom) in 1957. But Euratom has had only limited success, primarily in the promotion of research and a few common projects, the JET fusion research program being the best recent example. The treaty of the European Economic Community, also signed in 1957, made no provision for other energy sectors, nor for the development of a common energy policy. Thus, energy policy remained fragmented and sectoral, emphasizing coal and nuclear fuel. The development of policy in other sectors could only proceed gradually, on a step-by-step basis, when there was unanimity among the member states, under Article 235. The fusing of the three Community executives in 1967 did not change the different and only partial treaty powers.

By the 1960s the availability of relatively cheap external oil supplies made petroleum a major European energy source, and coal began to decline. In 1972, just before the OPEC oil embargo, oil represented about 60 percent of Western Europe's energy consumption, and 99 percent of it was imported.[2] The embargo and subsequent oil price increases dramatized the dangers of this situation and provoked awareness of the need for more comprehensive and effective energy policies at the na-

1. The international context of the energy crisis and the immediate policy responses were previously analyzed in Wilfrid L. Kohl, "The United States, Western Europe, and the Energy Problem," *Journal of International Affairs*, vol. 30, no. 1 (1976), pp. 81–96.

2. Joel Darmstadter and Hans H. Landsberg, "The Economic Background," *Daedalus* (Fall 1975), p. 21.

tional and European level, although it is true that the Commission had made some proposals in this direction earlier—in 1968.

## ENERGY POLICY OBJECTIVES

At the Community level, the principal agreement reached was the December 1974 resolution of the Council outlining the Community's "Energy Policy Objectives for 1985." The Council approved the objective of reducing Community dependence on imported energy to 50 percent, and if possible to 40 percent, by 1985, as compared to 63 percent in 1973. Moreover, it was agreed that the rate of growth of energy consumption for the Community as a whole should be reduced in order to achieve, by 1985, a level 15 percent below January 1973 estimates. The pattern of energy used was to be altered to increase security of supply, especially by increasing the share of electricity produced by nuclear energy.

Several points are noteworthy about the 1974 resolution. First, whether or not the specific targets will be achieved, the objectives set were certainly positive and unavoidable, given the Community's situation of energy dependence. Second, it accepts the inevitable continued dependence on external supplies, but tries only to reduce the amount of that dependence. Third, the resolution has provided little more than a loose framework for nine separate national energy policies. Aside from agreement on a few common measures to conserve energy and cope with a further oil emergency, plus some ad hoc collaboration on research and development, and information gathering, subsequent efforts to obtain binding commitments at the Community level on

specific policies to achieve the 1985 objectives have generally failed.

## ENERGY COUNCIL

There has been no lack of effort on the part of the Commission, which has produced a stream of proposals for the consideration of the Energy Council, a body that has been meeting two or three times each year. For example, at the 30 May 1978 meeting of the Energy Council, the Danish presidency sought to achieve agreement on an energy package containing five items for proposed Community financial support:

1—demonstration projects in the field of energy-saving;
2—alternative energy sources such as geothermal, coal liquefaction, solar demonstration projects;
3—hydrocarbon exploration projects;
4—Community aids for intra-Community trade in power station coal;
5—the reduction of surplus capacities in the refining industry.

National differences prevented the Council from adopting the package, which was postponed. Although agreement in principle was expressed relating to regulations for demonstration projects on the first two items, major divergencies persist on essential subjects covering the coal and refining sectors.[3]

## EUROPE'S PRESENT ENERGY SITUATION

Recent trends in Western Europe's energy situation have increased, not diminished, the need for progress in energy policies. While it is true that there has been an overall reduction

3. *Agence Europe*, May 25, 31, and June 1, 1978.

in Community energy consumption, this reduction has been due primarily to the continuing economic recession of the past several years, as well as to some progress in energy conservation. The danger is that a return to prior economic growth rates may lead to a level of energy consumption by 1985 higher than the target figures, in which case the gap would probably have to be made up by imported oil.

In terms of the structure of EC energy demand, oil still remains very important—about 53 percent of energy consumption in 1977. Coal and other solid fuels are declining slightly. There is a more noticeable slowdown in the nuclear sector, which is not developing as rapidly as predicted. If nuclear power remains underdeveloped and electricity consumption continues to rise, as now predicted, there must be a corresponding increase in the consumption of solid fuels. Thus the state of the Community's coal industry continues to be a problem. If more coal is not produced, oil consumption will inevitably rise. Further reduction in oil use implies its replacement with natural gas.

In terms of energy imports, the Council's objectives projected a 50 percent external dependence. (In 1976 the Commission deemed the alternative goal of 40 percent dependency as unattainable.) Current forecasts show that net imports may be reduced by 1985 to the general target range of about 650 mtoe (million tons of oil or equivalent). Oil still makes up the major import share, accounting for about 80 percent of total energy imports. The Community has resolved that by 1985 oil should not exceed a net import figure of 500 million tons (10 million barrels/day).

## ENERGY PRODUCTION IN THE COMMUNITY

On the side of energy production, the Community situation can be summarized as follows:[4] While production of brown coal and peat is satisfactory in relation to Community targets, hard coal production is in decline. There are problems on the environmental side with deep mining, difficulties in financing the large investments necessary, and labor difficulties. As a result, coal imports have risen. In 1977 hard coal output was 152 mtoe, which was 4 percent less than 1976 (the 1985 target was 180 mtoe as set in 1974). The Commission has therefore recommended that the Council take urgent action to support Community coal and increase coal burning through investment in coal-fired power stations.

At present the Community produces 47.4 million tons of oil, 10 percent of oil consumption. The target for 1985 was set at 180 million tons. Current forecasts vary considerably, in large part because of the uncertainties connected with North Sea oil reserves. But it now seems unlikely that the 1985 target will be met unless major new discoveries are made. The situation is hampered by the current fall in oil consumption, due to the economic situation, and an apparent glut on the oil market. Moreover, there are also technical difficulties in drilling deep sea oil wells, not to mention great costs and uncertainty about profitability. Similarly, natural gas production seems

4. The following summary is based on two Commission documents: 1) "Second Report on the Achievement of Community Energy Policy Objectives for 1985," COM(77) 395 (29 July 1977); 2) "The Community and the World Energy Situation," COM(78) 101 (9 March 1978).

to be running less than forecasted and will probably also fall short of the target objective set for 1985, especially since yields are expected to fall off in present gas-producing countries by the end of the 1970's. In 1977 the share of natural gas was about 17.5 percent of overall energy production, amounting to about 144.4 mtoe (the 1985 target is at least 175 mtoe).

A major shortfall is the nuclear area where national programs have run into opposition from parliaments and environmental groups. Present total capacity is 22 GWe. The 1974 target for 1985 called for 160–200 GWe,* but this is now clearly not achieveable, and a revised forecast is nearer 90 GWe. The Community is trying to support more investment in nuclear reactors. The decline in the nuclear program results in a projected shortfall of 20 mtoe for electricity production—thus posing the danger of increased oil imports.

Considering these various shortfalls and other changes in the Community energy situation since 1974, the Council is now attempting to reach agreement on revised updated Community energy objectives for 1985.

## DIFFERENT NATIONAL RESOURCE ENDOWMENTS AND ENERGY POLICIES OF EC MEMBER STATES

Aside from the institutional inadequacies of the EC in the energy area, other causes of the failure to extend EC energy policy lie certainly in the differences among the member states in resource endowments and philosophies for dealing with the energy market. Among the Nine, Britain and the Netherlands are the

* GWe: Giga Watts effective, or a thousand million watts.

countries most rich in energy resources. They are reluctant to share these resources and, therefore, resist most strongly a common EC energy policy.[5]

### Britain

Great Britain's positive energy position derives mainly, of course, from the recently discovered reserves of oil and gas in the North Sea. In addition, Britain has extensive coal reserves and an advanced nuclear energy program, although the latter is no longer as strong as the efforts of France and Germany. Britain's first energy policy priority is the development of North Sea oil and gas, in order to achieve net self-sufficiency in energy production by 1980.[6] This effort is being directed by the state-owned British National Oil Corporation, established in 1975. Oil production is forecast to range from 90 to 110 mtoe in 1980 and 100 to 150 mtoe in 1985. Natural gas production is estimated at 35 mtoe by 1980 and will range from 35 to 45 mtoe by 1985. Already a good deal of the oil produced is being exported, thus improving the British balance of payments position. One contentious issue, however, is the

5. In addition to the specific documents cited, the following section is based on interviews with energy officials, and on two general sources: 1) *1977 IEA Reviews of National Energy Programmes*, International Energy Agency, Paris (pre-publication mimeo, 1978); 2) Guy de Carmoy, *Energy for Europe: Economic and Political Implications* (Washington, DC: American Enterprise Institute, 1977). See also Robert A. Black, Jr., "Plus ça Change, Plus C'est la Même Chose: Nine Governments in Search of a Common Energy Policy," in Helen Wallace, William Wallace, and Carole Webb, *Policy Making in the European Communities* (London: John Wiley, 1977), chap. 7.

6. See *Energy Policy—A Consultative Document* (London: HMSO, 1978), Cmnd. 7101.

British guideline that two-thirds of North Sea oil must be refined at home. In the 1980s, North Sea oil will provide an unexpected bonanza. However, even at peak, the amount of oil exported will only meet, at maximum estimates, something like 10 percent of EC oil needs. By the 1990s most of the North Sea oil will be depleted, and Britain must therefore plan to rely on other energy sources.

The development of coal reserves is another British objective, and a strategy to raise production to 125–35 million tons by 1985 has been jointly agreed on by the National Coal Board, the unions, and the government. This will require extensive government subsidies, since much of the coal must be deep mined. British strategy in the nuclear sector has not yet been fully determined, but it is planned to expand nuclear reactor development so that nuclear energy will meet 5.5 percent of energy requirements in 1981, and 6.4 percent in 1986—equivalent to 14.4 mtoe. Britain has no reserves of uranium, and is therefore interested in fast breeder reactor technology.

Conservation has been another element of British energy policy, especially since the country has traditionally used a large amount of energy per unit of output. According to the International Energy Agency (IEA), Britain has achieved some of the best energy conservation results through voluntary measures, stressing such actions as insulation in industry and private homes, and the promotion of increased automobile efficiency. Total British energy consumption has decreased every year since 1973.

In terms of EC energy goals for 1985, Britain is fairly close to target. The main difference is greater British stress on coal (31 per-

cent in 1985, instead of 17 percent for the Community), and a lag in nuclear power, which will probably not match half the EC mark of 13 percent. Cooperation with the European Community has been made difficult, however, by the presence of an avowed anti-Europeanist, Mr. Tony Benn, as head of the British Energy Department. In practice, Britain apparently prefers to cooperate more with the IEA in Paris than with the EC.

## Netherlands

The discovery of the Groningen gas fields in the 1960s made the Netherlands an energy rich country and a net energy exporter by 1974. At roughly the same time, the share of natural gas had become equal to that of oil in the domestic energy market. Coal mines have been closed down. Meanwhile offshore gas exploration has been successful in the Dutch sector of the North Sea, and gas imports have begun to replace the expected decline in output of the Groningen fields. Gas has been developed by an association of the public and private sectors in Royal Dutch Shell and Gasunie, a utility company which handles transport and sales. The Dutch government controls pricing policy.

According to Dutch energy policy, oil imports will be expanded to 48.3 percent by 1985, with natural gas declining to 37.7 percent of domestic consumption, to conform to an expected reduction in gas production. The Dutch government has decided not to renew gas export contracts after their expiration. The reintroduction of imported coal is being considered in the long run, with nuclear energy only to be enlarged when certain safety and environmental problems are resolved. Fuel switching is thus a major component of Dutch policy. In addition, substantial attention is being devoted to energy conservation.

## Italy

Those countries which have the most to gain from an extensive EC energy policy are the energy poor countries: Denmark, Italy, and Ireland; Belgium should probably also be included in this category. Of these countries, Italy, the most important in size, has hydroelectric power sites in the Alps, some medium sized natural gas fields in the Po Valley, but no coal resources, and a stalled nuclear program. There are some prospects for offshore oil in the Adriatic Sea. While per capita energy consumption is relatively low, the country is heavily dependent on energy imports (80 percent in 1973).

With heavy import dependence a given of the Italian energy situation, Italy's main energy objective is the diversification of import supplies and their sources. The instrument primarily responsible for this policy continues to be the Ente Nazionale Idrocarburi (ENI), a powerful state-run enterprise operating in the entire field of oil and gas industries, in Italy and abroad, with little competition. ENI is engaged in large-scale exploration programs in Italy and abroad. Supply contracts for natural gas have been negotiated with Libya, the Netherlands, Algeria, and the Soviet Union. A major gas pipeline is under construction from the Algerian Sahara to Tunisia, across the Mediterranean to Sicily, and to the mainland. ENI has also entered into a number of bilateral agreements with oil-producing countries, including drilling contracts.

Under a revised National Energy Plan which passed the Parliament in the fall of 1977, Italy's energy consumption is expected to grow during the period 1976 to 1985 at approximately 4.3 percent per year. Dependence on oil imports will be reduced over that period, from 66 percent in 1976 to 63 percent in 1985, but net oil imports are estimated to increase. The contribution from nuclear power is now foreseen to grow more slowly, although Parliament has recently approved the building of eight nuclear plants. A conservation effort is now just beginning, based on mandatory standards rather than on incentive schemes.

A major problem for Italy is the excess capacity in its petrochemical industry in the south. Italy is looking to Britain in particular, and the European Community as a whole, to subsidize its refining industry, or for more contracts to utilize it.

## Denmark, Ireland and Belgium

Denmark and Ireland have essentially no domestic energy resources. Denmark's principal energy policy objective is to reduce its high degree of dependence on imported energy, especially oil, which is supposed to decline from 87 percent in 1975 to 61 percent in 1985. This is to be accomplished through energy conservation measures, diversification of energy sources used (natural gas, coal, nuclear power and nonconventional energy), and further development of what indigenous energy resources are available. For example, it is hoped that 65 percent of electricity fuel input will be provided by coal in 1985, as compared with 35 percent in 1975. There are possibilities of developing small resources of domestic oil and gas.

Ireland also depends heavily on imported oil (70 percent in 1976). This dependence is projected by the Irish government to rise to 75 percent in 1985, despite other efforts to conserve energy, and to pursue vigorously a program of offshore hydrocarbon exploration.

Coal is the only indigenous energy resource in Belgium. However, in spite of significant reserves, production costs are high and heavy subsidies are required. While furnishing 12 percent of Belgium's energy requirements in 1976, coal is projected to decline to 8 percent in 1985. Oil imports are essential for Belgium and supplied 51 percent of energy demand in 1976. This oil share is expected to decline to 47.5 percent in 1985. The most important feature of Belgium's energy situation is probably the significant contribution made by nuclear power plants, which produce 25 percent of electricity generated. This is expected to be doubled by 1986. Conservation efforts have so far been weak.

*France and West Germany*

In between the energy rich and the relatively energy poor countries of Europe, there is a middle group composed of France and West Germany. In general, these two countries have been favorable to the development of a European Community energy policy in some areas, not in others.

Germany's strengths in the field of energy derive from large coal reserves and from its advanced program of light-water nuclear reactors. Its weakness is its heavy dependence on imported oil and gas. German energy policy over the past few years has been directed at decreasing overall oil consumption through nuclear power development, expanded use of domestic coal for electricity generation, increased natural gas imports, energy conservation, and the prohibition of new oil and gas-fired power plants. The Second Revision of the German Energy Program of December 1977 announced some shifts in emphasis, with greater attention to conservation and a scaling down of objectives in the nuclear area because of political resistance.

German oil imports, which account for about 50 percent of current energy requirements, are the largest in absolute terms of any European country. In keeping with forecasts for economic growth, oil consumption is projected to increase in absolute terms but decline relatively to 46.2 percent of total energy demand by 1985, and 42.6 percent in 1990. The gap is to be made up presumably by expanding hard coal production, although this requires subsidies, and the utilization of hard coal in electricity generation, plus a more modest expansion of nuclear power. Nuclear energy is to be developed "to the extent absolutely necessary to secure electricity supply, with priority being given to the safety of the population."[7] Further development of nuclear energy is contingent on new measures for waste management and nuclear safety. The use of imported natural gas is also seen as an important way to reduce dependence on oil.

The West German government is involved directly in the energy industry and exercises a major influence through several national companies: Veba-Gelsenberg, which

7. *Energy Policy Programme for the Federal Republic of Germany*, 2d. ed., Rev. (Bonn: Federal Ministry of Economics, 14 December 1977), p. 6.

controls some 20 percent of refinery capacity; Deminex, the oil-exploration group; and Ruhrkohle and Ruhrgas. West Germany has insufficient refining capacity and as a result imports petroleum products, especially from the Netherlands. Deminex is involved in one sector of North Sea oil development. Long term contracts for natural gas have been negotiated with the Netherlands, the Soviet Union, Norway and Iran, as well as Algeria. In the area of conservation, after a slow start, a law is under consideration to set standards and give some assistance for insulation of new buildings. In spite of this increasing government involvement, there remains a preference to preserve a free market in the energy field, and a reluctance to go too far with controls. This philosophy limits German support for future EC energy policies should they be too all-encompassing. The Federal Republic is especially interested in EC subsidies for coal production, but not if they cost too much.

France is also a country highly dependent on external energy sources. In 1973–74 the oil crisis placed a heavy burden on the French payments balance, and boosted general price inflation considerably, since the portion of imports in the overall energy balance was 77 percent (higher than the EC country average of 60 percent). Oil made up 67 percent of energy demand, almost all of it imported. France has small reserves of coal in the Lorraine, practically no fossil fuels, but the largest uranium deposits in Europe. There is some hydroelectric power. The strongest French card is the nuclear program, the largest in Europe. The French government essentially controls the entire energy sector via national companies: Compagnie Française des Petroles and Elf-Erap; Charbonnages de France as concerns coal; Electricite de France; and over natural gas with Gaz de France. The Commissariat à l'Energie Atomique is in charge of civilian and military atomic research and development.

The key elements of French energy policy are conservation, the development of natural resources, and diversification of energy sources.[8] A special conservation agency, the Agence pour les Economies de l'Energie, has been created, which has set a target of 15 percent reduction by 1985 in total energy consumed. In early 1975 the French government fixed a ceiling of 51 billion francs per year for oil imports and imposed restrictions on the use of fuel oil. Domestic oil consumption has been considerably reduced. The government revised its targets in 1976 and now hopes that oil will not exceed about 42 percent of energy consumption by 1985. Domestic coal production is scheduled to decline because of costs and difficulties of mining deep deposits. Natural gas imports are also expected to increase.

The key hope is clearly the nuclear program, which in 1985 is projected to supply about 24 percent of France's energy needs. In the nuclear field the French first built natural uranium graphite-gas reactors, beginning in 1963. Later they switched to light water reactors. Much research and development work by the CEA has been devoted to breeder reactors. Since 1976 France and Germany have cooperated in the field of advanced reactors. The French have also pro-

8. See, for example, the *Rapport de la Commission de l'Energie sur les Orientations de la Politique Energétique* (Paris: Ministère de l'Industrie et de la Recherche, Juillet 1975).

moted Eurodif, a large cooperative uranium enrichment plant, operating by the gaseous diffusion process, with Belgium, Spain and Italy. And they have joined with German and British groups to pool efforts in reprocessing nuclear fuels in United Reprocessors.

France is generally favorable to a more active EC energy policy in research and development. Like Italy, France suffers from excess capacity in her oil refining industry and seeks EC support in that sector. She is also interested in EC policies on gas and electricity, and on the development of new energy sources. In the nuclear area France is probably more reluctant to cooperate unless proposed actions harmonize with her already existing programs.

## THE FUTURE OF EUROPEAN COMMUNITY ENERGY POLICY

As the foregoing survey should make clear, there is a wide disparity among the Nine EC member states in their endowment of energy resources. National governments are jealous of their resources. This is not surprising, since energy policy is a vital motor of western industrial economies. It is an extremely sensitive area of national sovereignty. So far, more energy policy is made at the national level than at the European level, and this will probably continue to be the practice of the member states in the future. There are simply insufficient political incentives to do much more together at this stage.[9]

9. This conclusion differs from the viewpoint presented by N. J. D. Lucas in *Energy and the European Communities* (London: Europa Publications, 1977) where it is argued that the time is ripe for more ambitious EC energy cooperation.

The recent failure to achieve agreement, at the May 1978 Energy Council, on Community aids to the refining and coal sectors is a case in point. Italy has insisted on a special Community aid system, that provides for the payment of a fixed subsidy per ton of distillation capacity suppressed in the future, as compensation for the loss of economic activity due to closure of refineries. Italian intransigence is rooted in the particular situation of the Italian oil industry, primarily controlled by ENI, a state-owned company with few other possibilities for compensation. The United Kingdom and Germany, countries where the oil industry is more diversified, have so far refused to accept the Italian position. As for aids to coal, on the other hand, Italy has been reluctant to go along with other countries, partly out of a need to maintain this subject as a bargaining chip, partly because she produces no coal domestically and, therefore, would receive no benefit under any new Community scheme.[10]

Another reason for reluctance on the part of some EC states is, of course, the existence of another organization, the International Energy Agency (IEA) in Paris, of which most of them (but not France) are also members, and which some of them prefer to deal with. The IEA has broader membership and includes 19 countries, among them the United States, Canada and Japan. Aside from the agreement to share oil in case of a future embargo, the IEA does not take binding decisions, while the EC can. The Paris agency only makes recommendations. However, the IEA has received high level attention from member govern-

10. *Agence Europe*, 1 June 1978.

ments, and its recommendations therefore carry some weight. (For example, in October 1977 the member countries agreed to limit total oil imports to not more than 26 million barrels per day by 1985.) Moreover, it is producing very high level research reports on the energy situation in its member countries. While the IEA has no separate budget for subsidies, it has encouraged, through its long term program, a series of research and development projects between member governments. In addition, the IEA has become somewhat more closely associated with the recent North-South dialogue.

Since the oil crisis, Western European countries have, on the whole, responded with major revisions and improvements in their energy policies, and they have done so much more rapidly than the United States. Certainly, much more needs to be done. If the Community has not provided the major nexus for this European policy response, it certainly has, by its recommendations and prodding, contributed to the result.

At present the European Community seems limited to providing a framework for the national energy policies of the Nine. However, within this context the Community can undertake useful research and promote better understanding of energy issues. It can encourage coordination and harmonization of national energy policies. And it can establish common energy policies in areas where national energy policies conflict with one another. Whether it can do much more in the near future is doubtful, unless and until the process of European economic and political integration is further advanced. As in other areas, national policies will remain controlling in the field of energy.

ANNALS, AAPSS, 440, Nov. 1978

# European Industrial Policies: Balancing Interdependence and Interest

By DOREEN ELLIS

ABSTRACT: Following a short description of European industrial policy definition and strategies, policy choices are analyzed in terms of international inputs into the policy process and the substantive consistency of policy choices. It is argued that policy formulation is related to the type of interdependence of the unit and to the external policy objective. Vulnerability interdependence leads to fewer policies with integrative effects, as is the case with oil and energy policies. Beyond the external context for policy, the substantive relationships among objectives and strategies in industrial policy, emphasizing their consistency and contradictions, are discussed. These two modes of analysis provide depth in studying policymaking in international organizations while illustrating the strengths and weaknesses of European industrial policy.

*Doreen Ellis is a candidate for a Ph.D. at Northwestern University, and is currently an Instructor of Political Science at Virginia Polytechnic Institute and State University. Her research interests center in international political economy.*

POLICIES and ideologies for balancing power among European political–economic units have a long history. Shifting alliances and power distributions have reflected changing national attributes and diplomatic relationships. In one sense, the European Communities (EC) can be seen as part of this tradition. It is another international association for regulating European interactions. As a policymaking institution, the EC must account for national differences and relationship patterns.

Turning from this historical linkage of European institutions, we note two differences distinguishing the EC from past traditions. One is the present emphasis on economic matters. European Community activity centers on international agreements focusing on economic goals to maintain peace. Questions about institution building and management for political–economic security are intertwined with the second prominent distinction, the interdependence affecting modern policy definition and decision. In the past, European policies were directed inward, with occasional complications related to colonial activity. However, modern Europe focuses outward as well. Because it is integrated into a global capitalist system, dependent on trade, limited raw materials, and energy supplies, it is sensitive and vulnerable to international behaviors. In a sense, balance of power takes on a new meaning in present day interactions based on global interdependence. The balances must include the environmental inputs in negotiation and decision taking, and the internal consistency of objectives.

In this paper we will stress how this interdependence-based interaction and distribution relates to the creation of European industrial policy. Industrial policymaking unites some of the traditional problems of balancing national interests with the changed political-economic context. Following an introduction to the concept of industrial policy, the international pressures leading to European policy development will be considered and the substance of European policy will be examined within this background.

## INDUSTRIAL POLICY—AN INTRODUCTION

Most scholars note the changing governmental role in capitalist systems since Keynes. Growing government economic intervention in advanced societies and the lesser developed countries' (LDC) concern with industrialization have created an awareness of potential public policy inputs into industrial development, loosely termed industrial policy. However, governmental inputs into economic behavior have a longer tradition that also provides a context for present policymaking behavior. Internationally oriented trade policies affecting industrial development have analogues in mercantilist policies. Present industrial policies combine both of these strategies: internally oriented macro-economic concerns, especially employment, investment, and inflation; and externally focused trade trends, reflecting the context of a more internationalized capitalist economic system within a political realm emphasizing the nation.[1]

Because of the extremely broad

1. Micro-economic considerations tend to remain in the domain of private enterprise as we will see later. However, cost, price, and allocation are affected by the policies.

scope of policy targets and potential objectives, and the many different approaches to policy creation and implementation, no one definition successfully distinguishes industrial policies from other government activities. Rather, definitions attempt to draw some broad boundaries around policy concerns.[2] For example, Cairncross and others note that industrial policy affects the sectoral allocation of resources, the structural organization of industries, the development of technological innovation, and the maintenance of regional balance.[3] Yet this suggestion does little to simplify conceptualizations of national policy-making. Even greater complexity exists when dealing with the multi- and cross-level orientation, formulation, and implementation of industrial policy by an international organization such as the EC. In an attempt to make an inroad into this complexity, we will provide a short description of the substance of European policy and then consider the inputs to the Community policy process.[4]

2. Following a common approach, limiting industrial policy to those attempts formulated and implemented by the government to directly affect the nonagricultural, nonservice sectors, constrains the concept in two key ways: 1) the externalities prominent in economic interactions fall outside of the concept; 2) agenda setting, which may be important because policies straddle a thin line supporting liberal capitalist thought. However, most policy studies begin by examining particular or proposed legislation.

3. Sir Alec Cairncross et al., *Economic Policy for the European Community* (New York: Holmes E. Meier, 1974).

4. For further information see Michael Hodges, "Industrial Policy: A Directorate General in Search of a Role" in Helen Wallace, William Wallace, and Carole Webb, eds., *Policy-Making in the European Communities* (New York: Wiley, 1977); J. J. Boddewyn, "Western European Policies

The European Community Economic and Social Committee suggests:

It is perhaps fair to say that industrial policy is primarily a special type of approach to the interplay between individual policies which have an impact on industry (economic and monetary policy, social and labour market policy, regional policy, trade policy, environment policy, etc.). "Industrial policy" covers not only the general approaches adopted in the various relevant fields but also all concrete rules of conduct, support arrangements, and restrictions, which have a direct impact on the industrial situation.[5]

European policymakers emphasize that industrial policy is but one mechanism for attainment of a combination of objectives, including productivity improvement, a high employment level, increased competition among firms, and the improvement of quality of life and work conditions. The 1970 Colonna Memorandum first outlined the strategies for attaining these objectives. The major strategies include: the removal of technical barriers to trade, with particular emphasis on the cross-national extension of the right to tender for public supply contracts; promoting concentration and competition through the formation of European companies; a unified capital market, and other legal and fiscal harmonization policies; considering the

Toward U.S. Investors," *New York University Institute of Finance Bulletin* 93–95 (March 1974); and Steven Warnecke, "Industrial Policy and the European Community," Steven Warnecke and Ezra Suleiman, eds., *Industrial Policies in Western Europe* (New York: Praeger, 1975).

5. Opinions of the Economic and Social Committee in *Official Journal of the European Communities* (Brussels: C292/17; December 1977).

special problems of declining industries and advanced technology sectors; redeveloping a Community science and technology policy; coordinating information and education; and developing a unified policy toward nonmember states. Since 1970 various Commission, Parliament, and committee statements have reiterated the broad strategic plan, although tactics have varied somewhat.[6]

In 1976 the Commission reviewed industrial policy decision and implementation performance.[7] The Commission found limited progress on both counts. Council of Ministers' activity was slow and partial. Discussion and negotiation stagnated on issues pertaining to tax and legal harmonization, establishment of cooperative technological research, and declining industries. The Council was more successful in the area of eliminating technical barriers to trade, perhaps because this strategy is more directly deducible from the general Com-

6. Some of the statements include: Commission of the European Communities, "Industrial Policy," *Bulletin of the European Community* 6 (1972); Commission of the European Communities, "Towards the Establishment of a European Industrial Base," *Bulletin of the European Community*, Supplement (1973); Commission of the European Communities, "The Common Policy: the Field of Science and Technology" (Brussels: 1972); Commission of the European Communities, "Report on the Implementation of the Industrial Policy Programme," Resolution of 19 December 1973 (Brussels: May 1976); Economic and Social Committee of the European Community, "Opinion," *Official Journal of the European Communities* (Brussels: December 1977); European Parliament, *Working Documents 1973–1974* (December 1973).

7. Commission of the European Communities, "Report on the Implementation of the Industrial Policy Programme, Resolution of December 1973 (Brussels: May 1976 Com (76) 199 final).

munity ideological basis in trade liberalization. The Commission and Parliament made several suggestions for speeding Council of Ministers' activity. One proposal asked that decisions be aggregated into "bundles of directives" which would organize negotiations by balancing benefits and costs among individual nations during one bargaining session. Another suggestion was to simply transfer more decisionmaking authority to the Commission by redefining the policies as regulatory.

Although these suggestions were sent to a committee for evaluation, the chances for acceptance are small. They amount to a redistribution of decisionmaking authority which would shift power away from national interests represented by the Council. As it remains, policymaking attempts to balance the suggestions of an international bureaucracy and the national interests of the Council. Even this complicated negotiating act does not entirely explain the limited progress in industrial policy formulation and implementation. Indeed, occasionally policies surmounted the tensions, as with the institutionalization of a European Patent Office. Considering European industrial policy as balancing interdependent national and Community interests, within a complex context of objectives, external and non- or trans-national pressures, provides a focus in this web of interaction.

## EUROPEAN COMMUNITY POLICIES—BALANCING INTERDEPENDENCE

In an attempt to analyze trends in European integration, Haas poses a provocative question about the conceptual and theoretical bases for future European studies.[8] Regarding policymaking, he asks whether focusing on interdependence or integration will best aid in understanding European behavior.[9] He suggests that integration is a special case of interdependence, denying it a separate conceptual existence. This interpretation implies that the unit of analysis choice in regional integration studies artificially sets the boundaries of theory application. Interdependent interactions occurring beyond these boundaries may not be considered because of the "artificial" limits of the study.[10] Haas states that internationalization has a different impact on various issue areas. The effects on integration will vary accordingly, promoting uneven institutional development and hindering integration. Although Haas' argument has merit, it does not justify an end to studies of regional integration. Rather, it signals the need to understand the effects of present interdependences on coordinated policymaking.[11] Given the growing global inter-

8. Ernst B. Haas, "The Obsolescence of Regional Integration Theory," *Institute of International Studies Research Series*, no. 25 (Berkeley: University of California Press, 1975).

9. Haas, *Obsolescence of Integration Theory*, p. 89, defines interdependence as interconnectedness, which denies unilateral action and policy integration as harmonization of activities toward some objective, particularly interdependence coping.

10. This criticism can be generalized to other research activities which reify a concept or unnecessarily bound a study by the choice of the unit of analysis. It is a valid warning about the complexity of problem definition and testing judgments in the social sciences.

11. Interdependence is not a new phenomenon, nor is it necessarily of a significantly different magnitude compared with past linkages. However, there are certain characteristics of the relationship that may differ or promote different patterns.

dependence, one concept of importance for understanding European industrial policy is, indeed, context.

## International environment

The second World War left the European and Japanese economies with severe gaps. Restoring productive capacity and infrastructure required new investment of a scope impossible for capital-short countries. Counterpoised against the weakened European position, the United States was economically and politically strong. These relative strengths were reflected in the development of postwar institutions and ideologies such as the International Monetary Fund (IMF) and the General Agreement on Tariffs and Trade (GATT). The United States emphasized liberal political economics and a free trade ideology as the accepted means to attain economic and political security and provide peace. By basing the system development on equilibrium economic models concerned with exchange allocation and welfare efficiency, but not distributive justice, initial power and value distributions tended to maintain the dominance of the United States. Trade and investment relationships coordinated with the role of the dollar as the basic postwar monetary unit.[12] United States corporations benefited from their postwar technological, organizational, monetary, and economic advantages, and expanded into foreign markets offering great potential for profit. The

12. See Joan Spero, *The Political Economy of the International System* (New York: St. Martin's Press, 1976). The limited use of SDR's as an international currency has not approached the role of the dollar in the international monetary system.

European market was of special interest because of linked United States–European traditions, similarities in education, demand, and consumption pattern. United States government policies supported European reconstruction, perceiving potential growth and expecting European support, in exchange for the much needed capital the corporations could bring.

United States interests were divided over European integration attempts. Some suggested that a European Common Market would aid the reconstruction of war-torn allies, who could then support United States policies in the Cold War. Other interests feared that a strong Europe eventually would compete with United States policies and international plans. This division of interests surfaced as support for either the European Communities or a broader Atlantic Community. European Community growth was dominated by the United States, which remained external to the Community itself. The interdependent development of subsystem within a broader system during initial Community organization provides a history to Haas' interpretation of policy interdependence and integration. Concern with external actors shaped Community organization. Policy interdependence translated into integration institutions because European ability to act was limited by its relatively weak position in the system.[13]

More current European policy formulations reflect two changes in the international system that make interdependencies an issue rather than a conclusion. One shift is the increasing European power relative to the United States since 1960. The over-valuation of the dollar until 1971, and its effect on monetary agreements, investment flows, and internationalization of production, as well as the eventual lessening of Cold War tensions, changed European bargaining capacities relative to the United States. Although sensitivity interdependence within the Atlantic Community grew during this time, European–United States asymmetry and vulnerability lessened. The second change is broadly associated with the North–South dialogue. In addition to the changes in commodity and raw material markets, newly industrializing nations increased global competition in certain sectors, such as light manufacturing. These changing interdependencies affect industrial policy formulation and objectives.

Although welcomed as a strengthening of the Western Alliance, the direction of European growth in the 1960s concerned some scholars and practitioners. Several publications suggested that the United States' technological advantage would maintain its predominance and growth in the global system.[14] Additionally, this advantage permitted successful exploitation of market advantages, especially through the multinational corporation (MNC). In a more powerful international position following Community's unification, the Commission began work on an industrial policy for more competitive European exploitation of common market scale advantages. The initial

13. However, we cannot determine whether regional organization would have developed any differently had Europe been stronger.

14. Examples are: Christopher Layton, *Transatlantic Investments* (New York: The Atlantic Institute, 1967), and his *European Advanced Technology* (London: Allen & Unwin, 1969); and Jean Jacques Servan-Schreiber, *The American Challenge* (New York: Atheneum, 1967).

European corporate response to integration followed the United States pattern of national concentration and transnational expansion. To alleviate regulation problems with this response, the Commission proposed concentration through cross-national mergers, fiscal and legal harmonization, and coordination of information and education to promote further European competition with the United States, while promoting transnational integration and potential regulation. Preliminary policy development was two pronged: redistribution from the United States to Europe, but also from national to transnational domains. Additional proposals focused on United States MNCs but did not culminate in Community action.[15]

European industrial policy developed in a context of shifts in the international distribution of power. The industrial policy was expanded to cover political problems associated with the maintenance of free trade and regulation of decisions previously considered as purely internal matters. Lessened European vulnerabilities in international affairs promoted European competitiveness and enhancement of its international standing.

The vertical shifts of the North–South dialogue and energy crisis affected EC industrial policymaking in different ways. Traditions of hierarchical relationships evolved into the Yaoundé and Lomé Conventions, linking Europe to its past colonies through trade preferences combined with aid and investment policies in a modern arrangement. The historical sphere of influence and dominance now takes into account European vulnerabilities in commodity and raw material markets, and competition with industrializing nations in certain sectors, such as textiles. The Lomé agreements recognize this shift by accepting some Third World demands while maintaining European dominance through aid and investment arrangements. European industrial policy addresses these external shifts by promoting internal changes. Again, industrial policies relieve sectoral crises indirectly, dealing only with the internal structural malfunctions initiated by external changes.[16]

Present European production utilizes oil to produce energy. With limited petroleum reserves, the climate of uncertainty following the quadrupling of oil prices and the related worldwide inflation followed by recession struck hard on the Community. However, Community action and industrial adaptation was limited. Community industrial policy proponents emphasized production cost efficiencies based on scale and externalities to balance the higher input costs. In addition, coordinated research and development, education, and reevaluation of regulations, technology assessment, and investment incentives were to support industry. These strategies are not new mechanisms for considering a new prob-

15. Some discussion of direct foreign investment regulations occurred. Division among EC members on this issue prohibited action. In addition, such action would have disrupted the international economic agreement upon which the postwar system stability is based. See Boddewyn, *Western European Policies* for further information.

16. Note how this decision provides some boundary for European industrial policy. Although the Lomé investment strategies will have a direct impact on European industry, it is not integrated into the European industrial policy.

lem. What has limited new policy development?

There are two possible explanations for this policy lack. The first is simply that insufficient time passed for policy development to be integrated with industrial policy. The second explanation is twofold. It suggests that the more basic the issues are for national industry, the less likely is decisionmaking power to be reallocated to the supranational authority.[17] The highly vulnerable position of certain European states (those without any reserves) makes them unwilling to give up any further control. A subsidiary suggestion is that allocation of industrial costs and benefits is much more difficult than policies assuming growth. Therefore, national interests play a larger and more disintegrative role. To this point the energy crisis provided limited incentive for further industrial integration.

Two sets of propositions can be distilled from these examples of policy externalization and EC industrial policy development. The first concerns interdependence and the potential for integrated policymaking. As Haas has indicated, the potential for integrated policymaking is related to the "structure" of interdependence sensitivities and vulnerabilities in the network. When unit vulnerability is very great, interdependence limits or bounds action towards objectives. With highly vulnerable interdependence, marginal increments of authority are not reallocable. The focus for determining the costs of interaction may be within the EC or with external nations. Both are important considerations in industrial policy, as illustrated by energy policy and competition. Outside of highly vulnerable situations, sensitivity to external actors promotes common action through the realization that no one country can achieve its ends unilaterally.

Previous analyses tended to be static. Consideration should be given to time and feedback based on external changes, inputs, and past traditions or attitudes. In addition, the balances based on considerations of sensitivity and vulnerability to external interdependencies may change because of: 1) changes in the power distribution, 2) changes in the network of interaction, and 3) unit internal redistributions.

To take a less pessimistic view than Haas about the future of integrated policymaking; it can be suggested that if there is a developing tradition of international interaction, as there has been in the EC, although crises may not be dealt with immediately, in the long run adjustments to extreme vulnerabilities underlying them may be met by coordinated action lag. Crisis vulnerabilities further explain limited international interaction in terms of crisis decisionmaking theory. Limiting information through selective perception and decreased numbers of advisors are common reactions to the stress of crisis.[18] When time expands the situation boundaries, more potential integrated interaction may develop.

17. European Commission of the European Communities, "The Common Policy: the Field of Science and Technology" (Brussels, 1972) suggested a similar problem in coordinating research.

18. See for example C. F. Hermann, ed., *International Crises* (Beverly Hills: Sage, 1969) or any textbook such as K. J. Holsti, *International Politics: A Framework for Analysis*, 3d ed. (Englewood Cliffs, NJ: Prentice-Hall, 1977).

## Regions

Regions may be territorial or sectoral subsets of policy, illustrating particular problems that complicate the allocation of policy costs and benefits. Industrial policy affects regional interdependencies in allocation. Territorial regional policies include external region relationships—Lomé countries, other affiliated areas, enlargement process —and internal inequalities in industrial development; the most obvious examples are the Mezzogiorno and Ireland. As noted above, external regional considerations affected industrial policy as do international inputs or national balance of power politics.

Focusing internally, discrimination and incentives for regional development are industrial policies attempting to overcome international and sectoral political-economic dysfunctions. The problem of development poles and redistribution, so well documented by Third World integrationists, is nonetheless important in Europe.[19] Within a liberal orientation of expanding welfare, recognition that failure to share the gains from integration will prohibit further institutional development is revolutionary. While the less developed regions have less power in the traditional economic or political sense, proportionate EC voting schedules required their

19. For example, Francois Perroux, "Multinational Investment and the Analysis of Development and Integration Poles" in *Multinational Investment, Public and Private, in the Economic Development and Integration of Latin America* (Bogota: Inter-American Development Bank Round Table, 1968); Lynn K. Mytelka, "The Salience of Gains in Third World Integrative Schemes," *World Politics* 25, 2 (1973); and Lynn K. Mytelka, "Fiscal Politics and Regional Redistribution," *Journal of Conflict Resolution* 19 (1975).

support for decisiontaking. Concern with unit territorial regions is a reaction to inequalities caused by interdependence; it harmonizes integration by providing for national objectives.

Sectoral problems reflect the changing competitiveness of European industry in the global market, especially facing the new competition from nonindustrialized countries. The Community responded to the problems of declining industries in two ways: 1) support for making them more competitive, and 2) assistance to displaced workers. The problem of declining industries is not specific to the EC. However, the Community-wide policy attempts are novel solution strategies. Basically, the EC proposes to take advantage of scale economies for efficiency and competitiveness while developing new industrial strengths, especially in high technology industry. EC policymakers implied that internal actions designed to increase competitiveness were necessary to adapt to the changing international environment and maintain the European position in the international division of labor. Political interaction could address the problems associated with sensitivity in the international system without threatening the internal balance of power. Industrial policies that focus upon the subsystem to whole system interdependence balances (rather than within unit balances) have more uniform appeal until the questions of distribution become an issue.

## SUBSTANTIVE BALANCES IN INDUSTRIAL POLICY

Within the context of interdependence, policies imply substantive balances, too. However, European industrial policymakers overlooked many tensions in the policies themselves and in their interaction with other behaviors. An examination of the industrial policy focus on European transnational business mergers will illustrate some of these problems.

The promotion of transnational business mergers and competition is one of the major directions of European industrial policy.[20] It could be hypothesized that the closer a particular policy is to other well-accepted policies—both across decision levels and across substantive areas—the greater the likelihood of its implementation. It may be that the limited success of cross-national mergers to date can be explained by cross-level conflict and problems of substantive balance. Four dimensions of the substantive content of policies will be considered, bringing in questions of cross-level conflicts where applicable. The four problem areas are: public versus private tensions, concentration and efficiency, structural improvements for competition, and information coordination.

## Public versus private policies

The fundamental European industrial policy tension is between

20. Again, the reasons for this direction include: 1) the potential advantages to scale which include a) efficiency in production and marketing and cost competitiveness, b) efficiency in energy, c) ability to spread costs of technological research and development, and d) regional planning; 2) the resultant competitiveness in the international division of labor, associated with U.S. direct foreign investment, and preventing loss of markets through cost competition with industrializing countries, based on their cheaper labor and fewer technical or fiscal barriers; and 3) permitting an adaptability to changing environments both internal and external to the Community.

public and private economic activity. Although this trade-off exists in most advanced societies, the limited legitimacy and layers of interests in the EC makes the balance more complex. The EC movement, as part of the postwar emphasis on freeing trade, is based upon liberal political-economic market allocations rather than planned economy. Yet the speed of change and structural dysfunctions associated with the intra-European freeing of trade, harmonizing policies, and the changing European international role are politically unpopular. Part of the Commission answer was to promote competition through transnationally regulated concentration. Policies continually emphasize that individual firm freedom would be maintained, that individual action was necessary for competition. However, the EC did not specify means of reconciliation of private behavior and public regulation, beyond stressing efficiency and economies of scale. This tension is basic to industrial policy itself. At this point scholars and policymakers remain uncertain as to how the links can be made.

## Concentration and competition

European industrial policies consistently emphasize the positive impact of concentration on increased international competitiveness. This orientation is based on the expectation that increased firm size is related to increased efficiency in capturing the gains from European scale. The gains include production, marketing, research and development cost efficiencies, transnational regulation, distribution of the profits and benefits, and the positive political and economic externalities associated with the process. As impetus to cross-national mergers among small to medium sized firms, rather than already large companies, the EC continued its effort to prevent restrictive agreements. Some of the assumptions and tensions in this policy choice will be reviewed.

The first problem begins with the relationship of firm size to scale efficiencies including technological advance. Although some minimum scale is required for efficient production and allocation of resources to research and development, there is uncertainty about what constitutes optimal size centering around the problems of bureaucracy and including unwieldy decisionmaking apparatus and risk aversion.[21] In terms of the economic goal of efficiency, much can be gained by vertical integration of production and marketing processes, but this consideration is not mentioned in policy strategies, nor are there special incentives for such action. Part of the problem may be that vertical integration would not necessarily occur within European boundaries. Therefore regulatory problems would exist. The problems of scale and efficiency interface with those of private versus public decisions in a manner not considered by EC policymakers. This complication hinders policy choice for either of the objectives, efficiency or competition.

Further consideration of the concentration and competition link exposes potential contradictions among objectives such as: 1) concentration, technology, and energy, and 2) concentration, technology, and employment. Reaping economies of

scale through technological advances for increasing productivity frequently uses large quantities of capital and energy. The substitution of cheaply-priced oil for coal in postwar Europe illustrates a problem basic to advanced industrial development. High technology consumer and capital goods tend to use a great deal of energy. Although short-run efficiencies from economies of scale may exist, the longer-run problem of energy consumption is addressed only by promoting research and development in EC industrial policies. The association of high technology standard of living, and energy is not considered as a potentially conflictual problem in industrial programs, requiring some discussion of trade-offs among objectives.

Another potential contradiction, associated with concentration and present organization and technology use in production, concerns the objective of high employment levels. Advancing technology frequently substitutes capital for labor. This may lead to unemployment in certain sectors. Structural dysfunctions may limit the transfer of skills or labor among industrial sectors. Thus, concentration and advancing technology imply structural unemployment, contradicting Commission goals. Perhaps the policy process is at too early a stage to consider these problems. But outcomes of regional plans, declining industry policies, or any other strategies may be affected by the trade-offs and the externalities of chosen policies for other objectives. We may consider integrated policy performance a failure, without proper understanding of the reason for the failure, and therefore have limited hope of solving the problem. This is the opposite side to the suggestion that

21. See Keith Norris and John Vaizey. *The Economics of Research and Technology* (London: George Allen and Unwin, 1973).

congruent objectives and foci will aid implementation.

## Structural improvements for competition

Another incentive for transnational business cooperation is structural policy harmonizations. Those proposed in EC industrial policy include both "negative" and "positive" integration effects.[22] Comparing policy implementations, we find that the negative policies, such as removing technical barriers to trade, have been the most successful. In an effort to explain this success, we will examine three types of proposed harmonization relevant for transnational concentration: tariff barriers, fiscal harmonization, and legal harmonization.

Within the postwar context of liberalizing trade institutionalized in GATT, temporary regional discriminations were suggested to permit strengthening of subsystems. Regional elimination of obstacles to trade hopefully would increase trade and aid international integration. Firms could exploit comparative advantages for production, marketing, and servicing without hindrances. Linking industrial policy to the basis of the EC would ensure performance success, explaining the discrepancy in implementing policies noted above. However, traditional, commonly noted technical barriers to trade regulations providing production standards are but one type of barrier affecting one flow, that of goods and services. In addition, other barriers exist which may be more difficult to surmount because they are generated directly by national interests and sovereignty, and no international culture modifies their strength. Fiscal policies are one such barrier.

Two fiscal harmonization approaches were suggested by the Commission: the elimination of restrictive taxation barriers and the creation of a transnational capital market. The elimination of double taxation and other national fiscal discriminations were facilitators but not incentives for concentration.[23] The building of a European capital market, through cooperation among national financial institutions and further collaboration with the European Investment Bank, was to provide the same potential. Such harmonization coincides with the state goals of an economic and monetary union, thus suggesting additional support for implementation. Yet whether performance will aid cross-national mergers or direct foreign investment is not certain.

The second additional barrier is the maze of national legislation. Industrial policy emphasized legal harmonization, including uniform regulations for societes anonymes, the formation of a European Patent Office, and the attempt to cross-nationalize tendering for public supply contracts. These policy formulations aim to promote information and comparative advantage efficiencies on a European scale, change historical attitudes and national prestige demands, and promote spillover into the cultural domain.

Generally speaking, the harmonization policies coordinate with the more general orientation to customs unions and integrated decision-making. Although they require some minimal acceptance of supranational

22. John Pinder, "Positive Integration and Negative Integration: Some Problems of Economic Union in the E.E.C.," Michael Hodges ed., *European Integration* (Middlesex: Penguin, 1972).

23. Commission of the European Community, "Industrial Policy," *Bulletin of the European Community* 5 (1972), p. 21.

legitimacy, they do not emphasize radical redistributions of power to such authority or among national interests. As Chown notes, "Harmonization does not mean 'equalization' or 'standardization.'"[24] Harmonization policies attempt to alleviate the most obvious institutional discrepancies limiting the objective of integration. The proposals suggested frequently expand the role of an existing institution, the European Investment Bank, or create new ones rather than cut back on power or discretion of actors. As noted, the more congruent policies promoting transnational mergers are to general integration policies, the more successful is implementation.[25]

### Coordinating information institutions

The last policy group provides a good illustration of the EC emphasis on growth rather than choice hinted at in the previous example. Considering political goals, growth is cheaper in terms of lost support than redistribution. Industrial policies to coordinate institutions are part of the growth ideology that hinders recognition of trade-offs. Three institutional developments are emphasized by the EC: organizations for science and technology research, statistical information, and the "marriage bureau" information service for merging firms. Each of these strategies represents an attempt to distribute the costs of information, which are often too high for individual nations. The program objectives coincide with the general aims of the

EC Treaty, including rational use of energy and raw materials, protection of the environment, industrial restructuring, employment increases and working condition advances, and competitiveness. Again, coordinating information like harmonizing policies does not require immediate distributive decisions among EC goals, or recognition of their interlinked nature. Information is depoliticized by Community policy strategy.

Focusing more specifically on the science and technology policy, the Commission has created a framework for coordinating national policies while implementing common research programs. Four criteria for EC project selection (effectiveness, transnational nature, large market, and common requirements) link science and technology policy to concentration, competition, and industrial policy goals.[26] Based on the questions raised above about the relation between technology and macro-economic concerns, these criteria fail to recognize the substantive balances that may be required in allocating benefits in an interdependent system.

### SUMMARY

EC industrial policy has developed in fits and starts. Most scholars emphasize the traditional, national versus supranational authority and interest divisions, as explaining the lack of success. We have attempted to dig deeper into the policy process to note relative successes and failures and their relation to European participation in the global system. We also focused on the internal consistency of policies within this context.

24. John Chown, *Taxation and Multinational Enterprises* (London: Longman, 1974), p. 232.

25. This overlap does not necessarily imply spillover but some jointly distributed outcome.

26. Commission of the European Communities, "The Common Policy: The Field of Science and Technology," (Brussels, 1972).

Annals, AAPSS, 440, Nov. 1978

# The External Relations of The European Community

By Michael B. Dolan and James A. Caporaso

ABSTRACT: The European Community (EC) has been in existence for over twenty years and its permanence is no longer seriously questioned. This recognition of the EC as a permanent component of the global system is partially acknowledged by the shift of scholarly research from the internal problems of Community development to its external relations. Here a number of important questions are unresolved: Is the EC a coherent global actor or only an arena where representatives of nation states carry out their foreign policies? Does the EC operate effectively in the political arena or is its power limited to economic matters? The authors address these questions by dividing their subject matter up into EC relations with the advanced industrial societies, and relations with the developing countries. In the former category they examine EC external policy in agriculture and energy. In the latter category the EC's attempt to formulate a development policy is examined from six different perspectives. Regardless of the degree of common purpose and cohesion evident in the EC's activities, it clearly is an important actor for both the industrial and nonindustrial countries.

---

*James A. Caporaso is the Andrew W. Mellon Professor of International Studies at the Graduate School of International Studies of the University of Denver. He is author of* The Structure and Function of European Integration, *co-editor of* Quasi-Experimental Approaches: Testing Theory and Evaluating Policy, *editor of a special issue of* International Organization *on dependence and dependency, and author of articles on integration and dependence in* American Political Science Review, International Studies Quarterly, *and* International Organization.

*Michael B. Dolan is Assistant Professor of Political Science at Carleton University, Ottawa, Canada. He has published articles on the theory of regional integration in* International Studies Quarterly and Peace Science Review. *His current research focuses on the relationship between the European Community and the less developed countries.*

INHERENT in any discussion of the external relations of the European Community (EC) are three ambiguities which are not easily resolvable, and are therefore likely to limit understanding of the subject from the start. The first of these concerns the nature of the external role of the EC. Can this external role be described as one of a coherent foreign policy or should it be designated more modestly as external relations? To speak of external relations is only to admit that the existence of the EC has consequences for the outside world. These contacts and consequences need not involve any overall purposive actions, indeed any consciously formulated policy at all. To speak of foreign policy, by contrast, implies the existence of consciously formulated and executed plans of actions. An EC foreign policy suggests at a minimum the existence of purposeful actors at the European level, a minimal unity of goals on substantive matters, and a working agreement on procedures.

The second ambiguity is related to the first. Is the EC merely an arena, a place where foreign policy is conducted, a kind of multilateral stage operating at the regional level, or is the Community a new global actor? There are those who see the EC as merely a convenient place where national representatives, fully instructed and controlled by their national capitols, harmonize the details of their foreign economic policies. On the other hand are those who see the EC as an important independent actor, with aims and resources far exceeding those of the separate nation states.

The third ambiguity from which our analysis proceeds concerns the issue of economic versus political power. Few would argue with the statement that the EC is a potentially powerful economic area; yet few see it as an emerging superpower, equipped with the full range of political functions, and capable of entering into the power calculations of the United States or the Soviet Union. This is because its power, such as it exists, is limited to the pursuit of economic goals with economic means. The diplomacy of the EC is what one observer calls a "business suit diplomacy,"[1] suited more to technical questions of tariffs, agricultural surpluses, and balance of payments than to national security, missile reductions, German reunification, and dissolution of the major cold war blocs.

Finally, and this is a kind of summary statement of the three preceding ambiguities, there is a dichotomy between those who see the EC as an emerging global monolith and those who see it as a harmless collection of rival nation states. On the one hand, there are the exaggerated fears of those who see every rumbling of EC cohesion, every pro forma call for political unity, every summit meeting, as a signal for the return of European diplomatic ambitions. Indeed, for this group, the existence of political cohesion is unnecessary. The mere occasion for the exercise of power, in the form of existing economic resources, is enough to justify the political conclusions. On the other hand, there are the inveterate liberals who forever see economic and political actions as occurring in separate spheres with no linkages between them. For this group, no amount of economic resources counts

1. W. Hartley Clark, *The Politics of the Common Market* (Englewood Cliffs, NJ: Prentice-Hall, 1967), p. 130.

because there are no political institutions—let alone political will—to convert this potential into political influence.

## THE TWO FACES OF THE EUROPEAN COMMUNITY

The EC presents two different images to the world and, depending on which one is played up, different conclusions will be drawn about the EC's external role. The first Europe we might refer to as "the Europe of potential," a Europe bulging with economic muscle, rich in economic resources, and impressive in its economic productivity, its foreign trade, and its international competitiveness in technology and capital. Wittingly or not, this is an image of a Europe of consequence for others, a European community perhaps powerful in spite of itself. This is a Europe of power without purpose and of consequences without intentions.

There is another image of the EC. This one emphasizes the Community's goals and purposes, as well as consequences, and speaks of political will and institutions, as well as resources and capabilities. It stresses the emerging policymaking capacity of the EC in the areas of commercial policy, energy, foreign agricultural policy; and it plays up the coherent role of the EC in international negotiations, such as the Kennedy Round of tariff negotiations, the Conference on Security and Cooperation in Europe, and the Law of the Sea Negotiations. In sum, to the EC's already impressive resources, one now adds coherence of goals, political will, and an institutional capacity for achieving its goals. It is not by accident that this view of Europe has aroused more fears on the part of nonmember states than the first image.

### Economic potential of the EC

Several authors have referred to the EC as a "non-military" or a "civilian power."[2] Presumably this refers to the considerable resources at the disposal of EC countries, and the limited use of power within sectoral contexts—in tariff policy but not in security policy. It is true, as one observer put it, that

If the Community evolves beyond a customs union—an evolution which seems more likely since the Paris summit meeting of October 1972—the United States would confront an integrated European economic area with a GNP of, say, $700 billion, and a population of 270 million. . . . Its $60 billion or so of foreign exchange reserves and its annual revenues in the public sector of $250 billion would represent more than a match for the United States economy.[3]

Similarly, we have the opinion of Pierre Hassner who feels ". . . the only respect in which Western Europe does constitute a power is the economic one" and that "it is mainly through this sphere that she irritates her Western allies and attracts her Eastern neighbors."[4]

To provide a concrete example of the growing economic power of the EC, one has only to look at the relevant trade statistics. In 1970, if one adds together the value of trade among EC member states and trade between the EC and nonmember states, the EC accounts for 30.3

2. See for example, Pierre Hassner, *Europe in the Age of Negotiations*, The Washington Papers, no. 8 (Beverly Hills, CA: Sage, 1973).
3. James Chace, "The Concert of Europe," *Foreign Affairs*, vol. 52, no. 1 (October 1973), p. 99.
4. Hassner, *Europe in the Age of Negotiations*, p. 2.

percent of world imports and 31.7 percent of world exports.[5] In addition, the EC has become more self-sufficient over time, which is to say that the ratio of internal EC trade to total trade has increased. Intra-EC trade in 1970 represented 48.4 percent of total trade (intra EC plus inter EC and nonmembers) compared to 29.6 percent in 1958.[6]

However, to downplay the importance of political institutions and a coherent European foreign policy toward the industrialized countries is not to rule out the serious consequences of the Community's existence. The evolution of the EC has had an impact on most of the outside world, not the least on the industrial world. By 1968, the completion of the removal of internal tariffs and the establishment of the customs union had necessitated adjustments in the policies of the US, Japan, and the members of the European Free Trade Association (EFTA).

### EC—a political entity

The question can be legitimately asked: Can the EC play *only* an economic role? Is it possible? Is it desirable? Can the EC limit its role to questions of the production and distribution of goods and services without stimulating public conflicts with nonmembers concerning the consequences of its activities. What is or is not political is not fixed eternally but depends on the reactions of those affected by private activity. The common agricultural policy (CAP) may be concerned with the optimal allocation of resources in the agricultural sector, but this economic activity assumes a political content when such policies start to eliminate the markets of others. For some time after the adoption of the major parts of the CAP (in 1962, 1963, and 1964), there was little response to the EC policies of domestic stimulation of production (well above levels needed for internal consumption), subsidies, and export rebates. The EC had succeeded in "privatizing" a potentially controversial area. Later, of course, the CAP became a major political issue in the foreign policies of the United States, Canada, and many African countries.

In addition to the political content of specific EC policies, the EC assumed a political role as a balancer, with varying shades of economic and political content, for nonmember industrial countries, primarily for those not incorporated into one of the major economic blocs. Thus, one author sees Europe as "Canada's last chance" in its role as a counterweight to the US.[7] The European option became particularly attractive after Nixon's protectionist measures of August 1971 and the enlargement of the EC in January 1973.[8]

The Nordic balance also provides a case in point. This balance has to do with a system of relationships among Norway, Sweden, Finland, Denmark, Iceland, and the Soviet Union. The membership of Denmark, Norway, and Iceland in the North Atlantic Treaty Organization (NATO) is balanced by Finland's close ties with the Soviet Union, including joint military plans in the event of an attack on the

5. *Bulletin of the European Communities*, vol. 5, no. 6 (Brussels: Commission of the European Communities, Secretariat of the Commission, 1972).

6. Ibid., p. 38.

7. Peter C. Dobell, "Europe: Canada's Last Chance," *International Journal*, vol. 27, no. 1 (Winter 1971–1972), p. 113.

8. Ibid., p. 116.

latter. Finland's buffer role on the northern flank of the Soviet Union is supplemented by the fact that neither Denmark nor Norway permits foreign troops on their soil.[9] The centerpiece of this balance is Sweden, whose armed neutrality and strong economic role are critical to the stability of East-West relations in Europe.[10]

While Sweden's military position in Europe is stable, and has indeed been reinforced by the Conference on Security and Cooperation in Europe, her economic position is not, and this has been due largely to the necessity of adjusting to the dynamic role of the EC in Europe as a whole. The reasons are clear. The economic ties between Sweden and the EC, even without Great Britain's membership, are substantial. Over a third of the Swedish GNP is accounted for by trade, and of this amount over one-fourth goes to the EC countries.[11] With Great Britain as Sweden's largest market, and the Federal Republic of Germany as her biggest supplier, the enlarged EC promised to account for almost 70 percent of Sweden's markets. Given these facts, it is not surprising that there was strong economic pressure for Swedish membership and, indeed, this option was seriously considered by the Swedish government. The fact that Sweden ultimately rejected membership was due to political variables, to the fear of political union in the EC,

the loss of neutrality, and the consequences of such a loss for the European balance. Sweden, apparently, had a difficult time separating the economic and political content of Community membership.

## THE EC AS A COHERENT FOREIGN POLICY ACTOR

Although the EC is far from a perfectly integrated supranational actor, with a powerful executive and streamlined bureaucracy, imitating its national counterparts, it is also much more than a loose collection of nation states. The Six and the Nine have operated cohesively on a variety of fronts, often presenting a common front in NATO, caucusing to achieve a common position in the United Nations, as well as speaking with one voice in the area of commercial policy.

For an actor to effectively pursue goals, it must have more than potential power. In order for this power to become effective, there must exist some common denominator of political will, and in order for political will to be effective, there must be political institutions. Here we are not speaking only of institutions such as the Council of Ministers or the Commission of the EC, but also of organized ways of bringing power to bear on competitors in concrete situations. One general practice that the EC member countries have found useful is banding together for market power, which some see as a strategy to be followed in relation to state-trading companies[12]; it has had a limited success in the EC foreign economic

9. Toivo Miljan, "The Nordic Countries: Europe's Reluctant Partners," in Peter Stingelin, ed., *The European Community and the Outsiders* (Ontario, Canada: Longman Canada Ltd., 1973), p. 120.

10. Ibid.

11. M. Donald Hancock, "Sweden, Scandinavia, and the EEC," *International Affairs*, vol. 48, no. 3 (July 1972), p. 424.

12. John Pinder, "An Ostpolitik for the Community," in P. P. Everts, ed., *The European Community and the World* (Rotterdam: Rotterdam University Press, 1972), p. 45.

policy toward the United States and Japan.

## Foreign policy in agriculture

One area in which the EC has cultivated and utilized its economic power self-consciously is agriculture. Parts of the CAP were oriented toward increasing the efficiency of agricultural production, while others were simply directed toward stimulation of production. As part of the institutional organization of the CAP, there was an elaborate system of price supports, target prices, and the protectionist variable levy (a tax levied on agricultural goods imported into the EC). This policy so stimulated production, that it led to gigantic and costly surpluses, which were in turn cleared by supplying export rebates to the very countries which had produced the surpluses. Not only did this hurt the less developed countries, many of whom relied on agricultural exports, but also the industrial countries, particularly the United States, Canada, and Australia (as exporters of grain).

These aggressive foreign economic policies can be expected to continue because they are grounded in the domestic political situation of the member countries. As one observer put it, in the coming years increased unemployment is likely to be less tolerable than the cost of maintaining surpluses and, consequently, EC governments will pursue policies designed to keep the workers on the land.[13] Furthermore, the EC will follow agricultural policies designed to satisfy the demands of powerful agricul-

tural pressure groups organized at both the national and supranational levels.[14] In addition, there is another structural force pushing agricultural policies in the direction of the cycle of greater production, protection, and export: the chronic balance of payments problem faced by most major European governments which has been substantially aggravated by the increased price of petroleum.[15] Agricultural surpluses have become a European trump card, and excess food production has taken on a new commercial importance in the post-OPEC era.

The primary reasons for the successful formulation and implementation of a foreign agricultural policy are two: one, this policy rests on a domestic consensus of the individual nation states; two, the relationships among the member states and the global system are not divisive. Though there is often conflict in these relationships, so far this conflict has not split the members internally. It should be noted that the existence of a coherent foreign policy in agriculture is partially tied to a confluence of interests which are not likely to be duplicated in other sectors. The attempts of the EC to fashion a common energy response to the OPEC embargo and price increase provides a good example of this.

## Foreign policy in the energy sector

The details of the energy crisis are by now well known. In October 1973 the OPEC countries disrupted the supply of petroleum to the United States and the Netherlands

13. Denis Bergman, "Agricultural Policies in the EEC and their External Implications," World Development, vol. 5, nos. 5–7 (May–June 1977), p. 412.

14. Adrien Zeller, L'Imbroglio Agricole du Marché Commun (France: Calmann-Levy, 1970).

15. Bergman, "Agricultural Policies," p. 412.

and brought about a four-fold price increase for the consuming countries, including the EC countries. The response of the EC was mostly one of disarray, with individual national responses and initiatives carrying the day. The Germans appealed to both Atlantic and European solidarity and eventually joined in the November pro-Arab EC declaration so as to assure themselves the necessary levels of supply. The long-term picture was also dominated by national initiatives. As Wilfrid Kohl pointed out, France has signed a long-term agreement with Saudi Arabia involving the exchange of French weapons for a secure oil supply. Libya and Italy have also come to terms, linking Libyan oil to Italian technological assistance. The United Kingdom, on the other hand, banked on the existence of oil deposits in the North Sea.[16]

While the major reactions were national, there was also an international component. This response did not center around the EC but was larger than the Community, involving an internationalization of the EC effort by the United States and other oil-consuming countries. This phase, already in existence by early 1974, centered around the Energy Coordinating Group (ECG) flowing from the US initiative in setting up the Washington Energy Conference. In addition to eight of the nine members of the EC (France joined as an observer only), the United States, Canada, Norway, and Japan also joined, in an attempt to bring together a group of countries with effective market consumer power. This larger grouping accounted for much more oil consumption than did the EC alone.

The reasons for failure in the development of a foreign policy in energy are clear. The first is that each of the member states is endowed with different natural resources, and at least one (Great Britain) hoped for an optimal solution at the national level. There were also important cleavages along financial lines with "The division of the EEC into essentially three classes of states—Bonn, with its hugh export potential, its strong *deutsche mark*, its trade and payments surpluses; Italy and (at least until the North Sea oil comes to the rescue) Britain at the lower end; France and the Benelux countries in between—makes cooperation and internal cohesion more difficult."[17]

The second factor concerns the different linkages between EC members and the global system. France has pursued a more pro-Arab policy than other member states, whereas the Netherlands has taken a strong pro-Israeli stance. Italy has strong historical ties with Northern Africa, a fact which encouraged her to look to the oil producers there for some relief. With respect to the United States, not all Community members were of one mind. Germany's fascist experience and military defeat in World War II forced her to play a cautious role in reentering the global system. A fully armed Germany,

16. Wilfrid L. Kohl, "The United States, Western Europe, and the Energy Problem," *Journal of International Affairs*, vol. 30, no. 1 (Spring/Summer 1976), pp. 81–82; and Kohl, "Energy Policy in The Communities," This issue.

17. Stanley Hoffmann, "No Trump, No Luck, No Will: Gloomy Thoughts on Europe's Plight," in James Chace and Earl C. Ravenal, eds., *Atlantis Lost: US-European Relations After the Cold War* (New York: New York University Press, 1976), pp. 23–24.

unchecked by a major power was unacceptable; thus a foreign policy of close reliance on the United States and the EC, and a firm commitment to Atlanticism evolved. France's historical experience was, of course, quite different. Her humiliation over the pattern of Great Power decisions during the second World War, her resentment over the special relations between the United Kingdom and the United States (the Anglo Saxons), the failure of the United States to support French interests in Suez, the dominance of the United States in the military commands of NATO, all led France to a different policy. Striving for independence in foreign relations, and avoiding domination and constraints on an independent global role, in whatever guise—integration, Atlanticism—became basic French policy goals. The result of these different international linkages is that France and Germany, both short of oil resources, responded to the United States energy initiatives quite differently.

This discussion suggests that it may be misleading to ask whether the EC is a coherent foreign policy actor in general terms. One should instead ask this question on a sector by sector basis. In some cases, the EC reaction is little more than a series of uncoordinated national responses, while in others, the unity is impressive. Sometimes the EC seems too big for an effective response and at other times too small. It is sometimes outflanked by national societies from below and by other forms of international solidarity (Atlanticism, trilateralism) from above. Given the complexity of global politics, this should not be surprising. There is no a priori reason to suppose that the EC is

the optimal level of response for all international problems. As a former Commission member in charge of the external relations of the EC put it:

. . . this European union cannot be and will not be a self-confident, self-happy, self-sufficient bloc in a world of blocs. We have no intention of looking upon the world as one in which only large political units have a place. We believe instead that the world should remain varied, and that there are many ways in which people can define their own position in a world of peaceful interrelations. We do not believe that the 'bloc' notion of world politics pays sufficient attention to the complexity of relations even between gigantic developed nations like the United States.[18]

## THE EC'S RELATIONS WITH THE THIRD WORLD

In the Rome Treaty the relations of the EC with the developing world were limited to member states' dependencies, most of which were in Africa. The member states, Belgium, Italy, and especially France, did not want to lose their ties with these dependent territories as a result of joining the EEC. The other member states, especially Germany, balked at the special treatment given to these colonial empires, but France made her EEC membership conditional upon the association agreements.

Through the early 1960s, the EC's relations with the developing world were limited to the member states' remaining territories, to newly independent former colonies (in the 1963 Yaoundé Convention with the eighteen African and Malagasy States (AASM), and to preferential and nonpreferential economic and aid

18. Ralf Dahrendorf, "The Foreign Policy of the EEC," *World Today*, vol. 29, no. 2 (February 1973), p. 57.

agreements with several Mediterranean countries (Greece, Turkey, Iran and Israel). In the 1968–1972 period the EC negotiated a host of new preferential agreements with African and Mediterranean countries. The Arusha Convention of 1968 linked the EC with three Commonwealth countries, Kenya, Tanzania, and Uganda, after which individual agreements were negotiated with Morocco, Tunisia, Spain, Yugoslavia, Malta, Egypt and Cyprus.

After Britain entered the EC in 1973, the EC negotiated the Lomé convention, signed in 1975, with 46—now 54—African, Caribbean, and Pacific (ACP) states, which included both the former Yaoundé states (the AASM) and the non-Asian developing countries in the Commonwealth. Since then the EC has again turned its attention to the Mediterranean region. In 1972 the EC undertook to establish a global Mediterranean policy, and has negotiated agreements with the Maghreb (Algeria, Morocco and Tunisia), and the Mashrek countries (Egypt, Jordan, Lebanon, and Syria).

This brief inventory indicates the evolution of the nature and size of the EC's external relations with the Third World since the Rome Treaty. The EC now has preferential agreements with all of the Mediterranean rim countries except Libya and Albania, and with all of Arab and Black Africa except for Angola and Mozambique, who have thus far declined the EC's offers. The distinguishing feature of the EC's development program is its regional exclusivity; preferential agreements outside of Africa and the Mediterranean are limited to a small group of Caribbean and Pacific countries in the Lomé Convention. Thus the EC has established a development policy that is limited to the former colonies of Britain and France, as well as the rest of the member states, and to the Mediterranean rim countries.

The EC's rationale for the exclusiveness of its development policy varies according to the source. Some simply point to the historical or special relationships that Europe has had with these countries. Others argue that many of the countries within the ACP bloc are among the poorest in the world, and therefore require additional assistance. Still others blame France for the exclusivity of the EC's development policy. In any event the rest of the developing world has not been wholly ignored.

In 1972 the EC agreed to work toward a global cooperation policy. The generalized system of preferences (GSP), which was the first of its kind when it was installed in 1971, constitutes the only substantive progress in this direction. The GSP allows a limited amount of preferential treatment to many industrial, and a few agricultural, products from all of the Third World. The EC also has signed several nonpreferential trade cooperation agreements with other developing countries: Bangladesh, Brazil, India, Mexico, Pakistan, and Sri Lanka. Until recently the EC gave only food aid and technical assistance, in export promotion and regional integration, to nonassociated countries. Now the EC gives very limited assistance to Asian and Latin American countries to develop food production, and a more substantial amount to the United Nations Emergency Program. Finally the EC has working relations with a number of other regional integration groups: the Latin American Free Trade Association, the Andean Group, the Caribbean Common Market, the Central American Common Market, and the Association of South East Asian Nations.

In sum, EC development policy has evolved from a policy limited to the colonial empires of some of the member states to a three track system: associated, semi-associated, and nonassociated status. The associated states consist of the original ACP states of the Lomé Convention who receive the most preferential treatment and the bulk of EC financial aid. The special or semi-associated states consist of the Mediterranean countries which also receive preferential treatment and some aid, but less than the ACP states. Finally the rest of the developing world constitutes the non-associated track, which benefits only from the GSP and a very limited amount of financial aid.

## PERSPECTIVES ON EC DEVELOPMENT

Different images or perspectives on EC development policies convey the complexity of the factors involved in the EC's relations with the developing world. The official EC development view is a largely uncritical perspective emphasizing the EC's good will and the interdependence of Europe and the developing world; another much more critical view offers a perspective of economic imperialism. Each is examined briefly below. Since the totality of these perspectives explains only a limited amount of the EC's development policies, four additional perspectives are necessary for a more complete understanding.

### The official EC perspective

We begin with the EC's own, predictably benign, views on its overseas development policies.[19] The official EC position is that, as a result of an increase in member states' awareness of Third World development problems, it has substantially strengthened its development policies. The inventory of agreements with developing countries that was presented above certainly supports this view, for the 1970's have brought preferential agreements— via Lomé and the "global" Mediterranean policy—to three times the number of countries which received preferential treatment in the 1960's. In a more limited fashion, the EC's GSP gave preferential treatment to all of the developing countries. The Lomé Convention, which is the core of the EC's development policy, is touted by the EC as a revolutionary break with previous EC development agreements, and as a model for North-South relations.[20] Such praise is heaped upon the Lomé Convention by the EC because of the Convention's inclusive membership— 54 ACP states as compared to 17 in the 1969 Yaoundé II Convention—and because of its trade and aid provisions. Most heralded among the latter is the STABEX arrangement, which guarantees the ACP states export earnings on a limited number of mainly agricultural products.[21]

The increase in Community awareness of Third World development

19. A brief introduction to the EC's development policy as seen by the EC is *The Development Cooperation Policies of the European Community: from 1971 to 1976*, Commission of the European Communities (Luxembourg: Office des publications officielles des Communantés européenes, April 1977).

20. See the "Lomé Dossier," a special issue of *The Courier*, 31, 1975.

21. Lomé Convention Title II, the text of the Convention is published in the "Lomé Dossier."

needs is a result of the developing countries' ability to back their proposals with a unified front. The EC has taken pains to indicate that it was ACP solidarity which prompted strong responses to EC proposals in contrast to earlier association negotiations. For example, the EC's plan to offer several alternative frameworks for the convention was successfully rejected when they substituted their own framework. Thus the EC has stressed the transition from the "association" bargaining style of the Yaoundé and Arusha negotiations to the "partnership" bargaining style that characterized the negotiations for the Lomé Convention. To the uninitiated, it should be mentioned that the term "association" had come to be tainted with neocolonialist overtones in many of the nonassociated and associated developing countries.

While the EC cites ACP solidarity as a major determinant of the new style of North-South relationship characterized by Lomé, it realizes that solidarity alone cannot explain why the Lomé Convention was "founded on equality between the partners,"[22] or why it was "a relationship very much based on equal terms between the two partners."[23] Equality in a bargaining relationship assumes that each side has roughly equal bargaining strength. In the view of the EC, the bargaining chips of the ACP states are their raw materials, including oil and uranium, as well as their markets for EC exports and private investments. In an uncritical assessment, Isabel Gruhn describes the Lomé Convention as "creeping interdependence."[24] Gruhn suggests that

the ACP states followed the OPEC example and learned to bargain effectively with their raw material resources; the EC had to face this new reality. To a certain extent this view is part of the official view; the EC has not claimed that the motives behind its development policies were entirely altruistic. In fact the EC explicitly recognized the relationship between the raw materials base of the ACP states and the terms of the Convention. At the signing of the Lomé Convention, the then chairman of the EC's Council of Ministers, Dr. G. Fitzgerald, commented:

These (ACP) countries are major, suppliers of raw materials and this close link must be to Europe's advantage: and I am certain that it is to their advantage because of the terms (of the Convention) we managed to settle in negotiations.[25]

In sum, the official EC view is that the Lomé Convention, and its development policies in general, are the result of a desire to assist Third World development, and the EC's need for Third World resources, trade, and investment markets. Finally, the EC rationalizes the exclusiveness of its preferential agreements by noting that many ACP countries are among the poorest in the Third World, and that to further increase the number of countries receiving preferential treatment, besides being beyond its capacity, would water down the preferences already given.

*Economic imperialism perspective*

While the official EC perspective points out the gains made by

22. "Lomé Dossier, " p. 12.
23. Ibid., p. 7.
24. Isabel Gruhn, "The Lomé Convention: Inching towards Interdependence," *Inter-*

*national Organization* 30, no. 2 (1976), pp. 241–62.
25. "Lomé Dossier," p. 7.

the EC as a result of the Lomé Convention, the main thrust is upon ACP gains, or at least upon the mutual beneficialty of the convention, a quid pro quo from which both sides prosper. In contrast to the benign official view, the economic imperialism perspective emphasizes the EC's tactics and its resultant gains at the expense of the Third World. In the most critical pronouncement, Kwame Nkrumah of Ghana labeled the EC's development policies "collective colonialism." Johan Galtung has argued that the EC's development policy was one of "exploitation, defined as vertical division of labor, fragmentation, and penetration."[26] Exploitation refers to having manufactured goods dominate the flow of EC goods to the developing countries, while raw materials constitute the bulk of the Third World exports. Fragmentation refers to the divisive effects of the nonuniformity of the EC's development policy, the EC's division of the Third World into associated and nonassociated classes. By penetration Galtung indicates the identification of elites in the associated countries by European elites and the dependence of the latter on the former.[27]

Galtung's argument was based upon the exclusiveness of the Yaoundé agreements and, at the same time, the paucity of benefits gained by the associated states (the AASM). The Yaoundé Conventions were very protectionist; needed raw materials were allowed into the EC, but competitive food and agricultural products were not. These Conventions in effect created industrial free trade areas, and since very few industrial goods were produced by the associates, the EC was the main beneficiary. One indicator of the paucity of benefits gained by the associates was that over the 1958–1969 period, the average rate of increase in exports to the EC was greater for the nonassociated Third World countries than for the associated states.

The negotiation of the Lomé Convention served to blunt some of Galtung's criticism.[28] Nevertheless others have drawn critical arguments against various aspects of the Conventions which address themselves to the spirit of economic imperialism.[29] The critics point out that while large in the number of countries, the ACP bloc of the Lomé Convention includes only 268 million people, (98 percent of whom are African) out of a total Third World population of more than two billion people. Further, the ACP states have attempted on several occasions to prevent the EC from improving the GSP so that the level of preferential treatment for non-ACP products would not approach that received by ACP products. This divisiveness also occurs in the Third World: for instance, in 1976 at a preparatory meeting for the United Nations Conference on Trade

26. Johan Galtung, *The European Community: A Superpower in the Making* (Oslo: Universitetsforlaget, 1973).

27. Ibid., p. 68.

28. Johan Galtung, "The Lomé Convention and Neo-Capitalism," *The African Review* 6, no. 1 (1976), pp. 33–42.

29. Michael B. Dolan, "The Lomé Convention and Europe's Relationship with the Third World: A Critical Analysis," *Journal of European Integration* 1, no. 3 (May 1978); Reginald Herbold Green, "The Lomé Convention: Updated Dependence or Departure Toward Collective Self-Reliance?" *The African Review* 6, no. 1 (1976), pp. 43–54; and David Wall, "The European Community's Lomé Convention: 'STABEX' and Third World Aspirations," Trade Policy Research Centre, London, 1975.

and Development (UNCTAD IV), the African states quarreled with the other members of the Group of 77 over the treatment of commodities in the New International Economic Order (NIEO), because of the preferential treatment already accorded to them by Lomé.[30]

The Lomé Convention had also been criticized for the meager and sometimes differential benefits received by the ACP countries. STABEX, the export earning support mechanism, has not overcome the balance of payments problems of the ACP countries, and has tended to favor the more developed ACP countries. The aid provisions of the Lomé Convention are even less bountiful than those contained in the previous Yaoundé agreements; the aid per capita in real terms is less than half of the development fund in Yaoundé II. In sum, the Lomé Convention is seen largely as a continuation of previous EC association agreements. The main difference from this perspective is that, as a consequence of British entry into the Community, the non-Asian developing countries of the Commonwealth have been included. As a result the EC now has an agreement with nearly all of Black Africa. The mentality of exclusiveness and an economic sphere of influence remains.

These two hypotheses do not appear to adequately explain EC development policies. Other points of view need to be exposed and analyzed to comprehend EC-Third World relations.

## The EC United States perspective

Seen from the perspective of economic imperialism the EC's de-velopment policies are an attempt to carve out and dominate chunks of the Third World. However, such an explicit policy would be necessary only if the EC perceived competition from other industrial states. The premise of this assumption is that the EC development policies are, to a large extent, a result of industrial state rivalry for limited resource, trade and investment areas in the Third World. The EC's competition comes mainly from the United States, and to a lesser extent Japan.

The US has been very critical of the EC's Mediterranean and African agreements on two points. One is reciprocity, or reverse preferences, which allows preferential treatment for EC products so that the EC has a competitive advantage over other countries.[31] Some critics also argue that reverse preferences may be harmful to the economic development of the Third World states. The second issue is the EC's predilection for regional trade discrimination agreements in the Mediterranean, Africa, and the Caribbean; and that these agreements are in violation of the General Agreement on Treaties & Tariffs, GATT, although waivers are commonly given for agreements with developing countries such as the ACP group. Although the EC can argue, under Article 24 of the GATT, the legality of discriminatory agreements with Greece, Turkey, Israel,

30. Dolan, "The Lomé Convention."

31. See, for example, Stanley Henig, "Mediterranean Policy in the Context of the External Relations of the European Community 1958–1973" in Avi Shlaim and G. N. Yannopoulos, eds., *The EEC and the Mediterranean Countries* (Cambridge: Cambridge University Press, 1976), pp. 305–324; and Jacqueline D. Matthews, *Association System of the European Community* (New York: Praeger, 1977).

Spain and Portugal, because they are putative members either of the EC itself or of an enlarged free trade area, the same does not hold for the other Mediterranean agreements. However, in the latest round of EC agreements with Mediterranean countries, reverse preferences have not been included except with those countries just listed. Apparently, because of the United States position, several ACP states would not have signed the Lomé Convention had the EC not dropped its insistence upon reciprocity.[32]

There are, however, several aspects of the Lomé Convention designed to give the EC member states a competitive edge over economic rivals, especially the United States. In the Convention, for purposes of defining originating products, the ACP is considered as a single area.[33] This should facilitate rationalization of production, but because of their size this clause will probably be more beneficial for Multinational Corporations MNC's than for indigenous firms. To obtain this clause, the ACP were compelled to accept an extensive list of specific processes that do not confer ACP originating status on products made from imported raw materials.[34] This list, which takes up more than one-fourth of the document, gives EC components an advantage over non-EC components because the former can reenter the EC duty free. Correspondingly, this might give EC MNCs an advantage over non-EC MNCs.

Nevertheless, the EC is presently

very concerned about its investment in the Third World since it has effectively stagnated since 1972; in that year, in real terms, there were $1253 millions, compared with $1232.7 millions in 1976.[35] The EC's explicitly stated fear is that this stagnation will allow its American and Japanese competitors to capture trade and investment markets. To remedy this situation the Commission is presently recommending to the Council of Ministers a community investment package which would set up and promote specific investment projects and guarantee the investments. The Commission argues that a Community level approach would supplement national guarantee systems in that European MNC's could be protected under this scheme.[36]

Aside from the ACP as a trade and investment market, Europeans rely upon this area, especially Africa, as an important source of raw materials. Black Africa has proven oil reserves of 4,100 m. tons, with prospects of much more, and all of the present African oil producers have long standing ties with European companies. Africa also has an abundance of uranium, another critical energy material for which Europe is dependent upon external sources; while the United States and the Soviet Union have domestic sources, Europe and Japan have none. The *Economist* described the Lomé Convention as a "big business coup" because in return for "short run gains" for the ACP states, it would give Europe a decided advantage over industrial competitors for scarce energy materials.[37]

---

32. Wall, "The European Community's Lomé Convention."

33. Lomé Convention Protocol 1, Title 1.

34. Lomé Convention Protocol 1, Annex II.

35. *Europe Documents*, no. 985 (2 February 1978), pp. 2–7.

36. Ibid., p. 2.

37. The *Economist*, 1 February 1975, p. 52.

Europe's need for ACP oil and uranium have received considerable attention, but the EC is also very dependent upon many Third World nonenergy raw materials such as cobalt, copper, iron ore, manganese, phosphates, tin and tungsten. The EC attempted to include a clause in the Lomé Convention that would assure access to raw materials in return for aid, but the ACP states effectively opposed it. Since then the EC has become more concerned about Third World raw materials because the percentage of EC mining exploration in the Third World has decreased substantially, from 57 percent of the total financial effort in 1961 to 13.5 percent in 1973–74.[38]

In the EC–US competition for Third World markets and raw materials in the 1970's, the EC has labored to better its relative position by portraying itself as the better friend of the Third World. It has pointed out that the EC is the largest market for developing country exports (taking 32 percent in 1975), and the largest market for developing countries' imports, (providing nearly 38 percent in 1972).[39] The EC is also the largest source of aid to the Third World—providing nearly 50 percent of the total—and its aid, as a percentage of national income, is substantially higher than that of United States. In 1971 the EC instituted the first generalized system of preference; the US GSP did not emerge until 1976. These "facts," which the EC uses to bolster its image as friend of the Third World, were evident in the

North-South dialogue when the EC attempted to establish itself as the "mediator" between the developing countries and the United States. In the dispute between the developed and developing countries, "the voice of reason came in the first instance from the EC," referring to the Lomé Convention and the STABEX agreement which the EC touts as models for North-South relations.[40]

*Member state competition perspective*

This perspective views the EC as a single entity reacting to external factors, and the development policies of the EC as the result of these relationships. Various studies have shown that the external relations of the EC are the result of many different and often conflicting member state policies, and this view regards the content and evolution of EC-Third World development policies as the result of internal competition among the member states. Thus, evolution of the development policies in the Community's twenty-year history was greatly affected by the Franco-German rivalry and the ascendancy of Germany in the Community's changing balance of power. The unsuccessful British entry attempts in the 1960's, and her eventual entry in 1973, were catalysts for much of the conflict within the EC over its development policies.[41]

The Treaty of Rome limited development policy to colonies and

38. *Europe Documents*, p. 2. The renegotiation of Lomé, beginning in 1978, will again see the EC attempt to include raw material access.

39. "Development Cooperation Policies of the European Community," p. 4.

40. "The Raw Materials Dossier," Information: Development Aid (109/X/76-E) Commission of the European Communities (Brussels), p. 3.

41. The description of this perspective benefited greatly from the research of Carl Lankowski at Columbia University.

countries that had special relations with member states, which primarily meant France and Belgium. The other EC states, especially Germany and the Netherlands, were very critical because they might be subsidizing, the continuation of French hegemony over these African dependent states through the aid program. Germany feared that the inclusion of the associates in the treaty would harm its relations with developing countries in Latin America and Asia, but France made the Association a condition for her signature and Chancellor Adenauer acceded to the French insistence.

From the outset, then, the development policies of France and Germany, and their corresponding development objectives at the Community level, were at cross purposes. France wanted a tightly-knit, homogeneous and exclusive association, while Germany and the Netherlands favored an open policy that would not be limited to African colonies. During the early years of the Community, the French policies dominated.

In 1963 the Yaoundé Convention was signed by the EC and by eighteen newly independent African and Malagasy associates (AASM). This convention was similar in most respects to the trade preference and aid system established in the Rome Treaty. The Germans unsuccessfully argued to replace the preference system with a commodity stabilization scheme; the Dutch also failed in their attempt to include the Commonwealth countries. Again the French prevailed; however De Gaulle's veto of British entry came in this period and the other EC member states symbolically delayed the signing of the Convention for six months. More lasting in effect were the German and Dutch initial

decisions to reject the Convention; this forced the French to agree to the *Declaration of Intent* which invited other African countries with economic structures comparable to the AASM to apply for Community association. As a result, in that same year Nigeria opened negotiations with the EC. The French objected to Nigerian association because Nigeria would be the beneficiary of two preferential agreements: the EC's and that of the Commonwealth. Negotiation finally resulted in agreement in 1966, but the Nigerian civil war precluded its ratification. It is perhaps worth noting that France's support of Biafra in the Nigerian civil war also staved off Nigerian attempts to establish a West Africa economic zone which would have ended the French zone. Therefore France was able to thwart the Nigerian association, although for the first time in the EC her development plans were not followed. Three former British colonies, Kenya, Tanzania, and Uganda did become associates of the EC in the Arusha Convention of 1968.

During the negotiations for Yaoundé II (1969), the clash continued between France on one hand and Germany and the Netherlands on the other; Belgium and Italy sided with the anti-French coalition. The main issue was trade reciprocity, or reverse preferences. The second conference, New Delhi, 1968, had called for their elimination, and within the EC only France advocated their retention. The French won out, but the end of their dominance was near. The devaluation of the franc in 1968 indicated the weakness of the French economy relative to Germany, and the ascendance of German influence within the EC followed De Gaulle's retirement in 1969. In terms of development policy, the first indication of the changing power structure within the Community was the GSP (1971) which was much closer to German and Dutch development objectives. The GSP was strongly advocated by the Group of 77 in the first two UNCTAD meetings, and was supported by the Germans because it was aligned closely with their own economic and development interests. The GSP was open to all of the developing world, not just to the associated states, and it was nonreciprocal. German support at this time was self-serving not only because of the German global investment pattern, but also because it enhanced a German foreign economic goal which was to lessen inflationary pressures by increasing its direct foreign investment and decreasing its export surpluses. The French influence was not moribund; France succeeded in including many qualifications and limitations so that the original GSP was meagre in its benefits for the Third World. However, liberalizing changes have been introduced in succeeding years.

In terms of rhetoric at least, the EC changed its development policy objectives in 1972 to include all of the developing countries. This should not necessarily be construed as a French defeat because the EC's development policy was tracked into an association policy and a development policy for the nonassociated states, that is, the rest of the Third World. Since France has tried to carve out a special role for herself between the North and the South, the 1972 EC policy statement allowed France to allay Third World criticism while maintaining the EC's association policy.

Part of the reason for French support of eventual British entry in 1972 was to counteract the increasing German influence. But French influence continued to decline in the post-1972 period. British entry into the EC was predicated on the inclusion of the non-Asian developing Commonwealth in some type of association with the EC. The substance of the ensuing Lomé Convention indicates the extent of German influence in the EC. The French originally wanted the Commonwealth and associates in separate tracks and attempted to split the ACP group, but the Germans successfully supported ACP unity. The French wanted the retention of trade reciprocity but in the face of unified EC and ACP opposition, this too was finally rejected. The Germans were happy with STABEX because it was in line with their economic philosophy of individual commodity treatment and no price intervention. The Germans were responsible for limiting the development fund to 3,000 million units of account; they had grown tired of subsidizing the French and, given their position, they now could put a limit on it.

In sum, this perspective views the nature of the EC's development policies as the result of competing French, German, and Dutch interests, with the ascendancy of Germany in the changing balance of influence within the EC. It would be ill-advised to conclude that the EC has become a German preserve; German development positions within the EC are not sacrosanct. For instance, at the March 1977 summit meeting, the EC member states overcame strong German opposition and advocated the establishment of a Common Fund. However, Germany and the United States have successfully weakened the structure of the Common Fund proposal of the industrial states, the Group of 8, in the North-South dialogue, so that an agreement has not yet been reached with the developing countries.[42]

## Internationalization of production perspective

The EC agreements with Africa and the Mediterranean were viewed by some as attempts to maintain, consolidate, and protect economic blocs as sources of raw materials and markets for European manufactured products. Thus, development agreements were seen as a continuation of the old international division of labor, with European manufactured goods entering the Third World markets and raw materials going in the other direction. This perspective views the Lomé Convention and the GSP as the result of an emerging new international division of labor, juxtaposed to the old division of labor, creating a trend toward a new international division—an internationalization of production.[43] In this context Stephen Hymer has argued that:

If present trends continue, multinationalization [of production] is likely to increase greatly in the next decade

as giants from both sides of the Atlantic . . . strive to penetrate each other's markets and to establish bases in underdeveloped countries. . . . This rivalry may be intense at first but will probably abate through time and turn into collusion as firms approach some kind of oligopolistic equilibrium. A new structure of international industrial organization and a new international division of labour will have been born.[44]

MNC's are increasingly establishing their production facilities in developing regions in order to take advantage of lower labor costs; low level production takes place in the Third World, while research and development in high level technology, and the decision-making control, remain in the advanced countries. The result is "a hierarchical division of labor between geographical regions corresponding to the vertical division of labour within the firm," and a development program caused partly by the needs of the new international division of labor.

The Lomé Convention, in tune with the needs of MNC's in the new international division of labor, allows the duty-free entry of manufactured goods into the EC as did the earlier Yaoundé agreements. However, compared to Yaoundé, the emphasis of Lomé is upon trade rather than aid; the Lomé aid in real per capita terms is less than one-half of Yaoundé II aid. Lomé also stresses industrialization in the ACP states, with a Committee of Industrial Cooperation and a Centre for Industrial Development being established.[45] The EC ex-

42. Stephen Taylor, "EEC Co-ordination for the North—South Conference," *The World Today* 33, no. 11 (November 1977), p. 439; and Geoffrey Goodwin, "The UNCTAD Common Fund—Challenge and Response," *The World Today*, 33, no. 11 (November 1977), pp. 425–32.

43. This perspective is developed by Lynn K Mytelka in "The Lomé Convention and a New International Division of Labour," *Journal of European Integration* 1, no. 1, pp. 63–76.

44. Stephen Hymer, "The Multinational Corporation and the Law of Uneven Development," in H. Radice, ed., *International Firms and Modern Imperialisms* (Baltimore: Penguin Books, 1975).

45. Lomé Convention Title III.

plicitly acknowledges the role of the ACP states in the new international division of labor:

The fact that industrial cooperation is one of the priorities of the Community's policy of cooperation with the ACP States is also a reflection of the changes taking place in international economic relations, as a result of which the developing countries are acquiring a growing share of industrial production and of international trade in manufactures.[46]

This perspective views development policies largely as the result of MNC needs, with the real competition between MNC's on the one hand and those firms in Europe that have not moved production facilities into the Third World— and the affected labor unions— on the other. The implication of the perspective is that the MNC's are winning, but it would be erroneous to conclude either that the struggle is over, or that Europe's opposition to the MNC strategy has not had an effect on the development agreements. One need only read the various agreements and conventions to find the sensitive areas and products: those for which preferential treatment is limited to some extent. However, the trend over EC development agreements is that the number of sensitive products is diminishing progressively.

*Strategic perspective*

Strategic implications help to determine development policies too, even though such a perspective would seem to be the least probable because European defense is within the purview of NATO rather than the EC. Yet, the strategic motivations of the Mediterranean policy,

presented by Wolfgang Hager, Ari Shlaim and Stanley Henig, are based on the regions political instability and the new economic power of Middle Eastern and North African oil.[47] The curtailment of oil exports by the Arabs in 1973, brought home to the EC the necessity of addressing this politically sensitive problem. Finally, the decreasing United States naval superiority in the Mediterranean Sea is rivalled by a greatly increased Soviet presence.

The strategic argument, in view of these realities, is that Europeans have come to realize the necessity of a unified Mediterranean policy. Since Europeans have neither the will nor the military might to replace the United States military presence in this region, they decided to use their substantial economic prowess as a policy instrument. The Community institutions were a ready-made arrangement through which to pursue a European economic policy. It is unclear whether this civilian power is designed to complement or counter United States policy, but for its part the United States has complained bitterly to the EC over preferential agreements with the Mediterranean countries. From its point of view, the EC's Mediterranean and African policies constitute a Third Force which is not consistent with United States needs.

If the EC's Mediterranean policy was guided by strategic implications, these motivations were frus-

46. "Development Cooperation Policies of the European Community," p. 28.

47. Wolfgang Hager, "The Community and the Mediterranean," in Max Kohnstamm and Wolfgang Hager, eds., *A Nation Writ Large* (London: Macmillan, 1973), pp. 209–215; Avi Shlaim, "The Community and the Mediterranean Basin," in Kenneth Twitchett, ed., *Europe and the World* (London: Europa Publications, 1976), pp. 77–120; and Stanley Henig, "Mediterranean Policy."

trated in the 1960's; the EC's external relations with Mediterranean countries in this period are notable for their lack of coherence or of a unified approach. This mosaic of disjointed bilateral treaties was the result of Mediterranean countries seeking preferential treatment and relief from the CAP for their agricultural exports on which their economies largely depended. And if the EC was seeking greater influence in this region, it is not attested to by the general niggardliness of the preferences granted to the Mediterranean countries in the various treaties. In fact, the dissatisfaction of the Mediterranean countries probably decreased the European influence in the 1960's.

In 1972, the EC moved to establish a global Mediterranean policy. The political objective of this policy was "a first step toward an increased European presence in the Mediterranean area, as a factor for equilibrium and peace, relieving the strains and pressures felt by the countries bordering the Mediterranean."[48] The EC official line is that through the association agreements, the Mediterranean countries will achieve greater economic development and, ultimately, political stability. The EC policy rationale, which is also applicable to the ACP countries, suggests that stability will foster and protect the EC's trading and investment markets. Certainly the EC has traditionally been concerned with fostering political stability in the Mediterranean region. For instance, the EC-Greek association in 1962 was partly the result of an EC desire for Greek stability.

Some have advocated that the EC

attempt to use its Mediterranean policy to establish a sphere of influence. For several reasons the likelihood of this is small. Such a policy would probably fail because the Mediterranean countries are suspicious of neocolonialism and the EC is dependent upon the region's oil. Also, given the EC's cumbersome policymaking system, it is doubtful that the EC could effectively establish a political sphere of influence. Thus far the member states have carefully separated the political consultations of member states from the EC institutions. But equally important is the lack of necessity for a political sphere of influence. If the EC were successful in enhancing its economic position, and tying the region into the European market, overt political control would be unnecessary. In an economic sphere of influence its influence would be less direct but just as useful; the threat of an Arab oil embargo would be diminished if not extinguished.

Recent trends have changed the focus of the EC's association policy for the Mediterranean so that it has taken on a more Arab cast. First was the 1973 Arab action which prompted the initiation of the continuing Euro-Arab Dialogue; and, secondly, the Greek, Spanish and Portuguese requests for EC membership, which will obviously remove them from association status. With notable exceptions the EC's global Mediterranean policy will consist predominantly of Arab countries. In fact the EC already has some type of association agreement with ten of the seventeen Arab League members. From this perspective, the EC has used its development policies to ensure the continued flow of Arab oil, and therefore has increased the

48. As quoted in A. Shlaim, "The Community and the Mediterranean Basin," pp. 79–80.

preferential treatment given to the Mediterranean nations.

## CONCLUSION

The EC's relations with the more and less developed countries cannot easily be reduced to generalizations, but we can raise and highlight several themes which emerge from our analysis.

First, although there is a certain amount of conflicting evidence as to just how cohesive the EC is in formulating and pursuing foreign policy goals, the weight of the evidence seems to be strongly in favor of the position that the EC is a political reality in global relations. It is clearly a significant actor in foreign agricultural policy and energy policy, as well as in the gamut of development policies with respect to the LDC's.

Second, it appears to us that the EC is considerably stronger and more united in its negotiations with the LDC's than with the advanced industrial countries, and that this contrast is particularly sharp if one compares development policy to energy policy. Although this is offered as a hypothesis rather than a conclusion, it is a hypothesis that has some plausibility. One could reason that the greater the bargaining power flowing from a cohesive position, the greater the incentive for member states to unite. In its relations with the less developed countries, a united EC is certainly in a strong bargaining position. Such was not the case in energy, however, where a thoroughly unified EC was an inadequate counterweight to the Organization of Petroleum Exporting Countries.[49] Here the additional weight of the United States, Japan, and Norway was needed to achieve an effective consumer response.

Finally, we should underscore what is perhaps obvious from the preceding discussion, the multilateralization of international relations. While the nation-state is still the elementary unit in global politics, in the sense that it has the ultimate authority to say "yes" or "no" in the global arena, in reality, the attainment of foreign policy goals is increasingly linked to international levers and mechanisms. With respect to energy, one thinks of the EC, Norway, Japan, Canada; in development policy, the EC, OECD, the ACP countries and the European-Arab Dialogue; and in agriculture, it is difficult to imagine foreign economic policy without the CAP, the EC, and the United States. The current global system is one of large economic units because only these can effectively compete in the international environment. From this perspective, we expect the EC to play an important role in the global system in the decades ahead.

49. See Kohl, "Energy Policy in the Communities," this issue.

ANNALS, AAPSS, **440**, Nov. 1978

# The Community in Perspective: Public Policy and Political Structure

By STUART A. SCHEINGOLD

ABSTRACT: It is now clear that the original integrative goals are beyond the reach of the European Community. At the same time it is equally clear that the Community has been playing an increasingly important part in relations among the member states and has been functioning as a bloc in an imposing range of international negotiations. The Community's policy role varies, however, within and among sectors in ways which resist generalization and explanation. This article traces patterns in the Community's policy record and relates those patterns to discontinuities in the political structure of the European Community—in particular, to weak linkages between Community institutions and grass roots and elite politics at the national level. The result is a Community which can be expected to play a prominent but decidedly derivative role in the political, economic, and social problems facing Western Europe in the years immediately ahead.

Stuart A. Scheingold is Professor of Political Science at the University of Washington. He has written extensively on the European Community and, more generally, on problems of law and politics in the United States and Western Europe. His publications include The Rule of Law in European Integration; Europe's Would-Be Policy, with Leon N. Lindberg; and The Politics of Rights.

IT HAS NOW been twenty years since the Common Market and Euratom joined the Coal and Steel Community as the institutional carriers of Jean Monnet's vision of a united Europe. Today's consolidated and enlarged European Community is firmly entrenched and a prominent feature on the political and economic landscape. Not only has it grown from six to nine members, it has also developed links with a significant number of nonmember states scattered around the globe. An extensive bureaucracy has been established in Brussels, and the scope of Community activities has increased over the years. Within the member states, no major political force questions the legitimacy of the Community, and internationally it figures conspicuously in a host of important negotiations.

The European Idea has certainly come a long way, but despite all of its successes the European Community has turned out to be an immense disappointment to its most ardent early advocates. Europe has not been united, and the nation states have not withered away. Whatever early impetus was generated in that direction has long since abated. Indeed, the development of the Community has proceeded apace with the recovery and reconsolidation of the European nation states, which were so badly shaken by World War II. The simple truth is that the initial hopes of Jean Monnet and those whom he inspired have not and will not be realized in the foreseeable future.

The Community thus finds itself facing the last two decades of the twentieth century in odd and unanticipated circumstances. It seems securely established and an acknowledged presence in domestic and international politics, but its original raison d'etre is no longer within reach. This new situation poses problems of evaluation. With the uniting of Europe no longer a viable objective, what standards are we to use to judge the success and chart the progress of the Community? It does not seem to make much sense to continue asking whether, and in what measure, each new development furthers the integrative process. But if we turn away from what is after all the defining issue of integration studies, what questions *are* we to pursue?

My own inclination is to focus on the Community as an instrument of public policy: To what extent is the European Community relevant to the present condition and future prospects of Western Europe? Since the Community's policy record turns out to be uneven, a second question comes quickly to mind. How are variations in the policy record of the European Community to be explained? This second question leads from policy per se to the interaction between policy performance and institutional capabilities. Two themes which run through this anniversary volume will, therefore, be juxtaposed in this article: the policy performance and the political structure of the European Community. I hope in this fashion to provide one way of synthesizing two rather distinct perspectives and thus to offer a useful overview of the achievements of and outlook for the European Community.

Accordingly, the first task of this paper will be to search the policy record for underlying regularities which will help us make sense out of what is on the surface a perplexing tangle of successes and failures in a wide variety of policy arenas. The principal conclusion that emerges from this search for regularities is that the Community seems able to play a *facilitative* policy role, mediating conflicts and working through administrative difficulties, but is not really capable of taking the kind of *constitutive* (or leadership) role associated with mobilizing support for departures from accepted policy paths. All of this will have to be explained in greater detail, of course, but it is readily apparent that these regularities transcend particular policy arenas and relate instead to the political structure of the European Community, which will be the focus of a separate section of this paper. The essential message of that section is *not* the familiar complaint that the Community has failed to develop truly supranational institutions with the power to override the member states. Instead, I conclude that the Community's problems stem from the incomplete interpenetration of national and Community political structures and, most particularly, from the virtual absence of links between Community institutions and grass roots politics within the member states.

Taken together, these arguments lead to conclusions reminiscent of those drawn some years ago by Stanley Hoffmann. What Hoffmann claimed was that integration was bound to stop well short of an authentic political community at the European level. While acknowledging that the Community system had taken on many of the responsibilities of the member states, Hoffmann contended that none of these responsibilities were associated with that core of "high politics" that defined the vital interests and,

therefore, the life blood of national political communities. Hoffmann illustrated his argument with striking metaphors—likening, for example, nationhood to the heart of the artichoke from which integration was merely stripping away the leaves while the core of national existence remained intact.[1] As I have already asserted, it now seems clear that Hoffmann was correct and that integration does not pose a serious alternative to the existing nation states.

While my analysis shares a good deal of common ground with Hoffmann, there are some important differences. He was primarily concerned with the shortcomings of the Community, but I am equally interested in its capabilities and its limitations. That is to say, I am more concerned with fitting the Community into the contemporary European policy context than in measuring it against some long range integrative goals. For this reason, I avoid Hoffmann's elusive search for the essence of political community, and concentrate instead on the political resources available to Community institutions, and on the kind of policy role that these resources enable the Community to play. I also steer clear of the distinctions Hoffmann wishes to make between high and low politics, or between politics and economics, as others have posed the issue. It is not, in my judgment, so much the characteristics of particular policy arenas as the basic features of the Community political structure that account for what the Community can or cannot accomplish. But despite these differ-

1. For one of his more extended analyses, see Stanley Hoffmann, "Europe's Identity Crisis: Between the Past and America," in *Daedalus* 93 (Fall 1964): 1244–97.

ences of purpose and perspective, there remain significant continuities between Hoffmann's work and the latter portions of this paper.

## THE POLICY RECORD OF THE EUROPEAN COMMUNITY

On the surface of things, the Community seems to be playing a wildly erratic role in the policy problems of Western Europe. Brussels is the acknowledged nerve center of European agricultural policy. In contrast, the Community seems altogether beside the point when it comes to matters like Eurocommunism, or the crises of civil authority in France in 1968, and more recently in Italy. Between these poles of relevance and irrelevance lie the many policy areas in which, as the articles in this volume make abundantly clear, the Community has been active, but with only mixed results. It is also important to realize that the Community's record has not only been erratic from issue area to issue area but within issue areas as well. In antitrust matters, for example, it has been possible to establish an effective mechanism for dealing with agreements in restraint of trade, but it has not been possible to get a merger policy off the ground. Similarly, a Regional Development Fund has been created, but the Community has not been able to agree on an overall development program. One finds these same patterns of partial success in energy and monetary policy, and in other matters as well.

This is not the place for a detailed review of Community policymaking, but rather for an effort to find the patterns which lie beneath all of the surface variations.[2] Two such patterns can be discerned.

The first pattern, and one on which most students of European integration would agree, is that the Community's reach regularly exceeds its grasp. That is to say, the Community regularly promises comprehensive programs to deal with regional problems, the energy shortage, monetary imbalances, restraints on competition, and the like. What it delivers are ad hoc schemes for coping with particular aspects of the general problem, or for heading off impending crises.

From the supranational perspective, this would all be dismissed as trivial or self-defeating. Rather than progressing towards union, the Community has, according to this way of thinking, chosen to function as a creature of the member states, with the crucial decisionmaking power residing in the Council of Ministers. Indeed, in the case of monetary policy, these decisions are in the hands of central bankers, and Community institutions are kept at arm's length. This is a far cry from the European Monetary Union which was supposed to refuel the expansive logic of sectoral integration in the seventies.[3] Only in agriculture has a comprehensive and effective Community program been established, and agricultural policy developed so long ago as to be of little

2. For a comprehensive analysis of the Community's policy record, see the excellent recent collection edited by Helen and William Wallace and Carole Webb, *Policy-Making in the European Communities* (London: John Wiley, 1977).

3. For details see Robert W. Russell, "Snakes and Sheiks: Managing Europe's Money," in Wallace, Wallace, and Webb, *Policy-Making*, pp. 69–89, and Michael Brenner, "Monetary Policy," this issue.

help in understanding the Community as we now know it.

The supranational perspective can, however, be misleading, because despite the failure to push systematically ahead towards integration the Community has shown remarkable staying power and even some capacity for growth. Established programs, like those for freeing the movement of labor, regulating agreements in restraint of trade, and maintaining the customs union, have continued to thrive. The Community has also taken on added responsibilities—for the Regional Development Fund and the harmonization of laws governing business practice, for example. Finally, the Community has decidedly become a factor to be reckoned with in international affairs. Although displaying the same sectoral variation in its external relations as in internal affairs, the European Community has become, as Dolan and Caporaso put it, a "coherent foreign policy actor" even beyond the scope of the Treaty. There has been cooperation in NATO and the United Nations and concerted action on agricultural and energy matters as well as in development policy toward the LDC's.[4]

The first kind of pattern which can be discerned in the Community's policy record is, therefore, somewhat perplexing in its own right. On the one hand, we have a Community system which promises more than it delivers and, in particular, has failed pretty much across the board to develop programmatic solutions to the policy problems it has tackled. On the other hand, a picture emerges of a developing bloc of nine states integrally, if problematically, linked to one another and increasingly turning a common face to the outside world on an important and growing range of issues.

Whatever we may learn from these loose generalizations, we cannot draw from this sort of analysis any insight into the reasons why the Community's policy record has developed in such an inconclusive fashion. For that insight we must adopt a different frame of reference, which takes us closer to issues of political structure and political resources. The argument put forward here is that the Community's notable policy failures— no European Monetary Union, no comprehensive energy plan, no overall regional program—are all due to the fact that these matters were too closely associated with the basic distributive bargains on which the legitimacy of the member states ultimately rests.

Once the major political forces at the national level have composed their differences and have accepted a policy plan, only two alternatives are open to the Community. A least common denominator solution established at the point of convergence among national policies is one option. Thus, it was possible to agree on a Regional Development Fund but not on a single Community scheme for distributing regional development monies. Such decisions have been left to the member states, since regional development is so integrally tied to sensitive national problems like inflation and separatism.[5] Similarly, restrictive practices

4. Michael B. Dolan and James A. Caporaso, "The External Policy of the Communities," this issue.

5. Helen Wallace, "The Establishment of the Regional Development Fund: Common Policy or Pork Barrel?" Policy-Making, pp. 137–63.

have been brought within the ambit of Community policy processes, but mergers are too integrally linked to ideological issues and to disputes over the economies of scale.[6] The other option is a kind of ad hoc pulling together in the face of some outside threat—the kind of defensive reaction that the Community finally mounted to the energy and monetary crises of the mid-70s. Coordinated community programs are only possible, however, on matters which are not directly tied to the basic distributive politics of the member states.

It is worth noting that the explanation that has just been offered for the failure of common policies to emerge and to be institutionalized avoids many of the conventional ways of approaching the problem. My position is not based on the countervailing interests of the member states, nor on the resistance of one or another state to the surrender of sóvereignty. Similarly, my argument is not rooted in the slippery distinction between economics and politics, nor on the assumption that the Community can operate effectively only when its Treaty mandate is clear and detailed. Whatever may be the merit of these explanations, my focus is elsewhere: on the political structure of the European Community.

The message of this section is that while the Community has developed impressive capabilities for composing differences among the member states and for administering even the most complex kinds of policy programs, Community institutions are in effect cut off from the wellsprings of national politics.

Accordingly, these institutions have no real resources for mobilizing consent for Community programs or, to put the same point in slightly different terms, for composing a political base at the Community level. These constricted decisionmaking capabilities are, as we shall see in the next section, reflective of the basic strengths and weaknesses of the political structure of the Community.

## THE COMMUNITY'S POLITICAL STRUCTURE

A necessary first step towards understanding the political structure of the European Community, as Rosenthal and Puchala have pointed out in this volume, is to abandon the supranational perspective that has dominated a major portion of the research on the institutions of the Community.[7] The focal point of supranationalism is on the aggregation of decisionmaking power at the Community level. Even more narrowly, the focus is on the Commission, the Parliament, and the Court of Justice which are the most manifestly supranational agents of integration. In contrast, the Council of Ministers and the Committee of Permanent representatives (COREPER) are viewed as creatures of the member states and, thus, as potential threats to integration. Since the Parliament has been largely impotent and the Court of Justice caught up in arcane legal conflicts, major attention is, in practice, directed to the struggle between the Commission and the Council for primacy in Community decisionmaking.

6. David Allen, "Policing or Policy-Making? Competition Policy in the European Communities," Policy-Making, 91–112.

7. For an earlier formulation, see Peter Busch and Donald Puchala, "Interests, Influence, and Integration: Political Structure in the European Communities," in Comparative Politics 9 (October 1976): 235–54.

The alternative perspective which will be employed in this section directs attention to the nature and extent of interpenetration of Community and national political institutions. According to this way of looking at things, it is less important that the Community institutions be capable of imposing their wills on the nation states than that the national and Community institutions be linked together in mutually relevant decisional processes. Busch and Puchala make roughly the same point: "The strength of EC is, then, a function of the degree of *structural integration* in the system, by which we mean the degree to which Community policies and programs facilitate the maintenance of influence structures permitting leaders to distribute rewards downwards and outwards." In other words, attention is directed away from the hierarchical images associated with supranationalism to the extent of continuity in the "system of linkages among elites."[8] What we shall discover is a complex picture of intense interpenetration coexisting with sharp disjunctures, and it is these continuities and discontinuities that help us understand patterns of policy relevance just discussed.

The major discontinuity in the Community system is between the general public and Community institutions. No provisions whatsoever have been made for popular participation in these institutions. Although there may be a modest change in this situation once the direct election of members of the European Parliament commences in 1979, this change will be meaningful only if a directly elected Parliament manages to gain a more

influential role in Community decision making. Adding to the problem is the esoteric and highly technical nature of much of the Community's business, which seldom engages attention at the grass roots. The Community is also unable to generate any significant symbolic attachments. All this means that there are no lines of communication, responsibility, or control between the general public and Community institutions.

The result is not only a manifestly undemocratic institutional structure but also the isolation of the Community from the public and, hence, from popular support. The immediate consequence of this discontinuity in the political structure of the European Community is not opposition but rather apathy. Studies of European public opinion continue to turn up what Leon Lindberg and I once referred to as a "permissive consensus" in favor of Community institutions and integration more generally. There is, however, a hollow ring to this endorsement. As Wildgen and Feld put it:

There appears to be a mild pro-integration consensus which, upon analysis, becomes unspecific and unarticulate. Using some of the best predictive variables uncovered by social science, we are still confronted by a direction of public opinion that is only marginally better than random in statistical terms. The masses of Europe, on this question, are enigmatic and seem to view integration with more tolerance than enthusiasm . . .[9]

In other words, interpenetration stops well short of the grass roots, thus depriving the Community of

8. Ibid., pp. 248 and 237.

9. John K. Wildgen and Werner J. Feld, "Evaluative and Cognitive Factors in the Prediction of European Unification," in *Comparative Political Studies* 9 (October, 1976): 331.

the sustenance which could be provided by an engaged citizenry.

At the opposite extreme are the legal and administrative processes of the Community. Here interpenetration is extensive. Individual firms caught up in Community rules, as well as the officials charged with implementing these rules, tend to behave in ways that obscure the boundaries between Community and national institutions.

At the heart of the matter is the emerging rule system which has been accepted as authoritative. The result is that a fairly normal pattern of legal and administrative relationships have been established. A study that I conducted in the mid-1960s indicated that even at that time lawyers and judges within the member states tended to accept the Community system as authoritative. While this did not preclude objections and occasional resistance to particular regulations and procedures, the objections themselves were drawn into established channels, thus further normalizing the Community legal system.[10] A parallel process seems to have developed among Eurocrats and national civil servants charged with a kind of joint responsibility for administering the more successfully integrated policy areas like agriculture, competition, and the customs union itself. While the relationships may not always operate smoothly, and are surely not free of conflict, there seems to be an understanding of mutuality and interdependence in a collective enterprise.

10. Stuart A. Scheingold, *The Law in Political Integration: The Evolution and Integrative Implications of Regional Legal Processes in the European Community*. Occasional Papers in International Affairs, no. 27. (Cambridge, MA: Center for International Affairs, June 1971).

It would be wrong, however, to think about legal and administrative interpenetration in terms of conventional notions of integration. The willingness to cooperate probably has more to do with careerism than Europeanism. The narrow career interests of lawyers and bureaucrats are served by interpenetration. The lawyers serve their clients by finding alternative avenues of legal recourse, and the bureaucrats, who see their jobs as technical, can obviously work better in a situation in which conflict is minimized and efficiency maximized. Indeed, one might even speculate that bureaucratic interpenetration is facilitated by the technocratic careerist orientation of the current crop of Eurocrats, who have replaced the committed Europeans who flocked to Luxembourg and to Brussels in the 1950's.

In between the discontinuity dividing the Community and national systems at the grassroots, and the emerging symbiosis of administrative and legal personnel, is the partial interpenetration of political elites. Contacts among cabinet level officials and their Community counterparts, the Commissioners, is maintained by frequent meetings of the Council of Ministers, and the intensity of these contacts is extended through the Committee of Permanent Representatives. As Rosenthal and Puchala point out in their article, this interpenetration even includes so-called political matters by way of "(c)hannels of fairly regular liaison (which) now link all of the foreign offices of the Nine and counterpart channels (which) tie in the Commission and the COREPER."[11] But while contact at

11. See Glenda G. Rosenthal and Donald J. Puchala, "Decisional Systems," this issue.

the highest levels may be regular and intense, the decisionmaking systems operate in relative isolation from one another. They do not really interpenetrate below the highest levels.

This restricted interpenetration can be explained by a kind of asymmetry between the national systems and the Community system. The national decisionmaking systems are rooted in patterns of political party and interest group competition. In other words, the governments depend on party support and the interaction between interest groups and executive agencies to develop and nurture political programs. But the Commission has only limited access to these vital political forces. It is true that there is a semblance of a party system in the European Parliament, but these parties are derivative— that is delegated by, and beholden to, the national parties—and the impotent Parliament is, in any case, unable to provide any programmatic support for the Commission. The interest group picture is a little less bleak, because there are a great many Eurogroups which make Brussels rather than the national capitals their home and focal point. These groups could provide the access and support that the Commission needs. This point has been made by William Averyt as follows:

Under certain condition (and these conditions often occur in industrialized democracies) *government agencies need interest groups to carry out their programs*. The interest groups are not simply buffers placed between the state and the individual, . . . rather they are instrumental for the state. They are integral parts of the long process whereby government policy is carried through to the citizenry.[12]

12. William Averyt, "Eurogroups, Clientela, and the European Community," in

Yet the bulk of interest group activity remains focused at the national level. Even the Eurogroups seem more strongly attracted to the Council of Ministers and the Committee of Permanent Representatives than to the Commission. The reasons for this, nicely detailed by Averyt, are less important for our purposes than the fact that they are deeply rooted and not likely to change in the foreseeable future. Thus, interpenetration is inhibited by the relative isolation of the Commission from important structures of political support and action. This is, moreover, a permanent condition of the partial discontinuity between the Community and national systems.

PROCESS AND POLICY

It is now time to put the two pieces of this analysis together—to make explicit the relationship between continuities and discontinuities in the political structure of the European Community and the erratic patterns of policy relevance discussed near the outset of this article. Briefly put, I am arguing that the European Community is an administrative or bureaucratic reality, but that its political existence is problematic. Hence, the Community's authority is limited because its legitimacy is circumscribed.

The Community is well-endowed with technical capabilities required to formulate policy and to implement policies once they have been accepted. There are, however, only limited leadership capabilities of the sort required to generate consent for policy initiatives. Because Community institutions have virtually no access to the minds and imagina-

*International Organization*, vol. 29 (Autumn 1975), p. 959. Italics in the original. As Averyt points out, this argument is drawn from the work of Joseph LaPalombara.

tions of its "citizenry," the Community is utterly without resources for shaping the values which ultimately determine the directions that politics will take. This simple schema, thus, leads to some sober but not necessarily gloomy conclusions about the policy relevance of the European Community.

One of these is that policy relevance is severely restricted by the Community's modest access to political party and interest group structures, and by its virtual isolation from the people of Europe. An initial expectation of supporters of European integration was that the Community might foster new patterns of political authority by tapping the political loyalties of an emergent European citizenry. Without this grip on the popular mind, the Community is in no position to participate in any of the basic distributive issues that are at the core of politics and public policy. There is, in other words, no reason to expect Community institutions to play any meaningful part in, or exercise any direct influence upon, the problems of economic, political, and social justice. If politics is really, as Harold Lasswell wrote, "who gets what, when, how" then the European Community is not truly political. All of these problems must necessarily be mediated through the structures of power established at the national level. Policy of this magnitude, thus, comes to Community decisionmaking processes prepackaged and beyond reconsideration. Similarly, it was at one time thought that Community institutions, that is the Commission, had capabilities for manipulating influential elites and thus for mobilizing support for policy initiatives. Given the very limited penetration of party and interest group structures by Community institu-

tions, it is now clear that such activities are beyond the capabilities of the European Community.

Some years ago I complained that students of integration were devoting too much attention to the process of integration and not enough to its consequences.[13] With more policy studies emerging and with less emphasis on supranationalism, some of the grounds on which my complaint rested no longer obtain. But in more general terms, the challenge posed in that article has not been answered. My appeal was that we should look at the consequences of integration on a grander scale—asking questions about the contribution that the European Community has (or has not) made to peace and security, as well as to the more equitable distribution of power and wealth within and beyond Western Europe. The analysis presented in this article suggests why no such investigations have been undertaken. On issues of that magnitude, the politics of the European Community has been and is likely to remain derivative. The Community simply does not have an independent role to play but must necessarily reflect the values and outlooks established in the member states.

We are left then with the European Community as an essentially facilitative, technocratic structure. Community institutions are convenient and effective mechanisms of policy coordination and are increasingly called upon to cope with matters which are outside the precise scope of Treaty defined activities. When this occurs, elabo-

13. Stuart A. Scheingold, "Domestic and International Consequences of Regional Integration," in Leon N. Lindberg and Stuart A. Scheingold, eds., *Regional Integration: Theory and Research* (Cambridge, MA: Harvard University Press, 1971), pp. 374–98.

rate steps are usually taken to distinguish an ex officio rubric for dealing with these matters and, in particular, for downplaying the role of the Commission. These efforts are, of course, an index of the general unwillingness to extend the progress of integration as such. On the other hand, the patterns of co-operation and consultation which have been nurtured by the Community, when added to the formidable legal/administrative apparatus, tend to guarantee that the member states will concert policy with one another. Moreover, it seems reasonable to believe that the member states will continue to work together either within or in conjunction with the institutions of the European Community.

## CONCLUSION

Only a more intrepid social scientist than I would attempt to forecast the future of the European Community. It seems a forbidding enough task to make sense out of the past and present—what with the recurrent crises, the sharp variations in institutional capabilities, and the checkered patterns of policy relevance. Still the linking of policy performance and institutional capabilities in this article does suggest certain long-term trends which may well obtain in the near-term future. Thus, it seems that the future of the European Community is reasonably secure but rather unexciting. The Community is useful and well established enough not to be at risk. Moreover, in contrast to the heroic days of Monnet and Hallstein, the Community is probably without the will and/or the means to provoke a crisis in the hope of advancing some integrative objective.

Under what circumstances might this change? First, it is possible but unlikely that direct election of members of the European Parliament might reduce the isolation of Community institutions from the grassroots. Whatever reservations one may have about the effectiveness of voting as a means of policy control, or as a way of assuring responsive political institutions, the symbolic importance of voting seems incontrovertible. Voting binds the citizen to the political system because it is a collective political act, preceded by the imposing campaign ritual which points up issues of concern, engages people's attention, and links officeholders to the general public. From quite another perspective, one can imagine economic crises of sufficient magnitude and duration that they would surely engulf the Community. It is, therefore, possible to work out scenarios which would threaten the prevailing tranquility.

It seems, however, more reasonable to project a stable future. Just as the Community seems unable to exert any appreciable impact on the fundamental problems of member state politics, so too does it seem largely untouched by such problems. Difficulties of much more restricted dimensions have, upon occasion, engendered strong if transient grassroots opposition to the Community. Indeed, it is ironic, given the aspirations of the founders, that in those rare instances when the public has been aroused by the Community, it has been in opposition to integration—the British left and the French farmers come most immediately to mind. But these brief storms were more the occasion for adjustments than for any serious threat to the stability of the Community. There is, in other words, a kind of silver lining that attaches to the Community's cloud of isolation from the national polities. Isolation becomes insulation, and is reinforced by the integral links that have developed among the member states as well as by the benefits of the emergent foreign policy bloc. Thus, we are left in the final analysis with strong reason to believe that the European Community will play an ever more prominent role in European and world affairs without ever moving any further along the integrative path plotted by its founders.

# MINKOFF

Chemin de la Mousse 46 — 1225 Chêne-Bourg / GENÈVE (Suisse)

## HISTORY OF THE SECOND INTERNATIONAL
## 1889 - 1914

The complete facsimile collection comprises:

**22 volumes in-8 and 1 volume in-4 bound in skivertex**

**The price of the complete collection is SF. 4.500.—.** Each volume may be bought separately.

Each Congress has been presented by a historian, either **Georges Haupt** or **Michel Winock** (with a preface in French and English).

For ease of reference, we have standardized book size, added a new page order and, where necessary, an index. It is hoped to publish the same documents in French, English and German.

Throughout the history of the Second International Workmen's Association, from 1889 to 1914, the socialist movement gained ground, first in Europe, and then in the other continents, as one of the major social and political forces of the contemporary world.

The sources of the Second International we are presenting are of two types. The main documents concerned are those relating to the periodical congresses that punctuate and most often constitute the history of the International, from that held in Paris in 1889 to that held in Basle in 1912. Besides these, for the last part of the period concerned (1909-1914), we have at our disposal the valuable periodical bulletin of the International Socialist Bureau, a central organ set up in 1901.

On the subject of these sources, which the Minkoff printing firm has undertaken to reproduce for the benefit of researchers, journalists, writers and students, the historian Georges Haupt writes as follows:

"Consultation of the minutes of the congresses and the documents of the I.S.B. is essential for all study of the efforts to coordinate socialist action on an international scale; the same is true for the reports on activities presented by the associated parties, for an understanding of the history of labour, of the introduction and progress of the socialist movement in the various countries.".

Up to this day, the sources of the history of the Second International have been confined to a small number of specialized libraries in Europe or belonged to private collectioners; it is for this reason that we trust a reproduction in extenso of these original texts will prove extremely valuable.

### VOLUMES DE LA COLLECTION

DOCUMENTS GÉNÉRAUX

1. Max BEER
Fifty Years of International Socialism. Londres, 1935.

2. Thomas KIRKUP
A History of Socialism. Londres et Edimbourg, 1892.

3. LES CONGRÈS SOCIALISTES INTERNATIONAUX
Ordre du jour et résolutions / La Manifestation Internationale du 1er Mai. Die Internationale und der Weltgrieg. Gand, Bruxelles et Leipzig, 1902, 1906 et 1916.

4. Jean LONGUET
Le mouvement socialiste international. Paris, 1913.

5. C. STEGMANN. – C. HUGO
Handbuch des Sozialismus. Zurich, 1897.

6.-7. CONGRÈS INTERNATIONAUX SOCIALISTES DE PARIS 1889.
Le Congrès marxiste.
Le Congrès possibiliste.

8. CONGRÈS INTERNATIONAL OUVRIER SOCIALISTE
Bruxelles, 16-23 août 1891.

9. CONGRÈS INTERNATIONAL OUVRIER SOCIALISTE
Zurich, 6-12 août 1893.

10.-11. CONGRÈS INTERNATIONAL SOCIALISTE DES TRAVAILLEURS ET DES CHAMBRES SYNDICALES OUVRIÈRES
Londres, 26 juillet - 2 août 1896.

12. A. HAMON
Le socialisme et le Congrès de Londres. Etude historique, Paris, 1897.

13. CONGRÈS SOCIALISTE INTERNATIONAL
Paris, 23-27 septembre 1900.

14-15. CONGRÈS SOCIALISTE INTERNATIONAL
Amsterdam, 14-20 août 1904.

16-17-18. CONGRÈS SOCIALISTE INTERNATIONAL
Stuttgart, 6-24 août 1907.

19-20-21. CONGRÈS SOCIALISTE INTERNATIONAL
Copenhague, 28 août-3 septembre 1911.

22. CONGRÈS INTERNATIONAL EXTRAORDINAIRE
Bâle, 24-25 novembre 1912.
LA CONFÉRENCE INTERNATIONALE SOCIALISTE DE STOCKHOLM 1917.

23. LE BUREAU SOCIALISTE INTERNATIONAL
Bulletin périodique du Bureau socialiste international 1909-1913.
Nos 1-11 et suppl.

**15 volumes disponibles**

### PLEASE ASK FOR OUR DETAILED CATALOGUE

## Protest at Selma

*Martin Luther King, Jr., and the Voting Rights Act of 1965*

David J. Garrow

The first detailed account of how the Voting Rights Act of 1965 came into being and how the strategy of Martin Luther King, Jr., and the Southern Christian Leadership Conference at Selma won this landmark victory for Southern blacks.

"A significant contribution to civil rights literature."—*Library Journal*
Illus. $15.00

## Quaker Experiences in International Conciliation

C. H. Mike Yarrow
Foreword by Anatol Rapaport

As far back as the early 1900s, the Quakers have been engaged in a program of quiet private diplomacy that won them a Nobel Peace Prize in 1947. During the turbulent 1960s, they acted as unofficial conciliators in several tense situations. This comprehensive study of Quaker peacemaking activities focuses primarily on the variety and effectiveness of their efforts in Berlin from 1962 to 1973, in India/Pakistan in 1965, and in Nigeria from 1967 to 1970.
$10.00

## The Origins of the Second World War

Maurice Baumont
translated by
Simone De Couvreur Ferguson

"Baumont has produced a solid diplomatic history of the six years preceding the outbreak of World War II. He brings to his subject an unrivaled command of the literature, an incisive intellect, and a style which is both graceful and pithy. . . . All in all, this volume must be seen as the exposition of the 'French' view of the origins of the war."
—*Library Journal*   $22.00

## The Presidential Election Game

Steven J. Brams

In this book Brams applies the tools of modern decision theory and game theory to the analysis of presidential campaigns and elections. His use of scientific modeling to illuminate all aspects of the presidential election process—from state primaries and national conventions to coalition politics and Richard Nixon's resignation—adds a new dimension to our understanding of this important aspect of American politics.

"The examples are contemporary, the writing is crisp, and the insights are prodigious. In short, the reading is rewarding."—*Library Journal*
Cloth $15.00   Paper $3.95

## Southeast Asian Transitions

*Approaches through Social History*

edited by Ruth T. McVey
with the assistance of
Adrienne Suddard

In six major essays written to honor the late Harry J. Benda, an international group of scholars focuses on a particular concern of Benda's—the impact of advanced colonialism on Southeast Asian societies and the attempt of the Southeast Asians to develop ideological and institutional responses. The authors have approached the subject from the angle of local history, showing through the study of significant small-scale events how people far from the centers of political power reacted to the pressures for change.
$17.50

## Yale University Press

New Haven and London

# Book Department

|  | PAGE |
|---|---|
| INTERNATIONAL RELATIONS AND POLITICS | 169 |
| AFRICA, ASIA AND LATIN AMERICA | 174 |
| EUROPE | 189 |
| UNITED STATES | 192 |
| SOCIOLOGY | 200 |
| ECONOMICS | 212 |

## INTERNATIONAL RELATIONS AND POLITICS

PETER BOYCE. *Foreign Affairs for New States*. Pp. x, 289. New York: St. Martin's Press, 1978. $19.95.

This small and readable volume, by Professor Boyce of the University of Queensland in Australia, does not actually deal with foreign affairs for the new states, as its title implies. It is primarily a study of the professional machinery available to foreign offices in the Third World. Despite this rather courageous attempt to supply meaningful data and to discern patterns where so far there has only been an analytic void, the finished product is a rather pedestrian description of the obvious. Although allusions are made to the classical manuals of European diplomatic practice by Harold Nicolson and Ernest Satow, the Boyce study strenuously seeks differences in Third World diplomatic behavior. Some distinction and a separate treatment are justified by the existence of such elements as a greater fluidity in foreign policy, an increase in international disputes, the expression of "moral indignation," new and subtle forms of dependencies, and a numerical preponderance in international organizations, leading to their politicization.

Professor Boyce assembles a convincing mass of material although drawn only from the Commonwealth states of Asia and Africa. He equates statehood with a capacity to negotiate treaties, explains the metropolitan influence in the foreign affairs machinery, and analyzes political leadership in foreign policymaking. In the process, executive control is limited to one page, foreign ministers are seen as travelling more and serving longer, and the influence of media, opposition and interest groups are described as minimal. The foreign offices are relegated to being "relatively unimportant in policy formulation," and their modus operandi is "the letter, the telegram, the telephone call and the personal visit." (p. 89) Occupational hazards for diplomats include "political loyalty, personal safety and intestinal fortitude" (p. 106). Diplomatic representation "must be weighed against available resources" (p. 149), and sanctions should be applied only "in a gradual crescendo of severity" (p. 162).

It is difficult to generalize about a small volume on Third World diplomacy without lapsing into the obvious. The reader is also treated to three case studies: on Papua, New Guinea; Malaysia; and Singapore. These are too brief to be useful and factually too dispersed to enlighten on diplomatic practice. On p. 226, Malaysia's cabinet makes a "unilateral decision about expelling Singapore" from the Federation, a statement changed one page later to "Singapore's secession." There are other assumptions that are questionable and other prescriptions which are doubtful. Unfortunately, the presentation is marred by a lack of proofreading, evidenced on almost every page. Despite these shortcomings, Professor Boyce needs to be commended for seeking to simplify what is a complex problem for any one country, without speaking about the ninety countries of the Third World whose only common denominator is the timing of their independence.

HANS H. INDORF
Washington, DC

LAWRENCE FREEDMAN. *US Intelligence and the Soviet Strategic Threat*. Pp. xv, 235. Boulder, CO: Westview Press, 1977. $22.50.

ERNEST J. YANARELLA. *The Missile Defense Controversy: Strategy, Technology, and Politics, 1955–1972*. Pp. xi, 236. Lexington: The University Press of Kentucky, 1977. $17.25.

These books parallel each other more closely than their titles might suggest. Freedman defines a Soviet strategic threat "as one of a set of conceivable changes in the Soviet force structure that would, in the absence of counter-measures, seriously diminish America's strategic strength" (p. 5). He distinguishes between threat assessments and intelligence estimates; the Soviet activity which the intelligence community monitors becomes a threat only when it enhances, or is perceived as enhancing, some American vulnerability. His survey of the intelligence community is directed largely to the question of how much the intelligence estimates remain independent of policymakers' judgments about vulnerabilities. Through much of the 1960s, the strategic vulnerability most debated among policymakers was the lack of an ABM defense. Thus, much of Freedman's book deals with the same issue as Yanarella's; while Yanarella's as well as Freedman's, though more briefly, sets the missile defense controversy into a longer time sequence demarcated by its predecessors and sequels in strategic debate.

Although both deal largely with the same issues, and both began as doctoral dissertations, the two books differ greatly in style. Freedman's pages of small print are dense with data, the argument closely reasoned, much interpretation left to the reader. Yanarella is more boldly interpretative, more willing to draw from his case study large generalizations about national policy formulation. Yanarella's book is also considerably easier to read and seems to have drawn more attention even among serious academicians. For it to continue to do so would be unfortunate; Yanarella's study is factually thorough and intellectually stimulating, but Freedman's probes further into nuances and complexities.

Yanarella takes as his point of departure the frequently stated assertion that it is technology that governs strategic-weapons policy, that what can be done technologically will be done. Conceding that much can be said for this argument, he seeks to return, however, to the men and institutions whose assumptions continue, he insists, to give direction to technology. He argues that while Secretary of Defense Robert S. McNamara hoped to restrain the arms race, McNamara also gave the race added impetus. McNamara retained certain crucial assumptions of his predecessors, notably that the United States is challenged by a determined adversary with a dynamic weapons technology, and that offensive weapons always get through. By reducing interservice rivalry, McNamara furthermore removed a curb upon each of the service's development. Hence an unrestrained, centralized research and development network in the Department of Defense in fact gave technological development almost free rein. American weapons development competed not against the Soviets but against itself, the designers of offensive weapons competing against the designers of the defense. McNamara's assumption that the offense will always get through gave an advantage, however, to the development of offensive weapons. The bias in favor of the offensive was critical in causing the rejection of the ABM, while accepting, with few misgivings, the MIRV, a "far more dangerous destabilizing" breakthrough than the ABM, but "developed without the faintest understanding of its revolutionary character" (pp. 165, 166).

Freedman is not so sure that the MIRV is all that revolutionary, and it is the value of Freedman's book to demonstrate that even Yanarella's complexities are not quite complex enough. For example, Yanarella plays down a bit too much all outside influence on American weapons development. It is Freedman who reminds us, at the heart of Yanarella's case study, that the concern of the NATO allies over not being consulted on American moves toward a hardpoint anti-Soviet ABM defense was important in turning McNamara toward an anti-Chinese system. In the end, furthermore, one of Freedman's major conclusions is not far distant from the theory of self-generating technology with which Yanarella begins, but Freedman has added considerable sophistication: ". . . the key arguments over the sources and character of United States strategic strength tend to be organized around the vices and virtues of particular weapons systems. . . ." It is through the arguments over specific weapons systems that "strategic doctrines become more explicit in order to provide convincing rationales as to why a particular weapons system should or should not be deployed" (p. 191).

These are excellent and remarkably complementary books.

RUSSELL F. WEIGLEY
Temple University
Philadelphia

WALTER LaFEBER. *The Panama Canal: The Crisis in Historical Perspective*. Pp. xii, 248. New York: Oxford University Press, 1978.

This study should have been required reading for every adult American—starting with Ronald Reagan—during our recent, seemingly interminable debate on the new Panama Canal treaties. Before they were narrowly ratified last spring, these treaties threatened to bring the United States government to a halt. If Professor LaFeber's book had been read and understood by the members of the Senate and the electorate, one feels that near paralysis could have been avoided—assuming, of course, that the Senate and the nation are both rational and educable.

That is not an assumption one can make

with equanimity on the basis of this assessment of the history of U.S.-Panamanian relations. LaFeber takes pains to show that "Panama did not magically materialize at Theodore Roosevelt's command," that Panamanian nationalism preceded TR's big stick diplomacy by several centuries, and that the historical facts will not support the view that the Canal Zone is sovereign United States territory like Alaska or Florida. While myth making is an honored American political pastime, these myths have so obscured the colonialism inherent in United States-Panamanian relations since 1903 as to have invested much of the debate in this country over the new treaties with a chest-thumping air of unreality that has been both dangerous and absurd.

That the relationship has been and remains a colonial one is clear from nearly every page of this study and, as LaFeber notes in closing, "such a colonial relationship had begun to be historically outdated in Asia and Africa even in 1903 when it was established between the United States and Panama. Certainly it was a dangerous anachronism by the mid-1970's." Colonialism implies not simply the exploitation of a weak power by a stronger one, but the nearly total dependence of the former on the policies and whims of the latter, often with the result—especially in instances of informal or extra-constitutional colonialism, such as this one—that the imperial power, at best, ignores its colony and, at worst, cheats it, reneging on commitments. Both tendencies are evident in the history of United States-Panamanian relations.

My suggestion that LaFeber's study be required reading does not imply that it's tough going. Thoroughly researched —including interviews in Panama and Washington—and lucidly written, the book is entertaining as well as enlightening. One can only wish that Oxford Press had employed a copy editor to exorcise whatever impish spirit produced such embarrassments as "less riskier ventures" (p. 9), "doubtlessly resulted" (p. 31), and "will doubtlessly endorse" (p. 208). These should not, however, obscure the sanity and balanced judgment of this excellent history.

LYNN H. MILLER

Temple University
Philadelphia

ROBERT J. MADDOX. *The Unknown War with Russia: Wilson's Siberian Intervention.* Pp. ix, 156. San Rafael, CA: Presidio Press, 1977. $9.95.

This little book is ambitious in attempting to debunk Woodrow Wilson's gilded image in foreign affairs. Professor Maddox has brought new evidence to light, organized his material carefully, and laid out common-sense conclusions (one suspects in a Puritan spirit) in plain language. I think this essay will enjoy greater significance as a milestone in research into the American presidency than as a gravestone over Wilson's reputation. That may well be Maddox' goal and, if he has intervened in the dispute over the Wilson legacy with goals so limited, he may legitimately claim to have scored some points in a fight with no knock-downs.

Granted that Wilson's first reaction to Bolshevik success was one of antipathy, one must next inquire what policy measures embodied this antipathy. The record, as Professor Maddox presents it, is tantalizingly suggestive. During those halycon days in the transition between two epochs, Wilson and his advisors ". . . knew little more than what appeared in the press" before the first sketchy reports from the American embassy arrived. An entire cabinet meeting on November 9 was devoted to Russia, following which, according to the semi-official *New York Times*, the Cabinet adopted a wait-and-see attitude. No official record of that meeting has seen the light of day. Yet Secretary of State Lansing speculated on the same day that some "strongman" might emerge who would unify the nation. On November 12, in a public address, the President characterized the new Russian leaders as "idle dreamers." This is at least a shockingly casual comment from a head of government if that government had genuinely adopted a temporizing policy a

mere three days before. Recalling that the last period of Wilsonian "watchful waiting" led to intervention in Mexico, it seems at least arguable that the Washington government: (1) had better sources of information than Maddox credits them with; (2) put forward the "wait-and-see" story as a *laissez-entendre* through the *New York Times*; and (3) quite possibly resolved in Cabinet, on November 9, to do whatever appeared feasible to facilitate the emergence of a government that could preserve democracy and continue the war.

As Maddox notes, "Decisions made behind the scenes strongly suggest that President Wilson opposed the Bolsheviks from the outset. . . ." The concatenation of events alone is indicative. On November 11, four days after the Bolshevik coup, two days after a Cabinet meeting without surviving notes, and one day before the President's slighting reference to "idle dreamers," the Russian Ambassador announced that he would not recognize the Bolshevik regime—but would continue to represent "Russia" until a legal successor regime appeared! It would of course be impossible for a diplomat without credentials to occupy and administer an embassy complex without the tacit support of the host country. Maddox characterizes this situation as "an item of diplomatic *curiosa*," but it seems to signal clearly that the Administration was already *partipris* in the Russian political struggle.

"Provocative" is the only word to describe the evidence Maddox has selected to illustrate the leverage the Administration exerted on this new fulcrum. The Russian embassy's assets, valued at more than fifty-six million dollars (deposited at Citibank) were expended to arm both Whites and Czechs with the active assistance of United States government agencies. Twice the State Department interceded to induce the bank to defer collecting obligations, previously floated on the money market, which would have severely reduced the embassy's ability to execute contracts. One of the ancillary conclusions Professor Maddox does not draw is that if the Soviet government consented to make a token payment on the imperial bonds repudiated by Lenin, it would be symbolically subsidizing intervention! This is heady stuff indeed.

When Wilson did decide to send troops to Siberia, in uneasy collaboration with the Japanese in July 1918, N. D. Baker, the Secretary of War who had previously opposed the decision, in effect took himself out of the chain of command by handing General Graves the President's aide-memoire without any specific military instructions. Graves adhered scrupulously to the injunction to avoid siding in Russian internal politics. Thereby he gave offense to every other armed force in Siberia. Further, he accurately predicted Admiral Kolchak's downfall as Supreme Ruler in Omsk. In Maddox' view the military were the most objective observers of the alien Russian scene, whereas American diplomats' views were colored by their close associations with various representatives of Russian social opinion. Is there a moral here?

To conclude, what is presented as a study in intervention takes on the appearance of a Puritan homily on the sins of the imperial and liberal presidency. This interpretation could be innocently misleading. It suggests a perception of Wilson as a liberal Prometheus whose historical reputation is ravaged by the claws of Professor Maddox. But in ranging himself among the opponents of Bolshevism Wilson would have been lost among a large majority of Russians; far from appearing heroic, he adopted the policy of the average man. The problems he faced in trying to "reconcile the American people to the need for intervention . . ." flowed from the weakness of his position rather than its strength. This is the opposite of the situation in a truly imperial state in which *quod principi placet leges habet virorum*. Yet to condemn intervention as a "total failure" appears overly narrow and hence overly harsh.

The prosaic truth is that geography, circumstances, political institutions, and military capacity dealt Wilson a weak hand. The titular head of a second-class power adopted a strategy of no trump— with the usual results. But he eschewed overcommitment and maintained acceptable relations with the first-class powers while Congressional opposition deterred him from an improvident squandering of resources of the kind that destroyed the myth of the later imperial presidency. It could have been worse. Military intervention in foreign politics, concealed by domestic subterfuge, is not a practice to be recommended to democratic governments.

DALE LA BELLE
Columbia University
New York

FRANS N. STOKMAN. *Roll Calls and Sponsorship: A Methodological Analysis of Third World Group Formation in the United Nations.* Pp. x, 338. Leyden: A. W. Sijthoff, 1977. $34.75.

In many ways, this is not one book, but two: one proposes a methodology for analyzing voting behavior in legislatures; the other, explores aspects of the behavior of developing nations in the United Nations. Both books are of interest, but it is possible that two quite dissimilar audiences will find some profit in this work.

The methodological explication is comparatively clear, for a complex matter, and was probably written for a general audience of political scientists. Anyone who has a survey course in statistics should follow the procedures with careful reading. For methodologists, there will be frustrations, because proofs are usually omitted and, for more detailed explanations, reference is repeatedly made to a paper given at a conference in Munich or to a work in preparation by Dr. Stokman and his colleagues in the Netherlands.

Two sets of techniques are advanced and used in the volume. One set involves measuring the distance between two delegations at the UN based on roll call voting on colonial and economic issues. The techniques are based on a minimum of assumptions but involve the use of an estimated probability of a particular vote (i.e. yes, no, abstain). The author demonstrates that different probability estimates give different results; in such a situation, one wonders why Bayesian techniques were not employed. Also, Dr. Stokman

(p. 98) claims that the distances with one of his measures ($C_4$) have normal distribution; if this be true, one wonders why confidence testing of these differences was not performed. The author states that the techniques could be used with profit by analysts of any legislature, and this reviewer agrees.

The second set of techniques involves the concept of cosponsorship of General Assembly resolutions, and the author rejects frequency of sponsorship as a measure. Instead, networks of cosponsorship using graph theory is used and the object of the technique is to be able to make a statement about leadership.

Space limitations of the review prevent a detailed discussion of the numerous uses to which the various measures were put. The analysis was divided into four time periods (1950–1955+, 1956–1959+, 1960–1963+, and 1965–1968) and focused on developing nations. Much of the analysis compared Asian, African, and Latin American nations. In general, the study found that during the 1950s Latin America was more influential than Africa or Asia; subsequently there was a shift to Asia, then Africa. Today, all three groups cooperate within the "Group of 77," but Africa and Asia are much closer to each other than Latin America is to either. Yugoslavia is included in the Stokman analysis, as a member of the Afro-Asian group, and proves to be the leader on socioeconomic issues, while India leads on the colonial isues. Within Latin America, Brazil is the colonial issue leader and Argentina the socioeconomic issue leader.

In summary, this is a very interesting book which has information of value to a number of different specialties within political science: methodologists, area specialists, and United Nations analysts. It also details an approach that could be of value to those students of American, or other national, politics who are interested in legislatures. Probably, no one will agree with all of the findings or the approaches in this book, but there will be few who cannot learn something of value.

O. ZELLER ROBERTSON, JR.
University Center
Michigan

## AFRICA, ASIA, AND LATIN AMERICA

TONY BARNETT. *The Gezira Scheme: An Illusion of Development*. Pp. 192. Totowa, NJ: Frank Cass, 1977. $30.00.

There are two types—or more precisely, two ends of a continuum—of radical or critical social scientists: those who bring their insights, formulations, and commitments to a study and find themselves in a struggle to recognize, acknowledge, and cope with a very complex and subtle reality; and then there are those who struggle to fit anything encountered into a preordained and rather simplistic framework of analysis and assertion. The results in the former case, frequently a bit messy, sometimes seem to fall between two stools, and yet they usually strike one as exhibiting good faith and considerable good sense. The results in the latter case, usually very neat, seem to be airtight, even stifling and suffocating; one has the sense that conclusions were established long ago and that the study is a perfunctory ritual, the faith involved being directed toward established doctrines rather than the spirit of inquiry.

I regret to say that the work in question, Barnett's *The Gezira Scheme*, seems to me to lean rather toward the second type of work, toward the doctrinaire, the preordained, the perfunctory, the simplistic, the closed, and the mean spirited. I regret to say this because *The Gezira Scheme* is an on-the-ground fieldwork-based study of an important development scheme, field studies are a considerable improvement over ideological pronouncements, and serious studies of development schemes are few and much needed. But I regret even more that an opportunity for an open-minded, sensitive, and balanced assessment has been squandered, and that the reader is likely to be convinced of little more than the author's very definite point of view.

The Gezira scheme—which Barnett characterizes in his subtitle as "An Illusion of Development"—is a large scale cotton production system, based upon extensive irrigation in the area between the White and Blue Niles in central Sudan. Established under the British colonial regime and continuing to the present day, it produces the high quality cotton that is one of the Sudan's most important exports and sources of foreign earnings. It was and is run as a formal organization under government supervision. The main participants in the scheme are the government, the organization, and the tenants, assisted by laborers.

Barnett's central argument is that the scheme has been run as a part of the international capitalist system, with production of cotton and its sale for profit as the primary and almost exclusive goal, and with relatively little concern for the social and economic welfare of the tenants. There are three aspects of the difficult status of the tenants: first, as a result of the terms of tenancy, they have been wrenched out of their traditional social milieu and have become more or less atomised. Second, they have very little control over their conditions of work, because they are at the lowest level of a hierarchical, formal, authoritarian, and mechanistic organization. Third, after the costs of labor and of loans to carry them through difficult periods, and in the face of high costs of imported food and consumer goods, the tenants realize relatively little from their efforts. Added to all of this, and exacerbating it, is the advantage that those who came into the scheme with resources have, and the high standard of living of the scheme officials.

Barnett supports his case with documents and interviews to show that the production of cotton is the main goal of the organization and that attempts at decentralization to give the tenants a greater degree of participation and control have failed. He provides statistical analysis to show that tenants cannot, in most phases of their family cycle, provide the labor necessary to work their allotted plots. Case studies are given to illustrate "the manipulation of water and the manipulation of men" by the better off tenants for their further betterment. Background material on the scheme officials is set out to show why they are conservative, and stress formal rules and technical problems rather than social problems. And all of this is set within a sketchy

historical framework to show the underpinnings of the scheme in government policy.

There is no doubt that Barnett has put his finger on many of the shortcomings and costs of the scheme. But his overall assessment seems less than balanced. He acknowledges that tenants have a regular and secure living, while emphasizing that the standard of living is too low. He recognizes throughout, the importance of the Gezira cotton to the national economy of the Sudan, but stresses the constraints that this places upon social innovation. He points up the costs of the scheme but is not able, or at least makes no attempt here, to suggest alternative modes given the constraints of the national economy. And while dwelling upon the difficult conditions of the tenants, he makes no attempt to consider what their circumstances would be without the scheme, or how they fare in comparison with other cultivators in the Sudan. In short, Barnett presses the point that the tenants are badly off, but he does not indicate in contrast to whom, or in relation to what realistically conceivable alternative arrangements, they are badly off. This lack of comparative framework undercuts his conclusions and makes his approach suspect.

How much good Cass has done by publishing this book is open to question; that they will do well seems certain with a price of $30 for a 192 page book.

PHILIP CARL SALZMAN
McGill University
Montreal
Canada

JEFFREY BUTLER, ROBERT I. ROTBERG, and JOHN ADAMS. *The Black Homelands of South Africa: The Political and Economic Development of Bophuthatswana and Kwazulu.* Pp. 260. Berkeley: University of California Press, 1977. $12.50.

This work originated as a study for the Office of External Research of the Department of State but, fortunately, its official origins do not in any way detract from its value. Four of its chapters are devoted to the ethnic, geographic, and historical context, the legislative, administrative, and political arrangements of the so-called Homelands. The final three concentrate on finance and economic development. The whole constitutes an excellent compendium of facts about the Homelands and their political and administrative development up to 1976. It is analysis surprisingly free of interpretative content. Interpretations are implicit rather than explicit, although the reader cannot fail to make his own from the facts presented. It is all the more devastating for that.

The Homelands represent an effort to reconcile what has always been the fundamental problem for white South Africa: to achieve a balance between the desire for opulence and the need for internal defence. The Homelands can remain, like politically independent Botswana, Lesotho, and Swaziland, catchments for labor, while providing the opportunity to 'rusticate' the unemployed and the disaffected. Yet the final chapters of this book demonstrate that the Homelands have become something else. They have become the means by which the old 'reserves' can be penetrated by white capitalist enterprise. They are in fact political window dressing for economic integration, not so much acts of internal decolonization as acts of internal neo-colonialism. Perhaps the most telling sentence in the book comes in the final chapter: "Accelerated development will lead to greater dependency."

Nonetheless, there may be a political paradox. The most significant development of recent years (and here the book has to a certain extent been overtaken by events) has been the radicalization of the black Homeland leaders. They have been forced along a radical path in order to attempt to maintain their support among Homeland expatriates who are employed by whites elsewhere in South Africa (66 percent of all Tswana and 49 percent of all Zulu live outside their Homelands). These leaders have found themselves able to say things that would land them in detention but for their political role in the Homelands. No country is prepared to recognize the independence of Homelands like the Transkei, yet the Homeland leaders have an international position that has placed them beyond the reach of the South African police and security forces. There are ample signs that the Homeland leaders have not radicalized themselves nearly enough to satisfy their constituents on the Rand, but the increase in detentions and repression generally, since this book was published, is further indication of the opportunities open to them. In creating this connection between Homelands and white cities, the South African regime has created its own destabilizing element.

This book is an exceptionally valuable source which, moreover, disproves its own subtitle. The Homelands are far from being about development. It is to be hoped that this volume, and the report on which it was based, have been carefully read in the State Department.

JOHN M. MACKENZIE
University of Lancaster
England

MARTIN CHANOCK. *Britain, Rhodesia and South Africa, 1900–1945: The Unconsummated Union.* Pp. vii, 289. Totowa, NJ: Frank Cass, 1977. $22.50.

Rhodesia is the last great problem for British colonial policy, but it is far from being a problem of recent making. Throughout the history of colonialism, Rhodesia has been a thorn in Britain's side. On several occasions the British Government has attempted to extract that thorn. On each occasion it has simply succeeded in driving it deeper. This book is about Britain's efforts to find a policy for Rhodesia in the context of southern Africa.

The dilemma facing the British was what to do with Middle Africa. Policy for western and eastern Africa was reasonably clear, certainly by the 1920s, even if not always consistently directed. But where was the southern frontier to lie — on the Limpopo or on the Zambezi, or indeed beyond? Were the Central African states to be part of eastern or of southern policy, or was an entirely separate policy possible, even the creation of a great central African state straddling the Zambezi. The difficulties lay in the chartered company origins of the central territories and in the presence of white settlers there; they were exacerbated by Jan Smuts' ambitions to create a united states of southern Africa which would incorporate: the High Commission territories of Bechuanaland (Botswana); Basutoland (Lesotho); Swaziland; and the territories of the British South Africa Company in Southern and Northern Rhodesia, extending as far north as captured German territory in Tanganyika.

Chanock's aim is to revise the old trusteeship interpretations of these events, as expressed for example in Ronald Hyam's *The Failure of the Expansion of South Africa*. For Hyam, as the shape of South African native policy emerged, Britain woke up to her trusteeship responsibilities and inflicted a series of defeats on South Africa. Chanock sees the development of the Union of South Africa not as a defeat for British liberalism, but as a victory for British neoimperialism. South Africa remained, even under nationalist governments, within the British sphere. Policy for Rhodesia was directed towards securing that end, and was always subordinate to it. Rhodesia was, in short, designed throughout her history to be a counterpoise. Cecil Rhodes's conception in occupying Rhodesia in 1890 had been the outflanking and ultimate taking over of the Boer republics. Later, Rhodesia was to be seen as the means of keeping Smuts and the loyal Afrikaners in power. This was the internal counterpoise. When that failed, a great Central African dominion was planned (the Federation of 1953) to attempt to guide Nationalist South Africa along the paths of British righteousness by precept and example. This was the external counterpoise. Yet, despite all this talk of counterpoise policies, Chanock admits that British colonial policy cannot be seen as a monolithic grand design: rather was it a series of inconclusive incompetencies.

This book is essentially a political and diplomatic history. Therein lies its weakness. Chanock himself notes that ultimately politics were irrelevant in the maintenance of the British economic ties with South Africa. Smuts' ambitions in Rhodesia foundered on the bourgeois nationalism of the Southern Rhodesian white electorate in 1923. British ambitions for a Central African Federation foundered on a rising tide of black nationalism in Northern Rhodesia and Nyasaland. Yet the economic geography remained consistent. The economic frontier never lay either on the Limpopo or the Zambezi. South Africa and the ex-company territories, Rhodesia and Zambia, have remained part of the same economic system regardless of the regimes in Pretoria, Salisbury, or Lusaka. Mining and other capitalist interests would no doubt have preferred some such grand political designs as that of Smuts, but it is a combination of their adaptability, and the power of the geography of railway lines and the like, that have rendered the twists and turns of British decision making ultimately irrelevant. Minerals in rocks speak louder than policies in shifting sands.

JOHN M. MACKENZIE
University of Lancaster
England

RICHARD E. BISSELL. *Apartheid and International Organizations*. Pp. xiii, 231. Boulder, CO: Westview Press, 1977, $17.50.

With activist undergraduate students and concerned clergymen, there has been a slow, but steady drive on several American university campuses to urge university boards of trustees to sell their stock in multinational corporations with investments in the Republic of South Africa. This campaign of disinvestment, coupled with the stress of the Carter Administration upon the Helsinki Accords and other international manifestations of concern for individual human rights, suggests the need for greater clarification of the complexities of Southern African racial politics in the era of decolonization. The author, who is affiliated with the Foreign Policy Institute in Philadelphia, and is the managing director of the prestigious foreign affairs quarterly *Orbis*, has provided the lay and specialist reader with an eminently readable and remarkably objective analysis of the patterns of interaction between the Republic of South Africa and the welter of international organizations (including the United Nations family as well as the Organization of African Unity) which have been used, with greater or lesser success, to redress the imbalance of power within South Africa, thus hoping to terminate the system of minority white rule described as apartheid.

Dr. Bissell's book, which grew out of his 1973 Fletcher School of Law and Diplomacy doctoral dissertation, "Conflict Control among International Organizations: The Apartheid Dispute," devotes almost no attention to those transnational organizations called nongovernmental organizations (see pp. 152–153) and deliberately excludes Namibian (South West African) affairs from detailed consideration (p. 50). Such deletions allow him to focus much more sharply on what the Pretoria regime has long insisted are its own domestic affairs, supposedly outside the purview of U.N. consideration under the domestic jurisdiction clause of the U.N. Charter. His discussion (on pp. 13–16) of the "internationalization of the apartheid dispute" in the introductory chapter is one of the most prescient and insightful that this reviewer has ever seen in print. Dr. Bissell draws attention, in a nontechnical way, to the game that is being played in the United Nations (pp. 15 and 33) with respect to this issue, thus linking it with the larger treatment that one finds in the provocative study by Abraham Yeselson and Anthony Gaglione, *A Dangerous Place: The United Nations as a Weapon in World Politics*. The author is able to unravel the dispute in such a way as to demonstrate the cleavage between form or rhetoric, on the one hand, and substance, on the other hand (pp. 73–74). He interprets the clash between South Africa and its African foes and their allies in the United Nations as one of "symbolic conflict" (p. 144). African hostility regarding apartheid has involved what the author regards as "spillover" (pp. 48 and 85) into arenas beyond the United Nations, such as the Commonwealth of Nations, from which South Africa was in effect forced to resign.

The Africans, in contrast to those who are loathe to interfere in the internal affairs of other nations, deem apartheid to be "static aggression" (p. 95) and, therefore, the object of a just war in the medieval sense. These states, as Dr. Bissell so correctly avers, are acting as the agents of the disenfranchised majority polity in South Africa, namely, the African people themselves who do not have the requisite sovereignty to fight this battle in international forums open only to nation-states (p. 166). The foes of apartheid have been most successful in sensitizing world public opinion to the nature of apartheid, thanks to a vigorous campaign of public education via United Nations-sponsored media, but they have had the least success in those endeavors which involved economic or military force, epitomized by the United Nations Security Council and the International Bank for Reconstruction and Development. The Western Powers, whose nationals have considerable investments in South Africa, and whose regimes prefer gradual rather than radical reform, are able to utilize their vetoes or weighted votes in these two bodies which, unlike the General Assembly, the Africans cannot dominate by sheer force of numbers. Thus, contends the author, "The dispute . . . has arrived at a remarkably stable condition: freedom for the General Assembly to pass any and all resolutions, and the freedom for South Africa to ignore them. The Africans won the battle for social sanctions in international organizations, and apartheid remains" (pp. 162–163).

Although Dr. Bissell uses U.N. documents with great deftness, his touch is less sure when dealing with the domestic and diplomatic history of South Africa. He appears to be unaware of the contributions made by James Barber, Amelia Leiss, and Robert Good in this area and he makes no use of the debates of either House of the South African Parliament, which would illustrate lucidly the South African perception of the external threat and interpretation of political reality. In all of his 41 pages of endnotes and in his three page preface, no mention is made of any interviews that the author may have conducted with either U.N.

officials or national permanent missions to the U.N. in New York; and it would appear that none of the research for the book was conducted in South Africa. He fails to draw attention to the considerable number of American, British, and South African doctoral dissertations which would further illuminate the topic, and he unwittingly may have offended many by his use of the term "native" (pp. 7 and 10) and "Bantu" (pp. 11 and 169) when referring to Africans in South Africa who regard such terms as pejorative. It would have been helpful to the general reader had passages in French (pp. 36–37) been translated and more information had been given in his "note on sources" (pp. 175–176) about how the specialized reader can secure access to the documents of the Organization of African Unity.

RICHARD DALE
Southern Illinois University
Carbondale

HERBERT FELDMAN. *The End and the Beginning: Pakistan 1969–1971*. Pp. 210. New York: Oxford University Press, 1978. $14.50.

ROBERT G. WIRSING. *Socialist Society and Free Enterprise Politics: A Study of Voluntary Associations in Urban India*. Pp. xiv, 214. Durham, NC: Carolina Academic Press, 1977. $11.00.

These two excellent volumes provide valuable insights into the political transformation that was under way in Pakistan and India prior to the break-up of Pakistan in late 1971, and the proclamation of national emergency in India in June, 1975. Feldman's book is a macrostudy of the Yahya Khan period (March, 1969, to December, 1971), Wirsing's a microstudy of political and social change in the central Indian city of Nagpur.

Herbert Feldman has lived in Pakistan since its birth, and has therefore been in a unique position to observe the passing scene in that distressful country. His trilogy on political developments from 1958 to 1971, during the Ayub Khan and Yahya Khan periods—*Revolution in Pakistan, From Crisis to Crisis*, and now *The End and the Beginning*—constitutes

probably the clearest and best overview of these eventful years.

Major factors in the demise of the old Pakistan, in Feldman's view, were: the policies and mindset of Ayub Khan, whom he holds "largely responsible for the dissolution of Pakistan," (p. 6); the "negligible understanding" in West Pakistan "of the ferment which led to the break-up of 1971" (p. 5); the dissolution of West Pakistan into its four former constituent provinces in 1970; and the movement for greater autonomy in East Pakistan, "which preceded the Six Point formulation" of Sheikh Mujibur Rahman "by years" (p. 5).

Separate chapters are devoted to the legal Framework Order of March 30, 1970, which the author sees as "no contribution to a solution of the constitutional problem" (p. 68); and the first national general elections on the basis of universal adult suffrage in the history of Pakistan, in December 1970. The elections, which polarized the country and opened up the prospect of a reversal of the roles of East and West Pakistan, were followed by "a bizarre game of three-way political chess" (p. 111), involving three major political elements, "the armed forces represented by Yahya Khan, the Awami League led by Shaikh Mujib, and the Pakistan People's Party" led by Z. A. Bhutto (p. 108). The "holocaust" that followed the breakdown of negotiations "is, perhaps, the most controversial chapter in the entire history of the old Pakistan" (p. 127). Feldman tells the main story clearly in six chapters: the Pakistani butcheries beginning on the night of March 25–26, 1971, the East Pakistani "carnage against Biharis and West Pakistanis," the relations between Yahya Khan and Bhutto after March 1971, ("each was using the other, or thought he was") (p. 152), the Indian involvement, the December Indo-Pakistan war, and the final disruption of Pakistan.

Feldman is concerned with recording and analyzing the death and re-birth of a nation—Wirsing with the political dynamics of a single Indian city. However, as Wirsing states in the preface, his book is not only a study of voluntary associations in a single city of central India, but it is also "an inquiry into both the process and the meaning of power sharing in urban India" (p. vii). His study is based mainly on interviews with more than 300 persons in Nagpur, between January 1969, and March 1970, most of whom were active in the municipal election of 16 March 1969. He documents convincingly the interrelationship between voluntary associations and politics in Nagpur, with some fascinating case studies and other arresting examples.

Voluntary associations in Nagpur encompassed a wide variety of institutions, including "the relatively recent and government-promoted institutions of educational management and cooperativism . . . , but also . . . communal organizations, wrestling and gymnastic societies, neighborhood committees, and such conventional groups as trade unions, business and professional societies" (p. 40). Wirsing describes many of these organizations, particularly cooperative associations and educational societies. Since many of these associations had influence and funds, they inevitably attracted politicians of all kinds. Indeed, Wirsing argues, "the politics of the city is, in significant ways, the politics of voluntary associations" (p. 5).

Hence Wirsing is led into the broader arena of political life in Nagpur. His book is in fact an excellent case study of "the pattern of urban politics in India," to borrow the title of Chapter 2. He gives special attention to: "the politics of language;" "the politics of caste;" the nature and changing role of factions—"by far the most pervasive and powerful medium of political organization in India" (p. 102)— the role in Nagpur and in Indian politics of the Jana Sangh, which "is undergoing a fundamental transformation away from a goal of cultural revitalization and towards one of cultural accommodation" (p. 152); and the election campaign in Nagpur in preparation for the fourth municipal election in the city since India's independence in 1969.

In his concluding chapter Wirsing raises the basic question: "Can impoverished India *afford* the luxury of meaningful popular political participation?"

(p. 195), such as seems to be developing in Nagpur. He recognizes that "the burden of political participation is incontestably great in India and . . . is growing even greater. . . . the public decision making process at all levels is clearly threatened with inundation by seemingly insatiable demands" (p. 196); but he warns that "scrapping democracy may transfer power without rendering it any more capable, just, or effective" (p. 198). His conclusion, the validity of which seems to be reinforced by the experience of Pakistan under Bhutto, and by India during the emergency of 1975–77, should be taken to heart by all who are concerned with political development in the developing world: "Repressive government may restore stability, but much more than that is required to overcome India's problems. The worst mistake of all may be to victimize democracy" (p. 199).

NORMAN D. PALMER
University of Pennsylvania
Philadelphia

THOMAS R. H. HAVENS. *Valley of Darkness: The Japanese People and World War Two*. Pp. xi, 280. New York: W. W. Norton & Co., 1978. $9.95.

Although there is a fast growing and excellent literature in English on Japan's road to the Pacific war, her overseas conquests and policies in occupied lands, her military defeats, surrender, occupation, and recovery, and the high-level diplomacy of it all, there has been surprisingly little written on wartime Japan itself. The U.S. Strategic Bombing Survey tells the story of devastation from the air for those who care to dig it out from the plethora of American Occupation reports; there are several (rather old and inadequate) studies of the Japanese war economy, and a number of interesting studies of wartime ideological controls.

But aside from Donald Keene's excellent article on "Japanese Writers and the Greater East Asia War" (Journal of Asian Studies, 23, Feb. 1964), there is little on the mood, to say nothing of the lives, of the Japanese people during the war. Of course, there has been a goodly amount written in Japanese, and it is the great merit of Havens' study that he has utilized a wide variety of these Japanese materials in his book, which constitutes the first full fledged social history of Japan during the war years written in English.

It is fascinating history with not a few surprises. To the Japanese it was *not* a passionate war. It developed incrementally from the Marco Polo Bridge incident in China (July 1937), which itself was no big thing. One of many China "incidents," it only dimly intruded on the consciousness of the Japanese people, whose world was generally stable and prosperous at the time.

War controls were not rigorously applied at first. Anti "dangerous thought" laws were invoked sporadically and used to hound a relatively few intellectuals. The Welfare Ministry, established in 1938 to strengthen "the nation's military potential," seemed more like a friendly civilian health care program to the populace (pp. 47–49), and the "totalitarian" Imperial Rule Assistance Association complained that community groups were "ignoring" its orders as late as October 1943 (p. 81). Of course, conscription was taking young men, more women were in the work force, inflation and shortages were beginning to be felt, but it was only during the last two years of the war (1943–1945) that the sufferings of war at home became real. Then they accelerated rapidly. A blackmarket in food began to operate extensively in 1943, and in October of that year the government decided on a program of evacuation of nonworking people from the major cities. Promulgated in December as a voluntary program, few paid heed until, in July 1944, the Government ordered the evacuation of 6th grade children from a dozen major cities. From then until the end of the war the flight to the countryside and the interaction of urban evacuees and country people becomes the principal theme of Haven's story, as "ten million outsiders piggy-backed on forty-two million country people" (p. 171).

Havens concludes that "fierce and brutalizing though it was, the war scarcely affected the deep underlying structures of society at all—particularly the family patterning of small groups." However, it hobbled the military, declassed the landlords, and opened the way for businessmen to share a "post-war triangle of power" with bureaucrats and politicians (pp. 203–4).

This is an important and well written book of social history.

HILARY CONROY
University of Pennsylvania
Philadelphia

JAN S. PRYBYLA. *The Chinese Economy: Problems and Policies*. Pp. xiii 258. Columbia: University of South Carolina Press.

This book's objective is stated to be the examination of China's aim to become a modern industrial power by the year 2000. However, the achievement of this goal depends on the outcome of the race between population growth (reasonably estimated at an annual rate of 1.5 percent on more than 900 million people) and the increase of supplies through man's total socialization—by the merging of the individual in the mass.

Despite the undoubted progress of China's economy, the determination of the rate and quantity thereof is inhibited by the absence of any reliable current estimates, probably because these are unattainable. Consequently, no meaningful comparison can be made with the progress of Taiwan, Japan and India.

The pros and cons of the communist process are well considered under the chapter headings: Population, Agriculture, Industry, Money and Banking, Transportation and Communications, Domestic and Foreign Trade, and Public Health and Education.

Emphasis is on improving the existing agriculture land through drainage and irrigation work rather than on additions of new land through reclamation.

There has been a gradual shift of small and medium scale industrial plants from the commercial east to the rural west, yet Shanghai retains its dominant position in the industrial landscape. Account must be taken of political objectives and social aims so that growth cannot be maximized at their expense. Profit, as an investment motive, is not alien to decentralized state planners but must yield to social goals. While the objective may be the elimination of individual, competitive, material incentives, and their replacement by collective, comparative, moral ones—and eventually by endogenous work enthusiasm—at present the most skilled production worker gets about three times the wage of unskilled workers in the plant.

As the influence of university professors was brutally diminished, higher education is seen as in a mess.

The author notes that China is scrupulous in maintaining equilibrium between her exports and imports but concludes that if the promise of oil on the mainland and in offshore areas materializes, she may emerge as one of the world's major earners of foreign currency. The book is well written readable and amply annotated and indexed.

ALBERT E. KANE
Washington, DC

AFAF LUTFI AL-SAYYID-MARSOT, *Egypt's Liberal Experiment, 1922–1936.* Berkeley: University of California Press, 1977.

Professor al-Sayyid-Marsot's book traces the chequered political history of Egypt from the end of World War I until the signing of the Anglo-Egyptian treaty of 1936. In her view the era was one in which Egyptian leaders sought to introduce into the country liberal, parliamentary institutions. While she thinks that the experiment was doomed to failure because the foundations of a democratic society were lacking (a well-developed communications network, literacy, and high standards of living), she argues that the Egyptians deserve more credit than most scholars have given them for almost succeeding.

Her history is highly personalized, sometimes irritatingly so, but she writes with verve and her insights are always perceptive. A great deal of the story would appear to be based on her own experiences and her associations with members of that ruling elite. She was the niece of Egypt's leading liberal intellectual, Ahmad Lutfi al-Sayyid, and she mentions in the preface that she spent long hours talking with her uncle, her father, and another important political personality, Bahi Eddine Barakat. These conversations have afforded her a deep and personal feeling for the period. But they also present a problem of assessment and evaluation to the reader, for some of her generalizations are not supported with documentary evidence. For example, Professor al-Sayyid-Marsot claims that when the Wafd first came to power in 1924 it "set the behavior pattern for successive cabinets . . . (and) encouraged the spoils system of party patronage whereby Wafd supporters were appointed to government posts and their opponents dismissed from office." (p. 76) But she offers no statistics on the number of offices that changed hands, and the reader is compelled to take her word for this assertion.

Most historians of interwar Egypt have tended to stress the importance of individuals and personality clashes in explaining national political events. Professor al-Sayyid-Marsot carries this tendency quite far; hers is a story of leading persons fighting jealously with one another for high office. Social and class analysis do not get much attention, confined, as they are, to a single chapter toward the end. It is also clear, as one might expect in a story dominated by individuals, that she has personal heroes and villains. On balance, Zaghlul emerges as a malevolent force, his thirst for power preventing timely compromise and making conciliatory parliamentary democracy difficult to implant. The Liberal Constitutionalists are the most praiseworthy, dedicated in her view, to gradual, practical implementation of the new liberal order.

It seems to me that she is forced to employ a host of casuistical arguments to account for the Liberal Constitutional Party's abrogation of the constitution in 1928. Even more troublesome to her is Ahmad Lutfi al-Sayyid's joining of this anticonstitutional ministry, which is excused on the grounds of his not wanting to rebuff his friend, Muhammad Mahmud. These would be areas in which I would want to change the emphases. But the essay is full of understanding and rewarding to read.

ROBERT L. TIGNOR
Princeton University
New Jersey

JOSEF SILVERSTEIN *Burma: Military Rule and the Politics of Stagnation.* Pp. ix, 244. Ithaca: Cornell University Press, 1977. $16.50. Paperbound, $4.95.

In 1959 and again with a second edition in 1964, Professor G. McT. Kahin edited *Governments and Politics of Southeast Asia* (Cornell University Press). This text, designed for undergraduate area courses on Southeast Asia, had been prepared almost exclusively by "graduate fellows in the Cornell Southeast Asia Program." Each chapter, following in the main a similar outline, was authored by a young scholar who had specialized on that country. Kahin, in a brief foreword to the title here reviewed, indicates that the subject matter treated in the earlier effort could no longer "be subsumed within the covers of a single book." Hence, he, as general editor, offers us this new series of separate volumes on the "larger Southeast Asian countries" and related topics.

Professor Josef Silverstein of Rutgers University, who contributed the chapters on Burma in the 1959 and 1964 editions of the earlier one-volume text, has the "lead" position and about twice as much space in this new series. Once again he "scores" with a competent, clearly written, amply documented text, eminently suitable as an undergraduate "area" text on Burma for a course on post-World War II Southeast Asia.

*Burma: Military Rule and the Politics of Stagnation* is divided into seven substantive chapters and "Some Concluding Observations." (The book also includes an adequate though modest bibliography and index.) Necessarily, several of the chapters such as "Sources

of Burmese Political Culture," "The Contemporary Setting," "Constitutional Government, 1948–1962," and parts of others, "The Economy . . ." and "Foreign Policy . . . ," for example, are rewritten, occasionally expanded sections of the one-volume text mentioned above. Other chapters and sections devoted to the post-1962 coup period represent the new material implied by the title of the book.

Silverstein belongs to the generation of post-World War II scholars who, by interest and preference, became "area specialists"; in his case, Southeast Asia in general and Burma in particular. Despite the decline in academic, foundation, and government support for area studies, and the difficulties of living and studying in Burma, he has for the past quarter century persistently ploughed his chosen field. The result is clearly evident in this small but sure and fair book. His concluding paragraph, hardly debatable, is worth noting:

Neither the indifferent approaches to the problem [improving the well-being of the people] by the civilian leaders before 1962 nor the authoritarian methods of the military afterward appreciably reached the people in the countryside. The gap between the governing, urban-centered elite and the masses that was evident in the 1950s persists and may have widened in the 1970s. The problem cannot be solved quickly or easily. Patience and understanding are needed, as well as a new leadership sympathetic to tradition and able to use it to get the people to change and to voluntarily accept direction.

There are, however, several conceptual and historical issues, on which this conclusion is based, worth debating especially if Silverstein were to bring out a second edition. He holds that both the civilian government and the military regime failed to solve the problem of the "minorities" and thereby bring about "national unity" so essential for true nationhood. (In a dogmatic and unhistorical statement he asserts that "Burma is not and never has been a nation.") Though the earlier civilian government had adopted a democratic federal type of constitution not unlike that of Yugoslavia, and the military adopted an authoritarian unitary type of constitution for all citizens and districts of Burma, neither regime, though not for lack of trying, resolved the problem. Silverstein hardly explores this crucial issue. Was political structure at fault? Or was it "men" not "laws?" What have been the consequences of communist insurgency (begun in March 1948 with support of Moscow, and later Peking, and continuing to today) on the countryside and the government? How much "ethnic" insurgency is communist, how much, romantic nationalism? How much of the failure should be assigned to belated quasi-feudalism in the Shan States and how much to "tribalism?" What does it mean to say that Burma is divided between a "traditional" peasant society and urban, Western educated elite? (Actually, the Burmese "elites" are probably more rooted in their own countryside than any other society in southeast Asia excluding Laos/Cambodia!)

There are other debates on the "economy," and I should like to mention one here: How does one evaluate the success of those members of the Burmese "traditional," agrarian society who turned to jute farming as against members of the same society who remained mired in the present unprogressing patterns of paddy or rubber farming?

In sum, I would hope, that for his next edition, Professor Silverstein would put some hard questions, currently ignored or at best superficially examined here, to his own text. The results would benefit all of us who for better or worse are "Burma Hands."

FRANK N. TRAGER
New York University
New York City

ROBERT G. SUTTER. *China-Watch: Toward Sino-American Reconciliation.* Pp. xiii, 155. Baltimore: The Johns Hopkins University Press, 1978. $10.95.

CHIN O. CHUNG. *P'yŏngyang Between Peking and Moscow: North Korea's Involvement in the Sino-Soviet Dispute, 1958–1975.* Pp. x, 230. University, AL: The University of Alabama Press, 1978. $15.00.

Those following closely the changing relations between China, the USSR, and the United States, and the position of North Korea during these changes, may have their own scorecards of the diplomatic ups and downs for each country. They have little to gain in reading either of these books, unless it be to check their own tallies. For those who have not continuously graphed the changing patterns, both books provide useful reviews for the last three decades. Each gives a chronological account of the tactical moves, positions, and standings of the four countries, and the two volumes complement each other as to East Asian relations.

Sutter concentrates on the changing situation for China and the United States, with an eye on the USSR, focussed as the Communist Chinese view the other two powers, whereas Chung views the changing complex of Russian, Chinese, and American relations from the Korean perspective. Both differentiate between public stances, as presented in official releases, and the quiet diplomatic maneuvers by the participants, these two expressions more than occasionally being superficially contradictory. Both use wire service news reports, radio broadcast translations, foreign affairs journals, diplomatic statements, and domestic public utterances of national leaders in their accounts. Much of this material has not been widely available either to specialists or the general public. Sutter devotes the opening chapter to the subject of Sino-American relations, as an element in the balance of power in Eastern Asia, and a second one to the efforts of the Communist Chinese to cultivate sympathetic treatment by the United States during World War II and immediately afterward. The failure of these latter efforts is accounted for, but the reaction of older readers may well depend on the personal patterns of ideological commitment to the Nationalists or the Communists in China. Five chapters then trace the consequent efforts of the Communist govern of China to effect a rapprochement with the United States in order to offset the growing power of the USSR in Eastern Asia.

Chung provides an initial background chapter on the establishment of North Korea as a Soviet satellite, and on the role of the five factions who sought control of North Korea. Seven chapters then chronologically trace the changes in positions, and the successive diplomatic leanings of North Korea toward either the USSR or China. Caught between the two powers and dependent on one or both, North Korea is shown to have sought to maintain relations with both but to stand aloof from the specific rivalry between the two, insofar as this was possible under difficult economic constraints.

Sutter's conclusion is that current Sino-American relations are quite narrowly based, on strategic grounds alone, unsupported by such factors as trade, moral affinity, common heritage, or cultural objectives, but that the two countries will continue their efforts to maintain a balance of forces bearing on East Asian relations. Chung concludes that North Korea must either pay a heavy price for taking sides, or continue to endeavor to stand aloof, so long as the Sino-Soviet rivalry continues. Both provide copious source notes and good bibliographies.

JOSEPH EARLE SPENCER
University of California
Los Angeles

TAKETSUGU, TSURUTANI. *Political Change in Japan: Response to Postindustrial Challenge.* Pp. xii, 275. New York: Longman, 1978. Cloth, $12.50; paper, $6.95.

Postulating that societies grow through three stages—traditional, industrial, and postindustrial—the author identifies Japan as in the third stage by virtue of three facts: first, the service sector of the economy employs a majority of the labor force; second, the output of this sector is above 50 percent of the total; third, affluence is such that scarcity is no longer a major social problem. Else-

where the author also mentions such features as a high level of mass material well-being and a decline of work ethic and material values. He notes further that Japan entered into postindustrialism in the 1960's and currently shares this status with seven other nations—Canada, Sweden, Britain, Belgium, Denmark, Australia, and the United States.

Advanced industrialism, according to Dr. Tsurutani, typically generates certain problems which may conveniently be grouped into these categories: (1) politicization of costs of industrialism, (2) status politics, (3) expressive politics, and (4) trivialization of politics. In plainer English, the first refers to issues that cross class stratifications: for example, air pollution concerns the rich as well as the poor. The second means struggles for more recognition by groups such as women, senior citizens and welfare recipients, often with the support of established groups that are politicizing the issues. The third category denotes the tendency of people to engage in political action more for the sake of expression than for the sake of influencing the decision making of society. The fourth deals with the triviality of some of the political issues today, which the author attributes to general boredom as a result of the leveling effect of advancing industrialism and popular immunization to radical appeal.

The main purpose of the book is to study the response of Japanese politics to the new situation brought about by postindustrialism. The author chooses to concentrate on two main areas: the political parties and the patterns of popular involvement in politics. He explains in detail why the ruling Liberal Democratic Party, whose president is automatically the prime minister, responds the least to voter feelings at the grassroots level. Because of ties to big business, the seniority system, and factionalism within the party, the prime minister owes his appointment less to voters than to politicians and business leaders. This fact renders the central government leaders insensitive to the changing circumstances in the country at large. By contrast, the Japanese Communist Party and the Clean Government Party, "because they are not constrained by ties and alliances with any major force of industrial society," respond better to the felt needs of the voters and may in time exert pressure on the national government.

Advancing industrialism has, according to the author, also radically altered the political ecology of Japan. Voters are younger, better-educated, and therefore more prepared for direct involvement in politics. Hence, the growing importance of the citizens' movements which, the writer finds, are led by "middle Japanese in age and social status," include a large number of women, and concern themselves with issues rather than with the party affilations of political candidates. Since the citizens' impact is far greater on local than national government, Dr. Tsurutani sees an acute conflict arising out of national and local politics. This national-local tension, he believes, has replaced the old urban-rural dichotomy, which is disappearing as a result of the leveling effect of affluence. To the author's mind, the future of Japan lies in the adaptation of national politics to the exigencies of post-industrial conditions.

Several comments might be made on the merit of this book. On the one hand, it is clearly stimulating, innovative, and well-written. On the other, a devil's advocate may question some of Dr. Tsurutani's stands. For instance, he seems to regard postindustrialism as an unmixed blessing, which somehow will eradicate human selfishness. Thus, he speaks of the mutuality of interest among citizens, and the necessity of the government to focus on the well-being of the collectivity. In this a pious hope or a scholarly forecast? Again, while public sentiment can undoubtedly influence politics, it is less certain that the citizens' movements can become a major positive political force. Granted all the advantages of modern times—rising education, increasing leisure, can voters in Japan, or any country, really be competent to judge political issues? In passing, one may also question the degree

of relevancy of some of the features discussed in the book. An example is Dr. Tsurutani's finding that vote-winners in Japan are younger in age than their partisan losers. This fact may simply reflect a leaning toward the youth cult, which is modern but certainly not exclusively postindustrial. A look at some other countries will make this clear. Political leaders in both Taiwan and the Chinese mainland are getting younger than their predecessors. Yet neither is postindustrial. In fact, a decline in the average age of the leaders may not have much to do even with democracy.

YI C. WANG

Queens College
New York

LYNN T. WHITE, III. *Careers in Shanghai. The Social Guidance of Personal Energies in a Developing Chinese City, 1949–1966.* Pp. xiv, 249. Berkeley: University of California Press, 1978. $13.50.

Chinese Communists, like ruling Communists anywhere, fervently believe the absolute virtue of detailed regulation of the entire range of social life. The book by Lynn White provides us with an example of the practice of such "totalitarian" belief: the attempt of the Chinese Communists to regulate the career pattern of the people. But the focus of White's study is Shanghai.

Of all possible activities relevant to career decisions, Lynn White chooses to study four: education, rustification of urban youth (the "youth to the countryside" movement), occupational opportunities, and residential policy in Shanghai from 1949 to 1966. These topics, as Lynn White notes, used to be treated separately by scholars. His approach is to relate them in terms of "career guidance." Each chapter of the book excepting the "introduction" and "conclusion" describes how Communist leaders attempted to regulate one of the four activities, over the years, and the reactions from society. The latter aspect of his analysis is stressed at the outset of the book to show that "China is not completely totalistic," and that there has always been a balance between central and local power.

The quality of White's study is uneven. Each chapter, whether on the school system, the rustification movement, job opportunities, or residential requirements, presents a well organized historical and factual account of the policy of the Communist Party and the ways lower level leaders adapted central policy to local circumstances. The book is thus valuable in imparting information on specific activities in Shanghai from 1949 to 1966.

However, White's study falls short of accomplishing the stated purpose of linking those four activities in a new way, that is in the frame of "career guidance." First, the linkage of the four activities to careers in Shanghai is too diffuse. Any study of "careers" or "career guidance" should first point out the major careers available in a society or community. After that it is possible to discuss the ways public authorities guide or fail to guide the people to those careers. Lynn White does not point out what careers are available in Shanghai. His discussion on job opportunities in Shanghai focuses on factory work; surely that is only *one* of numerous possible careers.

White's discussion on the school system and the rustification movement in Shanghai is so general that linkage between them and the careers of Shanghai youth becomes obvious. For example the only distinction in education that White makes is technical and nontechnical. Nothing is said about the careers possible for those who receive "technical" and those who receive "nontechnical" education. If there is need for substantial "career guidance," then certainly it occurs within these broad categories. On the access to education and careers, White dwells on class origin of the students only. He does not take into account other possible factors such as sex, religion and race.

Second, a major variable—citizenship—that the author uses frequently to explain "career guidance" in Shanghai is never clarified. The same is true concerning the variable, "respectability."

Implicitly, White equates both "citizenship" and "respectability" in Shanghai or China with "rustification." That is a major error. What White fails to provide is a clarification of the Chinese Communist concept of "citizenship" or its equivalents ("the people," "Communist youth," "model worker," etc.). If that had been done, then he could have discussed how the authorities in Shanghai or China manipulated the acquisition of those qualities of "citizenship." Instead, White mentions "citizenship" here and there in the book as if it were self-evident. He also makes an inapt analogy between "rustification" in China and the "adult rite" in primitive societies. The former is a fiat imposed by authorities and resisted vigorously by many; the latter is part of a culture accepted by all members of the community.

Third, a fundamental flaw of White's book is his seemingly not knowing what general and conceptual framework to use to interpret his empirical data. He fails to mention a whole corps of literature on the sociology of occupations; instead, he mentions psychoanalytic studies of great leaders like the George's study of Woodrow Wilson. He does not, as he should, make use of the accounts of former students in China who discuss specifically the problems of career decisions, such as *The Thought Revolution* by Tung Chi-ping. Since Lynn White went to Hong Kong to interview former residents in China, one wonders why he failed to inquire about the career decisions of his informants whose experiences could have been very illuminating. Consequently, it is not correct for the author to conclude that his discussions of the Communist Party's policies on schools, rustification, factory employment, and residential requirements "all had effects on individuals' career motivations in Shanghai" (p. 207), because he has not established such a cause and effect relationship. The data on "individuals' career motivations" are not in White's book.

Whereas specific linkage between the various public policies and career motivations of Shanghai people is missing in Lynn White's study, we find awe-inspiring "behavioral scientific" linkages proposed by him such as: "the relation between urban supply and career guidance can be thought of as a hump-shaped curve" (p. 216), or "if residence control is thus related to urban supply in a hump-shaped manner, and if net immigration is related to residence control in a linear inverse way, then it follows mathematically that there would be a U-shaped relation between net immigration and urban supply." (p. 217) One wonders what purposes statements like that serve.

In conclusion, if one is interested in learning how the Communist Party attempted to regulate the schools, rustification of youth, factory employment, and residential requirements of Shanghai after 1949, then Lynn White's book is highly recommended. But if any "China specialist" seeks to find in White's study how the Communist regime manipulated career opportunities in Shanghai before 1966, he (or she) will be disappointed.

ALAN P. L. LIU
University of California
Santa Barbara

JOHN D. WIRTH. *Minas Gerais in the Brazilian Federation, 1889–1937.* Pp. xx, 322. Stanford: Stanford University Press, 1977. $17.50.

John D. Wirth's book, *Minas Gerais in the Brazilian Federation, 1889–1937* is the first of three monographs focusing on important states as centers of regional power, and on their changing relationship with the national government. As such, this study represents a significant breakthrough in North American historiography on Brazil. The in-depth analysis, firmly based on a wealth of information, will allow scholars to better understand the socioeconomic forces that shaped the modern nation. Wirth's study, then, and, most probably, the two companion studies that follow (on Pernambuco and São Paulo by Robert M. Levine and Joseph L. Love, respectively) are positive steps toward a reexamination and resynthesis of Brazilian national history.

Because this is the first of the trilogy, the book begins with a concise statement by the three authors setting forth the themes and goals of their parallel investigations. Their common hypothesis is that decisions made at the state level have played a major role at a critical phase of national political integration. Wirth then presents three general, introductory chapters on Minas Gerais: one on geography, developing his concept of the "Minas mosaic"; another on the state economy, showing its uneven development; and the third on society and culture, focusing on the "traditional Mineira family" and elite values and career patterns. In Chapters 4–8 Wirth presents his findings on internal state politics and the changing relationship between the state and the federal government. In so doing, he discusses such topics as: *coronelismo*, cooptive politics, the durability of hierarchical political structures, and the political elite and its effective participation in national affairs.

Among the most noteworthy of Wirth's contributions is his concept of the "Minas mosaic," a phrase which refers to the fact that the state is a heterogeneous combine of seven subregions. This theme surfaces in his subsequent analysis of the various factors that contributed to this disparate subregional development. He concludes that Minas is a political unit, not a unified economic whole. This discrepancy between political and economic boundaries hindered state integration and allowed one or two of these subunits to dominate the others.

Another contribution of note is Wirth's treatment of the informal aspects of the political process. On a macrolevel of analysis, he shows how cooptive politics assured the adaptability of the formal hierarchical structures to change, and weakened attempts to organize alternate horizontal structures among nonelite groups. The challenge to the system, therefore, did not come from within, but from without, that is, from centralizing changes in the federal capital. Accommodation with the federal government in the 1930s explains the enduring political power of the state at the national level, despite a relative economic decline vis à vis São Paulo.

On a microlevel, however, Wirth fails to carry his analysis to its logical conclusions. The traditional Mineira family (TMF), friendship networks or *panelinhas*, and consanguineous and affinitive kinship ties are central to his discussion of the economic elite. Wirth considers personal contacts essential for sustaining economic and social power by providing access to information, and to the powerful, at the local, zonal, state and national levels. Yet, in his subsequent prosopographical analysis of the political elite, he fails to consider fully the actual or potential *informal* control over politics of certain groups. The author found that *fazendeiros* (landowners) were underrepresented in the political elite, although he suspects "that many, perhaps the majority, of this elite held fazendas and/or were closely related to fazendeiros." He, nevertheless, continues saying that "Despite conventional wisdom, . . . 'the fazendeiros' as a group did not control Minas politics at the state elite level." The key word here is "control." It may be true that fazendeiros did not formally control state politics, but might not the fazendeiros have exercised "behind the scenes" control? Could not those with formal political power be the spokesmen for agrarian interests? These seem like plausible hypotheses given the evidence that Wirth himself presents regarding, for example, the fazendeiros' multiple careers, their contacts through family and friends, and the outcome of certain political questions—on land taxes, to cite just one—that were decided in their favor. Similarly, he describes coronelismo as patron-client politics run by rural bosses, but stops short of documenting how local individuals or families dominated municipalities, which would have been one way to approach the often elusive aspects of informal power and influence.

Other problems of the study are relatively few and unimportant. One is the lack of perspective. Preoccupied with writing a book that could be compared easily to the studies of Pernambuco and São Paulo during the same period, he does not provide enough background information to determine the relative development of Minas Gerais in temporal terms. The author assumes the reader has a detailed knowledge of Brazilian history. The non-Brazilianist, however, has no way of knowing whether the state was decadent, stagnant, or ascendant at the end of the Empire. Also, perhaps because of the comparative nature of this study and the requirements of adhering to a preconceived outline, the book reads mechanically and fails to create a sense of feeling for the subject. These relatively minor shortcomings, however, should not detract from what otherwise is an emulous example of historical research and writing.

S. RAMIREZ-HORTON
Ohio University
Athens

## EUROPE

ANTHONY ADAMTHWAITE. *France and the Coming of the Second World War, 1936–1939*. Pp. xxii, 434. London: Frank Cass, 1977. $27.50.

Anthony Adamthwaite has written a long, detailed, and important study of French diplomatic history, focusing on the years 1936 to 1939, from the German remilitarization of the Rhineland to the outbreak of the second World War. The account begins with a perceptive examination of the post-Versailles setting and the beginning of France's eclipse as a great power. It explores the internal political and social crises of the 1930s and then takes up almost day by day the diplomatic maneuvers involved in the Rhineland episode, the Spanish Civil War, the annexation of Austria, the Munich crisis, the German incorporation of Czechoslovakia, the belated diplomatic revolution leading to guarantees by the French and British to Poland, Greece, and Romania, and the final crisis of August–September 1939. A valuable section of the volume interrupts the narrative flow to examine critically and analytically the personalities and the machinery involved in the making of French foreign policy.

There are striking vignettes of such major figures as Edouard Daladier, Paul Reynaud (in a French context is it fair to characterize Reynaud as right-wing?), and Georges Bonnet. Bonnet, in particular, intrigues the author who, although he does not wish to white-wash him, and strongly scores his memoirs as falsified history, still tries to rescue him, not quite convincingly, from the role of chief appeaser and villain. He sketches him more as a muddler than a schemer, especially in August 1939. The section succeeds in illuminating the role of the cabinet, the legislature, the parliamentary committees, the Ministry of Foreign Affairs, the armed forces, and even the press and the political parties in these years; some analysis of the presidency, ineffectual though that office was, might have been included. It makes possible a sophisticated recognition of the interplay between political leaders, circumstances, the bureaucracy, and military capabilities, and at times a "horrifying lack of liaison" between the Quai d'Orsay, the War Ministry, and the political leadership. The dependence on Britain, not surprisingly, appears as a strong determining factor in French indecision, and some damaging new evidence surfaces of the condescending attitude toward the French ally.

We emerge with a sad and unedifying tale. The three-year period begins and ends with broken promises; and at the end, the failure to do anything of military significance to honor the Polish commitment meant fulfilling the letter but not the spirit of the alliance with Poland. Neither London nor Paris had been willing to construct a grand military alliance to thwart Germany; Soviet participation was only belatedly sought. Disaster was preordained because of the timidity of the political and military leaders who were convinced they were no match for Germany; because of the deep divisions within French society (which the political leaders helped only to widen); and because of the somewhat less than mature dependence on British

support. At the outbreak of war in September 1939, Britain and France were militarily only slightly better prepared than they had been the previous year— what price appeasement? The maneuvers, the day to day dispatches and cables, the reports and assessments, the official statements and the notes on cabinet deliberations are all here. The author has made extensive use of all the available diplomatic sources, British, German, French, and American. He is able to cut through earlier more speculative accounts based on self-exculpatory memoirs. So wrapped up does he become, at times, in his documents that the forest is lost for the trees and one longs for the perspective and the cadences of a Churchill who, in the insightful sentence quoted by the author, could sum it all up without footnotes: "It must be recorded with regret that the British government not only acquiesced but encouraged the French government in a fatal course."

It is interesting to note how a book completed as this was, in 1974, will unselfconsciously use the verb "to stonewall." The inordinate delay between completion and publication of the volume made it impossible for the author to consult, as he himself notes, D. C. Watt's *Too Serious a Business: European Armed Forces and the Approach to the Second World War*, where it would have been instructive to do so. But there is little else that the author has failed to consult, as the end-notes, bibliography, and several appendices all make clear.

JOEL COLTON
The Rockefeller Foundation
New York

GEOFFREY PARKER. *The Dutch Revolt.* Pp. 327. Ithaca: NY Cornell University Press, 1977.

A major difficulty in writing about the Dutch civil wars, says Geoffrey Parker in the foreword to his *The Dutch Revolt*, is "to find a credible framework which is flexible enough to fit the experience of all the seventeen provinces of the Low Countries where, in the sixteenth century at least, particularism was more potent than patriotism." "Particularism," for Professor Parker, meant that the Dutch could not maintain the unity and directedness which effective self-government and opposition to Spain required. It meant, too, that any action on Spain's part provoked a multitude of Dutch responses, and it ensured that any unified external force could call the shots. For Professor Parker, then, the history of the Dutch revolt is generally the story of confused and multiple Dutch reactions to external stimuli, largely Spanish. This belief differs markedly from that of the great nineteenth century historian John Lothrop Motley, for whom the creation of the Dutch Republic was another stage in the growth of the "ancient rugged tree of Netherland liberty—with its moss-grown trunk, gnarled branches, and deep-reaching roots."

However, much of Professor Parker's evidence suggests that there may have been Dutch motivations towards unity and that the Dutch were not all reactive. The flourishing economy and demography of the Low Countries in the mid-sixteenth century receive ample treatment in the first chapter of his book; in the final chapter, he speaks of the extraordinary growth in population, commerce, and industry which Holland underwent in the late sixteenth and early seventeenth centuries. One wonders whether the pressures of growth were not working, independently of Spain's policies, to create more powerful and effective forms of government (central included), and to produce special social tensions. To what extent were the Dutch civil wars and the creation of the Dutch Republic the products of changing social and political needs and values? No doubt future research into the as yet little explored area of Dutch social history will help answer these questions.

The bibliography is extremely useful, with full references to guides to archival materials. Strangely enough, though, it contains no references to Henri Pirenne's classic and formative *Histoire de Belgique*, J. S. Smit's brilliant article "The

Netherlands Revolution," or the *Algemene Geschiednis der Nederlanden*. A statement by Professor Parker about where he places his book in the vast bibliography of works on the Dutch civil wars would also have proven valuable.

WILLIAM A. WEARY
Bowdoin College
Maine

WILLIAM SAFRAN. *The French Polity.* Pp. 332. New York: Longman, 1977. $12.50.

JANE MARCEAU. *Class and Status in France: Economic Change and Social Immobility 1945–1975.* Pp. x, 217. New York: Oxford University Press, 1977. $13.95.

Thus, once again, the French seem to have demonstrated their attachment and devotion to a socioeconomic system they appeared so anxious to overhaul only a few weeks before the first round of the March legislative elections. No doubt, the temptation will be great among political scientists to see in this apparently contradictory mode of behavior a vindication of those "paradoxes" so often invoked in scholarly efforts to explain the operation of the French political system.

To be sure, had he been aware of the outcome of the electoral campaign, William Safran might, himself, have yielded to such temptation. In any event, one must be grateful to him to have produced a work which has the essential merit of not accepting at face value the countless *idées reçues* one can find in the literature on French politics. For example, Safran is critical of the "dysfunctional" impact generally assigned to the "peculiarities" of French political culture. He views France "neither hopelessly backward or blocked nor at the threshhold of a post-industrial era," and he argues convincingly that "the incompleteness of institutional 'Americanization' and the persistence of pre-modern patterns are not necessarily detrimental to system cohesion or democracy." These points are important and, indeed, refreshing, especially in view of the fact that *The French Polity* is a textbook with a potential for a large audience of undergraduate students.

The body of the work itself is rather conventional and shows, in the author's own words, "a deliberate institutional bias." Under these conditions, the economic and social environment of the French political system and its foreign policy and economic outputs do receive some coverage. But such subjects as the constitution, political parties, interest groups, and the relationship among the executive, Parlement, the bureaucracy, and the courts take the lion's share.

The topical discussion is generally competent and draws on the most recent literature, thus providing a useful overview of scholarly debates. Yet, one may wonder whether its formalism can bring satisfactory answers to such key questions as the *problématique* of the concept of "stalemate society." To the extent that Jane Marceau tries to come to grips with this very question from a more relevant interdisciplinary and sociological perspective, the reading of *Class and Status in France* was particularly enlightening and rewarding.

Subtitled "Economic Change and Social Immobility," Marceau's work focuses on change in France in the postwar period. Its basic thesis is that, in spite of widespread economic transformations leading to the emergence of a consumer society, access to social rewards has increased within, rather than among, social groups, thus perpetuating a pattern of unequal opportunities and access to power. Relying on the theoretical framework developed by Pierre Bourdieu and his colleagues at the Ecole des Hautes Etudes en Sciences Sociales in Paris, Marceau explains this enduring phenomenon in terms of differential access to education and the "legitimizing" function of French culture.

One may, of course, disagree with the author's underlying neo-Marxist assumptions (which are still widely debated in France), as well as with her pessimistic conclusions about the possibility of further change within the current political regime. Yet, her case study provides solid empirical evidence lending credence to some aspects of the stalemate society interpretation of French politics while, at the same time, casting French society within a general analysis of industrial societies which makes meaningful comparative evaluations of the French system possible.

To sum up, although the premises of these two books are quite different, both are representative of the increasing uneasiness felt by many social scientists (including myself) in regard to the ethnocentrism, excessive specialization, and lack of empirical foundations characterizing much of the study of France. Inasmuch as *The French Polity* and *Class and Conflict in France* embody long overdue efforts to correct these flaws, they can be viewed as important contributions toward a more balanced and accurate understanding of the French political system.

JACQUES FOMERAND
United Nations
New York City

*UNITED STATES*

S. RUFUS DAVIS. *The Federal Principle: A Journey Through Time in Quest of Meaning.* Pp. 248. Berkeley: University of California Press, 1978. $11.50.

The dust jacket prediction that this book "will surely become a modern classic" cannot be correct; the work has too many flaws. Author Davis, an Australian professor, set out to find the origins of and the changes in the meaning of "federalism." But his methods were faulty and his presentation confusing. To begin, he admitted that a more complete older work existed. Yet instead of modernizing the scholarship, he replowed old ground, and he did so eclectically, ignoring examples which he himself asserted could not be overlooked. He also chose his sources peculiarly. On the Achaean League, he depended exclusively on several modern scholars for data and interpretations. His discussion of the Holy Roman Empire was based on the work of late medieval scholars writing contemporaneously. On modern federal systems, he again limited his view to other scholars' writings. Only rarely in these sections did any of the research or analysis seem to be Davis' own. And the writers whom he selected did not even share a like relationship to what they described. Only in the chapter on the American constitution was Davis' "quest" directed to the ideas of the participants themselves.

Throughout, Davis failed to give "meaning" to "the federal principle," as he promised. Every chapter includes pages of endless rhetorical questions, which are almost never answered. Even when dealing with the primary sources of 1787 America, he asked what "did the delegates understand by the new language . . . ?" and presented as the answer the words of one delegate, "[I]t seemed now so strange and obscure." The quest for meaning fell short here. Nor was it better satisfied by quoting Madison for three pages without explanation except to call the comments "revealing" and to conclude that they were "different." Why revealing and how different, Davis never explained. Historians are supposed to interpret data, not just relay them.

Readers then learn almost nothing about what federalism meant to those who proposed to live by it. Instead we are treated to reprehensible diction— "diadic taxonomy," "morbific identification," "epiphenomena"—or to unpardonable tense shifts—"Livy's . . . classification . . . *is* familiar" to the medieval scholars who "found little difficulty [emphasis supplied]"—that would be merely irritating if there were no other lapses of clarity. We must demand better writing than appears in this book.

The final chapters on the present and the future collapsed for lack of a solid foundation. Davis' premise was correct: the federal idea *has* fallen on hard times, when American states are free to decide little more than whether to allow right turns on red lights. A good book on what federalism is supposed to mean would be very valuable today. But this one will not do.

W. T. GENEROUS, JR.
Choate Rosemary Hall
Wallingford
Connecticut

DONALD J. DEVINE. *Does Freedom Work? Liberty and Justice in America.* Pp. xii, 192. Ottawa, IL: Caroline House, 1978. $10.00.

This is another in the endless parade of books designed to show: (1) that only a free market society (for example, the United States) can provide liberty and justice to its citizens; (2) that increasing government involvement—primarily the taxing and spending policies of the national government—in welfare, and social and racial integration has endangered, indeed lessened, the American achievement; and consequently (3) that if we are to become a free and just society again, we must abandon such political encroachments and rely instead on voluntary associations and local governments.

As Devine puts it: Americans still believe in "the values of liberty, justice, and morals." But our intellectuals, including politicians—"They are intellectuals since they manipulate symbols!"—tend to be disenchanted with these "bourgeois values" and "force their values upon society through government regulations." They forget that "law can do very little" to enhance "economic and social well-being"— indeed, blacks, the poor, and the aged have been more aggrieved than aided by the welfare state, which is why it "is approved by almost no one"— and that "almost all social and welfare functions can be handled locally or privately." As a result, "there are declining liberty, increased governmental control, and increasing state-caused injustice."

This celebration of the free market system, tempered by altruism, will of course readily convince the faithful, who need no convincing. It will only amuse or irritate others, because the argument is beset by fatal methodological and substantive difficulties.

At the methodological level, I note but two points. First, much of Devine's "evidence"—we are a religious nation because 94 to 98 percent of the American people personally believe in God—is drawn from Gallup, Harris, and Roper polls, though not from Yankelovich, whose findings have often been significantly different. The author seems unaware of the obvious fact that behavior is not the same as belief, especially stated belief, and that in-depth interviews have clearly shown the inadequacies of initial replies to pollsters' questions. Second, most of his citations are from articles in The Public Interest —none, of course, from Dissent—and from books by spokesmen of the Right. The arguments of major liberal and socialist thinkers are unmentioned, and thus uncontested.

Of the more numerous substantive problems, I again limit myself to but two. The author thinks Locke's defense of private property is a defense of the contemporary capitalist (free market) system. However, Locke's notion of a handicraft individual working his small piece of land is a far cry from present day, large-scale corporate ownership, and contemporary capitalism can hardly be equated with Adam Smith's market. Further, he argues that "as the result of free cooperation rather than coercion, most [Americans] now live together reasonably well." If it is true that most Americans now live together reasonably well, what evidences demonstrate that this is not in fact the consequence of welfare state policies? To assert, for example, that there have been six recessions in the United States since the commitment to planning allegedly began in 1946 is neither to show that those recessions were caused by governmental policies nor to account for each recovery.

The publisher's blurb informs us that Devine is an associate professor of government at the University of Maryland, and an announced candidate for Governor of that state. This book may, perhaps, serve as a propaganda tract, but it contributes nothing to scholarly knowledge, and its publication has denuded our forests of some valuable trees.

DAVID SPITZ
Hunter College
New York City

ROBERT J. DINKIN. Voting in Provincial America: A Study of Elections in the Thirteen Colonies, 1689–1776. Pp. x, 284. Westport, CT: Greenwood Press, 1977. $16.95.

In his Voting in Provincial America, Robert J. Dinkin attempts to "provide the first comprehensive analysis of voting in provincial America" (p. ix). Relying heavily upon secondary materials, along with some analysis of untapped primary sources, Dinkin provides readers with a sound and valuable synthesis. Since his work is a synthesis, it exhibits both the strengths and weaknesses of that particular type of monograph.

When Dinkin writes about voting, he is interested primarily in provincial or colony-wide voting, as opposed to local or town voting. Admittedly, there was little to separate the two in colonial America, but the reader should not approach the work looking for a discussion of all types of voting. Rather, under valid analytical categories, Dinkin examines all aspects of the provincial voting process, including the electorate (specific restrictions upon suffrage), the candidates (their qualifications and desires for office), nominations (development of the caucus system), electioneering (methods of campaigning), voting procedures (balloting procedures), turnout (percent of adult white males voting), and voting behavior (factors motivating active participation in the election process). Since each colony had its own distinctive forms and styles for conducting provincial elections, variety characterized electoral procedures in colonial America. And although these electoral procedures were initially patterned after those in England, they quickly diverged from that example, becoming less aristocratic in style and increasingly democratic in form.

Dinkin's book contains no methodological surprises for the untrained, especially in the form of statistical analyses or interdisciplinary techniques. Tables included are straightforward and easy to understand. It is unfortunate that Dinkin did not make better use of interdisciplinary sources or materials, for much of what is exciting and thought provoking in the book is the result of his readings in political science. Especially noteworthy is his use of constructs from political science, in chapter eight, where he tries to understand eighteenth-century voting behavior through a working model of voting behavior developed by another discipline. Furthermore, the book is heavily documented and provides a sound bibliographical essay for those unfamiliar with the historiography of voting in provincial America.

To conclude, Dinkin's study of voting in provincial America can be read with profit by the general reader and by those scholars interested in a one-volume synthesis of secondary findings on the subject, but for those interested in significant new approaches to the subject, Dinkin's work is disappointing.

RICHARD S. SLIWOSKI
University of New Hampshire
Durham

WILLIAM G. DOMHOFF. *Who Really Rules? New Haven and Community Power Reexamined*. Pp. xiii, 189. New Brunswick, NJ: Transaction Books, 1978. No price.

Lyndon Johnson is reputed to have said that the first objective of a politician must be to be reelected to office—for only then will he be able to acquire the seniority (power) and prestige among his fellow legislators necessary to significantly affect legislation (in a nonrevolutionary, pluralist context, of course). One of the defects of the publish or perish rule in academia is that scholars are frequently driven to publish prematurely. By so doing they save their careers; having survived, it becomes possible for them to pursue their research and for their most important work to find the light of day. At least for this reviewer, Domhoff's previous books have seemed to have an unfinished and (in retrospect) premature quality; apparently they were the means by which he survived so that he could write *Who Really Rules?*—a capstone of all that he has previously written.

Ideally, significant scholarly work should clearly state a controversy between two theoretical positions (no straw men, please); bring forward new and relevant data; show where the opposition "went wrong"; provide a model for others who want to replicate the methods used to test the theory in other contexts; and clearly state the theoretical implications of the position that the scholar's data have demonstrated. Domhoff clearly and succinctly lays out the controversy between his own class theory and Dahl's pluralism, brings new data to bear on community power in New Haven, reexamines Dahl's data (with Dahl's cooperation) and presents a reasonable argument on where Dahl "went wrong."

He also provides a research model that transcends the limitations of the community power structure studies of the fifties and early sixties, limitations which were built into the comparative studies of the mid-sixties and early seventies. Finally, Domhoff presents clearly the theoretical implications of his work, linking local class and power structure with national class and power structure theory and research. Those who take the pluralist position in socio-political analysis should be especially grateful for this clear, nonpolemical challenge to their position, and it is to be hoped that they will respond in a like manner or gracefully yield the field.

Domhoff and his publishers are to be congratulated. Readers of the *Annals* are urged to read the book.

LEONARD BLUMBERG
Temple University
Philadelphia

HOWARD I. KALODNER and JAMES J. FISHMAN, eds. *Limits of Justice: The Courts' Role in School Desegregation*. Pp. 624. Cambridge, MA: Ballinger, 1978. $22.50.

The central points in these pages—the intractability of problems arising from race and class differences, the unwillingness or inability of political leaders to deal with them, and the inadequacies of courts as a means of solving them—have been made before. But seeing these generalizations as they emerge again and again from the specifics of various historical moments and geographical places gives this book an impact that other studies do not have.

There are eight case studies in all: Boston, Brooklyn, Denver, Detroit, Indianapolis, Mount Vernon (N.Y.), San Francisco, and Winston-Salem. In addition, there is an introduction by Howard Kalodner, and two specialized articles. One of the latter, by Derrick A. Bell, Jr., discusses the ethical problems confronting civil-rights lawyers in class-action suits, such as the problem of possible conflict between their own views and those of the class or parts of the class. The other, by Forbes Bottomly, deals with the specific difficulties of educators and judges in working together to develop and implement judicial decrees in desegregation cases.

What emerges in this volume are serious questions as to the value of using courts to go further in the desegregation process rather than the dismantling of legally imposed dual school systems based on race. Attempts to undo segregation stemming from neighborhood schools and segregated housing patterns often create situations in which the issue is posed as one of educational excellence versus forced race mixing. The editors include some critical comments (at the end of the Bell article) insisting, on the contrary, that the issue is whether or not a constitutional right is to be denied merely because some persons will manipulate, disrupt, or undermine the public school system rather than permit the right to be enforced. Yet Kalodner's position, that it is unrealistic to expect courts to solve an essentially political problem, cannot be dismissed merely by repeating the phrase "constitutional right."

The basic problem examined in this volume lies not in legal identification of the *wrong* (although the author of the Winston-Salem case study states that the courts erred in this respect), but in providing an effective *remedy*, particularly in the face of "white flight." In dealing with the latter, courts have gone beyond decrees mandating desegregation to those specifying the kind and quality of education to be offered. The import of this volume seems to be that such remedies will be effective—if at all—only when undertaken by legislatures, executives, and school boards; which is to say that the problem is "political," not "legal," at this stage, yet no real hope of action by these bodies is held out. (Another view, that the basic problem is a failure to define the wrong with sufficient breadth, is not addressed in the book, although it fairly begs for articulation at several points.)

This summary cannot do justice to the diversity of viewpoints, the variety of facts, and the nuances found in this volume. Hopefully, however, it will convince judges, lawyers, educators, and political activists involved in the strife and tension of desegregation efforts that this is an indispensable book of caution, criticism, and guidance.

ROBERT NEIL JOHNSON
Adelphi University
Garden City
New York

J. R. POLE. *The Pursuit of Equality in American History.* Pp. xv, 380. Berkeley: University of California Press, 1978. $14.95.

This book analyzes the idea of equality as an issue in American public policy from the Great Awakening to the present. Pole focuses most of his attention on the influence various concepts of political, legal, religious, and social equality have had on the status of white Protestants, immigrants, women, and, especially, blacks. Lacking comprehensiveness, this volume provides only summary treatment of several potentially fertile areas, such as policies directed at Indians, class differentiations, distinctions based upon age, and disparities between geographic regions.

Central to Pole's historical perspective is the insight that the idea of equality has shaped major policy debates only at infrequent intervals. Despite a plethora of empirical contradictions, most Americans traditionally have shared Tocqueville's belief that an "equality of conditions" exists, and they have consigned critics of inequity to the periphery of American history. Unfortunately, however, Pole's data base, which consists largely of the writings of jurists, politicians, and scholars, precludes detailed examination of conventional wisdoms at the popular level. Pole, for instance, ignores the role of Horatio Alger tales and other "bound to rise" literature in prompting most Americans to assume a greater degree of equality of opportunity than actually existed.

The years since World War II are unique, constituting the only period of sustained effort by the federal government to redress inequities in American society. The renewal of heavy black migration to the North during the second World War transformed "the Negro problem" from a sectional dilemma into a national concern at a time when distinctions based on race or religion suffered from an identification with Nazi ideology. Moreover, a reorganized Supreme Court placed the federal government in an activist role in the "spread of constitutionally decreed egalitarianism" (p. 272). One wonders, however, whether the rising conservatism of the late 1970s indicates a period of impending quiescence for egalitarianism.

The chief merit of this volume pertains to the questions it raises. Is equality an absolute or a relative condition? Does equality refer to outcome as well as to opportunity? Eschewing polemics, Pole illuminates the nuances and variations that have made the concept of equality a chimera. Highly attuned to the influence of specific vantage points on perceptions of equality, as evidenced by his critique of affirmative action, Pole, lucidly and with dispassion, ele-

vates the discussion of equality to a sophisticated level far above the prevailing shibboleths. As Pole emphasizes, the great disputes are not between "equality and inequality but between one concept of equality and another" (p. 358).

WILLIAM M. SIMONS
State University of New York
Oneonta

JAMES REED. *From Private Vice to Public Virtue: The Birth Control Movement and American Society Since 1830.* Pp. xvi, 456. New York: Basic Books, 1978. $17.95.

This useful and interesting work provides a quite comprehensive review of the development of birth control in the United States. It includes an eight-page bibliographic essay, together with 54 pages of notes. Part I is devoted to a review of contraceptive technology and changes in the conception of the family and sexual standards in nineteenth-century America, along with the emergence of the movement to suppress contraceptive information and attempts to win a place for contraception in medical practice.

Part II deals with the life and career of Margaret Sanger, with her early American and subsequent European experience, her ascent to leadership of the American birth control movement, her contribution to the diffusion of contraceptive information and practice, and to her philosophy. Young readers will find baffling the Comstock-Sumner world through which Margaret Sanger had to fight her way.

Part III treats the work of Robert L. Dickinson (1861–1950) and the Committee on Maternal Health, along with Dickinson's efforts to focus the attention of medical research upon sex, obstetrics, and birth control.

Part V deals with Clarence J. Gamble (1894–1966), birth control entrepreneur and philanthropic pathfinder. "In succession, Sanger, Dickinson, and Gamble [who had been recruited by Dickinson] provided the innovative leadership in the birth control movement between the two world wars" (p. 226). Reed describes Gamble's involvement in the promotion of birth control, the establishment of standards for contraceptive products, and the conduct of experiments in population control in Logan County, Virginia and by the North Carolina Public Health Department. Chapter 20 provides an interesting account of conflict within the birth control movement.

Part IV deals mainly with "birth control in American Social Science: 1870–1940," especially with the response of social scientists to the decline in the fertility of the native born during the post-Civil War period of heavy immigration and with rising concern lest unfavorable reproductive selection was taking place. Inasmuch as birth controllers were blamed for the alleged decline in the quality and quantity of population, more attention began to be directed to spreading birth control to the "lower classes" (see chapters 15–16).

Part VI deals with the spread of attention to the need for birth control in "a crowded world," the failure of simple methods, and the founding of the International Planned Parenthood Federation. Part VII treats the development of "the pill." In Part VIII the alleged failure of "family planning" is examined along with the causes of this failure.

Social scientists will find this fine study very interesting and informative as well as suggestive of problems likely to arise in some countries.

JOSEPH J. SPENGLER
Duke University
Durham
North Carolina

HOWARD N. RABINOWITZ. *Race Relations in the Urban South, 1865–1890*. Pp. xxii, 441. New York: Oxford University Press, 1978. $17.95.

"Jim Crow"—creation of the antebellum South, post-Reconstruction "Redeemers," or late nineteenth- and early twentieth-century forces? All of these, asserts this detailed study. In a sense it was the product of Reconstruction as well, and even of blacks themselves.

Southern urban blacks, on whom Professor Rabinowitz focuses his attention, played a key role in the gestation. With slavery's end, many landless, unskilled freedmen drifted into cities where the races came in close proximity and often competed economically. By the 1890s blacks had developed (to a degree unrealizable in rural life) a society of their own, and even with Negro freedom and voting, social contacts with whites were highly circumscribed.

Suffering from military defeat, southern whites resented the influx of rural blacks as causes of instability and social disruption. Urban problems surfaced in Dixie as elsewhere, and freedmen were equivalent to the flood of foreign immigrants in the North. Desperately seeking some means of social control, whites came up with segregation, first in private areas, then generally by custom, and finally (accompanying lessened northern concern and essential denial of the ballot to blacks) by law.

Much of this is familiar, but de jure segregation was delayed for a number of reasons. Slavery and the Johnson provisional governments had virtually excluded urban blacks from city services. Under Radical Reconstruction, most Carpetbaggers and practically all Scalawags desired racial separateness, with inferior facilities reserved for blacks. When Redeemer regimes favored more separation and even less equality, older Negroes (seeing even this as preferable to outright exclusion) tended to acquiesce. Our present and persisting Negro ghetto problem has its roots in these developments.

This revised dissertation relates an evolving problem to an entire region, though it concentrates on five cities. Readers may question if Montgomery, Raleigh, Atlanta, Richmond, and Nashville are truly typical, but Rabinowitz's case for his selections indicates they are probably as representative as any quintet. Some quantitative methods and a host of source materials are utilized; documentation is copious. In places tendentious or tautological, replete with names and examples, and with a few chronological zigzags, the volume delves into nearly all aspects of black urban society, and seems as well organized as is possible for such a compendium. Essentially, the author makes his points: working for black teachers for their children, even Negroes were promoting segregation; when the black vote threatened to become an effective balance of power, it was nullified or extinguished. And when younger, more militant, blacks started resisting discrimination, Southern whites began formally legalizing already established practices. In balance, a worthwhile study.

DONALD H. STEWART
State University of New York
Cortland

LISLE A. ROSE. *The Long Shadow: Reflections on the Second World War Era.* Pp. 224. Westport, CT: Greenwood Press, 1978. $16.95.

Lisle A. Rose has written a thoughtful and interesting book, surveying leading political and intellectual developments in the United States from the period of the New Deal to the scandal known as Watergate. This book, *The Long Shadow: Reflections on the Second World War Era*, is appropriately entitled, for the author carefully examines the manifold consequences resulting from World War II. The focus of the book is on the United States, but this exposition is presented and discussed in an international context. And the author comprehensively traces and demonstrates the critical development of America's international role, from the 1930s on, to the cataclysmic World War —the long shadow—and points to its commitment in Vietnam.

Although the author does not break any new ground, he presents an excellent synthesis of this entire period. The special merit of this work is its contemporary quality. By taking an historical approach to current issues and problems, Rose addresses himself to the outstanding questions of the 1970s. Some of the pertinent questions discussed are the legacy of Nazism, the responsibility for the Cold War, United States involvement in Vietnam, and the causes of Watergate. The author is also au courant with the leading intellectual

figures and ideological movements which have shaped our time. The most influential secular ideologists are shown to be Thomas Jefferson, Adam Smith, Charles Darwin, Karl Marx, and significantly, Sigmund Freud. In citing Freud, whom he credits with bridging "the chasm between facile late-nineteenth-century assumptions of progress through violence and our own century's morbid preoccupation with violence for violence's sake" (p. 5), he recognizes the influence that Freud has had in shaping contemporary thought. Additionally, in this vein, Rose is cognizant of the contributions now being made by the new field known as psychohistory. He has a more extensive discussion on the legacy and current manifestations of racism, Nazism, Marxism, and the revisionist historians in the United States. Rose's critique of the revisionists, who attribute the Cold War to the United States, is thorough. Their basic premise, that this country waged a cold war for economic reasons, because it sought to safeguard its markets and acquire others, is amply refuted. Rose, however, states that there were two cold wars (and suggests that future historians may discern additional phases), the first one lasting from 1946 to 1950 and the other from 1950 to 1970. The summer of 1950 demarcates these two periods because American statesmen and their allies prior to this time acted defensively in the face of Stalin's contentious policies. But when the Soviet Union directed North Korea to attack South Korea, this aggression caused a change in the national mood. Thereafter, the United States developed into a "garrison state" and became more aggressive abroad, a posture ultimately leading to an intransigent involvement in Vietnam.

Where Rose takes an historical approach, his presentation is sound, but when he departs from this approach to become an essayist his interpretations become disputable. In his discussion of the youth of the 1960s, he resorts to an impressionistic sociology. He advances the opinion that the turmoil of this period was a form of generational continuity. The young people, in their opposition to the war in Vietnam, now had their own cause, as their elders had had, the Veteran generation of World War II, and like them, demanded conformity and discipline of their adherents. Such a generalization is too facile, for not all youth acted in the same manner. And there were regional variations, as well as generational, in the opposition to the lengthy war in Vietnam. There is another shortcoming. The documentation throughout the text is rather sparse, and the author relies essentially on secondary sources all of which are written in English. However, he has included a valuable bibliographical essay.

In sum, Rose's *The Long Shadow* is a highly readable book, at times gripping in its account. It will be useful for the general reader and especially for undergraduates.

JACQUES SZALUTA
United States Merchant Marine
    Academy
Kings Point
New York

## SOCIOLOGY

HENRY J. AARON. *Politics and the Professors: The Great Society in Perspective.* Pp. 185. Washington, DC: The Brookings Institution, 1978. $9.95. Paperbound, $3.95.

Conventional wisdom has it that the efforts of the Kennedy and Johnson administrations to declare "War on Poverty" and to create the "Great Society" failed because their programs were poorly planned, passed in haste, and inadequately funded. Dissatisfied with these undiscriminating and excessively general "explanations," Henry J. Aaron set out, as a Senior Fellow at the Brookings Institution, to find out what really happened to the once broad American consensus about the nation's problems and the best methods for solving them.

In individual chapters, analyzing programs created to eliminate poverty and discrimination, to create new educational and training opportunities, and to control unemployment and reduce inflation, Mr. Aaron illuminates the public and scholarly attitudes and beliefs about the effectiveness of public expenditures and programs. He shows how the legislative outpouring between 1964 and 1968 arose from convictions, born in the Great Depression and Second World War, that a benign government could efficaciously solve social problems and that quantitative tools of analysis had given social scientists the ability conclusively to inform debates about public policy. Then, in the late 1960s and early 1970s, public moods and governmental modes changed because people lost their faith in governmental actions as forces for good; because the coalition behind the civil rights movement dissolved after achieving formal victories; and because the intellectual accord about how to solve social problems collapsed as economists, the social scientists' *beaux ideal*, showed themselves manifestly unable to find ways of simultaneously controlling inflation and reducing unemployment.

Mr. Aaron's several chapters are fascinating intellectual journeys: detailed criticisms and suggestive analysis fill the landscape. Economic competition, instead of eroding racial and sexist discrimination, turns out, on closer analysis, only to reinforce it; the theory of human capital, that would have government spend money on the education of workers to increase either their actual productive capacity or their employers' perceptions of their capacity, is belied when poverty fails to yield to the meager increments in federal spending on education and training; and economic theories notwithstanding, government could not improve job opportunities for low-wage workers without sustaining rapid inflation.

As a result of faulty theories and the loss of public confidence, the roadblocks to the Great Society remain in place. Undismayed, Mr. Aaron concludes that we can still rationally hope to remove them "if we retain a bit of that sense of mutual obligation and community that flowed from economic catastrophe and the holocaust." Presumably, Mr. Aaron, as befits an Assistant Secretary in the Department of Health, Education and

Welfare (which is the office he now holds), places more hopes in wise political leadership to provide a new consensus than he does in social scientists, especially those who model themselves on physical scientists and mathematicians seeking simplicity and elegance in their theories. Procrustean attempts "to isolate individual influences, to make social and economic processes statistically and mathematically manageable through abstraction," he thinks, may well obscure more than they illuminate. Complex social reality, in his view, requires us to ignore what statistics may show "on the average" and instead to tailor policies to fit myriads of special conditions. Public policymakers should not employ the same tests of statistical significance that analysts use in testing hypotheses but rather, on the weight of all available evidence, act even before social scientists finish their research. Approvingly, he quotes James Sundquist's remark, that when one drives from the Atlantic to the Pacific, "one need not have a map of the entire route to know that he begins by heading westward."

RICHARD N. SWIFT
New York University
New York City

HAROLD X. CONNOLLY. *A Ghetto Grows in Brooklyn*. Pp. vii, 248. New York: New York University Press, 1977. $15.00.

Harold X. Connolly has written a well researched and perceptive record of the three hundred year old history of blacks in Brooklyn, with emphasis given to the evolution of the predominately black Bedford–Stuyvesant community. This volume, enjoyable to read, is a particularly welcome addition to the literature on black America since the black population of Greater Bedford–Stuyvesant presently exceeds that of Harlem, its more familiar Manhattan counterpart.

The author devotes appropriate and balanced attention to the social, economic, and political development of Bedford–Stuyvesant. He examines the role of various groups—some of which have their origins in the nineteenth century while others typified by the several poverty agencies are primarily the product of relatively recent Federal policy—in representing, articulating, and responding to the needs of the disadvantaged citizenry. Political scientists would find of special interest Connolly's discussion of black political power; his description and analysis of black social and economic leadership is of real value to urban sociologists.

Connolly examines the Twentieth Century transformation of Bedford–Stuyvesant from a largely white middle-class community to a black ghetto. Economic opportunities, brought about initially by the domestic industrial manpower needs of World War I, served as a magnet which attracted Blacks to Brooklyn, as well as other areas of the North. Continual black population growth has been accompanied by white resistance and eventual massive flight which has assured the development of the "intensifying ghetto."

This is a good book which is well written, informative, and carefully documented. Not only did the author make use of the usual library resources, but he also conducted interviews with individuals, or their descendents, who played a prominent role in the shaping of Bedford–Stuyvesant. In addition, Connolly perused and makes appropriate reference to the *minutes* of community organizations. The present-day despairing condition of Bedford–Stuyvesant can be better understood if one first reads and ponders over the material contained in this volume. History often does provide answers and insight into present major domestic problems confronting the polity.

NELSON WIKSTROM
Virginia Commonwealth University
Richmond

PAUL M. INSEL and HENRY C. LINDGREN. *Too Close For Comfort, The Psychology of Crowding*. Pp. xii, 180. Englewood Cliffs, NJ: Prentice-Hall, 1978. $8.95.

The aim of this book is stated by the authors on page 13: "It is our plan to present crowding as not only a social and ecological phenomenon but as a subject with many psychological contrasts." Insel and Lindgren choose as their guiding question, "Is there an ideal level of population best suited to human functioning?" (page xi). Since, they admit, there is no clear answer to this question, their book represents a review of a decade of studies in which the identification of the major elements of this query are examined.

Problems with the book emerge when the authors opt out of defining the term "crowding": "We shall instead talk about crowding as though everyone understands what it means." (page 16). Unfortunately, this decision leaves the reader without a conceptual or methodological guide in which to compare and evaluate the numerous studies that follow. The result is a potpourri listing of excellently selected studies that somehow are related to crowding. For example, in chapter 6, "Lines or Queues: Where Do They Lead?", the authors present nine pages of generalizations to conclude with the statement, referring to queues, "They are symptomatic of our crowded world." (page 109). Then in chapter 4, "The Social Cost of Crowded Homes," the authors present a concluding remark: "We have focused on the effects of crowding on mental development because it can be measured easily and reliably and hence makes a clear-cut case against crowding." (page 75). The reader was not aware that this chapter (or book) was a polemic against crowding. Also, one questions the authors' choice of this topic simply because it was easy to measure.

These examples demonstrate the effects of the atheoretical and non-conceptual nature of the method of inquiry Insel and Lindgren chose to investigate their topic. This approach (or lack of one) is also characteristic of the conclusion to the book in general. The authors state that the "desire for privacy" is the "essence of the psychology of crowding" (page 141). The authors rely on Westin's 1967 study to describe the four categories of individual privacy:

solitude, intimacy, anonymity, and reserve. These categories are vital functions that privacy offers each person in his/her necessary quest for "personal autonomy, emotional release, self-evaluation, and limited and protected communication." The book ends with a question and an answer: "Can we survive without the countryside and without space in which to find physical and psychological freedom? It is unlikely." (page 156). This conclusion seems simplistic and contradictory when compared to the cross-cultural differences in linguistic variations, perceptions and experiences of privacy that the authors insightfully presented earlier in the book (see pages 8, 9, 48–55). What, then, led Insel and Lindgren to this indiscriminate and overriding conclusion? Perhaps the lack of a guiding definition of crowding that would be cross-culturally valid.

Despite the methodological failing of the book, Insel and Lindgren have compiled an interesting selection of studies with insightful summaries. The authors also offer a useful bibliography (pages 157–168). Given these contributions, the book is easy to read and raises many lucid issues.

Joseph W. Weiss
University of Wisconsin
Madison

Rochelle Jones. *The Other Generation: The New Power of Older People*. Pp. 264. Englewood Cliffs, NJ: Prentice-Hall, 1978. $9.95.

The Other Generation: The New Power of Older People. It would appear that the first title is much the more accurate one, there is some real question, except for encapsulated areas, regarding the second. Old was and still is a pejorative term to which is assigned a negative social value. So much so that it is referred to in humor by a professor from a Florida university who stated, tongue in cheek, "you can call me senile but don't be calling me old!"

The concomitant factors which plague the older person is the main theme throughout. The first part of the book was a recitation of the different facets of what can, and often does, happen to different segments of the population who are over sixty-five years of age. The information was handled in much the same format as a debate, without a real effort to bring about a synthesis of the total material. We are, however, presented with an excellent synopsis of a number of emotionally controversial themes—namely, retirement, social security benefits and their failings, loss of self-image, sensory deprivation, and bottomless loneliness. As a result, the reader is left with the feeling that each chapter is either an article lifted from a previous expose or was written to definitely prove or illustrate the author's point. Therefore, nothing that could be classified as serendipitous really develops except to reinforce one's most grievous suspicion that old age is not necessarily so great—despite the poets.

In contrast, the second half of the book is where the author begins to develop some real analyses by taking a more comprehensive view of the universal problem of the older citizen in his present day social context. Comments on the relationships, as well as the social and personal dynamics, are introduced more heavily beginning in Chapter 7 and continuing to the final, eleventh chapter. The individuals who make up the older work force are depicted as being between the ages of forty-five and sixty-five.

The last part of the book is more acceptable to the reader who is a professional. For example, "What It Costs Society to Hide Older Adults," is the provocative title of Chapter 6. It is questionable, however, whether or not some of the popular misconceptions regarding social security are not carried forward in this book. Social security is described as a regressive tax and the poor person's welfare payment to the middle class. It hits hardest those least able to pay because it takes a bigger percentage of their earnings; and those who pay the maximum percentage in, get the smallest relative return on their contributions. Further, no mention is made that the section of the Social Security Act from which aged or retirees benefit is getting to be the smallest part of what social security covers. It is not necessarily the retirees' benefits which are putting a strain on the social security fund, but rather the more recent concept of the cradle to the grave coverage which includes: family endowments, educational benefits, accident and disability coverage, components which have been added over the years and were not part of the original concept of the plan.

The total book contains significant data clearly illustrating that older citizens adjust to, for, or against cultural restraints when they are up against a crisis—in this case, one which is primarily fiscal. This volume should be considered as a beginning in a new area of study relative to contemporary social anthropology that, heretofore, was not necessarily informally or formally acknowledged but is, without question, a real event in man's response to his ever-changing environment.

KENNETH G. SUMMERSETT
Newberry
Michigan

HARVEY H. KAISER. *The Building of Cities: Development and Conflict*. Pp. 217. Ithaca: Cornell University Press, 1978. $15.00.

In practice, urban planning reflects two strategies: redevelopment of the central city; or carving out nuclear entities in the urban fringe. Analysts and scholars, likewise, may adopt one of two strategies in investigating either focus of urban planning: emphasis on the substance or policies of such plans; or a major concern for the power-influence processes by which plans are adopted or thwarted. *The Building of Cities* (which is inaccurately titled, since it deals with the fringe rather than with the central city) is a brief case study of political processes that accompany the emergence of three "new towns" in the fringe developing between Rochester and Syracuse in the early 1970s. Essentially, the author seeks to account for apparent differences in local reaction to this form of urban planning in New York State.

This study plausibly approaches urban planning as a basic conflict over the nature and consequences of land development, though the specific instances deal primarily with private ventures in fringe development and thus are not yet applicable to large-scale public sponsorship of new towns and suburban nuclei in West European nations. Consequently, the author prefaces his detailed analyses with a process model of the land development arena and an adaptation of James Coleman's 1957 analysis of the dynamics of local controversy. In general, the author assumes that the probability of conflict is heightened by local sources of proposed change, by identification with narrow interests, by partial or vague presentation of plans, and by the economic or social class polarization prevalent in the affected area.

Very briefly, the three "new towns" had roughly similar processes, though with somewhat different timing of controversies. Lysander-Radisson (located northwest of Syracuse) was sponsored by a public agency, the state Urban Development Corporation, and had an early period of conflict, largely due to poor public relations and inadequate information for the residents of the neighboring area. But local acceptance was soon obtained, after the weakly organized opposition to the plan had expired. By contrast, Gananda (east of Rochester) was organized by a private developer, who was favored by good publicity and the support of locally esteemed financial leaders. Yet, as the community plan neared implementation, conflicts began to surface on matters such as education and jurisdictional issues. Finally, in Riverton (south of Rochester), the well-known Robert Simon, promoter of Reston, Virginia, carefully explained and sold the Riverton plan to local residents and authorities, generally forestalling controversy until the intervention of federal reviewing processes.

It is difficult to generalize about the political dynamics of planning new subcommunities from these instances. The author suggests, however, that, in the United States at least, the role of state and federal authorities and of bureaucratic intervention can be crucial in either facilitating or obstructing implementation. In fact, all three projects have been hampered by federal policy and by the economic recession of the 1970s—perhaps more significant than earlier local resistances. Perhaps, also, we are limited in what we can learn from the early and somewhat "unrealistic" phases of community development. We might more profitably focus on more advanced stages of conflict and accommodation, for example in the "older" new towns of Britain or in the evolution of Greenbelt since the New Deal years.

ALVIN BOSKOFF
Emory University
Atlanta
Georgia

ALFRED MCCLUNG LEE. *Sociology for Whom?* Pp. 236. New York: Oxford University Press, 1978.

To those familiar with the recent work of Alfred McClung Lee, it is obvious that the title of this book is a rhetorical question. In answering the question, the author presents a telling sociological analysis of establishment sociology as well as the humanistic sociologists' answer.

The relevance of the question posed by the title stems from the fact that social power is essentially people power, and that sociology may have the key to understanding and perhaps controlling social power. This power can be controlled and exercised either by the people or by power brokers such as politicians, financiers or religious leaders, and, therefore, sociology is ultimately for the service of one or the other of these groups.

Lee's analysis states that sociologists are unable and/or unwilling to contribute to the needs of the people to exercise and control this power, partially because of their selection and training, partially because of the types of careers they pursue, and partially because of the manner in which their professional organizations are structured.

Few sociologists have the intimate

and varied field-clinical experiences which are necessary to conduct defensible scientific work, which produces results of direct use to all classes of people. Further, political, economic and academic elites, through control of access to degrees, employment, promotion, and grants promote academic careerism, encourage, if not force, both training and work to be concerned with rationalization and propagation of the status quo.

This results in production of theories which are "nature centered," that is, the outcomes of individuals and humanity are the result of natural laws and, as such, are beyond human responsibility. When this type of theory is coupled with deindividualized views of people, and "scientific" methodology, the fact that the problems of life are of human origin and responsibility is obscured.

Positivistic establishment sociology, with its rhetoric oriented toward the status quo, is reluctant even to admit the possibility that coping with human problems means dealing with organizations which are in need of revision. Thus, the establishment sociologists find themselves allied with (lackeys of?) the power brackets. They become the source of knowledge of popular interests, needs, and fears, which is used by the brokers to manipulate the people. Even the professional organization of sociologists uses its code of ethics as a public relations device to rationalize and/or justify service to the power brokers (Chapter Eight offers real life examples of the type of responsibility and accountability to which this leads). Establishment Sociology's answer to the question posed by the title is obvious.

The correct answer for Lee and humanistic sociology is that sociology is for all classes of people so that they can participate in the control and employment of social power. To serve this end, sociologists should criticize, demystify, and clarify theories, drawing on knowledge gained from field-clinical situations. The historic and contemporary value of humanistic thought are presented forcefully, particularly in assessing the possibility of human survival. While these are important features of the author's argument for the humanistic approach, his position is most clearly stated in his suggestions for a more humanistic sociology: 1) development of a society of cooperative friends in search of social knowledge instead of one of competing prima donnas; 2) criticism of the abuse of power and privilege to exploit colleagues and students; 3) critical examination of fads in methodology and theory; 4) think of social problems as something more than developments which disturb various elites; 5) examination of the problems of those who do not have adequate food and shelter, not to mention human rights and dignity; and 6) exploration and publication of manipulative strategies and propaganda, exposing them for what they are.

No brief review can do justice to the author's humanistic sociology. Sociologists and other social scientists owe it to themselves to expose themselves and their students to the criticisms offered by this book and to ponder Lee's solutions as well as their own.

JERRY L. L. MILLER
University of Arizona
Tucson

AUGUSTUS Y. NAPIER and CARL A. WHITAKER. *The Family Crucible.* Pp. xiii, 301. New York, Harper & Row, 1978. $11.95.

*The Family Crucible* gives an excellent account of the rationale and technique of family therapy. It makes clear how family interactions are the problem and that no one individual can be blamed for his behavior. The approach this book takes is to alternate a description of the process of therapy with one particular family with theoretical and practical considerations of family therapy in general. This method makes it comprehensible to social scientists and even to interested laymen who do not work specifically in the field of psychotherapy.

Napier and Whitaker accept systems theory: a family is a system, that is, where any part affects the whole. The system may include subsystems, such as spouses, siblings, or a parent and child. Scapegoating can be part of a system where one child (sometimes a parent) is selected (unconsciously) as the target for the unsolved conflicts of the family. These conflicts more often than not derive from the unsolved conflicts of the parents with their families of origin, which are then reflected in the difficulties the spouses have with each other and result in entangling children in the situation with emphasis on one child in particular (the scapegoat as we have stated).

The uniqueness of this book is that through an informal, conversational style, it gets across the reality of the process of family therapy as no other book on the subject has done. Napier and Whitaker describe ongoing therapy with one family of parents and three children over a period of two years. Re-creations of the family's interactions are so vividly portrayed that the reader himself feels he is participating. Descriptions of the events that took place during a therapy session intermingle with discussions of the rationale for the way the co-therapists reacted in the session. The therapists never remain aloof but frequently delineate their worries about their own procedures and their frustrations when the family is not moving, as well as their excitment when they see real changes occurring in the patterns of family interactions. Furthermore, the therapists do complement each other's approach. At one point Whitaker attacks the mother quite strongly, and Napier comes to her defense, not by contradicting Whitaker but by exhibiting softness and empathy with how the mother is feeling.

Napier and Whitaker have two rather unique positions in relation to the conduct of family therapy. The first is that they adhere strictly to their rule of not fragmenting family sessions. No private sessions with individual members are allowed until the interpersonal problems are resolved. In this family everyone worked together until the children felt free from their parents' marital conflicts. At that time the spouses were seen together (although the children could come to the sessions if they so desired). It was not until the difficulties between the husband and wife were worked out that the therapists allowed the mother to be seen alone, at her request, as she wanted to work out some of her intrapsychic conflicts.

The second approach of Napier and Whitaker to family therapy is to include as many members as possible of the families of origin as consultants in the later stages of therapy. For example, the father's parents in the family under consideration were called in when he discovered that his father had secretly arranged a new job for him.

The last chapter of *The Family Crucible* deals exclusively with answering questions that might arise concerning practical matters about the management of family therapy. This is an unusual book in being all-inclusive but yet never becoming pedantic or uninteresting.

THEODORE ABEL
VÉGA LALIRE
University of New Mexico
Albuquerque

ERNEST PORTERFIELD. *Black and White Mixed Marriages: An Ethnographic Study of Black-White Families.* Pp. 189. Chicago: Nelson-Hall, 1978. $12.95.

Black-white marriage in the United States has not yet been heavily researched. The book under review here aims, at least partially, to remedy this situation. It consists of a systematic description of a population of 40 black-white families, a systematic review of research findings on such marriages covering the period from 1897 to 1964, and a brief historical survey of the phenomenon under study. In the final chapter the author contemplates the question of whether or not interracial marriage is a hindrance to the successful growth of black peoplehood.

Given the need for this kind of book, and the time and energy devoted to its publication, its final contribution remains somewhat disappointing. There are, in my view, two reasons for this. In the first place Dr. Porterfield's study somehow lost sight of the forest because of the trees. After reading the book the reader still remains very much uninformed about the exact nature of black and white intermarriage in this country. The author suggests at certain points in his discourse that the trend towards intermarriage will continue, and even increase gradually. He bases this assumption on the passage of civil rights legislation during the past decade and the 1967 United States Supreme Court decision which declared miscegenation laws unconstitutional. At the same time, however, his case materials repeatedly illustrate the growing rejection of racial intermarriage by blacks. What types, if any, of black-white marriage are likely to continue? Why, and under what conditions? Unfortunately, questions of this nature are not systematically raised, which gives the empirical part of the book a rather incidental flavor.

As far as the design of the empirical segment of the study is concerned, there is also a basic problem. The couples interviewed resided in four different locations: Illinois, Ohio, Alabama, and Mississippi. The obvious differences among these four settings do allow for a comparison and subsequent analysis of the possible association between the problems connected with racial intermarriage and its surrounding cultural milieu. But this type of systematic analysis is not presented; instead the subject families are most often simply lumped together and compared by criteria such as black-white marital combinations, marital happiness, and socioeconomic class. It is likely that the limited size of the research population necessitated such a combination of all regional categories, but I strongly suspect that the amount of variation introduced in this manner may seriously confuse the outcomes of the above comparisons. Furthermore, the research population only contained—by the nature of its selection—those interracial marriages which survived until the time of the research. To really understand the problematics of black-white marriage those unions which did not endure also should have been included.

In other words, what we are left with is an interesting, purely descriptive survey of a small population of black-white marriages. As stated above, in this social realm all data are welcome, and, as such, the book indeed contributes to our knowledge of how some of these kinds of marriages and families cope with their unusual circumstances. Unfortunately, that is about all we can learn from this study. One should hope that Dr. Porterfield continues his work in this area and provides us with more information in the future.

JETSE SPREY
Case Western Reserve University
Cleveland
Ohio

BOBBY BAKER and LARRY L. KING. *Wheeling and Dealing: Confessions of a Capitol Hill Operator.* Pp. 296. New York: W. W. Norton, 1978. $10.95.

GEORGE C. S. BENSON, STEVEN A. MAARANEN, and ALAN HESLOP. *Political Corruption in America.* Pp. xviii, 339. Lexington, MA: D. C. Heath, 1978. $21.95.

The Baker and Benson books are paradigmatic examples of the difference between the journalistic and scholarly approaches to politics. The former is impressionistic, anecdotal, simply written, and undocumented. The latter is written in formal language, is tightly organized, and includes extensive footnotes and bibliographical references. Yet despite their differing methodologies, both books illuminate dark corners of U.S. politics as they offer reconfirmation of the adage that politicians can't be bought—*cheaply*.

Baker, the former Senate page boy and secretary of the Democratic majority, rattles Capitol Hill skeletons in a way reminiscent of Suetonius' *De vita Caesarum*: he affords the same feeling of vicarious decadence and eroticism combined with moral superiority. He has a style so plain it is almost affectation, though the writing spouts with exuberance and at times frisks like a young colt. Indeed, throughout the book, the dominant tone is a page-turning combination of Potomac hubris and Carolina chutzpah. Baker, of course, was a notorious "doer," and the accounts of his services to Lyndon Johnson and Senator Kerr (he was Kerr's bagman) have about them something of the gathering suspense of a nineteenth-century realistic novel.

*Wheeling and Deeling* is flawed, certainly. It concentrates on the pre-Watergate, magnolia-scented Senate, and is thus outdated. It is really more about the author's passion for power and money than about the Senate. It avoids both theory and analytical argument. And, perhaps most damaging, it is written from an amoral, unrepentant perspective. Still, in fairness to Baker, it must be said that if he does not have a Boswellian craving to drop pretenses and tell the truth at any cost, he approximates that posture by avoiding cant about popular government and the ennobling virtues of representing the sovereign people.

More theoretical and systematic than *Wheeling and Dealing*, the Benson book is striated with useful insights and admonitory injunctions. The author, now President Emeritus of Claremont Men's College, summarizes a vast amount of scholarly and journalistic data regarding corruption, and at the end of each chapter boldly generalizes about aspects of the problem. Among his main conclusions are these: the federal government has least corruption, city governments the most; the varieties of corruption are limitless; there is no such thing as "honest graft"; the Truman Administration was the most corrupt in this century; and corruption is always dysfunctional, as it breeds widespread crime and cynicism and subverts the democratic representative process.

To praise the Benson book is not to agree with everything about it. The style, though generally clear, is rather pedestrian. Quantification is wholly eschewed. Watergate is barely mentioned. Little if any original historical material appears in the book. And, a minor point, the straight chronological approach, while making for clarity, is sometimes repetitive and a little deadening.

For all that, the Benson book is a first-rate addition to the literature of political corruption. And though its recommendations for "The Way Out of Corruption," set forth in Chapter 15, are cautious to the point of banality, its encyclopedic rehash of widely scattered materials makes it an invaluable research tool for scholars. There still is no such thing as a universally accepted theory of political corruption with a standard paradigm, but the Benson book may well be the next best thing. Too bad, therefore, that its inflated price will prove prohibitive for many who ought to read it.

FRANCIS M. WILHOIT
Drake University
Des Moines
Iowa

DIANE RAVITCH. *The Revisionists Revised: A Critique of the Radical Attack on the Schools.* Pp. xii, 194. NY: Basic Books. $8.95.

In *The Great School Wars*, a seminal work, Diane Ravitch demonstrated that educational reform does not merely reflect educators' convictions. Nor is it solely a story of changes in didactic methods or administrative restructuring. Comprising all these, it is also part and parcel of its times, inextricably interwoven with the political, economic, and cultural fabric of contemporary society. These concepts provide the rationale for her analysis of the radical assault on the public schools

Committed to the democratic-liberal tradition which created American public schools, she dedicates *The Revisionists Revised* to a defense against their assailants. In the 1950's conservative critics attacked them for alleged "fads and frills" and tolerance of radical ideas. Then radicals became the aggressors, charging schools with regimenting and indoctrinating children, stifling individualism, and processing pupils to become a permanent underclass in a capitalist society. These ideas grew out of the intellectual and emotional ferment of the late 1960's, in which the "New Left" charged the United States with racism and exploitation. Its adherents introduced a brand of politics that emphasized participatory democracy and confrontation as well as rejection of conventional American history as a "tissue of legends."

A brief but penetrating section considers the charge that the schools were instruments of "coercive assimilation," stripping minority children of their culture. This might occasionally apply to Indian schools. These institutions, however, were not established under a single, unvarying plan to oppress indigenous children, but under fluctuating policies, ranging from repression to cultural pluralism. More important, perhaps, is Ms. Ravitch's masterful exposition of European newcomers' relationships with the host society during the era of the "New Immigration." It indicates that the hope of advancement in a burgeoning economy persuaded most immigrants voluntarily to seek acculturation.

Have the schools failed to promote mobility, as the radicals assert? Neither observation nor research sustain the charge. The week the book was published, Ms. Ravitch was the principal speaker at a dinner in one of the nation's largest dining halls. Both the guest of honor, the outgoing Chancellor of New York City's schools, and the President of the Board of Education had risen far above their parents' stations. So, too, had most of the guests. Education had been indispensable for the progress of all. Social science literature now recognizes these facts.

Ms. Ravitch's critique of radical historians' methods is devastating. Apparently some have converted Voltaire's dictum, "History is philosophy teaching by examples" to "History is *my* philosophy teaching by *my chosen* examples." Unlike *The Great School Wars*, few if any of their works place educational reform in appropriate historical context. What is more, Ms. Ravitch's catalog of their shortcomings includes many of the first magnitude. One recalls Samuel Butler's assertation: "Though God cannot alter the past, historians can."

Ms. Ravitch generously credits her radical colleagues, nevertheless, with developing a fresh outlook on educational history that stimulates researchers in this area to ask searching questions and probe their specialties in greater depth. Perhaps a Hegelian dialectic between liberal education historians (thesis) and their conservative and radical counterparts (antithesis) may produce a synthesis, marked by a higher level of educational history.

Eventually this slim volume may exert a wide influence. It is axiomatic that teachers sway future leaders' minds. If this book's viewpoint gains widespread acceptance among educators, its ascendency may last for years to come.

FREDERICK SHAW

Office of Bilingual
   Education
Brooklyn
New York

STANLEY JOEL REISER. *Medicine and the Reign of Technology.* Pp. xi, 317. New York: Cambridge University Press, 1978. $14.95.

The history of technology and of medical practice (especially diagnosis) is blended in this painstakingly researched and well documented book in decidedly readable prose. The focus is on England and America and on the nineteenth and twentieth centuries. The author traces the origins of standard advances in diagnosis due to inventions: the thermometer, fluoroscope, microscope, stethoscope, ophthalmoscope, sphygmograph, electroencephalograph, electrocardiograph, x-ray, laryngoscope, and spirometer. Each in turn was destructive of "subjective" evidence— the patient's sensations and the on-the-spot physician's observations. Today there is a crisis, born of overwhelming "objective" evidence—laboratory tests and machines, including the eve of the computer age.

"The physician has become a prototype of technological man," a trend with dangers as well as benefits. The chemist, medical technologist, teams giving physical examinations, and the trend toward quantification are working against the old rapport between doctor and patient, born in intimacy and mutual interaction. Skills in using older techniques are in decline, while interpretation of new data is highly variable. Studies have shown doctors differing in diagnosis one out of five times; sharply differing when shown the same x-rays or EKG's; or making variable judgments on the same data after a lapse of time. Bored or half-educated laboratory staffs, totally ignorant of patients and their problems, may or may not give reliable information on a mass of tests (some only sought as protection against possible malpractice suits).

Here is a book to give your family physician (if he or she exists!) as a personal token of appreciation; or it will fascinate those sweating out months of slow recovery from hospitalization—for there are delicious quotes from old notebooks and diaries—and the bibliography will surely stimulate further reading. The director of the History of Medicine Program at Harvard Medical School is especially to be congratulated for realizing that historical research covering four centuries of medical diagnosis could provide food for intellectual stimulation (and pause) in our day.

The reviewer, as it happens, is a nicely recovering patient (half a year after myocardial infarction). He believes that the author has insufficient confidence in small town practitioners grouped about a small city hospital, although the implications of the book's case are that this patient was lucky to enjoy the personalized doctor/patient relationship born of having one physician for 14 years. Medical care outside the big cities is much better than the author thinks it is. Dr. Jack Kelly, president of the American Academy of Family Physicians, told colleagues on May 7, 1978, "The family physician is anything but a second-class doctor. He can handle 93 percent of a typical patient's problems, 85 percent of the time, in an office call or out-patient situation." He says that more than 50 percent of graduating family physicians are going into cities of less than 25,000. "Patients today want someone to care about them as persons," and costs are far less, he stated.

The present book could bring cheer to these doctors and their patients. To me, it appears to be a fine addition to the field of medical history and a sharp look at the dangers of mechanized medical practice.

VAUGHN D. BORNET
Southern Oregon State College
Ashland

DAVID SCHUMAN. *The Ideology of Form: The Influence of Organizations in America*. Pp. x, 196. Lexington, MA: Lexington Books, 1978. $17.95.

MASSIMO SALVADORI. *The Liberal Heresy: Origins and Historical Development*. Pp. xv, 248. New York: St. Martin's Press, 1978. $18.95.

Many books are now devoted to the dangers of what David Schuman's *The Ideology of Form* calls "tyranny without a tyrant" (p. 69). What Schuman means is that American politics has been sanitized by the preference for organization and administration (that is, for form rather than purpose) in the ideology of the "Federalist founding." Hence the invisibility of power, because only the impotent political order changes while the omnipotent social order persists. Hence the stifling of dissent through consensus rather than censorship. Hence the false reconciliation of individualism with public purpose, which assures neglect of both individual and collective selection of goals. Hence, finally, the mirror extremes of the all-American ideology of form, namely, organization theory, which attempts a technician's post-political objectivity; and violence, which promises a pre-political openness and a new start. In other words, the center as presently constituted will not hold, in a technological society whose liberal establishment can now enforce the Federalist formalism, because organization theory and other knowledge industries have, for the first time, provided the social tools required. The American ideology opposes a tyrant but sanctifies a provider—both in the name of liberty, of course.

Massimo Salvadori's *The Liberal Heresy* attempts to update the ideology of

Guido de Ruggiero by redefining its heretical, liberating element as opposition to the maximizing tendencies of authoritarianisms:

It is known empirically that the economists' law of diminishing returns applies to fields other than economic ones. This means that in many fields of activity, there is a point beyond which the disadvantages of whatever is done outweigh the advantages. That point is the *optimum*: whatever the efforts made, no one can ascertain how it can be established, except through trial and error. The *maximum*—to go as far as the ideal goal prescribes—is self-destructive. . . . Implicit in liberalism are rejection of the maximum, of the integralism which leads to authoritarianism, and the unending search for the optimum, essential for the peaceful coexistence of different tendencies on a level of equality. (pp. 31–32)

In this context, Salvadori refights Thermidor and Waterloo on a grand historical scale, so as to place liberal welfarism and revisionist socialism on the good side, and the spawn of Jacobin imperialism, which is to say hard-line Socialism and Fascism, on the bad side. His conclusion is that only the heretical notion that "theirs" and "mine" are equal in rights and respect, whether in matters of property or opinion, can protect the weak from the integralist maximizers.

Liberty existed in the past because monarchs, theocrats, and oligarchs could not control their intended victims, but "thanks to greater efficiency and larger populations the new absolutism is more frightful and frightening than the old. . . . Adding political subjection and monopoly of media and education to economic subservience, control over citizens becomes total. Scientific advances perfect control over consciences and minds. . . ." (pp. 217–218). The fate of the poor and the minorities within states, and of the fledgling nations in the international system, therefore depends on reviving that presently unfashionable, still heretical idea of the coequality of opposing interests.

Salvadori and Schuman have neatly reversed Walt Rostow's dictum that advanced industrialism cures the diseases of the transition to modernity. They represent the new dogma that the technological society implies bureaucracy and meritocracy, so that tyranny is transformed rather than replaced. Salvadori, an exile teaching in Britain and the United States since the collapse of Italian liberalism in the 1920s, looks to the traditional middle institutions of church, community, and property to hold up the walls of Liberal, Christian, and Social Democracy. Schuman, one of the new breed of political scientists, born at Berkeley and now reproducing in East Coast universities, looks to the creation of voluntary middle institutions like those advocated by the New Anarchists. Salvadori's rational heroes of the liberal tradition in Europe are therefore Schuman's insensitive liberal establishment in America. There are other differences as well: Salvadori's pessimism as over against Schuman's optimism; Salvadori's mistrust of and Schuman's faith in the masses; and opposing views of United States politics. More important, however, are their similarities: hostility toward conformist ideologies, belief in the treason of intellectuals, and preference for limited goals.

Neoliberalism and neoanarchism are, in fact, two of the major alternatives to the technological society which are in vogue because they promise to reintroduce democratic values into politics after one generation of prescriptive ideology and another generation of supposedly objective government. Salvadori's proposals for right thinking and Schuman's for right organization may exaggerate the power of ideas and forms in the preservation of democracy as compared with, say, Benveniste's *The Politics of Expertise*, Paul Dickson's *The Future of the Workplace*, and Amory Lovins' *Soft Energy Paths*. But Schuman, in particular, occasionally salts his criticism of Herbert Simon and his praise of Murray Bookchin with constructive suggestions for right action on alternative technology and community organization. Ben Wattenberg would accuse both Salvadori and Schuman of abetting the failure and guilt complex; ideologues of left and right would see in them a failure of will and purpose; and mainstream politicos would find little of a practical nature in their suggestions. But there is more than a rethinking of the end-of-ideology debate here.

THOMAS J. KNIGHT
The Pennsylvania State University
University Park

## ECONOMICS

LYNDA ANN EWEN. *Corporate Power And Urban Crisis in Detroit.* Pp. viii, 312. Princeton: Princeton University Press, 1978.

This is a rather simplistic book; it seems to carry the revisionist urge, better identified with international politics and recent American history, into the field of urban affairs. The book's central thesis is that the class struggle, as described and interpreted by Marx, is going to have to be taken into account in developing future alternatives for dealing with the urban crisis now confronting the various levels of government in this country. Detroit is the context in which some of the efforts of these various levels to cope with that crisis—albeit dismally, in the author's judgment—are briefly reviewed, and the case for a Marxist approach to dealing with that crisis presumably developed.

The author marshals an impressive amount of information in endeavoring to identify in some detail who comprise the haves and have nots in Detroit. The latter are treated both historically and functionally; the chronic problems associated with their non- and underemployment receive perceptive, careful treatment in the context of the increasing automation and industrialization, notably in automaking, so characteristic of that city in this century. An occupational profile of Detroit prior to large-scale manufacturing emphasizes employer-employee antagonisms. The lure of the automakers for largely unskilled laborers, the notable influx of black workers (and some whites) responding to these employment prospects, the stimulus of the two world wars further broadening those prospects,

and the bloody unionizing struggles of the 1930's all served to reinforce and extend the difficult relationships, in the author's judgment. Across time the effect of these occurrences is viewed as threefold: (a) a durable, tightly knit owner-manufacturer-financing group emerged capable of maintaining control over the means of production, and deploying these to its own ends and interests; (b) a skilled and semiskilled work force, part of it unionized, has been co-opted to support the owner-manufacturer-financing group's social and economic preferences, mainly because it benefits from them; and (c) a large, unskilled underclass with a liberal sprinkling of racial and ethnic minorities, has inherited the ills and disadvantaged of the prevailing social and economic order, and is seeking redress to no avail.

Such a perception of social and economic reality readily lends itself—at least in appearance—to a Marxist explanation. An economic elite rules in its own interest, it is alleged; it chooses to depress wages so labor will remain sufficiently cheap and abundant to satisfy expected production requirements. But one may ask whether the author really makes a case for this analysis in Marxist terms?

Not really. Demonstrating that both haves and have nots reside in Detroit does not establish the fact that the former caused the latter's socioeconomic condition. That it is in some way responsible will not be argued; however, the extent of responsibility is not clear. To allege conspiracy on behalf of the haves is not to prove it. Allegations as to the primacy or totality of responsibility on the part of the haves are not persuasively supported. The material provided in this book on this point is more akin to that marshalled by Floyd Hunter, not exactly a Marxist, in his argument on behalf of community elites and their influence.

Working from a Marxist perspective (despite evident weaknesses in crucial parts of the documentation), the author is led to the conclusion that the best interests of the have nots would be served if they were assured of participation in employment and public policy decisionmaking now dominated by the haves. The preferred model appears to be something like the popular front strategy pursued for political reasons by certain Marxist groups, notably in France, in the 1930's. This choice of a participatory, nonviolent role for the have nots contrasts sharply with the more violence-prone role prescribed for them by Marx vis-à-vis the haves. Nonviolence is at least recognized as a customary stance of the lumpenproletariat of America's urban centers. But so is nonideology, which seems to make the Marxist frame of reference as a way of approaching this study largely superfluous, when all is said and done.

In sum, this is an interesting, rather well-documented study of have–have not relationships in Detroit. However, as a demonstration of the correctness of Marx's explanation of how and why these relationships evolved, and what to do about them à la Marx, the book is disappointing.

HARRY W. REYNOLDS, JR.
University of Nebraska
Omaha

WALTER I. GARMS, JAMES W. GUTHRIE, and LAWRENCE C. PIERCE. *School Finance: The Economics and Politics of Public Education.* Pp. x, 466. Englewood Cliffs, NJ: Prentice-Hall, 1978. $14.95.

Any book like the one under review, which assists educators and school directors in the understanding of the complex subject of school finance, warrants endorsement. This volume draws upon the experiences of many states and a great deal of research in presenting a clear nationwide picture of school finance. The updating of the many changes at the federal and state level adds to the usefulness of *School Finance: The Economics and Politics of Public Education.* When one reads about the numerous court decisions and continuous development of new federal laws, one begins to comprehend the vast changes in educational policy which have come about in recent years.

*School Finance* is an excellent reference book, especially for school directors, and should be included on the special shelves for new school directors. It is a must for the preinduction term for new superintendents and new college presidents. Outstanding chapters are: "Present State of School Finance": "Collective Bargaining in Public Education"; "The Politics and Economy of Federal Education Policy"; and "Structure and Financing of Public Schools."

Some of those who have been deeply involved within the bureaucracies of the local, state, federal, and foreign governments lament the disinclination towards intergovernmental cooperation. The authors have not taken the time to denounce the attitude among many bureaucrats and legislators to spend federal funds just to reduce the balance to zero. Many of the same legislators who are careful to create the public image of being conservative with the funds for which they levy taxes at the same time are overzealous in the expenditure of federal funds. Many of us would support those involved in public expenditures if we could be assured that the funds would be carefully and judiciously expended.

It came as a surprise that there were no references to the fiscal problems of new towns or large-scale community developments in suburbia. When 3,000 to 5,000 new residences are erected after the assessment deadline and are occupied when school opens in September, a great many new residents escape a year's school taxes. At the same time the school budget for new teachers increases enormously and new facilities are usually required to be built while the homes are under construction. In Bucks County, Pennsylvania, Levittown had no need for double or triple sessions when a change in the law captured the formerly "lost" real estate taxes. The additional revenue permitted the local superintendents to stockpile over 100 teachers in the spring for whom there would not be any assignments until new pupils arrived in the fall. For the first few months there was an ample supply of teachers for special tutoring. Municipal revenue bond financing permitted school facilities to be constructed in advance of new residents.

The volume would have been enhanced if it had given more attention to economies in the planning and construction of new facilities. The use of "clinics" with the participation of all faculty members concerned, and the use of secondary school facilities by more citizens and high school students has served many Pennsylvania communities very well. A continuous review of state standards and laws, too, has resulted in lower costs. The academic credentials of all the authors account for, as one would anticipate, some of the theoretical recommendations. *School Finance* should be on your reading list.

CHARLES H. BOEHM

Morrisville
Pennsylvania

ZOLTAN KENESSEY. *The Process of Economic Planning.* Pp. viii, 400. New York: Columbia University Press, 1978. $16.50.

This is the book of a resolute partisan of central planning, "of overall intervention by government in order to achieve planned targets of growth" (p. 69). Dr. Kenessey believes that if properly managed, "the planned economy holds a number of promises: for a more efficient resource allocation from the overall social point of view" (p. 43); and that it can and should be blended with the market toward which it is not at all "antagonistic" (p. 98). Furthermore, "modern technology and modern society, in the long run, cannot function efficiently except in a planned manner" (pp. 60–61). All this does not mean, however, that Dr. Kenessey fails to perceive that there are significant shortcomings in planning—though he does not dwell excessively upon them—or that he doesn't see the general "social uses" of the market—though he warns us that both "planning and the market may be misused" in order to "foster special interests" (p. 99).

Dr. Kenessey is in favor of what he calls "humanistic" planning—based on the "humanistic ethics" whose "central value criterion is man's welfare" (p. 107)—as opposed to the totalitarian varieties. While he considers the Soviet planning experience as successful as far as growth is concerned, he recognizes clearly the deep imbalances and the great inefficiency of that economy, though he tends to attribute all this to the by now familiar caveat that "Russia was far from being the best testing ground for economic planning or for socialism in general" (p. 61).

Within this overall framework the book unfolds as a description of various institutional aspects of planning, of the ways of elaborating development strategies and plans, and of the manners in which they can be implemented—generously seasoned with well meant advice addressed to the potential planners themselves. The latter are advised, for instance, to "aid institutional reforms that can bring about the increased utilization of market forces" (p. 102); to take account of the fact that a "dispersed effort, owing to resource limitations, involves a slower development on a broader front" while "more concentrated development efforts usually lead to faster development" (p. 129); never to overlook during the elaboration of the development strategy "both the benefits and the costs of the envisaged growth" (p. 133); and, in general, "to have an open mind and considerable flexibility" in the vexing conflict between growth and the quality of life. There is more sound advice as to how one should look upon capital formation (p. 136), how and why one should avoid "the cardinal sin" of neglecting agriculture (p. 142), and how the planner should use the data and "cultivate his link to the statisticians" (p. 228)—but the list need not be lengthened further here.

While the author has dedicated his work "to those interested in the betterment of the human condition through planned social action" (p. vii), he has clearly not presented them with a book marked by either originality of thought or presentation. Much more can be found—without the advice to planners

—in the well-known books for under-graduates of Jan Tinbergen, *Central Planning* and *Development Planning.* And further, much more advanced litera-ture is, of course, available on this matter—part of which is quoted here and there by Dr. Kenessey. Maybe, how-ever, this personalized approach will be more successful and attractive to those who have to set up the institu-tional framework for planning in practice.

NICOLAS SPULBER
Indiana University
Bloomington

M. CARTER MCFARLAND. *Federal Gov-ernment and Urban Problems HUD: Successes, Failures, and the Fate of Our Cities.* Pp. xviii, 277. Boulder, CO: Westview Press, 1978. $20.00.

This readable treatise is in effect a manual on the Department of Housing and Urban Development; any person employed by or seriously involved with HUD ought to read it carefully from cover to cover. The author was a policy-making Eisenhower appointee in the Housing and Home Finance Agency, HUD's predecessor, and has been con-tinuously involved in or exceptionally close to U.S. urban policy development ever since. The book displays a lively and literate style, which is comprehen-sive and essentially fair. McFarland's biases are readily apparent but they do not get in the way of excellent reporting.

HUD, the reader should realize, is a governmental agency in Washington D.C. A book about HUD is not a book about America's cities, people or busi-ness, except as outside reality filters across certain desks in that agency. HUD in itself is significant, and hence worth reading about, because it does have impacts upon the real world. This book helps to show how little HUD is affected by the actual conditions of our cities. The department's mission has al-ways been assigned by the political process, which asks only that some ac-tivity be undertaken without making clear the ends to be served. Policymak-ers at HUD, then, have to select their own private criteria for success or fail-ure; this book is McFarland's report card for HUD, judging it by subjective stand-ards and primarily as an organization rather than a mission.

The first quarter of the book describes the genesis of HUD and evaluates its leadership to date. McFarland explains how key urban-related agencies dealing with transportation and home mortgages were kept out of HUD, and otherwise why HUD at best was bound to disap-point its advocates. He offers an explicit job description for HUD Secretary, along with candid, almost brutal judge-ments on each of the Secretaries from Weaver through Harris. Although he doesn't actually use letter grades it is easy to see that he gives Weaver top marks with a B+, Harris a condescend-ing B−, and others considerably poorer grades. George Romney seems to rate a C− for his "innocent and high-minded mistakes" (p. 43). Two chapters discuss the failure of city planning to deal with basic urban problems, which McFarland considers to be: the automobile, land speculators, and political fragmentation of metropolitan areas. A succinct, sad history of urban renewal follows a knowledgable critique of the block grant program. His comments on the model cities effort and on rehabilitation pro-grams seem entirely fair, and he predicts a reversion to categorical aids better targeted toward inner-cities. In just a few pages McFarland provides an excel-lent outline for a whole curriculum in planning.

About half of the book is given over to specific housing issues, unfortunately without painting any picture at all of the financial, economic or demographic magnitudes involved. The discussion of FHA's rise and fall is first rate, and there is the gentlest put-down of Opera-tion Breakthrough. A chapter on hous-ing discrimination would be better if it went a bit further into the dilemma of integration versus better housing as Federal goals. The treatment of housing subsidy programs and the cyclical per-formance of the market is much better. McFarland gives himself away in an al-most testy rebuttal to those who claim that subsidy programs are so limited in scale as to be mere tokens; he comes down four-square for tokenism. He also argues cogently for the use of fiscal rather than monetary policy in coping with national economic instability.

The last part of the book includes a perceptive criticism of urban research, and some slightly vague rationalizing for HUD's inadequate level of accomplishment. It is clear that McFarland is in sympathy with the concept of HUD and tends to blame either poor leadership or external factors for its failures. The book's introduction, by Paul Ylvisaker, while kind to McFarland's effort, is the most complete damnation of HUD likely ever to see print and a welcome counterpoint to the basic work.

WALLACE F. SMITH

University of California
Berkeley

BORIS S. PUSHKAREV and JEFFREY ZUPAN. *Public Transportation and Land Use Policy*. Pp. vii, 242. Bloomington: Indiana University Press, 1977. $18.50.

This book is the publication of a report undertaken by the authors for the Tri-State Planning Commission, at the Regional Plan Association of New York. As such, it is a "New York" book with most of its examples drawn from New York City and the surrounding suburban area.

Although not written by economists, the book's six chapter titles would be right at home in an economics book: Demand for Transit (two chapters), Transit Supply (two chapters), and Matching Supply and Demand. The analysis in the chapters, however, presents the planner-engineer perspective, with graphic analysis of multiple values assumed for various parameters.

Concern here is with the age old chicken and egg problem: does land use beget transportation demand or does transportation supply beget land use? This book strongly portrays the former as the most dominant, especially regarding transit, but certainly recognizes the sprawl influence of the urban radial expressways built from the 1950s on.

The main thrust of this study asks two basic questions:

1) What kind of transit service can be supported where, at what residential and nonresidential densities, at what cost?
2) How will the location and density of new residential and nonresidential development affect auto and transit use?

The demand chapters investigate the impacts of micro behavioral variables on transportation demand—money, time, disamenity—which are controllable in the short run by the suppliers of transport services; and the more macro impacts of land use and densities which are controllable in the long run by land use planners and the police powers (zoning) of the government. The micro demand analysis, not surprisingly, shows inelastic demands for public transit, and provides very incomplete bibliographic coverage, giving no discussion of the vast literature on behavioral modal split undertaken in the last five years. It seems clear that this book is not designed to be exhaustive but is designed for a less sophisticated audience of planners who would find a short, practical discussion appropriate.

The land use chapter is primarily concerned with explaining trip generation and auto ownership using conventional regression models. The models are not well discussed and, although yielding intuitively correct results, specification error may exist in the analysis. No elaborated a priori theory rests behind the regressions. Again this is probably sufficient for the intended audience, and the results of the demand analysis are certainly interesting, seeing what land uses and densities generate what level of transit and auto use.

The supply chapters define eight modes of public transportation which could compete with personal transportation by auto. These are taxi, dial-a-ride, local bus, express bus, light rail, light guideway transit, standard rapid transit, and commuter rail. The characteristics of each mode are described as to physical attributes and service, and estimates of capital and operating costs for existing systems are given, including energy costs and materials consumption for construction. The second supply chapter shows the relationship of speed to development density; for example, the auto is slowed relatively more than rapid rail transit as development increases. It also discusses access, station spacing, and peaking characteristics.

Chapter 5, Matching Supply and Demand, and Chapter 6, Summary and Interpretation, present the "meat" of the book. Chapter 5 shows what service can be provided, by frequency and cost, for each of the eight modes mentioned above, at each density.

The conclusions of the study are important:

1) While it is possible to expand the use of public transit by improving transit service, the costs are high and the results modest because of inelastic transit demands.

2) From the transit point of view, it is easier to gain riders by auto restraint or from increased density of urban development. Clustering nonresidential space, enlarging downtown size, increasing residential density near downtown, and concentrating apartments near transit will greatly enhance transit use. The tradeoffs of locating these developments at various places in the urban area are explicitly given.

3) Labor cost control is needed to control transit wages and transit automation needs to be explored.

4) Dial-a-Bus and light guideway transit aren't likely to be successful.

5) Commuter rail, conventional rapid transit, and express bus with foot access have limited applicability to large cities.

6) Express buses with park and ride access have very broad potential.

7) Rapid transit investment and expansion is best concentrated in existing lines, although some new lines could be constructed.

This book is an important one for its message: land use controls are needed if transit is to provide transportation services. This message has been heard before, but it needs strong advocates. Every strong advocacy position taken will bring us closer to land use controls which will make people *want* to choose public transportation; and automobile restriction, such as has been instituted in Singapore, all leading to more energy efficient development.

W. BRUCE ALLEN
University of Pennsylvania
Philadelphia

L. N. RANGARAJAN. *Commodity conflict, The Political Economy of International Commodity Negotiations.* 390 p. Ithaca: Cornell University Press, 1978.

Rangarajan's review of the international commodity issues after UNCTAD IV (Nairobi) provides some fresh thinking but suffers from insufficient economic analysis. The author points to the economic and political roots and consequences of the commodity problem, outlines the complex network of conflicting interests of many varied parties, and shows that with attention being paid either to efficiency or to equity it becomes difficult to negotiate and to observe commodity agreements. Rangarajan's treatment of the issue stresses its importance and indicates that it cannot be dealt with in isolation from other North-South problems.

Having recognized the complexity of the international commodity issue, he proceeds to evaluate existing simplistic judgments and solutions. While his sympathies are clearly on the side of the developing countries, he sees no basis for the accusation made of the well-to-do industrialized world that they plan to exploit the less developed periphery. He sees, however, an asymmetry between the rich and the poor providers of raw materials. This asymmetry was born, he suggests, of neglect and insensitivity shown by advanced countries, is further enhanced by the latter pursuing primarily their own interests, and by the operation of the more or less free economic system that favours the rich at the expense of the poor.

The gap between them should be decreased, but not by using recipes that are too generalized and demagogic, says Rangarajan. The author roundly criticizes the proposals for international multicommodity stocks or for indexation of commodity prices, offspring of the meetings in Nairobi and Manila. Global stocks, as proposed, would exclude energy (crude, gas, coal) and basic food products (cereals); moreover, they would be run in accordance with two irreconcilable aims—a search for stability and an assurance of above equilibrium prices. The author recognizes, however, that commodities such as coffee, cocoa, tin, and copper could benefit from buffer stocks. Indexation is objectionable because it would apply to some commodities only, leaving many poor countries outside its presumably beneficial influence. The instrument of indexation would ignore oil, the price of which has had more impact on less developed countries than that of any other single commodity. In addition, it would define the parity terms of trade on the basis of disparate and often conflicting criteria, such as the rate of world-wide inflation, fluctuation in the price of goods imported to the developing countries, and changes in the exchange rate.

Rangarajan outlines his own proposals that would recognize the multiplicity of goals and needs that exist in a world composed of many countries large and small, developed or not, net exporters or net importers of commodities, and producers of different mixes of primary products. The author is distrustful of markets and prices. The fact that most markets fail to behave like neat examples used in textbooks has led him to the conviction that free markets are a pernicious, or at least useless tool. He plumps, therefore, for a method which, for lack of a better name, could be called one of uncoordinated material balances. It is a model pleasing to a man fascinated by the methods of conflict resolution and the politics of international negotiations, but, in the eyes of an economist, hardly a coherent set of principles systematically leading to the achievement of any specific goal.

According to the author, an international Agreement on Commodity Trade (ACT) would provide the rules of negotiations, procedures (for instance, safeguards, exceptions, adjudication), and structures that would help countries to reach series of bilateral agreements. Each country, rich or poor, would come to the negotiating table, or rather to an array of negotiating tables, with a list of its objectives, such as improved access for one's manufactured products, specific pricing policy, or a list of concessions that might include assured access to supplies and an improvement in reliability. Hopefully, under the guiding light of the principle of reciprocity, but not necessarily of the equality of concessions, a quantity of bilateral agreements would be concluded to provide for expanded exchanges at prearranged prices. These agreements could be made between individual countries or between small groups of countries having similar characteristics for instance: "predominantly agricultural exporters, heavily dependent on one or two commodities" (p. 319). The next stage would consist of harmonizing the many agreements so concluded; this could be done most probably through a process somewhat reminiscent of the early GATT negotiations, such as the Torquay round. There is room for doubt as to whether integrating bilateral contracts using several variables (prices, quantities, duties, quotas, regulations) should be any easier than the task of coordinating the agreements concluded under GATT, which referred to rates of duties alone.

To an economist what is proposed sounds like a welter of contracts that may well be satisfactory from the static and narrowly partial equilibrium point of view. Whether waste or inefficiency is avoided, when one takes a more general equilibrium approach, is a matter of luck, as an economist would be tempted to say, or a matter of negotiating prowess, as would be implied by the author. When the dynamic approach is taken, the doubts of the economist increase even more, especially as flexible prices, those imperfect but workable devices of dynamic adjustment, are somehow left out of consideration. In L. N. Rangarajan's scheme no alternative means of signaling changes and apportioning gains is offered.

The book may be seen as a common sense attack on the exaggerated expectations of those who wish to see the problem of development tackled by organizing an international commodity market for the benefit of the less developed South. Alternatively, the book may be seen as the first draft of a nonpartisan proposal concerning the commodity issue, a proposal, however, that would require an injection of economic analysis.

STANISLAW WASOWSKI
Georgetown University
Washington, D.C.

STEPHEN R. SEIDEL. *Housing Costs and Government Regulations: Confronting the Regulatory Maze*. Pp. xv, 434. New Brunswick, NJ: The Center for Urban Policy Research, 1978.

With a substantial number of families living in substandard housing and construction costs rising more rapidly than average family income, there is a clear need for federal, state, and local governments to initiate action to reduce or limit the rate of increase in housing costs. Yet this new study is the first major investigation of the costs associated with governmental regulation of the residential housing industry since the Douglas and Kaiser Commissions released their reports in late 1968.

To collect data, building department officials in 100 "randomly selected municipalities" were interviewed relative to the administration of building codes, officials in 80 municipalities were interviewed relative to the administration of zoning and subdivision ordinances, and questionnaires were posted to more than 33,000 home builders and land developers. About 2,500 responded and 400 were contacted by telephone for additional information.

Major chapters are devoted to building codes, energy conservation regulations, subdivision regulations, zoning ordinances, growth controls, environmental controls, and financing regulations. While concluding that "the com-

plexity of today's construction methods" makes building codes necessary, Seidel found that codes increased "costs by requiring safety and quality features which are in excess of what can reasonably be defended as minimum requirements" (p. 305). Particularly disturbing is the influence of trade groups in the drafting of model codes that are adopted by many municipalities. The author also found that "subdivision improvement requirements . . . bear very little relationship to minimum health and safety standards, and therefore unnecessarily drive up the cost of housing" (p. 308).

The fractionated system of local government in most states raises costs since builders operating in more than one municipality often cannot use standard plans. One must disagree with the sweeping statement that "there is no reason for the existence of thousands of diverse local codes," (p. 306) as there are political reasons for the existence of the fragmented system of government and diverse codes.

The author correctly points out that "a principal obstacle to preventing an efficient building regulation system is the myriad of municipal officials who must inspect and approve a structure. . . ." (p. 86). He fails, however, to discuss adequately the technical and administrative qualifications of these officials and their low salaries that often invite corruption, or to present recommendations to correct the situation other than "mandatory training and licensing of building officials" (p. 305).

Reduction in frontage and lot size requirements is the major recommendation offered for decreasing the cost of subdivision development. Seidel believes that mobile homes can "become a very real option for low- and middle income families" (p. 310), and recommends changes in site design and taxing policies. His recommendation that states establish a procedure for reviewing the decisions of local officials, if adopted, often will result in additional delays and increased costs.

JOSEPH F. ZIMMERMAN
State University of New York
Albany

EDWARD R. TUFTE. *Political Control of the Economy.* Pp. xi, 168. Princeton: Princeton University Press, 1978. $10.00.

The literature of political economy has an important new addition: a study of political party-electoral forces, and their interactions with macroeconomic policies and outcomes, by Edward R. Tufte, a specialist in statistical analysis of political data at Yale. (The statistical aspect ought not mislead; the book has not a page of technical jargon, and the writing is sprightly, combining empirical analysis with anecdotal documentary materials.)

Effectively synthesizing his own analyses with other recent writings, the author has compressed into a slim volume three elements: a rounded picture of the assumptions held by politicians regarding the impact of short-run economic changes (in particular, changes in disposable income through spurts in transfer payments) upon the electoral chances of incumbent office holders; empirical testing of several propositions concerning both the impact of party ideology upon policy choices and the observable connections between economic performance and electoral outcomes; and some thoughtful paragraphs evaluating current reform suggestions by economists for depoliticizing economic policy and offering his own suggestions for simultaneously optimizing democratic control and technical effectiveness of economic policies. (The phrase "political control" in the title refers not to regulation of business, as a reader might imagine, but to party-electoral influences.)

One of the book's major themes is the cyclical nature of the relationships it discusses. Because political leaders believe that manipulation of economic policies is essential to their own success and also that they know what some of the policy imperatives are (Tufte's analysis suggests that they are right), economic policy is definitely constrained by political factors. The strongest such constraints exist, of course, in election years. Actions to stimulate boom conditions come easily in such years; austerity

measures—even if objectively called for by economic conditions—do not. Is it true that such things matter? The answer is definitely "yes," as indicated in some striking data presented by Professor Tufte related to the Carter vote in 1976. A table (p. 132) relating political party, income, and self-perception of family financial condition pre-election, as compared with a year earlier, shows such findings as Carter winning less than 3 percent of the votes of Republicans with incomes over $5,000 who perceived their condition as improved but 95 percent of the vote of Democrats who saw their condition as having deteriorated. Some other findings are also fascinating: for example, that among Democrats who perceived their own conditions as improving, 91 percent of those with incomes below $5,000 and 63 percent of those with incomes in the $15–25,000 range voted for Carter. Among Republicans in the $15–25,000 range, only 3 percent who saw themselves as better-off than they were a year earlier voted for Jimmy Carter, while the figure for those who perceived themselves as experiencing worsening conditions was 20 percent. On a broader level, the electoral-economic cycle is intriguingly described as one in which the early part of a presidential term calls forth efforts to build "business confidence," while a "liberal hour" of social welfare expansion and reduction in unemployment characterizes the near election effort.

Heretofore, much of the political science writing in political economy has been insufficiently empirical, as well as dull. The volume reviewed here is a distinct advance on both counts.

MICHAEL D. REAGAN
University of California
Riverside

ARNOLD R. WEBER and DANIEL J. B. MITCHELL. *The Pay Board's Progress: Wage Controls in Phase II.* Pp., xvi. 454. Washington, DC: The Brookings Institution, 1978. $12.95.

As an analysis of a public policy attempt to deal with the major domestic problem of inflation, the volume under review could hardly be more timely. Indeed, even the genesis of the Nixon "Phases" in congressional, political, opposition criticism of the President for not dealing effectively with rampant inflation, must give Jimmy Carter a distinct sense of déjà vu.

In its continuing service of chronicling the vagaries of United States wage-price policymaking over recent years (this is the fifth volume in the series of studies), the Brookings Institution has drawn upon the expertise of coauthors who are academic specialists in industrial management, former or present Brookings Fellows, and perhaps most significant, governmental inner-outer practitioners on the Pay Board.

The Pay Board administered wage controls under "Phase II" from October 1971 through the spring of 1973. Thus this book could be typed as a case study in administration. But to do so would do an injustice to the richness in the variety and range of questions of major interest to political and social scientists which are addressed. For, at one level, this is an account of institution building in an atmosphere of crisis. There is the hurried elaboration of a broad mandate; the frantic formation of a staff (initially relying heavily on detailees from other government agencies), and a history of chronic understaffing—in large part due to the President's own war on bureaucratic expansion.

There is also to be found here a description of internal decisionmaking processes and their evolution. In this connection the authors give ample testimony to a special variant of the "Lowi problem"—interest group liberalism. For the Pay Board was set up (for political reasons of course) as a tripartite body, representing the three traditional legs of the domestic tripod, business, labor, and public membership. Whereas other regulatory agencies are beset by clientele influence from a single area (such as communications or air travel), the Pay Board had to deal with the gamut of interests in all enterprises. (Samplings of the variety are given in case study accounts of wage regulation activities in coal, railroads, aerospace, and others.)

This, of course, led to heated controversy among the three organizational components of the Board. Within five months, Big Labor simply withdrew, having felt from the outset that the dice were loaded against it.

Finally, the authors make a stab at evaluation and impact. How effective was the Pay Board in inhibiting inflationary trends? The verdict is mixed due to the ambiguity of indicators, the state of the evaluative art, and the overriding fact that the Pay Board was designed assertively to be a temporary institution, to give way to the next policy increment of Phase III. Therefore the reader is treated to a macroanalytical study of a microscopic phase in the evolution of American economic policy making.

CHARLES E. JACOB
Rutgers University
New Brunswick

## OTHER BOOKS

BALDWIN, JOHN and MICHAEL McCONVILLE. *Negotiated Justice: Pressures on Defendants to Plead Guilty.* Pp. xvi, 128. Totowa, NJ: Biblio Books, 1978. $12.00.

BASILE, PAUL S., ed. *Energy Supply-Demand Integrations to the Year 2000.* Pp. xiv, 706. Cambridge, MA: MIT Press, 1978. $29.95.

BECKWITH, BURNHAM PUTNAM. *Liberal Socialism Applied.* Pp. ix, 331. Palo Alto, CA: B. P. Beckwith, 1978. $12.00.

BEQUAI, AUGUST. *Computer Crime.* Pp. xiii, 207. Lexington, MA: Lexington Books, 1978. $15.00.

BERGER, ALAN S. *The City: Urban Communities and Their Problems.* Pp. xv, 511. Dubuque, IA: William C. Brown, 1978. Paperbound. No price.

BÉTEILLE, ANDRÉ. *Inequality Among Men.* Pp. x, 178. Forest Grove, OR: ISBS, 1977. $26.25. Paperbound, $8.00.

BLOOD, BOB, and MARGARET BLOOD. *Marriage.* 3d ed. Pp. xvii, 653. New York: Free Press, 1978. $12.95.

BOULDING, KENNETH E. *Stable Peace.* Pp. xii, 143. Austin, TX: University of Texas Press, 1978. $9.95. Paperbound, $3.95.

BOURNE, L. S. and J. W. SIMMONS, eds. *Systems of Cities: Readings on Structure, Growth, and Policy.* Pp. xv, 565. New York: Oxford University Press, 1978. $9.00. Paperbound.

BRISTOW, EDWARD J. *Vice And Vigilance: Purity Movements in Britain Since 1700.* Pp. vii, 274. Totowa, NJ: Rowman & Littlefield, 1978. $22.50.

BROWN, DAVID. *Anglo-Saxon England.* Pp. 111. Totowa, NJ: Rowman and Littlefield, 1978. $12.50.

BRUCAN, SILVIU. *The Dialectic of World Politics.* Pp. xii, 163. New York: Free Press, 1978. $13.95.

BURCHELL, ROBERT W. et al. *The Fiscal Impact Handbook: Estimating Local Costs and Revenues of Land Development.* Pp. xxiv, 480. New Brunswick, NJ: Rutgers University Press, 1978. No price.

BURTON, ANTHONY. *Revolutionary Violence: The Theories.* Pp. ix, 147. New York: Crane, Russak, 1978. $11.95.

CANTOR, ROBERT D. *American Government.* Pp. xiii, 287. New York: Harper & Row, 1978. $6.95. Paperbound.

CATTELL, DAVID T. and RICHARD SISSON. *Comparative Politics: Institutions, Behavior and Development.* pp. xiv, 453. Palo Alto, CA: Mayfield, 1978. $13.95.

CHAPMAN, JANE ROBERTS and MARGARET GATES. *The Victimization of Women.* Pp. 282. Beverly Hills, CA: Sage, 1978. No price.

*Consumer Protection: Gains and Setbacks.* Pp. 209. Washington, DC: Congressional Quarterly, 1978. $5.95. Paperbound.

CUNNINGHAM, NOBLE, JR. *Circular Letters of Congressmen to Their Constituents 1789–1829.* Vols. I, II, III. Chapel Hill: University of North Carolina Press, 1978. $75.00.

CURRAN, BARBARA A. *The Legal Needs of the Public: The Final Report of a National Survey.* Pp. xxxi, 382. Chicago: American Bar Association, 1977. $25.00. Paperbound.

DAVIES, JOHN BOOTH. *The Psychology of Music.* Pp. 240. Stanford, CA: Stanford University Press, 1978. $13.95.

DAVIS, EDWARD M. *Staff One: A Perspective on Effective Police Management.* Pp. xii, 244. Englewood Cliffs, NJ: Prentice-Hall, 1978. $16.95. Paperbound, $10.95.

DEUCHLER, MARTINA. *Confucion Gentlemen and Barbarian Envoys: The Opening of Korea, 1875–1885.* Pp. xiv, 310. Seattle: University of Washington Press, 1978. $20.00.

DOOB, LEONARD. W. ed. *"Ezra Pound Speaking: Radio Speeches of World War II.* Pp. xv, 465. Westport, CT: Greenwood Press, 1978. $29.95.

DOWSLING, JANET and ANNE MacLENNAN, eds. *The Chemically Dependent Woman.* Pp. x, 115. Toronto, Canada: ARF Books, 1978. $4.95. Paperbound.

DUBY, GEORGES. *The Early Growth of The European Economy: Warriors and Peasants from the Seventh to the Twelfth Century.* Pp. x, 292. Ithaca, NY: Cornell University Press, 1978. $5.95. Paperbound.

DYE, THOMAS R. *Understanding Public Policy.* 3d ed. Pp. xii, 338. Englewood Cliffs, NJ: Prentice-Hall, 1978. $11.95.

EHNINGER, DOUGLAS, ALAN H. MONROE, and BRUCE E. GRONBECK. *Principles and Types of Speech Communication.* Pp. xix, 492. Glenview, IL: Scott, Foresman, 1978. No price.

ELLING, RAY H. and MAGDALENA SOKOŁOWSKA, eds. *Medical Sociologists at Work.* Pp. 347. New Brunswick, NJ: Transaction Books, 1978. $14.95.

ELWOOD, ROBERT S., JR., ed. *Readings On Religion: From Inside and Outside.* Pp. xv, 336. Englewood Cliffs, NJ: Prentice-Hall, 1978. $7.95. Paperbound.

FEIN, GRETA. *Child Development.* Pp. xv, 584. Englewood Cliffs, NJ: Prentice-Hall, 1978. $14.95.

FICKER, VICTOR B. and HERBERT S. GRAVES. *Social Science and Urban Crises.* 2d ed. Pp. xv, 332. New York: Macmillan, 1978. No price.

FISHER, ANTONY. *Fisher's Concise History of Economic Bungling: A Guide for Today's Statesmen.* Pp. xv, 113. Ottawa, IL: Caroline House, 1978. $8.95. Paperbound, $2.95.

FLEMMONS, JERRY. *Amon: The Life of Amon Carter, Sr. of Texas.* Pp. 520. Austin, TX: Jenkins, 1978. $12.95.

FLYNN, PETER. *Brazil: A Political Analysis.* Pp. xii, 564. Boulder, CO: Westview Press, 1978. $28.75.

*Foreign Relations of the United States, 1950: The Near East, South Asia, and Africa.* Vol. V. Pp. xvii, 1889. Washington, DC: U.S. Government Printing Office, 1978. No price.

*Foreign Relations of the United States: Asia and the Pacific.* Vol. VI. Pp. xi, 2276. Washington, DC: U.S. Government Printing Office, 1977. No price.

FREEDMAN, JONATHAN L., DAVID O. SEARS, and J. MERRILL CARLSMITH. *Social Psychology.* 3d ed. Pp. ix, 628. Englewood Cliffs, NJ: Prentice-Hall, 1978. $14.95.

FRIEDMAN, J. and M. J. ROWLANDS, eds. *The Evolution Of Social Systems.* Pp. xiv, 562. Pittsburgh, PA: University of Pittsburgh, 1978. $45.00.

GELLING, MARGARET. *Signposts to the Past: Place-names and the History of England.* Pp. 256. Totowa, NJ: J. M. Dent, 1978. $14.50.

GLOVER, MICHAEL. *A Very Slippery Fellow: The Life of Sir Robert Wilson, 1777–1849.* Pp. xiii, 224. New York: Oxford University Press, 1978. $14.50.

GOODWIN-GILL, GUY S. *International Law And The Movement Of Persons Between States.* Pp. xxvii, 324. New York: Oxford University Press, 1978. No price.

GREEN, I. M. *The Re-Establishment of the Church of England 1660–1663.* Pp. x, 263. New York: Oxford University Press, 1978. $20.50.

GREEN, STEPHEN. *International Disaster Relief: Toward A Responsive System.* Pp. xvi, 101. New York: McGraw-Hill, 1977. $3.95. Paperbound.

GREENBERG, MICHAEL R. et al. *Local Population And Employment Projection Techniques.* Pp. 277. New Brunswick, NJ: Rutgers University Press, 1978. No price.

GROB, GERALD N. and GEORGE ATHAN BILLIAS, eds. *Interpretations of American History to 1877.* Vol. 1. 3d ed. Pp. x, 454. New York: Free Press, 1978. $6.95. Paperbound.

GROB, GERALD N. and GEORGE ATHAN BILLIAS, eds. *Interpretations of American History Since 1865.* Vol. II. 3d ed. Pp. ix, 496. New York: Free Press, 1978. $6.95. Paperbound.

HAENDEL, DAN. *The Process of Priority Formulation: U.S. Foreign Policy in the Indo-Pakistani War of 1971.* Pp. xix, 428. Boulder, CO: Westview Press, 1978. $25.00.

HALL, PETER. *Europe 2000.* Pp. xii, 274. New York: Columbia University Press, 1977. $15.00.

HANSEN, OLAF, ed. *The Radical Will: Randolph Bourne Selected Writings 1911–1918.* Pp. 548. New York: Urizen Books, 1978. $17.50. Paperbound, $7.95.

HARROD, FREDERICK S. *Manning the New Navy: The Development of a Modern Naval Force, 1899–1940.* Pp. xi, 276. Westport, CT: Greenwood Press, 1978. $18.95.

HAYEK, F. A. *New Studies in Philosophy, Politics, Economics and the History of Ideas.* Pp. vii, 314. Chicago: University of Chicago Press, 1978. $15.00.

*Historic Documents Of 1977.* Pp. 969. Washington, DC: Congressional Quarterly, 1978. $37.00.

HORNE, THOMAS A. *The Social Thought Of Bernard Mandeville: Virtue and Commerce in Early Eighteenth Century England.* Pp. xii, 123. New York: Columbia University Press, 1978. $12.50.

HOWARD, DICK. *The Marxian Legacy.* Pp. xv, 340. New York: Urizen Books, 1978. $15.00. Paperbound, $5.95.

HUGHES, BARRY B. *The Domestic Context of American Foreign Policy.* Pp. xii, 240. San Francisco: W. H. Freeman, 1978. No price.

HUNT, E. K. and HOWARD J. SHERMAN. *Economics: An Introduction to Traditional and Radical Views.* 3d ed. Pp. xxxii, 608. New York: Harper & Row, 1978. $11.50. Paperbound.

IRISH, MARIAN D. and ELKE FRANK. *Introduction to Comparative Politics: Thirteen Nation-States.* 2d ed. Pp. ix, 469. Englewood Cliffs, NJ: Prentice-Hall, 1978. $14.95.

ISHAK, AZIZ. *Special Guest: The Detention in Malaysia of an Ex-Cabinet Minister.* Pp. x, 210. New York: Oxford University Press, 1978. $24.95.

JOHNSTONE, ROBERT M., JR. *Jefferson And The Presidency: Leadership in the Young Republic.* Pp. 332. Ithaca: Cornell University Press, 1978. $15.00.

JOUGHIN, LOUIS, and EDMUND M. MORGAN. *The Legacy of Sacco and Vanzetti.* Pp. xii, 596. Princeton: Princeton University Press, 1978. $5.95. Paperbound.

KENNEDY, EUGENE. *Himself! The Life and Times of Mayor Richard J. Daley.* Pp. xv, 288. New York: Viking Press, 1978. $10.95.

KING, RUSSELL. *Land Reform: A World Survey.* Pp. xvi, 446. Boulder, CO: Westview Press, 1978. $28.75.

KINNARD, DOUGLAS. *President Eisenhower and Strategy Management: A Study in Defense Politics.* Pp. xi, 169. Lexington: University Press of Kentucky, 1977. $13.75.

KNEI-PAZ, BARUCH. *The Social and Political Thought of Leon Trotsky.* Pp. xx, 629. New York: Oxford University Press, 1978. $34.95.

KOMONS, NICK A. *Bonfires to Beacons: Federal Civil Aviation Policy Under the Air Commerce Act, 1926–1938.* Pp. v, 454. Washington, DC: U.S. Government Printing Office, 1978. $8.00. Paperbound.

KORBONSKI, STEFAN. *The Polish Underground State.* Pp. ix, 268. New York: Columbia University Press, 1978. $16.00.

KOTTKE, FRANK. *The Promotion of Price Competition Where Sellers Are Few.* Pp. vii, 227. Lexington, MA: Lexington Books, 1978. $17.00.

LADD, EVERETT CARLL, JR. and CHARLES D. HADLEY. *Transformations Of The American Party System.* 2d ed. Pp. 406. New York: W. W. Norton, 1978. $5.95. Paperbound.

LAMBERTI, MARJORIE. *Jewish Activism In Imperial Germany.* Pp. xii, 235. New Haven: Yale University Press, 1978. $17.50.

LAND, STEPHEN K. *Kett's Rebellion: The Norfolk Rising of 1594.* Pp. 165. Totowa, NJ: Rowman & Littlefield, 1978. $15.00.

LAURENSON, DIANA, ed. *The Sociology of Literature: Applied Studies.* Pp. 283. England: University of Keele, 1978. $4.95. Paperbound.

LAWRENCE, WILLIAM J. and STEPHEN LEEDS. *An Inventory of Federal Income Transfer Programs, Fiscal Year 1977.* Pp. viii, 219. White Plains, NY: Institute for Socioeconomic Studies, 1978. $12.00.

LECOURT, DOMINIQUE. *Proletarian Science: The Case of Lysenko.* Pp. 170. New York: Schocken Books, 1978. $11.50.

LEHNE, RICHARD. *The Quest for Justice: The Politics of School Finance Reform.* Pp. vi, 246. New York: Longman, 1978. $11.95. Paperbound, $4.95.

LEWIS, MERLIN, WARREN BUNDY, and JAMES L. HAGUE. *An Introduction to the Courts and Judicial Process.* Pp. viii, 327. Englewood Cliffs, NJ: Prentice-Hall, 1978. $14.95.

LINDZEY, GARDNER, CALVIN S. HALL, and RICHARD F. THOMPSON. *Psychology.* 2d ed. Pp. xv, 709. New York: Worth, 1978. $14.95.

LOGORECI, ANTON. *The Albanians: Europe's Forgotten Survivors.* Pp. 230. Boulder, CO: Westview Press, 1978. $16.00.

LOXTON, HOWARD. *Pilgrimage To Canterbury.* Pp. 208. Totowa, NJ: Rowman and Littlefield, 1978. $13.50.

MACHADO, MANUEL A., JR. *Listen Chicano: An Informal History of the Mexican-American.* Pp. xviii, 196. Chicago: Nelson-Hall, 1978. $10.95. Paperbound, $7.95.

MACKENZIE, NORMAN, ed. *The Letters of Sidney and Beatrice Webb: Apprenticeships 1873–1892.* Vol. I. Pp. xx, 453. New York: Cambridge University Press, 1978. $47.50. 3-vol. set, $125.00.

MACKENZIE, NORMAN, ed. *The Letters of Sidney and Beatrice Webb: Partnership 1892–1912.* Vol. II. Pp. xv, 405. New York: Cambridge University Press, 1978. $47.50. 3-vol. set, $125.00.

MACKENZIE, NORMAN, ed. *The Letters of Sidney and Beatrice Webb: Pilgrimage 1912–1947.* Vol. III. Pp. xii, 482. New York: Cambridge University Press, 1978. $47.50. 3-vol. set, $125.00.

MACRIDIS, ROY C. ed. *Modern Political Systems: Europe,* 4th ed. Pp. xii, 532. Englewood Cliffs, NJ: Prentice-Hall, 1978. $14.95.

MARTIN, WILLIAM F., ed. *Energy Supply to the Year 2000.* Pp. xvi, 406. Cambridge, MA: MIT Press, 1978. $29.95.

McHALE, JOHN and MAGDA CORDELL McHALE. *Basic Human Needs: A Framework for Action.* Pp. 249. New Brunswick, NJ: Transaction Books, 1977. $5.95. Paperbound.

McVEIGH, FRANK, and ARTHUR SHOSTAK. *Modern Social Problems.* Pp. xix, 650. New York: Holt, Rinehart and Winston, 1978. No price.

MELLAART, JAMES. *The Archaeology Of Ancient Turkey.* Pp. 111. Totowa, NJ: Rowman and Littlefield, 1978. $12.50.

METCALF, MICHAEL F. *Russia, England and Swedish Party Politics, 1762–1766.* Pp. vii, 278. Totowa, NJ: Rowman & Littlefield, 1978. $35.00.

MILENKY, EDWARD S. *Argentina's Foreign Policies.* Pp. xvii, 345. Boulder, CO: Westview, 1978. $20.00.

MITRA, ASHOK. *Terms of Trade and Class Relations.* Pp. xi, 193. Totowa, NJ: Frank Cass, 1977. $25.00.

MOREY, ADRIAN. *The Catholic Subjects of Elizabeth I.* Pp. 240. Totowa, NJ: Rowman & Littlefield, 1978. $16.50.

MOROZ, HAROLD R. *The Republic of Vietnam.* Pp. 63. Hicksville, NY: Exposition Press, 1978. $5.00.

MULDER, JOHN M. *Woodrow Wilson: The Years of Preparation.* Pp. xv, 304. Princeton: Princeton University Press, 1978. $16.50.

NANDA, VED P., ed. *Water Needs for the Future: Political, Economic, Legal, and Technological Issues in a National and International Framework.* Pp. viii, 329. Boulder, CO: Westview, 1977. No price.

NELKIN, DOROTHY. *Technological Decisions and Democracy: European Experiments in Public Participation.* Pp. 114. Beverly Hills, CA: Sage, 1977. $7.95.

NEWELL, CLARENCE A. *Human Behavior In Educational Administration.* Pp. x, 261. Englewood Cliffs, NJ: Prentice-Hall, 1978. $11.95.

O'NEILL, TIMOTHY. *Life and Tradition in Rural Ireland.* Pp. ix, 122. London: J. M. Dent, 1978. $19.50.

*Outer Space: Battlefield of the Future.* Pp. xviii, 202. New York: Crane, Russak, 1978. No price.

PALMER, ROBIN and NEIL PARSONS, eds. *The Roots of Rural Poverty in Central and Southern Africa.* Pp. xviii, 430. Berkeley: University of California Press, 1978. $16.50. Paperbound, $5.95.

PENROSE, EDITH and E. F. PENROSE. *Iraq: International Relations and National Development.* Pp. xviii, 569. Boulder, CO: Westview, 1978. $28.75.

PERRY, STEWART E. *San Francisco Scavengers: Dirty Work and the Pride of Ownership.* Pp. 251. Berkeley: University of California Press, 1978. $10.95.

POPHAM, W. JAMES. *Criterion-Referenced Measurement.* Pp. ix, 260. Englewood

Cliffs, NJ: Prentice-Hall, 1978. $6.95. Paperbound.

PRITCHETT, C. HERMAN. *The Federal System in Constitutional Law*. Pp. ix, 394. Englewood Cliffs, NJ: Prentice-Hall, 1978. $7.95. Paperbound.

PURTILL, RICHARD L. *Thinking About Religion: A Philosophical Introduction to Religion*. Pp. xiii, 175. Englewood Cliffs, NJ: Prentice-Hall, 1978. $5.95. Paperbound.

QUARANTELLI, E. L., ed. *Disasters: Theory and Research*. Pp. 282. Beverly Hills, CA: Sage, 1978. No price.

RABINOVICH, ITAMAR and HAIM SHAKED, eds. *From June to October: The Middle East Between 1967 and 1973*. Pp. xxiii, 419. New Brunswick, NJ: Transaction Books, 1978. $19.95.

RHYMER, JOHN D. *Political Predictions For The Future: A Citizen's Manifesto*. Pp. 85. Hicksville, NY: Exposition Press, 1978. $10.00.

ROSE, RICHARD. *What is Governing? Purpose and Policy in Washington*. Pp. x, 173. Englewood Cliffs, NJ: Prentice-Hall, 1978. $5.95. Paperbound.

ROTBERG, ROBERT. *Black Heart: Gore-Brown and the Politics of Multiracial Zambia*. Pp. 377. Berkeley, CA: University of California Press, 1978. $15.00.

RUMMEL, R. J. *Conflict In Perspective: Understanding Conflict and War*. Vol. 3. Pp. 200. Beverly Hills, CA: Sage, 1977. $12.95.

SAVITZ, LEONARD D. and NORMAN JOHNSTON. *Crime In Society*. Pp. xii, 963. New York: Wiley, 1978. No price. Paperbound.

SCHUSKY, ERNEST L. and T. PATRICK CULBERT. *Introducing Culture*. 3d ed. Pp. x, 229. Englewood Cliffs, NJ: Prentice-Hall, 1978. $6.50. Paperbound.

SELTZER, MILDRED M., SHERRY L. CORBETT, and ROBERT C. ATCHLEY. *Social Problems Of The Aging*. Pp. 345. Belmont, CA: Wadsworth, 1978. No price.

SHAFFER, JOHN B. *Humanistic Psychology*. Pp. x, 198. Englewood Cliffs, NJ: Prentice-Hall, 1978. $5.95.

SHEPARD, JON M. and HARWIN L. VOSS. *Social Problems*. Pp. xvii, 533. New York: Macmillan, 1978. No price.

SHIMPO, MITSURU. *Three Decades in Shiwa: Economic Development and Social Change in a Japanese Farming Community*. Pp. 167. Vancouver, BC: University of British Columbia, 1977. $15.00.

SMITH, R. FRANKLIN. *Edward R. Murrow— The War Years*. Pp. vi, 156. Kalamazoo, MI: New Issues Press, 1978. $5.95. Paperbound.

SMITH, THOMAS C. *Nakahara: Family Farming and Population in a Japanese Village, 1717–1830*. Pp. viii, 183. Stanford, CA: Stanford University Press, 1977. $10.00.

SPODEK, HOWARD. *Urban-Rural Integration in Regional Development: A Case Study of Saurashtra, India—1800–1960*. Pp. 144. Chicago: University of Chicago Press, 1977. $6.00. Paperbound.

STRAUSSMAN, JEFFREY D. *The Limits Of Technocratic Politics*. Pp. xii, 164. New Brunswick, NJ: Transaction, 1978. $14.95.

TIHANY, LESLIE C. *The Baranya Dispute*. Pp. 138. New York: Columbia University Press, 1978. $11.00.

TILTON, JOHN E. *The Future of Nonfuel Minerals*. Pp. viii, 113. Washington, DC: Brookings Institution, 1977. $8.95.

TODD, MALCOLM. *The Walls of Rome*. Pp. 91. Totowa, NJ: Rowman & Littlefield, 1978. $14.50.

TREVOR-ROPER, HUGH R., ed. *Final Entries 1945: The Diaries of Joseph Goebbels*. Pp. xxxiii, 368. New York: G. P. Putnam's, 1978. $14.95.

TUDOR-CRAIG, PAMELA. *Richard III*. Pp. 74. Totowa, NJ: Rowman & Littlefield, 1978. $19.50.

ULLMAN, WALTER. *The United States In Prague, 1945–1948*. Pp. x, 205. New York: Columbia University Press, 1978. $13.00.

VALE, MARCIA. *The Gentleman's Recreations: Accomplishments and Pastimes of the English Gentleman, 1580–1630*. Pp. ix, 182. Totowa, NJ: Rowman & Littlefield, 1978. $13.50.

VYGOTSKY, L. S. et al., eds. *Mind in Society: The Development of Higher Psychological Processes*. Pp. x, 159. Cambridge, MA: Harvard University Press, 1978. $12.50.

WANG, K. P. and E. CHIN. *Mineral Economics and Basic Industries in Asia*. Pp. xxv, 358. Boulder, CO: Westview, 1978. $23.70.

WARREN, ROLAND L. *The Community in America*. 3d ed. Pp. x, 448. Chicago: Rand McNally, 1978. $14.95.

WATSON, JAMES L. ed. *Between Two Cultures: Migrants and Minorities in Britain*. Pp. viii, 338. Totowa, NJ: Biblio, 1978. $20.00. Paperbound, $9.95.

WHITE, BURTON L. et al. *Experience and Environment: Major Influences on the Development of the Young Child*. Pp. x, 566. Englewood Cliffs, NJ: Prentice-Hall, 1978. $18.95.

WICKMAN, PETER and PHILLIP WHITTEN, eds. *Readings in Criminology*. Pp. vii, 379. Lexington, MA: D. C. Heath, 1978. No price.

WILLIAMS, WILLIAM A. *Americans in a Changing World: A History of the United States in the Twentieth Century*. Pp. xvii, 523. New York: Harper & Row, 1978. $14.95.

WILSON, JOHN P. *The Rights Of Adolescents In The Mental System*. Pp. ix, 321. Lexington, MA: Lexington Books, 1978. $23.00.

WILSON, ROBERT, A. and DAVID A. SCHULZ. *Urban Sociology*. Pp. xiii, 368. Englewood Cliffs, NJ: Prentice-Hall, 1978. No price.

WINKS, ROBIN W., ed. *Other Voices, Other Views: An International Collection of Essays from the Bicentennial*. Pp. vi, 428. Westport, CT: Greenwood, 1978. $22.95.

WOELFEL, CHARLES J. *Accounting: An Introduction*. 2d ed. Pp. xix, 828. Santa Monica, CA: Goodyear, 1977. No price.

WOOD, DAVID M. *Power and Policy in Western European Democracies*. Pp. vii, 177. New York: Wiley, 1978. $6.95. Paperbound.

# INDEX

Adenauer, Konrad, 3, 34, 150
Advocates general, 44, 45
African and Malagasy States (AASM), 142, 146, 150
Afro-Caribbean-Pacific (ACP), 16, 17, 144, 145, 146, 147, 148, 149, 151, 152, 155
Arusha Agreements, 61, 143
Averyt, William, 164

Balassa, Bela, 4
Barre, Raymond, 24, 104
Benelux Memorandum, 6
Benn, Tony, 116
Brandt, Willy, 15
BRENNER, MICHAEL, Monetary Policy: Processes and Policies, 98
Bretton Woods, 103
Briand, Aristide, 2
British Energy Department, 116

CAPORASO, JAMES A., see DOLAN, MICHAEL B., joint author
Centre d' Etudes de Recherches et Education Socialist (CERES), 28, 31
Centre of Social Democrats (CDS), 25, 27
Chaban-Delmas, Jacques, 26
Cheysson, Claude, 15
Chirac, Jacques, 26
Cognitive Mobilization, 86, 87, 88, 89, 90, 91, 92, 93, 95, 96
Colonna Memorandum, 124
Committee of Permanent Representatives (COREPER), 7, 56, 161, 163, 164
Common agricultural policy (CAP), 23, 25, 31, 60, 138, 140, 154, 155
Common Assembly, see European Parliament
Common External Tariff (CET), 60
Common Market, 4, 6, 7, 9, 10, 11, 31, 58, 64, 71, 72, 73, 74
  see also European Economic Community 76, 78, 79, 97, 102, 157
Communist Party, 27, 29, 30, 31
COMMUNITY IN PERSPECTIVE: PUBLIC POLICY AND POLITICAL STRUCTURE, The, Stuart A. Scheingold, 156
Consensus building, 55, 62
  see also, decisional systems
Costa v. E.N.E.L., 47, 49
Coudenhove-Kalerghi, Count, 2
Council of Europe, 3
Council of Federations of Commerce, 8
Council of Ministers, 5, 6, 7, 10, 26, 49, 125, 139, 161, 164

Court of Justice, 5, 7, 34, 43
  administrative law functions of, 46, 51
  jurisdiction of, 45, 46
  supremacy of over national laws, 43, 50, 51, 53
  treaty interpretations, 50, 51
COURT OF JUSTICE: THE INVISIBLE ARM, THE, Werner Feld, 42

Davignon Report, 58
Debre, Michel, 25, 26
DECADE OF DIVERGENCE AND DEVELOPMENT, Pierre-Henri Laurent, 13
Decisional systems, 55, 63
  concert system, 55, 56, 57, 59, 60, 62, 63, 64
  political cooperation system, 55, 57, 58, 59, 63
  Rome system, 55, 56, 59, 60, 61, 62, 64
  summitry, 55, 57, 58, 59, 62, 63
DECISIONAL SYSTEMS, ADAPTIVENESS, AND EUROPEAN DECISIONMAKING, Glenda Rosenthal and Donald Puchala, 54
Deutsch, Karl W., 70
Directorate-Generals, 15
DOLAN, MICHAEL B. AND JAMES A. CAPORASO, The External Relations of the European Community, 135

Easton, David, 69
ECONOMIC UNCERTAINTY AND EUROPEAN SOLIDARITY: PUBLIC OPINION TRENDS, Ronald Inglehart and Jacques-Rene Rabier, 66
Einaudi, Luigi, 2
ELLIS, DOREEN, European Industrial Policies: Balancing Interdependence and Interest, 122
ENERGY POLICY IN THE COMMUNITIES, Wilfrid L. Kohl, 111
Erhard, Ludwig, 15
d'Estaing, Giscard, 15, 22, 23, 24, 25, 32
Euro-Arab General Committee (EAEC), 7
European Atomic Energy Committee (Euratom), 6, 7, 34, 36, 43, 45, 46, 47, 51, 112, 157
European Coal and Steel Community (ECSC), 2, 3, 4, 5, 7, 34, 43, 45, 46, 47, 50, 112, 157
European Council, 23, 26, 27
European Defense Community, 5, 28
European Economic Community (EEC), 6, 7, 34, 36, 45, 46, 47, 50, 51, 75, 76, 77, 78, 79, 95, 99, 101, 102, 103, 106

EUROPEAN INDUSTRIAL POLICIES: BALANCING INTERDEPENDENCE AND INTEREST, Doreen Ellis, 122

European Monetary Union, 159

European Parliament, 7, 10, 11, 14, 19, 26, 27, 29, 34, 35, 36, 37, 38, 39, 40, 41, 49, 67, 79, 80, 81 (Fig. 6), 82, 95, 96, 97, 117

European solidarity, sense of, 68 (fig. 1), 71 (table 1), 72 (table 2), 73 (fig. 2), 77 (table 3), 78 (table 4), 80 (fig. 5), 84 (table 5), 85 (table 6), 97

THE EXTERNAL RELATIONS OF THE EUROPEAN COMMUNITY, Michael B. Dolan and James A. Caporaso, 135

FELD, WERNER, The Court of Justice: The Invisible Arm, 42

F.E.O.G.A., 10, 29

FRANCE IN THE COMMUNITIES: PRESIDENTIAL AND PARTY ATTITUDES, Joyce Quin, 21

Free trade area, 60

Friedrich, Carl J., 8

Galtung, Johan, 146

de Gasperi, Alcide, 3

GATT, 126, 147

de Gaulle, Charles, 8, 9, 10, 11, 15, 22, 23, 30, 31, 61, 62

GEORG, 5

Guichard, Olivier, 26

Hague Summit, 58

Hallstein, Walter, 11, 62, 166

Heath, Edward, 10

Hoffmann, Stanley, 158

Industrial policy concerns, 124–126
  development of technological innovation, 126
  maintenance of regional balance, 126, 127
  sectoral allocation of resources, 130
  structural organization of industries, 133

INGLEHART, RONALD and JACQUES-RENE RABIER, Economic Uncertainty and European Solidarity: Public Opinion Trends, 66

International Energy Agency (IEA), 116, 120, 121

International Monetary Fund (IMF), 126

Jenkins, Roy, 24, 64, 99, 108, 109

Kennedy Round, 61, 137

Keynes, John, 123

KOHL, WILFRID L., Energy Policy in the Communities, 111

LAURENT, PIERRE-HENRI, Decade of Divergence and Development, 13

League for European Economic Cooperation, 8

League of Nations, 3

Lindberg, Leon, 7

Lipgins, Walter, 2

Lomé, 16, 17, 18, 63, 128, 130, 143, 144, 145, 146, 147, 148, 149, 151, 152

Louis Harris (France) Institute, 30

Manshold Memorandum, 61

Marchais, Georges, 29

Marjolin Committee, 99

Mazzini, Guiseppe, 2

Meade, James E., 4

Mitterand, Francois, 28

Monetary integration, 99
  currency integration, 100
  exchange rate union, 100
  financial integration, 100
  unification at the policy level, 100

MONETARY POLICY: PROCESSES AND POLICIES, Michael Brenner, 98

Monnet, Jean, 2, 3, 5, 34, 157, 166

Myrdal, Gunnar, 4

NATO, North Atlantic Treaty Organization, 138, 142, 153

Nkruman, Kwame, 146

Nuclear reactors, 117
  light water, 119

OPEC, 14, 112, 140

ORIGINS AND EVOLUTION OF THE EUROPEAN COMMUNITIES, Roy Willis, 1

Parliament, see European Parliament

PARLIAMENT AND THE COMMISSION, THE, Jean-Joseph Schwed, 33

Pirzio-Biroli, Corrado, 14

Pleven, René, 5

Pompidou, Georges, 11, 15, 22, 23, 25, 104

Popular Republican Movement (MRP), 25

Post Materialist value priorities, 86, 87, 88, 89, 90, 91, 92, 93, 96

PUCHALA, DONALD, see ROSENTHAL, GLENDA, joint author

QUIN, JOYCE, France in the Communities: Presidential and Party Attitudes, 21

RABIER, JACQUES-RENE, see INGLEHART, RONALD, joint author

Regional Development Fund, 159

ROSENTHAL, GLENDA and DONALD PUCHALA, Decisional Systems, Adaptiveness, and European Decisionmaking, 54

de Saint-Pierre, Abbe, 2

Sanguinetti, Alexandre, 25–

SCHEINGOLD, STUART A., The Community in

Perspective: Public Policy and Political
Structure, 156
Schmidt, Helmut, 15, 109
Schroeder, Gerhard, 10
Schuman Plan, 3
Schuman, Robert, 3, 34
SCHWED, JEAN-JOSEPH, The Parliament and
the Commission, 33
Smithsonian Agreement, 106, 107
Snake, 100, 106, 107, 108, 109
Socialists, 28, 29, 30, 31
Spaak, Paul-Henri, 6
STABEX, 16, 145, 147, 149, 151
de Sully, Duc, 2

Third World, 14, 16, 143, 146, 149, 152
Treaties of Rome, 5, 7, 9, 11, 14, 60, 64, 101,
149
Treaty of Paris, 14

Union of Handicrafts of the EC, 8
Union of Industries of the EC, 8
United Nations Conference on Trade and
Development (UNCTAD), 146, 147, 151

Value Added Tax, 61
Viner, Jakob, 4

Werner Committee, 105, 106
Werner, Pierre, 105
Werner Report, 105
Western European Union, 5
WILLIS, ROY, Origins and Evolution of the
European Communities, 1

Yaoundé, 15, 16, 60, 142, 146, 147, 150, 152

## FORTHCOMING FROM CMS

# THE POLITICS OF MIGRATION POLICIES

## THE FIRST WORLD IN THE 1970s
### by Daniel Kubat

This volume offers a time series of data on the movements and characteristics of migrants, as well as a comparison of migration policies by which countries respond to their diverse demographic realities. The text represents a reference work offering standardized information on the migration policies of some 22 countries of the West; it suggests analyses of the policies individual countries evolved to meet their migration needs; and, it provides the data on which the analyses are based.

### PARTIAL TABLE OF CONTENTS

| | | |
|---|---|---|
| I. AUSTRALIA | | *Charles Price* |
| II. CANADA | | *Daniel Kubat* |
| III. NEW ZEALAND | | *Jean L. Elliott* |
| IV. THE UNITED STATES OF AMERICA | | *Charles B. Keely* |

PART TWO: MIGRATION POLICIES OF AN EMPIRE
V. THE UNITED KINGDOM — *Tom Rees*

PART THREE: COUNTRIES OF IN-MIGRATION: NORTHWESTERN EUROPE
| | |
|---|---|
| VI. AUSTRIA | *Ernst Gehmacher* |
| VII. THE BENELUX COUNTRIES | *Gunther Beyer* |
| VIII. FRANCE | *Yann Moulier and Georges Tapinos* |
| IX. GERMANY | *Ursula Mehrländer* |
| X. THE SCANDINAVIAN COUNTRIES | *Altti Majava* |
| XI. SWITZERLAND | *Hans-Joachim Hoffmann-Nowotny and Martin Killias* |

PART FOUR: COUNTRIES OF OUT-MIGRATION: EXPORTATION OF LABOR TO NORTHWESTERN EUROPE
| | |
|---|---|
| XII. GREECE | *Theodore P. Lianos* |
| XIII. THE IBERIAN PENINSULA | *Maria B. Rocha Trindade* |
| XIV. ITALY | *Francesco Cerase* |
| XV. TURKEY | *S. Alias and Daniel Kubat* |
| XVI. YUGOSLAVIA | *Ivo Baucic* |

ISBN 0-913256-34-X. Tables. Index. 6 X 9.

*Order exclusively from:*
CENTER FOR MIGRATION STUDIES
209 Flagg Place
Staten Island, New York 10304